Economics: Theory and Researches

Economics: Theory and Researches

Edited by **Swena Lesley**

CLANRYE INTERNATIONAL
New Jersey

Published by Clanrye International,
55 Van Reypen Street,
Jersey City, NJ 07306, USA
www.clanryeinternational.com

Economics: Theory and Researches
Edited by Swena Lesley

International Standard Book Number: 978-1-63240-162-5 (Hardback)

Printed in China.

Contents

Preface

Scarcity is a problem that everybody is concerned about in this day and age and such a problem merits study. Economics then, becomes the study of this scarcity of resources. Each unit of a society, be it an individual, a family or an institution wants the maximum allocation of resources possible for itself. As such, economics helps in answering this extremely complicated process. Almost every decision made by an individual is centered in some way around an economic process, starting with an economic problem with various choices that affect the outcome, with the individual wanting the best possible outcome. When one realizes that such problem and subsequent process towards the solution is faced by every person around us, we realize the vastness of the field of Economics. Generally divided into two extremely broad categories- Macroeconomics and Microeconomics, there are innumerable sub-fields that are a part of Economics. Topics as diverse as household management and taxes to global trends of supply and demand and even how to maximize profit for a firm or increase GDP for a country- all come under the umbrella of Economics. As such, to better understand this field, rules and regulations as well as policies are often put up. Of course, such rules and policies have to constantly keep up with the current global scenario and look towards obtaining the highest benefit for the individual.

This book attempts to understand the basics of economics through collated data from past and present economic scenarios. I would like to thank the people whose research and data contributed to this book.

Editor

Responding to a Forest Catastrophe: The Emergence of New Governance Arrangements in Southern California

Brian Petersen[1] and Adam M. Wellstead[2]

[1] *Environmental Studies, Western Michigan University, 1903 West Michigan Avenue, Kalamazoo, MI 49008, USA*
[2] *Department of Social Sciences, Michigan Technological University, 1600 Townsend Street, Houghton, MI 49931, USA*

Correspondence should be addressed to Brian Petersen; brian.petersen@wmich.edu

Academic Editors: J. F. Negrón, A. Santini, and B. Schirone

The San Bernardino National Forest in southern California experienced an unprecedented bark beetle outbreak in the early 2000s. The outbreak, coupled with a looming threat of catastrophic wildfire, droughts, changing forest management priorities, and a legacy of poor forest management practices coalesced to create a challenge that existing institutions and management agencies could not address. In response, an interagency collaborative effort, the Mountain Area Taskforce (MAST), was initiated. Based on key informant interviews, this paper details how this new governance organization emerged and how it effectively addressed a landscape scale forest challenge. Forest governance analyses often focus attention on macroscales, overlooking the microlevel arrangements that set MAST apart from other responses to bark beetle outbreaks. Interagency collaboration has taken on greater importance in efforts to address forest management at landscape scales and this case study provides important insights into the challenges and opportunities of these new governance arrangements.

1. Introduction

In 2001, Southern California's forests experienced the largest bark beetle outbreak on record. The magnitude of the outbreak, which peaked between 2003 and 2004, led to unprecedented forest dieback, which dramatically altered the forest landscape and contributed to extensive socioeconomic consequences. Subsequent to the outbreak, devastating fires occurred across southern California in 2003. In the San Bernardino National Forest (SBNF) the "Old" and "Grand Prix" fires merged, burned 5,863 hectares of forest, destroyed thousands of homes, and cost more than $2 billion in firefighting and property damage [1, 2]. Another fire, in 2007, in the San Bernardino Mountains burned hundreds of more homes. The "Station Fire" in the Angeles National Forest just outside of Los Angeles in the fall of 2009 once again brought national attention to forest management issues in the region.

In this paper, we examine a systems-based collaborative effort, the Mountain Areas Safety Taskforce (MAST), that mobilized to address a forest health crisis in southern California's forests. We present two arguments about natural resource collaborative decision making. First, based on a three-level approach (Table 1), we argue that problems visible at a macrolevel (forest health crisis) require not only an examination of mesolevel governance arrangements but also the microfeatures of interagency collaborations such as MAST and the on-the-ground implementation of its programs. In this case, these microlevel arrangements contributed to an effective response to the crisis. We aim to illustrate how this effective response developed and how this example contributes towards a better understanding of how successful interagency collaboration can emerge. Bark beetle outbreaks posed significant challenges to land managers and policy makers across western North America. In southern California an integrated, collaborative response materialized that later served as a model for other areas facing similar challenges. This microlevel interagency collaboration sets this case apart from others, providing an opportunity to assess

Table 1: A three-level approach to policy logic.

System level	Political actors	Policy-relevant aspects	Policy focus
Micro: human agency/behavioral	Individuals representing agencies	Behavior/choice	MAST, collaborative dynamics/measures of program success
Meso: governance considerations	Government—civil society	Governance: state—societal relations	Institutional arrangements, policy network, instrument choice
Macro: systemic	Environment (landscape level problems)	Resources/constraints/ feedback	Problem definition

the relative importance of specific factors and arrangements in forest governance.

Second, focusing on the mesolevel, we argue that MAST represents a "new governance" arrangement. Recently, Tollefson et al. [3] and Howlett et al. [4] developed three-dimensional frameworks in order to determine if there had been shifts from government to new governance arrangements in US and Canadian natural resource sectors. Tollefson et al.'s [3] framework is employed here to examine the three dimensions of new governance (institutional, political, and regulatory) in the case of MAST. Contrary to the other case study applications in the natural resource sector, we argue that MAST represents a new governance arrangement. We apply indicators of new governance related to institutional, political, and regulatory dimensions to illustrate how MAST represents a new governance arrangement defined by an interagency collaborative response to an unprecedented forest crisis.

2. New Forest Governance Arrangements and the Necessity of Interagency Collaboration

Moving away from a mode of coordination based on hierarchical top-down, command, and control management, governments have increasingly experimented with new modes of governance that rely on the incentives provided by markets or the sharing of information in governance networks. Due to complexities embedded in resource and environmental issues, environmental policy has been a key venue for governance changes. Recent advances in the natural resource governance literature have sought to capture these governance dynamics and their effects on policy making [4]. A large literature on contemporary governance arrangements suggests that nonstate actors have gained an increasingly important role in policy making as the complexity of policy problems has increased, a process of institutional change which governments have both reacted to and facilitated [5, 6]. Lacking the knowledge or the mandate to govern alone, governments have increasingly chosen to try to construct policy consensus through more engaged and interactive forms of policy making and to allow nonstate actors to implement those policies within a broad framework of incentives, benchmarking, and private governance [7]. This is true in many areas where efforts have been made to develop "integrated strategies" such as forestry and coastal marine ecosystem management [8] and similar efforts are typical in both climate change mitigation and adaptation efforts [9]. In these new governance modes, the lines between public and private have become blurred [10].

New governance arrangements call for increased attention towards the microlevel and novel collaborative efforts. In the microlevel, leadership, communication, and collaborative dynamics emerge. Collaborative management, engaging government agencies and departments with the general public, has been touted as a viable approach for addressing complex forest and natural resource management challenges [11, 12]. In comparison, interagency collaborative efforts, involving multiple government agencies addressing natural resource management, have received far less attention. Most work on interagency collaboration has detailed how emerging partnerships have typically failed. Vangen and Huxham [13] found that "reports of unmitigated success are not common." Huxham [14] argues that "unless the potential for real collaborative advantage is clear, it is generally best if there is any choice to avoid collaboration." However, decision makers are increasingly recognizing that many natural resource issues cannot be adequately addressed in the absence of effective interagency collaboration. Additionally, dynamics of collaborative efforts and their relative success need to be understood in a larger governance context.

Understanding the role that mesolevel variables play in the governance of complex forest problems involves three specific dimensions: institutional, political, and regulatory. The first dimension is linked to the structure and pervasiveness of policy networks which address the balance of power between state actors and the societal actors and networks, which in turn are linked to the kinds of policy instruments that are chosen to give effect to new governance arrangements [15]. In this network dimension, the number and diversity of actors (state and nonstate) that exert some degree of power or influence over the outputs of the governance arrangements is a key facet of policy making [16]. In this respect, the concern of the analyst is to identify where political power lies in relation to society and the state [17, 18]. The challenge is to determine whether, and to what extent, in specific sectors and issue areas the state or its agents are directly dictating the outcomes that emerge from the governance arrangement, more loosely "steering" the arrangement, or alternatively whether ultimate power to determine outcomes rests with nonstate actors (e.g., corporations, unions, and environmental civil society organizations) [19].

The second dimension has to do with the rigidity of institutional policy-related arrangements, namely, their formal or informal nature. The institutional aspects of governance arrangement can be assessed in terms of factors such as precision (how closely it constrains private action); obligation (the "bindingness" of its commands); and delegation (the extent to which the power to adjudicate and enforce these obligations is retained by a regulator or delegated to an independent third party) [3]. Recently, Doelle et al. [20] explored these two dimensions in a study of climate-change-based forest governance arrangements in Canada, New Zealand, and USA.

Finally, the third dimension, the policy process, illustrates the dynamic features of governance arrangements by focusing on policy making and policy change. The policy cycle [4] and policy change frameworks (e.g., advocacy coalition framework, institutional rational choice, and structural choice) [21–24] are familiar approaches that draw upon the network and institutional dimensions and provide an even finer, more empirical lens to understand the complexity and challenges of governance. Stedman [25] utilized these approaches in their examination of climate change adaptation policy formulation in the Canadian agriculture, forestry, and water sectors.

In this paper, we also evaluate what interagency collaboration entails and what factors make it successful. Bardach [26] argues that collaboration encompasses "activities by agencies intended to increase public value by having the agencies working together rather than separately." Similarly, Thomas [27] argues that collaboration is "an unmandated effort by public officials in at least two local, state, or federal agencies to coordinate their activities or share resources." This latter definition highlights the important point that interagency collaboration often arises not from an official mandate but through a shared recognition of a need by the parties involved. Whether parties collaborate, however, depends on many factors, including the extent to which they depend on one another [27]. Empirical studies suggest successful interagency collaborative efforts that include allowing participants to have flexibility, motivating lower level staff, providing accountability, ensuring quality, adequately addressing financial matters, identifying common aims, and maintaining purpose over time [14, 26, 28, 29]. The interagency collaboration literature highlights three key indicators critical to interagency collaborative success: effective leadership, trust, and minimizing turf disputes (i.e., [13, 30–32]). These three indicators represent key components of interagency collaboration.

Applying a three-level approach, we now focus on MAST and its response to an unprecedented forest crisis. The bark beetle outbreak and subsequent fires in the SBNF occurred at a macrolevel. Addressing this problem initiated efforts at the mesolevel (new governance arrangements in the institutional, political, and regulatory dimensions) and microlevel (interagency collaboration) to address it. Rather than focusing on the macrolevel and a top-down approach, this case affords the opportunity to look at how bottom-up interagency collaboration and new governance arrangements coalesced to address this challenge. In addition, this paper focuses attention on the interagency collaborative effort that emerged and the extent to which it addressed the three key indicators (leadership, trust, and minimizing turf disputes) necessary for effective collaboration put forth in the literature.

3. Methods

This project began by visiting forest systems experiencing unprecedented bark beetle outbreaks and forest health crises. Site visits occurred in New Mexico, Colorado, Wyoming, and British Columbia, and also included interviews with forest managers in Montana, Idaho, Washington, and Oregon. We selected the SBNF because it was experiencing an unprecedented forest dieback, had initiated significant management responses, had changed public policy, had received significant state and federal resources to address the situation, and also created a unique, interagency collaborative response to orchestrate and facilitate actions. These features set it apart from responses initiated elsewhere. After selecting this case, we implemented a mixed method approach for data collection and analysis. This included conducting 80 in-person key informant interviews with individuals associated with MAST over a two-year period. Interviews primarily focused attention on individuals directly involved in MAST (US Forest Service, CalFire, San Bernardino County representatives, California State agencies, the Natural Resource Conservation Service, local fire departments, and private companies) but also included elected officials, academics, and concerned citizens engaged in responding to the forest health crisis.

We developed and employed a semistructure interview guide that focused its attention on the causes and responses to the bark beetle outbreak, specifically how MAST organized and operated. The semistructure interview guide allowed for each interview to engage the unique perspective and expertise of each respondent. Interviews were recorded, transcribed, and analyzed using a coding system. In addition to interviews, observations were made at regional meetings related to MAST activities, as well as community group meetings that dealt with new regulations and fire protection plans. Finally, primary documents from government agencies and financial records related to MAST were collected and analyzed.

4. Background: The San Bernardino National Forest

The SBNF encompasses over 273,837 hectares of public land and three ranger districts [33] in southern California (Figure 1). The national forest resides within San Bernardino and Riverside Counties and lies just outside of the city limits of the city of San Bernardino. Chaparral, oak, piñon/juniper, and scrub ecosystems dominate the national forest but also include forests that harbor Coulter (*Pinus coulteri*), Ponderosa (*Pinus ponderosa*), Lodgepole (*Pinus contorta*), sugar (*Pinus lambertiana*), and Jeffrey (*Pinus jeffreyi*) pines, incense cedar (*Calocedrus decurrens*), canyon oak (*Quercus chrysolepis*), and Douglas fir (*Pseudotsuga menziesii*). Unlike most national forests that have contiguous public lands, the SBNF surrounds private property and towns with significant population centers. This creates difficult challenges for public land management, including the necessity to prioritize actions that protect private property. A USFS district ranger noted: "the SBNF has more people living within its

FIGURE 1: The San Bernardino National Forest.

boundaries than any other forest in the country." Private property in-holdings exceed 59,549 hectares on the forest [33]. Its proximity also makes the SBNF one of the most heavily visited national forests.

In recent decades visitors and residents demanded new USFS management practices that favored aesthetic values and recreation over timber production. Timber harvesting disappeared from the region by the mid-1970s. Without timber management, funds for providing aesthetic and recreation values diminished. Over time, the USFS dramatically changed its workforce: by the early 1990s the forest had no foresters on staff. This made it difficult to conduct any forest management operations, such as thinning projects. The latest forest plan explicitly states, "Lands with a timber management objective are not suitable on southern California national forests. These national forests need to be actively managed for a variety of other purposes, including wildlife habitat and recreation opportunities" [34].

4.1. Macro Level: Unprecedented Forest Health Crisis in the SBNF. The emergence of an unprecedented forest health crisis in the SBNF can be traced to the simultaneous interaction of three interrelated natural phenomena (bark beetle, drought, and catastrophic fires) and a legacy of forest management (Table 2). Depending on forest conditions, the Western Pine beetle (*Dendroctonus brevicomis)* fluctuates in population size. Across North America, bark beetles have caused unprecedented forest disturbances [35]. These outbreaks have occurred in forests dominated by conifer species. Outbreaks interact with other forest disturbances [36] and affect fire regimes [37]. They have recently affected high elevation stands formerly buffered by cold temperatures [38] and have had considerable economic as well as ecological consequences [39, 40]. The SBNF bark beetle outbreak rapidly expanded beginning in 2000, and by 2002 represented a significant forest health crisis that policy makers and land managers had to respond to. By early 2003 70,000 hectares of the SBNF were affected ([41], cited in [1]).

Two major factors contributed to the unprecedented beetle outbreak: drought and fire suppression in the SBNF. Forest health acts as the primary control on beetle populations, as individual tree vigor is the primary defense against beetle outbreaks. Healthy trees have the ability to drive out beetles with resin [42], whereas drought and competition can reduce vigor, leaving trees more susceptible to attack. In the late 1990s a severe drought occurred across southern California. According to an ecologist working in the region, by the late 1990s, the SBNF forest landscape was in the "driest physical state it had been in since the 18th century."

Exacerbating the situation was a long history of fire suppression by government agencies. Past forest management contributed to a higher proportion of mature pine trees on the landscape and higher tree density levels [43]. Beetles preferentially attack mature pine trees and higher density levels increase tree competition for limited water and nutrients. We now turn to the meso- and microlevels to explore how MAST addressed this macrolevel crisis.

4.2. Mesolevel: The Mountain Area Safety Taskforce: A New Governance Arrangement. The threat of catastrophic fire and widespread tree mortality posed a significant risk to communities. The USFS in conjunction with a variety of other state and municipal agencies began discussions in November 2002 about addressing declining forest health. Preliminary meetings focused on finding ways to more efficiently address bark beetle and fire potential by cutting more trees and making communities less vulnerable to catastrophic fire. Collectively, there was a realization that no single agency could deal with such a complex problem. MAST, a coalition that included county, state, federal natural resource agencies, electric power companies, forest management contractors, and public safety agencies (Table 3), identified the following broad goals:

> to develop and implement an integrated and coordinated approach to address the disaster's immediate impacts on life, safety, and social and economic values, while implementing a long-range recovery plan resulting in safe communities and ecological sustainability.

Based on Tollefson et al.'s [3] three government to governance dimensions (institutional, political, and regulatory) we discuss MAST's organization and actions.

4.2.1. Formal but Voluntary: MAST's Institutional Dimensions. The nature of emergency management requires some degree of organization and formality. MAST efforts revealed strong

Table 2: Primary contributing factors leading to forest disturbances in the San Bernardino National Forest.

Contributing factor to forest disturbance	Context	Consequence
Drought	Driest physical state forests had been in over a century.	Trees died from water stress; those that survived had increased vulnerability to bark beetles.
Forest management practices	Shift from forest cutting to forest protection; managing for "park like" conditions; homeowner laws and public perceptions that limited or forbid direct forest management.	Tree densities increased, as did the age class of trees, contributing to a landscape with more mature trees, which bark beetles preferentially target, providing sufficient host material for the outbreak to occur.
Fires	Strict fire prevention practices and policies implemented; removal of natural fire regime across the landscape.	Lack of fire contributed to dense forests with older age classes. This created a continuous canopy that contributed to uncontrollable crown fires.
Beetles	Endemic beetle populations had access to increased host material due to drought and more mature trees on the landscape.	Controls that typically hold populations at low levels were lost. Populations exploded, killing trees at unprecedented levels.

Table 3: MAST member organizations.

Federal partners	US Forest Service Natural Resources Conservation Service
State partners	California Department of Forestry and Fire Protection (CalFire) California Department of Transportation California Highway Patrol
County partners	County of San Bernardino San Bernardino County Fire Department San Bernardino Office of Emergency Services San Bernardino County Department of Public Works San Bernardino County Sheriff San Bernardino County Solid Waste Management San Bernardino County Public Works/Hazardous Tree Removal
Local fire departments	Arrowbear Lake Fire Department Big Bear City Fire Department Big Bear Lake Fire Protection District Crest Forest Fire Protection District Running Springs Fire Department
Fire safe councils	Inland Empire Fire Safe Alliance Angelus Oaks Fire Safe Council Arrowhead Communities Fire Safe Council Big Bear Valley Fire Safe Council Lytle Creek Fire Safe Council Mill Creek Canyon Fire Safe Council Mountain Rim Fire Safe Council Wrightwood Fire Safe Council
Public utilities	Southern California Edison Bear Valley Electric Company

institutional dimensions. Table 4 lists important institutional indicators of new governance and how these indicators can be identified in terms of the MAST organization. These indicators relate to inclusive planning, an informal mandate and an inclusive consultation process. Initially, MAST adopted a degree of formality in its institutional arrangements. After the initial meetings, MAST created a voluntary-based structure that included a core group, a unified command group, a media relations group, a liaison group to the broader community, and four sections that formed the base of the day-to-day organization: operations, planning, logistics, and financial management. According to participants, this organizational approach addressed critical barriers to implementing actions, setting priorities, and generally shaping the organizational structure and direction.

Compared to other collaborative efforts, MAST adopted a more informal horizontal organization arrangement. This was critical for utilizing resources. There was no formal agreement binding participating agencies to the effort and external funding that came from state and federal government agencies, including $70 million through the Natural Resource Conservation Service. Despite government-wide budgetary cuts and diminished external funding, a decade later, MAST continues to operate in this manner. Interview respondents stated that MAST exceeded their initial expectations and critical land management actions were carried out in light of the catastrophic natural events. One person reflected a sense of optimism about the process: "It was amazing what we were able to do here. Absolutely amazing." Another said "I spent 40 years with the Forest Service, I have never seen a program run so effectively. It is probably, as far as I am concerned, the best example of how all levels of government can work together."

4.2.2. Shared Informal Decision Making: MAST's Political Dimensions. Interagency collaboration, as described above, has been proven to be difficult to achieve. Agencies defending turf or prioritizing their own as opposed to collective goals can derail interagency collaboration. MAST averted this problem in part due to their informal decision making process; Table 5 identifies the political indicators of new governance and highlights how they relate to MAST. Rather than create a top-down decision-making process that directed activities, MAST created an informal partnership. No organization had to formally join MAST and decision making, based on a gap analysis (see below), leveraged agency actions by allowing each agency to contribute in a way that protected their own interests but also contributed to the overall goals MAST established. Open meetings where partner organizations could contribute to discussions about

TABLE 4: MAST's institutional dimension.

Institutional indicators	MAST
Quantity and diversity of actors engaged in the institutionalized process in question	The most inclusive forest planning process in the region, MAST involved a comprehensive set of public and private interests in the decision-making process.
Origin and nature of mandate	Informal mandate agreed upon by diverse actors in response to looming forest catastrophe.
Nature and extent of consultation with affected interests	Created inclusive polycentric working group tasked with implementing shared goals and objectives.

TABLE 5: MAST's political dimension.

Political indicators	MAST
Quantity and diversity of actors with some degree of power or influence over decision/output	Rather than a top-down, hierarchy, MAST enabled all interested parties to contribute to decision making in collaborative fashion.
Actual formal decision-making power/actual not formal ability to influence decisions and outcomes	MAST partners collectively informally influenced decisions that led to interagency actions by participating groups and entities.

objectives and actions facilitated communication and shared decision making. MAST decisions enabled each partner organization to contribute based on their missions and abilities, while still making important contributions to established MAST priorities. MAST established a framework that enabled dialogue between partner organizations that had not occurred previously in the region. Interview respondents that participated in MAST suggested that the communication and joint decision making were the primary factors that enabled MAST to effectively organize a response to the forest health crisis.

4.2.3. Setting Priorities: MAST's Regulatory Dimension. Table 6 illustrates how MAST demonstrates regulatory indicators of new governance. MAST followed the "soft law" process. In a soft law process there is no formal entity with jurisdiction to institute or demand hard law outcomes and partners that contribute to decisions. MAST participants had no formal commitment, participating as equal partners with shared goals. It was organized in a way that gave voice to all participants. Rather than agencies and stakeholders working to meet their own objectives, MAST created a platform to allow an integrated response that focused on the forest system, not political boundaries. Actions taken thus dealt with pressing problems on federal, state, county, and private lands. MAST helped orchestrate policy changes at the state and county levels, as well as policies regulating vegetation management on private lands that facilitated their agreed upon objectives. Through this process, MAST garnered legitimacy both in a regulatory sense and also in terms of public perception. That legitimacy then enabled MAST to set priorities and implement actions.

MAST established three priorities early on that helped direct their efforts to effectively address the beetle outbreak and forest health crisis. First, they sought to protect communication sites such as radio towers and radio repeaters vital for ensuring effective communication during an emergency across the SBNF. In particular, these would help communication efforts in the case of evacuating all residents living in or near the SBNF. MAST identified those sites that needed protection and designed fuel treatments in the surrounding forest areas to divert fire away from them. Protecting evacuation corridors and putting in place an evacuation plan was MAST's second major activity. Only a few roads access the many mountain communities, housing developments, and individual houses in the SBNF. Trees falling over roads or fires hinder emergency evacuation and could also inhibit emergency services and firefighters from accessing communities in need. MAST identified key corridors needing tree thinning to ensure that blockages would not occur. Finally MAST set out a broad strategy of community protection. MAST identified those areas most in danger from fires and worked across agencies to put in place plans to remove dead trees near homes and undertake long-term fuel reduction projects on community edges in an attempt to lower the likelihood of fire and to divert fires away from communities. Such projects created breaks in forest canopies and fuel breaks to divert fires around communities and attempted to foster long-term efforts to ensure that forest regrowth would not recreate similar conditions conducive to another bark beetle outbreak.

The actions MAST took required a new regulatory framework. Previous to the bark beetle outbreak, agencies and institutions with jurisdiction over land management in and around the SBNF did not, and in many cases could not, effectively work in an integrated fashion. MAST created a voluntary organization that, coupled with policy changes, established an interagency collaborative framework to collectively take action. This hybrid system, including agencies and stakeholders working to meet their own objectives while simultaneously working to meet the broader goals established by MAST, enabled effective forest management to occur. MAST successfully implemented management actions that many respondents indicated had not occurred for decades and were long overdue.

4.3. Microlevel: Interagency Collaboration: The Nuts and Bolts of New Governance Arrangements. MAST faced

Table 6: MAST's regulatory dimension.

Regulatory indicators	MAST
Quantity and diversity of actors engaged in the regulatory arrangement	Formal and informal partners contributed to regulatory arrangement. Decisions followed a soft law process in which partners contributed to decisions (i.e., no formal entity had jurisdiction to institute or demand hard law outcomes).
Precision (how closely does the output prescribe and constrain private action?)	Precision: the decisions made had direct implications for federal, state, and county agencies, as well as private landowners (i.e., the decisions affected land of all types of land jurisdictions).
Obligation (how legally binding is the obligation?)	Obligation: policy changes at the state level as well as changes to county and property laws facilitated legally binding actions regarding forest and property management that did not exist prior to the outbreak.
Delegation (is the duty of adjudicating and enforcing the obligation vested in an independent third party or retained by the regulator?)	Delegation: Policy changes provided delegation of enforcement to MAST partners, supported by the public legal system.

multiple on-the-ground obstacles not readily observed in the mesolevel new governance literature. Successful interagency collaboration requires a continual contribution of its voluntary participants who support the efforts' objectives while balancing their own agency's goals. This proves particularly important when confronting unprecedented, landscape level problems where effectiveness requires innovation and flexibility, working effectively across both internal and external agency boundaries, moving away from short-term goals, and recognizing the need to maintain a long-term focus.

Within this unique new governance arrangement, there were a number of specific on-the-ground features that helped MAST successfully meet stated goals and objectives. These features cannot be captured in the mesolevel literature. Evaluating whether a program or effort is successful when faced with everyday problems can prove challenging. Challenges on the scale on the SBNF posed even greater obstacles. However, interview participants highlighted two primary indicators for program success: meeting short-term goals and facilitating long-term fuel modification work. The 2003 fires burned 60,700 hectares and destroyed over 1,000 structures [44]. The thinning work and tree removal efforts spared all the communication sites in the SBNF, thus allowing for communication to continue unimpeded. Uninterrupted communication was important for meeting the second short-term goal, implementing a resident evacuation strategy.

Interview respondents deemed evacuation efforts a success because law enforcement partners held public meetings, distributed materials, and used public service announcements to educate the public about the evacuation strategy. After the fires started, MAST partners initiated the evacuation plan. The County Sheriff Department brought in deputies along with search and rescue volunteers to provide residents with evacuation instructions and procedures. They used loudspeakers in neighborhoods to inform residents, implemented an emergency telephone system, and used helicopters to assess the situation and identify residents in need. On the roadways, established plans directed residents to evacuation routes and the county and state law enforcement agencies worked together to maintain order over the two days in which over 45,000 people were successfully evacuated [44].

The third and longer-range MAST objective was to reduce community vulnerability to fire through fuel modification work. Several fires, including the Grass Valley Fire in 2007 burned 199 homes. However, fuel modification efforts prevented more damage. In particular, an analysis of fire behavior showed that fuel modification efforts have decreased the intensity of fires and in several cases diverted fires around homes and communities [45]. A county fire marshal noted that "a $60,000 fuel break saved over 500 homes."

Promoting community fire safety occurred at three different levels. First, individual homeowners could apply for the federal Forest Care Program that funded the removal vegetation around homes. Homeowners who do not meet county ordinance requirements were still eligible for 75% reimbursement for fuel reduction work coordinated through Forest Care. According to a coordinator of the Forest Care program, 1275 homeowners utilized the program, treating over 265 hectares. Second, at the county level, the San Bernardino Hazard Tree Program undertook fuel modification work. The program treated over 15,059 hectares and removed over 300,000 trees in and around SBNF communities. And finally, the USFS also undertook fuel modification work throughout SBNF. According to a USFS regional forest manager, between 2003 and 2010 fuels reduction work on nearly 30,000 hectares was undertaken, representing approximately 11% of the SBNF's land base.

4.3.1. Factors Contributing to Interagency Success. The literature on interagency collaboration highlights the importance of leadership in promoting successful outcomes [13, 14, 26, 28–30, 46]. The SBNF forest supervisor provided strong leadership in initiating MAST's formation. As a result, other agencies contributed resources and personnel to the effort. The group of agency heads that directed the high level policy discussions for MAST established priority actions and goals that subgroups utilized to identify on the ground activities necessary to meet the broader MAST goals.

In addition to individual and organizational leadership within MAST, its partner organizations and individuals within those agencies illustrated key leadership regarding public relations. The MAST organization established threats and priorities that all participants agreed upon. This shared perspective created cohesiveness among those involved and more importantly a shared understanding of both the problems they collectively faced and the solutions to them. This unanimity allowed each person involved in MAST to serve as a spokesperson to clearly convey the approach MAST had undertaken to address the threats facing communities and homeowners across the mountain. MAST members held public meetings across mountain communities and talked about the role their particular agency played in the effort but also had the ability to speak competently about the broader MAST effort. This enabled MAST representatives to effectively communicate with the public to generate support for forest management actions that prior to the outbreak would not have found support. This played an important role in moving MAST objectives forward.

The interagency collaboration literature often raises the importance of participants having common aims. The impending and ongoing natural disasters in the SBNF contributed to a coherent aim across MAST organizations. Many individuals found that MAST shaped participant perceptions. As a respondent from CalFire put it "the experience of MAST caused the participants to view their own particular problem in relationship to how it impacted all the other agencies" and "that is probably the most unique factor out of MAST, the shaping of perceptions."

Turf issues and trust represent the other two primary issues affecting interagency collaborative efforts. In this case, the shared perception of an imminent threat to life and property brought entities with jurisdiction on the mountain together to address a common problem and facilitated trust and a shared understanding across MAST members. The creation of MAST helped galvanize trust and a common purpose across partner organizations. This led to partner organizations and individuals within them contributing without worrying about turf battles or seeking credit or attention.

Undertaking an institutional gap analysis represents one of MASTs most innovative and important elements. Respondents suggested that the gap analysis emerged during their efforts to identify how many partner organizations had jurisdiction across the mountain and to identify their mandates. From that baseline they then identified specific actions each entity could take and from that collective assessment identified what actions remained unaddressed. This process served to streamline action and reduce turf battles. MAST set out in early 2003 to undertake a gap analysis of all the entities with jurisdiction over land management or communities. The gap analysis identified the partner organizations, their responsibilities, and assessed whether they could meet their responsibilities given the forest health crisis. It also provided a means to identifying how partners could combine their efforts to expedite tree removal and fuel management projects. Without a gap analysis each partner would have continued to engage in efforts isolated from those taken by others. The gap analysis allowed both streamlining work and leveraging the actions of each partner to more strategically address broader MAST goals.

5. Conclusion

The bark beetle outbreak that erupted in the SBNF not only posed a significant threat to community safety but also rendered existing governance impotent to address an unprecedented landscape level problem. Occurring at a macrolevel, this forest health emergency necessitated a mesolevel response that included specific actions at the microlevel. The MAST emerged to meet the challenges posed. Dense housing in overstocked forests susceptible to catastrophic fire created a dangerous situation that compelled agencies to respond. The recognition that individual agencies could not alone address the issue necessitated a collaborative response. MAST formed expressly to maximize collective resources and work across agencies to initiate projects that reduce the threat fire posed to communities.

The literature on new governance highlights elements that differentiate MAST from traditional or "old" governance approaches. These include governance arrangements that blur the lines between private and public interests. As illustrated by institutional, political, and regulatory indicators, we argue that MAST represents an example of new governance. MAST strategically incorporated private actors in its decision making and more importantly in its on-the-ground actions. This included energy companies that had jurisdiction over power lines on the mountain, private contractors to undertake forest thinning projects, and individual property owners engaged in vegetation thinning across private property. More importantly, MAST embodied a new governance approach by introducing a flexible policy approach that engaged a large diversity of actors. MAST had a strategic, hierarchical planning process that enabled all actors to participate and inform decision making. No one agency had supremacy over others and each agency committed to following the process and decision made collectively by MAST. This organizational structure served to engage all actors, provide them a reason to participate, and has created a lasting governing structure that met short-term objectives and persists to address decades-long objectives related to maintaining forest health across the landscape.

MAST created an effective interagency collaborative effort. Particular elements contributed to this outcome. The literature on interagency collaboration singles out leadership, trust, and minimizing turf disputes as critical to effective interagency collaboration. MAST created a new governance structure that addressed these three elements. A gap analysis identified who could contribute and where vulnerabilities existed across agencies. In addition to those elements, other factors fell into place that enabled work to move forward. MAST helped coordinate an effort that led to effective measures to reduce the risk of fire to communities, protect communication towers, and the successful evacuation of residents threatened by fire. In some cases, analyses of fire behavior have shown that fuel modification work has successfully diverted fires away from communities.

Through the creation of a new governance arrangement to address forest health problems in Southern California, MAST has established a model that others can manipulate to address macrolevel problems through meso- and microlevel responses. Interagency collaboration will undoubtedly play a prominent role in addressing landscape level forest problems in the future elsewhere and MAST provides insights on how to create such an approach.

Conflict of Interests

The authors declare that there is no conflict of interests regarding the publication of this paper.

References

[1] M. L. Bond, D. E. Lee, C. M. Bradley, and C. T. Hanson, "Influence of pre-fire tree mortality on fire severity in conifer forests of the San Bernardino Mountains, California," *The Open Forest Science Journal*, vol. 2, pp. 41–47, 2009.

[2] A. E. Dunn, A. Gonzalez-Caban, and K. Solari, *The Old, Grand Prix, and Padua Wildfires: How Much Did These Fires Really Cost?* USDA Forest Service, Riverside, Calif, USA, 2005.

[3] C. Tollefson, A. R. Zito, and F. Gale, "Symposium overview: conceptualizing new governance arrangements," *Public Administration*, vol. 90, no. 1, pp. 3–18, 2012.

[4] M. Howlett, J. Rayner, and C. Tollefson, "From government to governance in forest planning? Lessons from the case of the British Columbia Great Bear Rainforest initiative," *Forest Policy and Economics*, vol. 11, no. 5-6, pp. 383–391, 2009.

[5] O. E. Williamson, *The Economic Institutions of Capitalism: Firms, Markets, Relational Contracting*, Free Press, New York, NY, USA, 1985.

[6] R. A. W. Rhodes, "The new governance: governing without government," *Political Studies*, vol. 44, no. 4, pp. 652–667, 1996.

[7] D. Sprinz and T. Vaahtoranta, "The interest-based explanation of international environmental policy," *International Organization*, vol. 48, no. 1, pp. 77–105, 1994.

[8] M. Howlett and J. Rayner, "Globalization and governance capacity: explaining divergence in national forest programs as instances of "next-generation" regulation in Canada and Europe," *Governance*, vol. 19, no. 2, pp. 251–275, 2006.

[9] J. Voss, D. Bauknecht, and R. Kemp, Eds., *Reflexive Governance for Sustainable Development*, Edward Elgar, Cheltenham, UK, 2006.

[10] A. Gatto, "The law and governance debate in the European Union," Discussion Paper, International Institute for Labour Studies, Geneva, Switzerland, 2006.

[11] J. M. Wondolleck and S. L. Yaffee, *Making Collaboration Work: Lessons from Innovation in Natural Resource Management*, Island Press, Washington, DC, USA, 2000.

[12] M. Nie, *The Governance of Western Public Lands: Mapping Its Present and Future*, University of Kansas Press, Lawrence, Kan, USA, 2008.

[13] S. Vangen and C. Huxham, "Enacting leadership for collaborative advantage: dilemmas of ideology and pragmatism in the activities of partnership managers," *British Journal of Management*, vol. 14, pp. S61–S76, 2003.

[14] C. Huxham, "Theorizing collaboration practice," *Public Management Review*, vol. 5, pp. 401–423, 2003.

[15] M. Howlett, *Designing Public Policies: Principles and Instruments*, Routledge, New York, NY, USA, 2011.

[16] D. Knoke, *Political Networks: The Structural Perspective*, Cambridge University Press, Cambridge, Mass, USA, 1987.

[17] S. Lukes, *Power: A Radical View*, Macmillan, London, UK, 1974.

[18] C. E. Lindblom, *The Policy-Making Process*, Yale University Press, New Haven, Conn, USA, 1977.

[19] D. McCool, "The subsystem family of concepts: a critique and a proposal," *Political Research Quarterly*, vol. 51, no. 2, pp. 551–570, 1998.

[20] M. Doelle, C. Henschel, J. Smith, C. Tollefson, and A. Wellstead, "New governance arrangements at the intersection of climate change and forest policy: institutional, political and regulatory dimensions," *Public Administration*, vol. 90, no. 1, pp. 37–55, 2012.

[21] T. Moe, "The new economics of organization," *Journal of American Political Science*, vol. 28, pp. 739–777, 1984.

[22] E. Ostrom, "Rational choice and institutional analysis: towards a complementary," *American Political Science Review*, vol. 85, pp. 237–243, 1991.

[23] E. Schlager and W. Blomquist, "A comparison of three emerging theories of the policy process," *Political Research Quarterly*, vol. 49, no. 3, pp. 651–672, 1996.

[24] P. Sabatier and H. Jenkins-Smith, "The advocacy coalition framework: an assessment," in *Theories of the Policy Process*, P. Sabatier, Ed., Westview, Boulder, Colo, USA, 1999.

[25] R. C. Stedman, "Risk and climate change: perceptions of key policy actors in Canada," *Risk Analysis*, vol. 24, no. 5, pp. 1395–1406, 2004.

[26] E. Bardach, *Getting Agencies to Work Together: The Practice and Theory of Managerial Craftsmanship*, Brookings Institution Press, Washington, DC, USA, 1998.

[27] C. W. Thomas, *Bureaucratic Landscapes: Interagency Cooperation and the Preservation of Biodiversity*, The MIT Press, Cambridge, Mass, USA, 2003.

[28] C. Huxham and S. Vangen, "Doing things collaboratively: realizing the advantage or succumbing to inertia?" *IEEE Engineering Management Review*, vol. 32, no. 4, pp. 11–20, 2004.

[29] S. Page, "Entrepreneurial strategies for managing interagency collaboration," *Journal of Public Administration Research and Theory*, vol. 13, no. 3, pp. 311–340, 2003.

[30] E. Bardach, "Developmental dynamics: interagency collaboration as an emergent phenomenon," *Journal of Public Administration Research and Theory*, vol. 11, no. 2, pp. 149–164, 2001.

[31] S. Vangen and C. Huxham, "Nurturing collaborative relations: building trust in interorganizational collaboration," *Journal of Applied Behavioral Science*, vol. 39, pp. 5–31, 2003.

[32] D. P. Moynihan, "The network governance of crisis response: case studies of incident command systems," *Journal of Public Administration Research and Theory*, vol. 19, no. 4, pp. 895–915, 2009.

[33] SBNF, San Bernardino National Forest, 2009, http://www.fs.fed.us/r5/sanbernardino/about/index.shtml.

[34] USFS. United States Forest Service, *Final Environmental Impact Statement, Volume 1. Land Management Plans: Angeles National Forest, Cleveland National Forest, Los Padres National Forest, San Bernardino National Forest*, R5-MB-074-A, USDA Forest Service, Pacific Southwest Region, 2005.

[35] K. F. Raffa, B. H. Aukema, B. J. Bentz et al., "Cross-scale drivers of natural disturbances prone to anthropogenic amplification: the dynamics of bark beetle eruptions," *BioScience*, vol. 58, no. 6, pp. 501–517, 2008.

[36] C. D. Allen, "Interactions across spatial scales among forest dieback, fire, and erosion in northern New Mexico landscapes," *Ecosystems*, vol. 10, no. 5, pp. 797–808, 2007.

[37] M. J. Jenkins, E. Hebertson, W. Page, and C. A. Jorgensen, "Bark beetles, fuels, fires and implications for forest management in the Intermountain West," *Forest Ecology and Management*, vol. 254, no. 1, pp. 16–34, 2008.

[38] K. F. Raffa, E. N. Powell, and P. A. Townsend, "Temperature-driven range expansion of an irruptive insect heightened by weakly coevolved plant defenses," *Proceedings of the National Academy of Sciences of the United States of America*, vol. 110, no. 6, pp. 2193–2198, 2013.

[39] M. N. Patriquin, A. M. Wellstead, and W. A. White, "Beetles, trees, and people: regional economic impact sensitivity and policy considerations related to the mountain pine beetle infestation in British Columbia, Canada," *Forest Policy and Economics*, vol. 9, no. 8, pp. 938–946, 2007.

[40] C. G. Flint, B. McFarlane, and M. Müller, "Human dimensions of forest disturbance by insects: an international synthesis," *Environmental Management*, vol. 43, no. 6, pp. 1174–1186, 2009.

[41] L. Merrill, "Bark beetles and tree mortality in the San Bernardino Mountains: current situation and outlook," Unpublished Report, USDA Forest Service, Region 5, Southern California Shared Service Area, San Bernardino, Calif, USA, 2003.

[42] N. E. Grulke, R. A. Minnich, T. Paine D et al., "Air pollution increases forest susceptibility to wildfires: a case study in the San Bernardino Mountains in southern California," in *Developments in Environmental Science, Volume 8. Wildland Fires and Air Pollution*, A. Bytnerowicz, M. J. Arbaugh, A. R. Riebau, and C. Andersen, Eds., pp. 365–403, Elsevier, Amsterdam, The Netherlands, 2009.

[43] R. A. Minnich, M. G. Barbour, J. H. Burk, and R. F. Fernau, "Sixty years of change in Californian conifer forests of the San Bernardino Mountains," *Conservation Biology*, vol. 9, no. 4, pp. 902–914, 1995.

[44] J. G. Taylor, S. C. Gillette, R. W. Hodgson et al., "Informing the network: improving communication with interface communities during wildland fire," *Human Ecology Review*, vol. 14, no. 2, pp. 198–211, 2007.

[45] G. Rogers, W. Hann, C. Martin, T. Nicolet, and M. Pence, "Fuel treatment effects on fire behavior, suppression effectiveness, and structure ignition. Grass valley fire, San Bernardino National Forest," Tech. Rep. R5-TP-026a, USDA Forest Service, 2008.

[46] L. J. Johnson, D. Zorn, B. K. Y. Tam, M. Lamontagne, and S. A. Johnson, "Stakeholders views of factors that impact successful interagency collaboration," *Exceptional Children*, vol. 69, no. 2, pp. 195–209, 2003.

2

Impact of Formal Financial Market Participation on Farm Size and Expenditure on Variable Farm Inputs: The Case of Maize Farmers in Ghana

Dadson Awunyo-Vitor,[1] Ramatu M. Al-Hassan,[2] and Daniel B. Sarpong[2]

[1] *Department of Agricultural Economics, Agribusiness and Extension, Kwame Nkrumah University of Science and Technology, Kumasi, Ghana*
[2] *Department of Agricultural Economics and Agribusiness, University of Ghana, Legon, Ghana*

Correspondence should be addressed to Dadson Awunyo-Vitor; awunyovitor@yahoo.co.uk

Academic Editors: D. Dave, M. Matsui, and M. Ransom

The study examined maize farmers' participation in the formal financial market and its impact on farm size and expenditure on variable farm inputs. A multistage sampling method was used in selecting 595 maize farmers from the seven districts in Ashanti and Brong Ahafo Regions of Ghana. A structured questionnaire and interview schedule were used to elicit information from the respondents. The impact of formal financial market participation on farm size and expenditure on variable inputs was estimated using Propensity Score Matching (PSM) method. The results of the study showed that formal financial market participation has the potential to significantly increase expenditure on variable inputs by farmers and consequently use of improved technology. Therefore, formal financial market participation should be encouraged through education and promotional activities.

1. Introduction

The formal financial sector has been identified as important in improving productivity by making financial services available to producers in the agricultural sector. This is because informal financial services are often considered to be unsatisfactory because of extraordinarily high interest rates on credit, and savings are not sufficiently secure [1]. It is therefore assumed that participation in the formal financial market would lead to larger farm sizes and adoption of improved technology through increased expenditure on variable inputs.

In view of this, several policies have been adopted by successive governments of Ghana to improve access to financial services. These policies include liberalisation of the financial sector to increase private sector participation in the provision of financial services. The sector has now expanded from the prereform period of two foreign banks and two state owned banks with virtually no nonbank financial institutions, to include many private financial institutions. The question then is: has the expansion in the formal financial sector increased participation of farmers in the market, and if so what impact does a farmer's participation in formal financial market have on their input usage and farm size? This paper empirically examines the impact of formal financial market participation on farm size and expenditure on farm inputs by maize farmers in two regions of Ghana (Ashanti and Brong Ahafo).

The literature on impact evaluation methods is extensive. Some authors [2–4] present very useful overviews. Khandker et al. [5] have also discussed in detail different methods that are applicable for impact evaluation and the data needed for each type. In their methodological review, they stress the need to address the fundamental question of the missing counterfactual data in impact evaluation, such as assessing impact of financial services on performance indicators in a nonexperimental context.

A cross-sectional data from an observational study [5] discussed the use of the propensity score matching (PSM) approach and pointed out that this method can be used under the conditional independence assumption and common support assumption [5]. The main thrust of these assumptions is that all factors influencing participation are observable, and individuals with similar characteristics have an equal chance of belonging to either group (participants and nonparticipants).

Owusu and Abdulai [6] used the PSM approach to evaluate the impact of nonfarm income on food security and poverty in rural Ghana. The authors argue that participation in nonfarm activities requires a decision by the individual, which is influenced by certain individual observable factors which place them in either group. A related study [7] examined the impact of maize varieties on farm output and income levels in Mexico. In both studies, the basis for the use of PSM is that the factors which influence selection into participation (adoption) and nonparticipation (nonadoption) groups are assumed to be observable.

Mutua and Oyugi [8] have evaluated access to financial services and poverty reduction in rural Kenya using propensity score matching. The study looked at the role access to financial services could play in addressing poverty and its related problems, especially in rural areas. They observed a strong link between access to finance and poverty reduction. A policy implication arrived at from their study was that a legal and regulatory framework which takes into account the banking needs of the poor should be formulated. Owuor [9] has empirically examined the impact of microfinance on smallholder farmers in Kenya using PSM. He used multistage sampling to identify respondents. Over all, 440 farmers were interviewed in a cross-sectional survey. His findings revealed that smallholders' participation in micro-finance credit (MFC) improved their incomes by a range of between US$ 200 to US$ 260 per hectare in a single production period.

2. Methodology

2.1. Sampling and Data Collection. Multistage sampling was conducted to select 2 regions, 7 districts, and 595 farmers for the study. Selection of the regions and districts (first and second stage) was guided by the level of agricultural activities and the level of maize production using official statistics from the Ministry of Food and Agriculture (MoFA) [10].

In Ashanti Region, districts whose maize production output in 2008 exceeded 20,000 metric tonnes were selected, while in Brong Ahafo Region, the 5 districts which had a minimum of 27,000 metric tonnes each of maize output in 2008 were selected for the study. A third stage of sampling involved identifying and listing maize farmers in the operational areas of the extension agents. Selection of respondents was guided by their involvement in maize production. A total of 595 maize farmers from the study area were sampled for the study.

A questionnaire was administered to the sampled farmers. The survey questionnaire contained detailed sections on demographic and socioeconomic characteristics of the farmers, household characteristics, variable input usage, farm size, and formal financial market participation.

2.2. Theoretical and Analytical Framework. Formal financial market participation is considered in terms of usage of any of the formal financial services or combination of these services by the respondents. Respondents are considered financial market participants if they responded yes to the question "have you used any financial services within the formal financial market segment?" We adopted and modified a method used by [7] to evaluate the impact of formal financial market participation on farm size and expenditure and on variable inputs as a proxy for technology adoption.

Becerril and Abdulai [7] employed PSM to evaluate the marginal impact of improved maize varieties on poverty in Mexico. Rosenbaum and Rubin [11] pioneered this method followed by many other improvements and applications in works by [12–14]. Propensity Score is defined as the conditional probability of participation given preparticipation characteristics. The main basis for the use of PSM is that participation and nonparticipation decisions may not be random but rather selective and depending on preparticipation variables: the estimation of the effect of participation may be biased by the existence of selectivity bias or confounding factors. For example, in order to evaluate the impact of financial market participation on farm size and expenditure on variable input, it is necessary to draw a counterfactual scenario about the productivity variables of farmers who participated in the formal financial market. This group of respondents is referred to as the treated group of farmers. The counterfactual would then be compared with farm size and expenditure on variable inputs of the treated (those who participated in formal financial market) in order to evaluate the impact of formal financial market participation on farm size and expenditure on variable inputs. For the treated, their counterfactual is the farm size and expenditure they incurred on variable inputs when they did not participate in the formal financial market segment. While for the untreated (farmers who did not participate in formal financial market) their counterfactual is their farm size and expenditure on variable input when they participate in the formal financial market segment. If we use φ to represent the impact of financial market participation on one of the outcome variables say farm size, then

$$\varphi = Y_1 - Y_0, \tag{1}$$

where Y_1 and Y_0 denote farm sizes of the respondents when they participated in the financial market and the counterfactual, respectively. The average treatment effect (ATE) of financial market participation can be calculated as

$$\text{ATE} = E(\delta) = E(Y_1 - Y_0), \tag{2}$$

where $E(\cdot)$ represents the average or expected farm size. The impact of treatment on farm size of the farmers who participated in the financial market (treated) can be estimated as

$$\text{ATT} = E(Y_1 \mid D = 1) - E(Y_0 \mid D = 1), \tag{3}$$

where ATT represents Average Treatment effect on the treated and D denotes the formal financial market participation indicator which equals one (1) if the farmer participated in the formal financial market and zero (0) otherwise. $E(Y_0 \mid D = 1)$ is the mean farm size of treated in absence of the treatment, that is, counterfactual farm size. In the case of nonparticipant (untreated or control) group of farmers, their average farm size can be estimated as

$$\text{ATU} = E(Y_1 - Y_0 \mid D = 0), \quad (4)$$

where ATU is the Average Treatment effect on the untreated. The estimation of ATT and ATU clearly depends on the counterfactual levels of farm size of the two groups, treated and control $\{E(Y_0 \mid D = 1) \text{ and } (Y_0 \mid D = 0)\}$, respectively, as explained above. In nonexperimental studies such as ours, it is impossible to assess the counterfactual farm sizes of the two groups of respondent formal financial market participants (treated) and nonparticipant (untreated or control) groups. It is possible to use the farm size of nonparticipants as a counterfactual for participants or the treated. However, this may lead to a biased estimate of the impact (ATT) as a result of selection bias (Rosenbaum and Rubin, 1983) as follows:

$$\Delta = E(Y_1 \mid D = 1) - E(Y_0 \mid D = 0). \quad (5)$$

Through expansion and rearrangement, we have

$$\begin{aligned} \Delta &= E(Y_1 \mid D = 1) - E(Y_0 \mid D = 1) \\ &\quad + E(Y_0 \mid D = 1) - E(Y_0 \mid D = 0), \\ \Delta &= \text{ATT} + E(Y_0 \mid D = 1) - E(Y_0 \mid D = 0), \\ \Delta &= \text{ATT} + \text{SB}, \\ \text{ATT} &= \Delta - \text{SB}, \end{aligned} \quad (6)$$

where SB is selection bias which arises as a result of unobservable characteristics influencing selection of respondents into treatment and control groups, respectively. If SB $= 0$ then the difference between the average observed farm size of treated and control groups of farmers would be given as

$$\text{ATT} = E(Y \mid D = 1) - (Y \mid D = 0). \quad (7)$$

However if SB is not equal to zero then there exists selection bias; thus the estimated ATT would not be the difference in the average observed farm size of the treated and untreated (nonparticipants).

It is possible that hard working farmers may be the ones who participated in formal financial market due to these institutions' screening process; thus SB $\neq 0$. Hence farmers who participated in formal financial market may have larger farm sizes even if they did not participate in the formal financial market compared to nonparticipants. As a result, average farm size of the untreated group is not a good comparison for the counterfactuals of the treated group in estimating the impact of formal financial market participation on farm size.

Therefore, [11] suggested the use of the propensity score matching approach as a way to correct for the existence of these confounding factors based on the idea that the bias is reduced when the comparison is performed using participants and control group of farmers who are as similar as possible [5]. This approach is based on the idea that by matching the outcome variables of treated and control respondents who are similar in observable characteristics, selection bias would be eliminated.

The PSM method summarizes preparticipation characteristics into a single index known as the propensity score, which makes matching feasible. The propensity score is a conditional probability estimator, and any discrete choice model such as logit or probit can be used as they yield similar results [14]. Thus, the PSM approach follows two steps; first, either the logit or probit model is used to estimate the probability (propensity score) of programme participation, in this case financial market participation, using observable characteristics which influence participation in formal financial market. In this study the logit model is specified as

$$\begin{aligned} P(X) &= P(D = 1 \mid X) \\ &= F(\beta_1 X_1 + \cdots \beta_i X_i) \\ &= F(X\beta) \\ &= e^{X\beta}, \end{aligned} \quad (8)$$

where $F(\cdot)$ denotes response probability which strictly ranges between zero and one, X is a vector of all observable characteristics (Covariates) which influence formal financial market participation, and β is the parameter of interest to be estimated.

This model predicts the probability (propensity score) of formal financial market participation. Given that the propensity score is a balancing score, the probability of formal financial market participation conditional on X will lead to distribution of farmers' covariates X, such that these covariates will be the same for treatment and control groups. Assuming that all information relevant to formal financial market participation and farm size are observable, then the propensity score will produce valid matches which can be used to estimate impact (ATT) of formal financial market participation on farm size and expenditure on variable input at the second stage. This is done by matching the two groups of respondents on the basis of the predicted propensity scores as follows:

$$\begin{aligned} \text{ATT} = \{&(E(Y_1 \mid D = 1 \cdot E(P(X)))) \\ &- E(Y_0 \mid D = 1 \cdot E(P(X)))\}, \end{aligned} \quad (9)$$

where $E(P(X))$ denote the expectation with respect to the distribution of the propensity score in the entire population and $E(Y_1 \mid D = 1, P(X))$, $E(Y_0 \mid D = 1)$ are as defined above under (3).

Three different matching algorithms which involve tradeoffs in terms of bias and efficiency are used to estimate ATT. These matching estimators are Nearest Neighbour, Radius, and Kernel Matching methods and are all conditional on the propensity score. Nearest Neighbour Matching (NNM) selects the control group with the smallest distance in propensity score to the treated group (farmers who access financial services). Generally, this is done with replacement, and it works well once the distribution of the propensity score of both groups (control and treated) is similar. However,

NNM may lead to poor matches when the nearest neighbours are far away.

Radius Matching (RM) or Calliper involves all neighbours with a maximum propensity score distance. This is normally defined *a priori*, and it corresponds to the common support assumption. Radius matching also helps to avoid poor matches which may arise through matching too distant neighbours [15]. Kernel-Based Matching (KM) was recommended by [16]. This is a nonparametric estimator that includes all respondents of the underlying sample of control group and weighs more distant observed characteristics among both groups (control and treated) down. Hence it indicates lower variance. Caliendo and Kopenig [14] noted that poorer matches could be obtained. The Kernel-based estimator of the ATT describes the mean difference in outcome while the matched outcome is given by the Kernel-weighted average of the outcome of the control group of farmers.

The PSM model works under two assumptions, namely, the conditional independence assumption and the common support or the balancing assumption. The conditional independence assumption postulates that all the covariates must be independent of participation. This means that the selection of farmers into both groups (treatment and control groups) is exclusively based on observable covariates X which influence the propensity score. In this case, farm size and expenditure on variable inputs of participants (treated) and nonparticipants (control group) are assumed to be independent of the treatment, conditional on observable characteristics or covariates X, respectively. Thus respondents' participation and nonparticipation decision is exclusively based on observable covariate X. The balancing assumption or the common support assumption (CSA) postulates that participation is shaped by preparticipation characteristics. Thus, this assumption rules out the phenomenon of perfect predictability of financial market participation ($D = 1$) given covariates X. This ensures that farmers with identical observable characteristics or covariates (X) have a positive probability of belonging to a particular group [16].

Good quality matches are those whose covariates are conditioned after the estimation of the propensity score and which are able to balance the distribution of the relevant variables between the treated and controlled respondents. For the standardized bias approach proposed by [11], the quality of matches is assessed by comparing the situation before and after matching to check if there remain any differences after conditioning on the propensity score. Sianesi [17] has also recommended an additional assessment of the matching quality which requires the reestimation of the propensity score of matched participants and matched nonparticipants. The matching procedure is expected to balance the covariates very well if the pseudo-R^2 after matching is fairly low, while the probability of the F-statistics is not significantly different from zero.

Furthermore, following [18] an appropriate control strategy of hidden bias is to examine the sensitivity of significance levels. It is important to assess the sensitivity of the estimated participating effect because this explained what happens when there is hidden bias. The symbol e^{γ} is used to present a measure of the degree of departure from a PSM result that is free from hidden bias [18]. Thus several values of e^{γ} are calculated to test the sensitivity of the significance level. This test helps to identify the critical impact level at which significance would be lost. This represents the level of unobservable covariate at which the inference about the treatment effect will be undermined [19]. In this study, the quality of the matches is evaluated by using the approach recommended by [17], and the sensitivity of significance levels was examined by using a method suggested by [18]. The first step in the PSM approach is the estimation of the participation model using a binary choice model. In this study the logit model was used to estimate probability of formal financial market participation or use of formal financial services.

The empirical model is specified as

$$\begin{aligned} \text{PART} = {} & \beta_0 + \beta_1 \text{GEN} + \beta_2 \text{YEDU} + \beta_3 \text{VALMOUTPU} \\ & + \beta_4 \text{OATIV} + \beta_5 \text{HSIZ} + \beta_6 \text{TASET} \\ & + \beta_7 \text{PROXIFA} + \beta_8 \text{LenProFOR} + \beta_9 \text{FSIZE} + e. \end{aligned} \quad (10)$$

3. Definition of Variables Used in the Logit Model

3.1. Dependent Variable: Participation in Formal Financial Market (PART). A dummy variable is used as the dependent variable as "use of formal financial services." This variable reflects respondent's use of formal financial services. It is specified as 1 if the respondent participates or uses any of the services provided by formal financial institutions and 0 otherwise.

3.2. Independent Variables

3.2.1. Gender (GEN). The likelihood of use of saving, credit, and money transfer services is assumed to be lower among female farmers. Relatively, female farmers are often poorer than male farmers. World Bank [20, 21] indicated that the female gender in the individual, household, and wider community and national context are affected by financial, economic, cultural, political, and legal obstacles which affect their demand for financial services.

Gender classification is important in this type of analysis because in Ghana as in many African societies, men and women have different levels of responsibilities and engage in different economic activities. Even if they engage in the same economic activities, it is at varying degrees of operation which have different implications on their use of financial services. The gender of the respondent is specified as a dummy variable which takes the value of 1 if the respondent is male and 0 otherwise. It is hypothesised that male farmers are more likely to participate in formal financial market compared to female farmers.

3.2.2. Years of Schooling (YEDU). Respondents who have attained higher educational levels are expected to have more exposure to the financial institution's policies regarding use of financial services. The higher the educational level is the more likely the farmer would be able to understand the needs of the financial institution in terms of requirement for access to their services. Therefore, it is hypothesized that education would have a positive relationship with use of services provided by formal financial institutions. Steiner [22] found a positive and significant relationship between higher education and use of formal financial services in Ghana. In this study we use the number of years of schooling to represent level of education.

3.2.3. Previous Year's Maize Income (VALPUT). The value of maize harvested is an important factor that would determine a farmer's use of services provided by formal financial institutions because this is a major source of their income. Where the value of maize harvested is low, the farmer has limited resources to save hence could not participate in the formal financial market by saving and may not be able to access credit as most institutions use savings as collateral for granting loans. Alternatively with a higher income from maize, a farmer may be able to save and demand credit therefore is more likely to participate in a formal financial market. This variable is specified as total value of maize sales from previous year's harvest, and it is hypothesised to have a positive effect on the demand for financial services.

3.2.4. Off-Farm Income Generating Activities (OATIV). Farmers may engage in off-farm income generating activities. Some activities require large amounts of capital and offer higher returns compared to others. In addition, formal financial institutions develop products which fit the revenue and expenditure cycles of off-farm income activities which encourage use of formal financial services. Therefore, use of formal financial services is assumed to have a positive relationship with engagement in off-farm income generating activities. This variable is specified as a dummy variable which takes the value of 1 if the farmer has a secondary income source and 0 otherwise.

3.2.5. Farmer's Household Size (HSIZ). The size of the household is assumed to positively influence the likelihood of using formal financial services. This is because larger households have more household members thus potentially may have higher consumption expenses which may affect their ability to save. Levels of saving tend to influence access to credit. Also larger households may have members who might occasionally be living outside their permanent residence and send money to or receive money from the household. For example, households may have a member in senior high school, whose fees may be paid through a formal financial institution. Chen and Chivakul [23] found family size to be a significant variable which influenced credit demand for household in Bosnia and Herzegovina. This variable is measured as the number of individual household members taken care of by the respondents. This variable is expected to have a negative effect on formal financial market participation.

3.2.6. Farmer's Household Assets (TASET). The value of the farmer's household assets is estimated as the sum of the resale value of household or domestic assets measured in Ghana Cedis (GH¢). This is used as a proxy for respondent's wealth status in line with [24]. It is expected that the higher the value of the asset is, the more likely farmers will participate in formal financial market by using saving and credit facilities as these assets can be used as collateral to secure loans which would support income generation and consequently savings. Therefore value of household asset is expected to have a positive effect on participation in formal financial market.

3.2.7. Proximity to Formal Financial Institution (PROXIFA). Farmers who live far from financial institutions are less likely to contact the financial institution easily for more information than those who live close by. Thus it is assumed that a farmer who lives at a distance of less than 2 km (walking distance) to a financial institution is more likely to use services provided by the institution because of lower transactions cost. This variable is specified as a dummy and takes the value of 1 if the farmer perceived the distance to be far, that is, beyond a walking distance (2 Km) to the nearest formal financial institution and 0 otherwise.

3.2.8. Farmers' Perception of Operational Modalities of Financial Institution (OPMO). Farmers pass through different processes to use formal financial services which are operational modalities of the institution. Depending on the institution, some of these processes can be time consuming and difficult to understand. Farmers may prefer to use financial services if they perceive operational modalities to be satisfactory. This variable is specified as a dummy variable which takes a value 1 if farmer perceive savings processes and lending procedures as cumbersome or unsatisfactory and 0 otherwise.

3.2.9. Farm Size (FSIZE). Farm size is measured in hectares and used as a proxy for the scale of operation, and it can also be used by lenders to estimate expected income of the farmer and therefore earning capacity. Farmers with large farm sizes are expected to increase the use of formal financial services as it influences savings and consequently credit.

4. Results and Discussion

4.1. Participation in Formal Financial Market. The data has been disaggregated into farmers who participated in formal financial market only, those who participated in informal financial market only, and those who participated in both formal and informal financial market. In all, 41% of the respondents participated in the formal market segment only while 13% used the informal market segment only. About eleven percent of the respondents used both market segments and close to 34% used neither formal nor informal financial intermediaries (see Table 1).

4.2. Factors Influencing Formal Financial Market Participation. The estimated coefficients of the logit model, along with the levels of significance and marginal effects, are presented

TABLE 1: Financial market participation among the sample.

Institution	Frequency	Percentage
Formal	243	40.84
Informal	79	13.28
Both formal and informal	70	11.76
None	203	34.12
Total	595	100.00

Source: Survey data.

in Table 2. The likelihood ratio statistics as indicated by chi-square statistics are highly significant ($P < 0.00001$), suggesting that the model has a strong explanatory power. The logit regression gave P value for Hosmer and Lemeshow goodness-of-fit test as 0.8602 which suggests that the model fits reasonably well. Given these goodness of fit measures, it is concluded that the logit model used has integrity and is appropriate.

The coefficient of education is positive and statistically significant at 1% level of significance. This implies that farmers with higher level of education are more likely to participate in formal financial market. This might be due to the fact that they can read and write hence understand benefit of using formal financial services and also are able to follow the procedures of the financial institution required for use of their services. A unit increase in number of years of schooling would result in a 1.72% increase in the likelihood of respondents participating in the formal financial market. The previous year's maize income has a positive and significant effect on participation in the formal financial market. This implies that if farmers earn more from maize production activities, they are more likely to keep their excess income with formal financial institution. A cedi increase in maize income increases the likelihood of using services of a formal financial institution by 1.83%.

Engagement in off-farm income generating activities significantly increases the likelihood of respondents participating in the formal financial market. This is because farmers who engage in off-farm income generating activities tend to generate additional income, which increases their demand for savings. This improves their savings and increases their account balance thereby increasing their demand for credit. Engagement in off-farm income generating activities increases the probability of using formal financial services by 11%. A farmer's total assets also have a positive effect on their use of formal financial services. This result indicates that wealthy farmers are more likely to participate in formal financial market.

The coefficient of a farmer's perception on proximity to the nearest formal financial institution is negative and significant at 1%. The result indicates that farmers who perceive that the distance between their residence and the location of the formal financial institution to be too far are less likely to participate in the formal financial market. Specifically farmers who perceive the distance to be far are 17.9% less likely to use services of formal financial institutions. This may be attributed to the fact that they would incur higher costs to transact business with the institution.

As can be observed in Table 2, the coefficient of operational modalities is positive and significant at 1%. Farmers who perceive operational modalities of formal financial institutions to be satisfactory are 37% more likely to use their services compared to their counterparts who perceive the operational modalities as unsatisfactory.

Farm size is related positively to participation in formal financial market. The coefficient is statistically significant at 5% level of significance. Based on the marginal effect, a hectare increase in farm size is likely to increase probability of farmer participating in formal financial market by 12.5% (Table 2).

4.3. Impact of Formal Financial Market Participation on Farm Size and Expenditure on Variable Inputs. Nearest Neighbour, Radius, and Kernel-based matching algorithms were used for the matching. The results of the propensity score matching on the impact of formal financial market participation on farm size and expenditure on variable inputs per hectare are presented in Table 3. All the matches gave similar results. The nearest neighbour matching estimate of the impact of formal financial market participation on farm size recorded an increase of about 0.11 hectare. However, this increase is statistically insignificant. In the case of expenditure on variable inputs, farmers who participated in the formal financial market recorded higher expenditure than nonparticipants (GH¢ 85.18), and this is significant at the 1% level. In the case of calliper or radius matching, we considered neighbours with a calliper of 0.01.

The result shows a 0.99 hectare increase in farm size, but this is statistically not significant. However, there is a GH¢ 79.42 increase in expenditure on variable inputs per hectare as a result of formal financial market participation by the respondents and is statistically significant at 1%. These results support the findings of [9] that farmers in Kenya who participated in microfinance programme had significantly higher productive income which can be attributed to higher input usage.

With regard to kernel-based matching algorithm, each participant is matched with a weighted average of all nonparticipants with weights that are inversely proportional to the distance between the propensity score of the participants and nonparticipants. In this study, we used a smoothening parameter of 0.06. The effect of formal financial market participation on farm size and expenditure on variable inputs per hectare shows an increase of 0.41 hectare and GH¢ 82.58, respectively. However, only expenditure on variable inputs is statistically significant at 1% level of significance. All the matching techniques produce consistent estimates of the effect of formal financial market participation on farm size and expenditure on variable inputs.

Table 4 presents results from covariate balancing tests before and after matching which gives an indication of matching quality. The results show substantial reduction in absolute bias for all the outcome variables for the three matching algorithms. As indicated in Table 3, the mean bias after matching lies below the 20% level suggested by [11].

TABLE 2: Logit model to predict the probability of participating in formal financial market conditional on selected observables characteristics. Dependent variable: participation or access to formal financial services ($Y = 1$).

Covariates	Odds Ratio	Marginal Effect
GEN gender of respondents	1.3387	0.0709
YEDU years of schooling	1.0742***	0.0172
VALPUT previous year's maize income	1.0285**	0.0183
TASET total asset	1.0003**	0.0007
OATIV engaged in off-farm income generating activities	1.5863**	0.1125
ACOM level of maize commercialisation	2.0473***	0.1757
PROXI proximity to financial institution	−2.2250***	−0.1799
OPMO operational modalities	7.1746***	0.3791
FSIZE farm size	2.0214**	0.1256
Number of obs = 577 LR χ^2 (14) = 168.41 Prob $>\chi^2$ = 0.0000 Pseudo R^2 = 0.2114		

*$P < 0.1$; **$P < 0.05$; ***$P < 0.01$.

TABLE 3: Estimated impact of formal financial market participation on farm size and expenditure on variable inputs per hectare.

(a) Nearest neighbour matching (NNM)

Outcomes	Average treatment effect (ATE)	Average treatment effect on untreated (ATU)	Average treatment effect on the treated (ATT)
Farm size	5.993	5.882	0.111 (0.21)
Expenditure on variable inputs	190.826	105.642	85.184*** (4.93)
No. of observations	218	180	

(b) Radius matching (RM) with a calliper of 0.01

Outcomes	Average treatment effect (ATE)	Average treatment effect on untreated (ATU)	Average treatment effect on the treated (ATT)
Farm size	6.0584	5.143	0.985 (0.66)
Expenditure on variable inputs	192.519	113.095	79.423*** (3.17)
No. of observations	190	174	

(c) Kernel-based matching (KBM) using smoothening parameter of 0.06

Outcomes	Average treatment effect (ATE)	Average treatment effect on untreated (ATU)	Average treatment effect on the treated (ATT)
Farm size	6.127	5.721	0.406 (0.65)
Expenditure on variable inputs	192.083	109.502	82.581*** (3.02)
No. Of observations	227	190	

t-statistics are in parenthesis.
Source: own calculations.
***$P < 0.01$.

This indicates that the variables were significantly balanced as a result of the propensity score matching procedure. In addition, the pseudo-R^2s after matching are fairly low with none of the F-statistics being significantly different from zero, suggesting that the proposed specification of the propensity score is fairly successful in terms of balancing the distribution of covariates between the two participants and nonparticipants [17].

Furthermore, following [18] the sensitivity of significance levels were examined. Here, several values of $\mathbf{e}^{\gamma}$ bounds are calculated on the significance level, and the null hypotheses of no effect of participation on potential outcomes, farm

TABLE 4: Indicators of matching quality before and after matching.

Matching algorithm	Outcome indicator	R^2 unmatched	R^2 matched	P value unmatched	P value matched	Mean absolute bias unmatched	Mean absolute bias matched	Absolute bias reduction
Nearest neighbour	Farm size	0.209	0.021	0.000	0.399	21.6	7.6	64.7
	Expenditure on variable inputs per hectare	0.209	0.020	0.000	0.308	8.2	12.1	47.8
Calliper	Farm size	0.209	0.017	0.000	0.555	21.6	5.8	73.0
	Expenditure on variable inputs per hectare	0.209	0.018	0.000	0.456	8.2	11.6	40.8
Kernel base matching	Farm size	0.213	0.026	0.000	0.268	21.6	5.6	73.0
	Expenditure on variable inputs per hectare	0.209	0.020	0.000	0.308	8.2	12.1	47.5

Source: author's calculations.

TABLE 5: Sensitivity analysis with Rosenbaum's bounds on probability values on farm size and expenditure on variable inputs.

	Upper bounds on the significance level for different values of $\mathbf{e}^\gamma$				
	$\mathbf{e}^\gamma = 1.25$	$\mathbf{e}^\gamma = 1.5$	$\mathbf{e}^\gamma = 1.75$	$\mathbf{e}^\gamma = 2$	
Using the single closest neighbour					
Farm size	0.0001	0.0072	0.0871	0.327	0.6324
Expenditure on variable inputs	<0.0001	<0.0001	0.0018	0.0211	0.1009
Using all neighbours within a calliper of 0.01					
Farm size	0.0005	0.0255	0.1884	0.505	0.785
Expenditure on variable inputs	<0.0001	<0.0001	0.0015	0.0171	0.0832
Using a biweight kernel function and a smoothing parameter of 0.06					
Farm size	0.0001	0.012	0.1254	0.4131	0.7202
Expenditure on variable inputs	<0.0001	<0.0001	0.0001	0.003	0.023

Source: author's calculations.

size, and expenditure on variable inputs tested, respectively, using the three introduced matching algorithms. Table 5 presents the result of the sensitivity analysis on farm size and expenditure on variable inputs.

Overall, robustness of the results produced by Rosenbaum's bounds are quite similar. Kernel-based matching produces the most robust treatment effect estimates with respect to hidden bias especially in the case of expenditure on variable inputs. Matched pairs might differ ($\mathbf{e}^\gamma = 2$) in unobservable characteristics, while the impact of participation on expenditure on variable inputs would be still significant at a level of 5%.

The same expenditure on variable inputs is robust to hidden bias up to an influence of $\mathbf{e}^\gamma = 2$ at a significance level of 10% following the radius matching approach. Also the nearest neighbour matching is robust to selection bias unobservable characteristics up to an impact level of $\mathbf{e}^\gamma = 1.75$ and $\mathbf{e}^\gamma = 2$, respectively. The estimated treatment effects on farm size are sensitive to hidden bias, at a smaller unobservable impact level of $\mathbf{e}^\gamma = 1.5$. Nevertheless, it has to be considered that these sensitivity results are worst-case scenarios, even though they indicate information about uncertainty within the matching estimators of treatment effects [18].

5. Conclusion and Policy Implications

The results from the logit model indicate that farmers' socioeconomic characteristics such as education, previous year's maize income, engagement in off-farm income generating activities, and farm size significantly influence their formal financial market participation positively. Thus improvement in the farmers' income levels through off-farm income generating activities and stable producer prices for maize would encourage farmers' participation in formal financial market or use of formal financial services.

Governmental and Nongovernmental Organisations that work to empower farmers' livelihood should train the farmers in off-farm income generating activities. This will encourage farmers' participation in formal financial market. Farm income improvement policy in terms of adequate remunerations for farmers (stable producer prices) is also an important policy option for increasing formal financial market participation.

Also, farm size expansion and a maize commercialisation policy will improve farmers' participation in financial services. Furthermore, availability of formal financial institution and use of friendly operational modalities will improve formal financial market participation by farmers. Thus, formal financial institutions should adapt their savings and lending modalities to the needs of the farmers (i.e., making it less cumbersome).

The results of the PSM analysis showed that farmers who participated in the formal financial market tended to spend more on variable inputs than nonparticipants. They also had higher farm sizes as compared with nonparticipants (albeit not statistically significant). Therefore, formal financial market participation should be encouraged through education and promotional programmes by formal financial institutions.

Conflict of Interests

The authors declare that there is no conflict of interests regarding the publication of this paper.

References

[1] S. R. Khandker and R. R. Faruqee, "The impact of farm credit in Pakistan," *Agricultural Economics*, vol. 28, no. 3, pp. 197–213, 2003.

[2] E. Duflo, R. Glennerster, and M. Kremer, "Using randomization in development economics research," *Handbook of Development Economics*, vol. 4, pp. 25–39, 2008.

[3] M. Ravallion, "Bailing out the world's poorest," *Challenge*, vol. 52, no. 2, pp. 55–80, 2008.

[4] R. Blundell and M. C. Dias, "Evaluation methods for non-experimental data," *Fiscal Studies*, vol. 21, no. 4, pp. 427–468, 2000.

[5] S. R. Khandker, G. B. Koolwal, and H. A. Samad, *Handbook on Impact Evaluation: Quantitative Methods and Practices*, The world Bank, Washington, DC, USA, 2010.

[6] V. Owusu and A. Abdulai, "Non-farm Work and Food Security Among Farm Households in Northern Ghana," non-farm_northern-ghana, 2009, http://www.pegnet.ifw-kiel.de/activities/research/.

[7] J. Becerril and A. Abdulai, "The impact of improved maize varieties on poverty in Mexico: a propensity score-matching approach," *World Development*, vol. 38, no. 7, pp. 1024–1035, 2010.

[8] J. M. Mutua and L. N. Oyugi, "Access to financial services and poverty reduction in rural Kenya," NEPRU Working Paper 108, 2006.

[9] G. Owuor, "Is micro-finance achieving its goal among small-holder farmers in Africa? Empirical evidence from Kenya using propensity score matching," in *Proceedings of the 25th International Conference of Agricultural Economists*, Beijing, China, August 2009.

[10] Ministry of Food and Agriculture, *Agriculture in Ghana Facts and Figures*, MoFA Ghana, 2009.

[11] P. R. Rosenbaum and D. B. Rubin, "The central role of the propensity score in observational studies for causal effects," *Biometrika*, vol. 70, no. 1, pp. 41–55, 1983.

[12] R. H. Dehejia and S. Wahba, "Causal effects in nonexperimental studies: reevaluating the evaluation of training programs," *Journal of the American Statistical Association*, vol. 94, no. 448, pp. 1053–1062, 1999.

[13] S. O. Becker and A. Ichino, "Estimation of average participation effects based on propensity scores," *The Stata Journal*, vol. 2, no. 4, pp. 358–377, 2002.

[14] M. Caliendo and S. Kopeinig, "Some practical guidance for the implementation of propensity score matching," *Journal of Economic Surveys*, vol. 22, no. 1, pp. 31–72, 2008.

[15] J. A. Smith and P. E. Todd, "Does matching overcome LaLonde's critique of nonexperimental estimators?" *Journal of Econometrics*, vol. 125, no. 1-2, pp. 305–353, 2005.

[16] J. Heckman, R. LaLonde, and J. Smith, "The economics and econometrics of active labor market programs," in *Handbook of Labor Economics*, O. Ashenfelter and D. Card, Eds., vol. 3, pp. 1865–2097, Elsevier, Amsterdam, The Netherlands, 1999.

[17] B. Sianesi, "An evaluation of the active labour market programmes in Sweden," *The Review of Economics and Statistics*, vol. 86, no. 1, pp. 133–155, 2004.

[18] P. R. Rosenbaum, *Observational Studies*, Springer, New York, NY, USA, 2002.

[19] T. A. DiPrete and M. Gang, "Assessing bias in the estimation of causal effects: rosenbaum bounds on matching estimators and instrumental variables estimation with imperfect instruments," *Sociological Methodology*, vol. 34, pp. 271–310, 2004.

[20] World Bank, *Finance for All? Policies and Pitfalls in Expanding Access*, World Bank, Washington, DC, USA, 2005.

[21] T. Jappelli, "Who is credit constrained in the U.S. economy," *Quarterly Journal of Economics*, vol. 105, pp. 219–234, 1990.

[22] S. Steiner, *Determinants of the Use of Financial Services in Rural Ghana: Implications For Social Protection*, Brooks World Poverty Institute, University of Manchester, 2008.

[23] C. K. Chen and M. Chivakul, "What drives household borrowing and credit constraints? Evidence from bosnia Herzegovnia," IMF Working Paper 08(202), 2008.

[24] M. A. Y. Rahji and S. B. Fakayode, "A multinomial logit analysis of agricultural credit rationing by commercial banks in Nigeria," *International Research Journal of Finance and Economics*, vol. 1, no. 24, pp. 90–100, 2009.

3

Education and Unemployment Patterns for Young Workers with Job Experience in Spain

Juan Acosta-Ballesteros, M. del Pilar Osorno-del Rosal, and Olga M. Rodríguez-Rodríguez

Departamento de Análisis Económico, Facultad de Ciencias Económicas y Empresariales, Universidad de La Laguna, Campus de Guajara, S/C de Tenerife, 38071 La Laguna, Spain

Correspondence should be addressed to Juan Acosta-Ballesteros; jacosta@ull.edu.es

Academic Editors: M. E. Kandil and M. Tsionas

This paper analyzes the education and unemployment patterns for young workers with some experience in Spain at the beginning of the current economic crisis, using the *ad hoc* module of the Spanish Labour Force Survey 2009. The results clearly show that educational level and field of study are crucial when explaining the instability of the first job and the difficulty in obtaining another one. Specifically, the lower is the educational level, the greater is the risk of unemployment, not only because it is less likely to keep the first job, but also because it is harder to find another one. Moreover, considering the field of study at a given educational level, it is detected that graduates from health and welfare are the best positioned in the labour market (especially university degree holders). For the rest of fields of study, and despite the differences in the risk of unemployment are small, it is observed that the lowest level of unemployment corresponds to sciences and technology, followed by social sciences and the rest of fields. The education and unemployment patterns detected in the paper may be useful to guide both policy and individual decisions.

1. Introduction

The high unemployment rate observed nowadays in the Spanish labour market has very negative consequences for young people, since they are especially sensitive to the business cycle. According to the Spanish Labour Force Survey, the unemployment rate for young workers in Spain was 34.09% in the third quarter of 2013, while this percentage was significantly higher than the national average of 25.98%. These figures reflect barriers in the school-to-work transition, which has been recently studied in the literature (see, e.g., [1–3]) Moreover, the high unemployment rate also affects young workers who have successfully found a first job and struggle to maintain it, since when they lose it their probability of unemployment is considerable.

In 2013, there were 7,249,800 active people under 35 in Spain; about 7.25% of them were looking for their first job, meaning that more than 6,700,000 active people in this age group had some previous experience. These young workers may be still working in their first job or, alternatively, they may be employed in a different one or unemployed.

Although this group of workers is really numerous, little has been said about their labour market situation in the literature. This paper partially fills in this gap. Moreover, as education (level and field of study) plays a crucial role in workers' career, the main objective of this study is to analyse the education and unemployment patterns for young workers with job experience in Spain. In order to develop this objective, the effect of education on the probability of maintaining the first job, as well as on the probability of being employed in another one or unemployed once they have gone out that first job, is studied. Analysing this issue is especially interesting in a period of crisis, which is especially affecting the Spanish economy, since the groups of young workers (according to these educational variables) who are handling it better can be identified.

The rest of the paper is organized as follows. Section 2 describes the sample and the variables included in the econometric analysis, while the model is specified in Section 3. The results obtained are shown in Section 4 and the paper ends with the main conclusions obtained.

2. Data and Variables

Empirical results are based on data from the *ad hoc* module on entrance of young people into the labour market, included in the Spanish Labour Force Survey (LFS, 2009). The choice of the LFS questionnaire is based on the fact that it contains crucial information that is not included in other sources, as the one related to educational level and field of study. Moreover, the module provides two important advantages: first, although it does not include information on the complete workers' career, it contains information about some characteristics of the entry job, and second, the current economic crisis had yet begun in 2009, so the groups of workers who are handling it better can be identified, as established in the objective of the study.

It is important to mention that the standard LFS used in this paper corresponds to 2009, but the module includes data related to the workers' first job. Thus, the individuals included in the sample obtained their first job after finishing school at different moments of time. This means that some of them might have been employed in different jobs before 2009. Then, the analysis does not necessarily refer to their employment/unemployment status immediately after leaving that first job.

The data includes the answers to the standard LFS questionnaire and the specific questions of the module for 23,286 workers under 35. Firstly, workers without a first significant job (i.e., with a duration of at least 3 months) after finishing school were excluded from the sample, since the paper focuses on young workers with some previous experience. Secondly, young people who remained in the educational system in 2009, those who were already working when they left school, self-employed workers, and members of the Armed Forces were also excluded. Finally, additional filters were applied to reject individuals with inconsistent answers and those who did not provide the necessary information for the analysis.

Thus, the final sample includes 7,850 young workers who have already got a first significant job. Sixty percent of them did not keep that first job in 2009. This instability is not surprising, since temporary employment in Spain represents around 25% of total employment and this percentage is even higher among young workers. In addition, about 29% of the individuals who did not hold their first job were unemployed in 2009. Therefore, a 17.34% of young workers in the sample were unemployed, whereby an 83.66% are employed, either in their first job or in another one.

With regard to the exogenous variables, educational level and field of study are basic in the analysis. According to the National Classification of Education (NCE-2000), and taking into account the limitations imposed by the need for an acceptable number of observations, a set of dummy variables is defined in order to provide a two-dimensional joint vision. In this sense, for general educational programmes (compulsory secondary or lower and noncompulsory secondary education) dummies for both levels are created; similarly, dummy variables for each of the four specializations considered for vocational training and university degrees are defined (i.e., 8 dummies): social sciences, sciences and technology, health and welfare, and other fields (education, arts, humanities, or services). Furthermore, dummy variables are included to differentiate the effect of higher relating to lower vocational training and long-cycle relating to short-cycle university degrees.

The rest of the explanatory variables are as follows.

Personal characteristics (gender and nationality) as well as socioeconomic background (the highest educational level of the two progenitors) are included. Whether the worker has got children or not has been considered in the analysis; therefore, the correspondent dummies appear interacting with gender in order to consider the possibility that family responsibilities have a different influence on the labour situation of men and women.

Workers are classified as overeducated in their first job according to an objective method previously developed in Rahona [4] and similar to the one applied in some of the literatures on overeducation in Spain. Furthermore, workers' potential experience (years elapsed since leaving the educational system until 2009) is considered when analysing the risk of unemployment of workers who are out of their first job; alternatively, the time since workers got their first significant job until 2009 is controlled in the analysis of the probability of maintaining it.

Additionally, information on first job characteristics, as part-time or fixed-term contract, is included, and finally, the activity sector, the GDP per capita by Autonomous Communities in 2009 (in relation to the national average), and the unemployment rate by gender in the quarter of the survey are also controlled.

A sample description is shown in Table 1. As most of the variables in the econometric analysis are dummies, Table 1 includes the sample frequencies for the most important ones. The sample average values for the continuous variables are also displayed.

3. Methodology

As previously stated, the main objective of the study is to analyse the effect of the educational variables (level and field of study) when explaining the employment/unemployment status of young workers with some experience in 2009. To this end, a bivariate probit model with sample selection is estimated. Thus, considering exclusively young workers who succeeded in the school-to-work transition, the model allows analysing two issues: the probability of maintaining their first job and, for the ones who do not maintain it, the probability of being unemployed.

As the observed unemployment data are nonrandomly selected for the set of workers who got a first job after leaving school, a bivariate probit model with sample selection is specified (see, e.g., [5, 6]).

Let us define y_1^* as the latent variable reflecting the probability of being unemployed and y_2^* as the latent variable

Table 1: Sample description: frequencies and average values.

Gender: female	46.3
Nationality: non-Spanish	7.1
Parents' higher educational level	
Compulsory education or lower	67.6
Noncompulsory secondary or lower vocational training	16.6
University or higher vocational training	15.7
Children	
Male worker	3.0
Female worker	3.9
Educational level and field of study	
Compulsory secondary or lower	36.8
Noncompulsory secondary	11.1
Vocational training (VT) in social sciences	8.4
VT in sciences and technology	12.8
VT in health and welfare	3.0
VT in other fields	4.4
Higher vocational training	15.4
University in social sciences	7.4
University in sciences and technology	6.0
University in health and welfare	3.8
University in other fields	6.4
Long-cycle university	12.4
First job	
Part-time	17.2
Overeducated	51.8
Fixed-term	67.3
Time since obtained first job	
Less than 2 years	13.2
2-3 years	19.8
4-5 years	15.1
6–10 years	30.4
More than 10 years	21.4
Potential experience	
Three years or less	12.3
3 to 5 years	14.0
5 to 10 years	34.3
More than 10 years	39.4
Unemployment rate by gender in the quarter of the survey*	21.5
GDP per capita by Autonomous Communities in 2009*	0.949

The frequency of the omitted category for variables with just two categories is not included since it is complementary to the one displayed in the table.
*Continuous variable (average).
Source: Spanish Labour Force Survey (2009). Own calculations.

indicating the likelihood of not keeping the first job. Then, the model can be specified as follows:

$$y_1^* = x_1'\beta_1 + \varepsilon_1, \quad y_1 = 1 \ \text{ if } y_1^* > 0, 0 \text{ otherwise,}$$
$$y_2^* = x_2'\beta_2 + \varepsilon_2, \quad y_2 = 1 \ \text{ if } y_2^* > 0, 0 \text{ otherwise} \qquad (1)$$

with (y_1, x_1) observed only when $y_2 = 1$.

In the above equations, y_1 indicates if the young worker is unemployed and y_2 if he does no longer hold that first job; x_1 reflects the variables determining the probability of unemployment; x_2 contains the variables explaining the fact of not maintaining the first job; and ε_1 and ε_2 are the error terms. When estimating the bivariate probit with sample selection, it is assumed that the error terms follow a bivariate normal distribution. As usual, these error terms have mean zero, variance equal to 1, and the covariance being ρ.

4. Empirical Findings

4.1. Parameter Estimates. The results of the estimations displayed in Table 2 indicate that women and foreign workers have a higher probability of not maintaining their first job, providing evidence on the well-known worse conditions faced by these collectives in the labour market.

This transition out of the first job is also more frequent among young workers with compulsory secondary or lower education and those with vocational training in social sciences, education, humanities, arts, or services. On the contrary, only university graduates from health and welfare have a greater chance of maintaining their first job than the ones with noncompulsory secondary education (omitted category). This result is interesting in the sense that not only the educational level but also the field of study influences the probability of maintaining a first significant job.

The shorter the time since the first job is found, the more likely is to continue in it. Furthermore, the probability of keeping that first job is lower if the worker had a temporary contract, as expected. Additionally, this probability is also lower if the worker was overeducated. This last result is in line with Alba [7], who also observes that Spanish overeducated workers are subject to higher employment mobility than the ones with a good educational match. On the contrary, having a part-time employment reduces the likelihood of being out of the first job. Finally, the estimates in Table 2 also show that there are significant differences across activity sectors and regions of residence.

Regarding the probability of unemployment for young workers who do not continue in their first job, the results reveal higher values for women and foreign workers. Male workers with young children face a lower probability of unemployment, while having children is not relevant for female workers.

Turning now to the main interest of the study, it can be pointed out that the risk of unemployment tends to decrease as the educational level increases. Nevertheless, when considering the field of study, different parameter estimates are obtained for university education.

The estimates suggest that workers with compulsory education are unemployed to a greater extent than the rest. Furthermore, as workers' educational level increases, their probability of unemployment decreases, being university graduates with the lowest likelihood.

It is important to mention that the field of specialization in vocational training does not imply significant differences in unemployment, while the level really does. Specifically, workers with higher vocational training are more likely to be employed in a different job after a first experience than those

TABLE 2: Parameters estimates for the bivariate probit with sample selection: probability of not maintaining the first job and being unemployed.

Variable	Not maintaining first job		Unemployed	
	Coefficient	t	Coefficient	t
Constant	0.154	1.83	−0.914	−5.47
Gender: female	0.235	5.80	0.234	4.70
Nationality: non-Spanish	0.312	3.99	0.283	3.74
Parents' higher educational level (ref. compulsory education or lower)				
Noncompulsory secondary or lower vocational training	0.274	5.95	−0.040	−0.70
University or higher vocational training	0.107	2.19	0.016	0.24
Children				
Male worker	−0.025	−0.24	−0.349	−2.82
Female worker	−0.095	−0.96	−0.034	−0.32
Worker's educational level and field of study: (ref. educational level: noncompulsory secondary; ref. field of study: general education)				
Compulsory secondary or lower	0.245	4.17	0.407	5.53
Vocational training (VT) in social sciences	0.197	2.41	0.141	1.41
VT in sciences and technology	0.110	1.41	0.102	1.07
VT in health and welfare	0.105	0.83	−0.092	−0.61
VT in other fields	0.326	3.32	0.176	1.42
Higher vocational training	−0.068	−1.09	−0.137	−1.80
University in social sciences	0.028	0.30	−0.371	−2.71
University in sciences and technology	0.006	0.07	−0.447	−3.18
University in health and welfare	−0.189	−1.89	−0.978	−5.44
University in other fields	−0.030	−0.34	−0.286	−2.16
Long-cycle university	−0.064	−0.94	0.096	0.85
First job				
Part-time	−0.890	−19.11		
Overeducated	0.262	7.62		
Fixed-term	0.953	31.76		
Time since obtained first job (ref. >10 years)				
Less than 2 years	−2.193	−33.61		
2-3 years	−1.335	−23.30		
4-5 years	−1.001	−16.68		
6–10 years	−0.482	−9.10		
Potential experience (ref. >10 years)				
Three years or less			0.524	5.16
3 to 5 years			0.268	3.32
5 to 10 years			0.015	0.29
Unemployment rate by gender in the quarter of the survey			0.011	4.50
GDP per capita by Autonomous Communities in 2009			−0.329	−2.66
Activity sector (ref. primary and industry sectors)				
Construction	0.136	2.25	0.330	4.76
Commerce	0.077	1.57	−0.200	−3.25
Transportation	0.306	4.11	−0.247	−2.65
Financial services	0.255	3.80	−0.084	−1.06
Public administration, education, and health	0.378	4.82	−0.205	−2.53

Table 2: Continued.

Variable	Not maintaining first job		Unemployed	
	Coefficient	t	Coefficient	t
Other services	0.115	1.41	−0.400	−4.08
Civil servant	−0.351	−4.53		
Regions (ref. Southwest)				
Northwest	−0.186	−3.57		
Northeast	−0.058	−1.21		
Central	0.097	2.06		
Southeast	0.010	0.20		
Correlation coefficient	0.239	3.51		
Number of observations	7,850		4,698	

The quarter of the survey has been controlled in the unemployment equation.

with lower vocational training. On the contrary, considerable gaps among university degree holders according to the length of the cycle (short or long) are not found, but a dependence on the specialization has been detected. Thus, the results clearly show that university graduates from health and welfare face the lowest probability of unemployment. On the other hand, degree holders from education, humanities, arts, or services have a greater risk of unemployment.

The results also show that the lower is the potential experience in the labour market, the higher is the probability of unemployment. Furthermore, there are some significant differences related to the sector of activity: the highest probability of unemployment corresponds to construction. This result is not at all surprising given the drastic drop of activity in this sector during the last years in Spain.

4.2. Education Impact on Unemployment: A Taxonomy. In order to highlight the importance of education in the analysis, a taxonomy of "educational labels" can be established depending on *instability* (probability of not maintaining the first job) and *difficulty* in finding another job (probability of unemployment given that the worker left the first job). Each "educational label" refers to a combination of educational level and field of study.

To this end, the parameters estimates of the model are used to calculate both probabilities for each "educational label." As they have been obtained evaluating the rest of variables in the sample mean, the differences in these probabilities quantify the effect of education per se on young workers' labour situation. Furthermore, this procedure allows calculating the complete set of probabilities including the probabilities of the omitted category in the econometric estimation. The results are presented in Table 3. Moreover, they are displayed in Figure 1 in order to show them from a visual perspective.

When the educational level is specifically analysed, a positive correlation between *instability* and *difficulty* is found. Furthermore, the specialization for each educational level affects *instability* of first job to a greater extent than *difficulty* in obtaining another one.

More specifically, a ranking of the "educational labels" can be established as follows.

(i) Workers with compulsory secondary or lower education are the most likely to suffer *instability* (almost 68% do not keep their first job), and they face the highest *difficulty* in getting a new employment (40% of those who are no longer working in their first job are unemployed).

(ii) Young workers with lower vocational training (except health and welfare) show a lower *difficulty* (30%), but *instability* depends on the field of study.

(iii) Higher vocational and noncompulsory secondary graduates show a similar level of *difficulty* (25%) and different degrees of *instability*. Moreover, instability across fields in higher and lower vocational shows the same pattern. The lowest instability corresponds to noncompulsory secondary.

(iv) There are no important differences in both indicators for workers with lower or higher vocational training in health and welfare. In any case, these workers hold a better position in the labour market than their peers from the rest of fields, as they suffer lower *instability* and *difficulty*.

(v) University graduates who left their first job (except graduates from health and welfare) face a probability of unemployment around 15–20%. This probability is slightly higher for long-cycle degrees, although *instability* is somewhat lower. Moreover, differences across fields of study are small for each level of education. Graduates from sciences and technology show slightly lower *instability* and *difficulty* indicators than workers with degrees in social sciences and other fields. Nevertheless, a better position could be expected for the former, but the above result can be explained by the greater impact of the crisis on the activity sectors, as construction, where this collective was employed in.

(vi) The best situation corresponds to university graduates from health and welfare, since their probability of

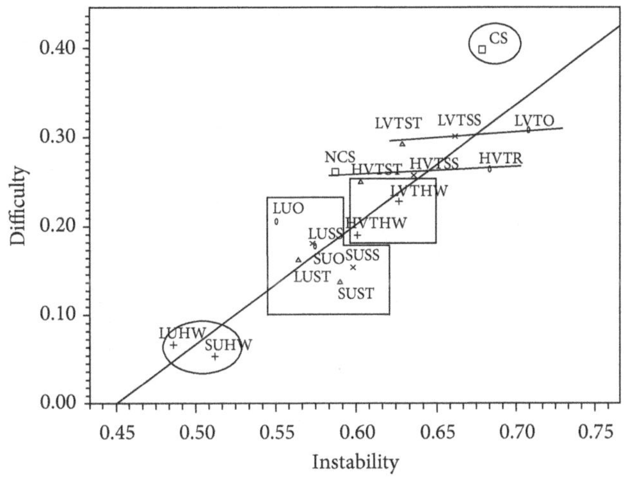

FIGURE 1: *Instability* of first job and *difficulty* in obtaining another one by "educational labels."

TABLE 3: Probabilities of not maintaining first job and unemployment given that the worker had left the first job, by educational level and field of study.

Educational label	Label	Instability*	Difficulty**	Probability of unemployment
Compulsory secondary or lower	CS	0.679	0.398	0.271
Noncompulsory secondary	NCS	0.587	0.262	0.153
Lower vocational training				
Social sciences	LVTSS	0.662	0.301	0.199
Sciences and technology	LVTST	0.629	0.292	0.183
Health and welfare	LVTHW	0.627	0.228	0.143
Other fields	LVTO	0.708	0.308	0.218
Higher vocational training				
Social sciences	HVTSS	0.636	0.257	0.164
Sciences and technology	HVTST	0.603	0.249	0.150
Health and welfare	HVTHW	0.601	0.190	0.114
Other fields	HVTO	0.684	0.264	0.180
Short-cycle university				
Social sciences	SUSS	0.598	0.154	0.092
Sciences and technology	SUST	0.590	0.137	0.081
Health and welfare	SUHW	0.512	0.054	0.028
Other fields	SUO	0.575	0.177	0.102
Long-cycle university				
Social sciences	LUSS	0.573	0.181	0.103
Sciences and technology	LUST	0.564	0.162	0.091
Health and welfare	LUHW	0.486	0.067	0.032
Other fields	LUO	0.550	0.206	0.113

These probabilities are calculated evaluating the rest of variables at the sample mean.
*Probability of not maintaining the first job.
**Probability of unemployment given that the worker had left the first job.

keeping the first job is around 50% and their probability of being employed in a different job once they have left the first one is around 93%. Thus, they are the ones who are better tackling the economic crisis.

The education and unemployment patterns for university graduates described above are in line with the results in Reimer et al. [8]. These authors point out that the educational expansion at the university level, such as that seen in Spain in the last decades, increases the differences in labour market employment chances of university graduates from different fields. Thus, in a context of educational expansion at the university levels, less able students are obtaining degrees and they are likely to graduate in soft fields, such as humanities or social sciences. As a consequence, graduates from these fields locate in lower labour market positions than their peers from hard fields, as health. In this sense, the results in this paper indicate that health and welfare as well as sciences and technology are the fields which better position workers in the labour market. Nevertheless and as already indicated, graduates from sciences and technology do not enjoy a more positive position due to the economic crisis.

Finally, both *instability* and *difficulty* jointly determine workers' risk of unemployment, that is, their probability of unemployment (last column in Table 3). The results obtained are similar to the above described since there is a positive correlation between the probability of maintaining the first job and the probability of unemployment given that the worker had left the first job. It can be concluded that educational level strongly determines success in labour market. Furthermore, specialization in health and welfare always implies a reduction in the unemployment rate given an educational level; this effect is stronger for university graduates. For the rest of fields of study, the differences in the risk of unemployment at a given educational level are small; nevertheless, the lowest level of unemployment corresponds to sciences and technology, followed by social sciences and the rest of fields.

5. Conclusions

This paper analyzes the education and unemployment patterns for young workers with some experience in Spain at the beginning of the economic crisis. Educational level and field of study are crucial when explaining the *instability* of first job and the *difficulty* in obtaining another one.

The results clearly show that the lower is the educational level, the greater is the risk of unemployment, not only because it is less likely to keep the first job, but also because it is harder to find another one. Moreover, for each level of education, it is also observed that (a) graduates from health and welfare are the best positioned according to both *instability* and *difficulty*, (b) graduating in the rest of fields of study mainly implies differences in *instability*, thus affecting the risk of unemployment, and (c) graduates from sciences and technology are closer positioned to workers from social sciences and other fields than to graduates in health and welfare because they have suffered the economic crisis to a relatively greater extent since it began.

It can be highlighted that university graduates from health or welfare were handling the economic crisis better than their peers from the rest of fields in 2009, since they had obtained more stable first jobs and they found another one more easily. Therefore, it would be also interesting to further explore if this collective still enjoys this privileged position in the labour market taking into account the cuts in the Spanish welfare state, including those in the public health system.

From an individual perspective, they indicate that the selection of a particular level and field of study have negative (or positive) consequences for future employment of young workers. Therefore, young people should take into account this fact when choosing their educational pathway. Moreover, from a social point of view, the education and unemployment patterns detected in the article may be useful to guide policy decisions, especially in the current context characterized by dramatic unemployment rates.

Thus, policy measures to be taken would include firstly, those designed to prevent a premature dropout the educational system, without achieving a minimum level of education. Secondly, it is also important to provide students in secondary education with wider information on labour market prospects associated with different educational programmes. Thereby, this information is interesting when deciding future studies. Thirdly, it is necessary to continue promoting enrolment in sciences or technology subjects, as the European Union recommends. And finally, it is necessary to extend the "practicum credits" in university degrees in Spain, especially in the more general fields, as Bologna reforms' attempt.

Conflict of Interests

The authors declare that there is no conflict of interests regarding the publication of this paper.

References

[1] C. A. Verdú, L. T. Cortés, and M. A. Davia Rodríguez, "To find or not to find a first "significant job"," *Revista de Economia Aplicada*, vol. 16, no. 46, pp. 37–59, 2008.

[2] A. Casquero, M. D. García, and L. Navarro, "Especialización educativa e inserción laboral en España," *Estadística Española*, vol. 25, pp. 419–467, 2010.

[3] A. Ugidos and C. Velásquez, "Inserción laboral de los jóvenes: quién encuentra un empleo acorde con el nivel y tipo de formación adquirido?" DFAE-II Working Paper Series 4, University of the Basque Country, 2007.

[4] M. Rahona, "Un análisis del desajuste educativo en el primer empleo de los jóvenes," *Principios*, vol. 11, pp. 45–67, 2008.

[5] W. Greene, "A statistical model for credit scoring," Working Paper EC-92-29, Department of Economics, Stern School of Business, New York University, 1992.

[6] W. Greene, *Econometric Analysis*, Pearson Prentice Hall, Upper Saddle River, NJ, USA, 6th edition, 2008.

[7] A. Alba, "Mismatch in the Spanish labour market: overeducation?" *Journal of Human Resources*, vol. 28, no. 2, pp. 259–278, 1993.

[8] D. Reimer, C. Noelke, and A. Kucel, "Labor market effects of field of study in comparative perspective: an analysis of 22 European countries," *International Journal of Comparative Sociology*, vol. 49, no. 4-5, pp. 233–256, 2008.

4

How Persistent Is the Occupation-Education Mismatch in Canada?

Xuyang Chen and Maxime Fougère

Employment and Social Development Canada, 140 Promenade du Portage, Phase 4, Gatineau, QC, Canada K1A 0J9

Correspondence should be addressed to Maxime Fougère; maxime.fougere@hrsdc-rhdcc.gc.ca

Academic Editors: J. Le Gallo and R. Wright

This paper investigates the duration of overqualification in Canada, the time-varying probability of leaving overqualification, and the wage consequences associated with the transition. The paper also applies a survival analysis approach to examine the impact of key driving factors on the probability of transitioning from overqualification to a job match using a proportional hazard (Cox) model. The analysis shows that within a 5-year period, an overqualified worker has a 22 percent probability of transitioning to an occupation that matches the education level. The probability of transition also decreases quickly over time, thus lowering the chances of finding a job match after 12 months. Regression analyses also provide evidence that overqualified workers with short tenure are more likely to transition than workers with medium to long tenure. Finally, job-related training nearly doubles the chance of transitioning out of overqualification.

1. Introduction

It is well known that the level of education has significantly risen in Canada during the past few decades. Over the same period, we also observe a trend increase in the incidence of overqualified workers. Human capital investment is a key determinant of economic growth. However, not only do we need to invest in the supply of skills to help support growth, we also need to ensure that the skills of Canadian workers are used efficiently. Carr and Chen [1] found that about one in three Canadian workers were overqualified for their jobs in 2008. Also, according to the OECD [2], overqualified workers earn about 20 percent less on average than their matched counterparts in Canada.

For an individual in a skills mismatch situation, overqualification may either be transitory, persistent, or permanent. In the case of a persistent or permanent mismatch situation, the cumulative loss in wages and productivity could become large and costly over time. Persistent overqualification also leads to skill obsolescence. While matched workers accumulate more human capital through experience, overeducated workers do not have the chance to use their skills and lose valuable work experience. This eventually leads to a depreciation of their human capital. Moreover, the persistence of overqualification inevitably reduces further the probability of finding an appropriate job that matches their skills set as firms use information on previous employment history in their hiring decisions.

Although there is a wide literature on the incidence of skills mismatch, the issue of persistence has not been studied much. Among the few studies, Green et al. [3], Johnson [4], and Jovanovic [5] argue that job mismatch would occur predominantly at the early stage of an individual's career and eventually disappear without the need for specific action or policy. In contrast, Spence [6] suggests that overqualification is a long-term situation and that individuals systematically acquire more skills than the jobs usually require. However, these arguments are mainly theoretical and to our knowledge not much empirical evidence has been provided on the degree of persistence of skills mismatch.

Overall, the extent to which the state of mismatch is transitory or permanent and how the transition probability evolves over time is unknown. This issue, however, is very important to help identify policy levers. If most mismatch situations are transitory and relatively short-lived, the need to develop policy instrument becomes questionable. On the other hand, if a significant proportion of skill mismatch remains persistent and eventually becomes permanent, the need for appropriate policy intervention should be more seriously considered.

This paper's key objectives are twofold. First, using the Survey of Labour and Income Dynamics (Panel 5, SLID 2002 to 2007), this paper seeks to investigate the duration of overqualification in Canada, the time-varying probability of leaving overqualification, and the wage consequences associated with the transition. Second, by specifying a survival model, the paper explores the impacts of key driving factors on the probability of transitioning from overqualification to a job match.

The remainder of this paper is divided as follows. Section 2 discusses the theoretical framework. Section 3 reviews some recent relevant literature. Section 4 discusses the data and methods used for the analysis. Section 5 presents the estimation results and marginal effects. Finally, Section 6 concludes.

2. Theoretical Background

Applying a simple form of matching function [7], the probability for an unemployed worker to find a job during a unit of time can be expressed as follows:

$$P = \frac{m(U,V)}{U}, \tag{1}$$

where U is the number of unemployed workers, V is the number of vacancies, and $m(U,V)$ is the number of jobs formed during a given time period. A job match can either be a transition from unemployment or from a job mismatch. If we assume that employed job seekers have the same search behaviour and reservation wage as unemployed job seekers, the same matching function can be applied to employed job seekers (see Petrongolo and Pissarides [8] for more details).

Muysken and Weel [9] have extended the theoretical framework developed by Pissarides [7] by introducing a matching process focusing on the transitions from underemployment (skilled workers working in unskilled jobs) to skilled jobs. This approach is mainly driven by labour demand: firms in skilled sectors create skilled jobs and seek workers having at least the level of skills (or human capital) $\hat{h}$ to fill the vacancies, while overqualified workers prefer to work in a skilled job that better matches their education for a higher wage. In this setting, U represents the number of underemployed workers (or overqualified workers) and V represents the number of vacancies of skilled jobs. Assuming that the probability of finding a job match remains constant over time and follows a stationary process, the mean duration of underemployment or search duration can be expressed as

$$D = \frac{1}{m\left(U,V,h/\hat{h}\right)/U}, \quad h \geq \hat{h}. \tag{2}$$

However, Pissarides [10], Devine and Kiefer [11], and Heckman and Borjas [12] reject the assumption that the probability of finding a job follows a stationary process. Instead, they argue that the skill of an unemployed or underemployed worker will tend to depreciate over time and accordingly, the probability of finding a job match will decrease with the duration of underemployment.

In this paper, we assume that the skill of an overqualified worker depreciates over time and express human capital endowment during the period of underemployment as

$$h_t = he^{-rt}, \tag{3}$$

where h is the original human capital at the beginning, h_t is the remaining human capital of an overqualified worker at time t, and r is the discount rate.

Over time, workers who remain overqualified become less attractive to employers due to human capital depreciation. Accordingly, the supply of skilled job offers will be reduced in the next period and the probability of transitioning from overqualification to match will decrease (Pissarides [7, 10] give a detailed description of the equation). Therefore, in period t, the matching probability between a skilled job and an overqualified worker will depend on the duration of overqualification, which we approximate by job tenure.

We assume that at the beginning of the overqualification period, workers' human capital endowment h matches the requirement for the skilled occupations $\hat{h}$. After a period τ, the level of human capital depreciates to h_τ which is lower than $\hat{h}$. In other words, after period τ, the overqualified workers who did not find a match are no longer attractive to employers from the skilled sector. This may be further examined in the empirical model by adding a time dependent variable $I_t(T > \tau)$ to measure the time point after which the remaining human capital of an overqualified worker falls below the requirement for a skilled job ($I_t(h_t > \hat{h})$).

On the other hand, taking job-related training or education may help restock an individual's human capital. Under this hypothesis, we assume that overqualified workers who take job-related training will increase their probability of transitioning to a skilled job match. Finally, a matching probability between an overqualified worker and a skilled job can be expressed as

$$p_{i,t} = f\left(T_{i,t}, Tr_{i,t}, I_{i,t}, X_i\right), \tag{4}$$

where $T_{i,t}$ refers to the duration of overqualification at time t, $Tr_{i,t}$ refers to the job-related training or education, $I_{i,t}$ refers to the indicator for the cut-off time of losing enough skill, and X_i refers to individual characteristics and behaviors.

3. Overview of the Skills Mismatches Literature

There is a growing body of literature on skill mismatch. In Canada, most studies so far have focused on the incidence of overqualification and its effect on earnings. For example, using the National Graduates Survey (NGS), Frenette [13, 14] and Finnie [15] find that roughly between 30% and 40% of recent graduates experience a skill mismatch. Using the Survey of Labour and Income Dynamics (SLID), Carr and Chen [1] find similar results among prime-aged workers.

These studies also find that the wage penalty associated with overqualification is substantial, compared with workers who have the right occupation-education match. In general, these results are in line with findings using American or other OECD country data [2].

Although there is a substantial literature on the incidence of overqualification, the issue of persistence has received little attention in Canada. One notable exception is Frenette [14] who briefly discusses the issue of persistence in overqualification among recent graduates. Based on an interview result from the NGS, he finds evidence that a significant proportion of workers remain overeducated between two and five years after graduation.

A few recent studies have examined the issue of persistence in overqualification for the US, Sweden, Australia, and Belgium. Overall, these studies present useful stylised facts on the duration of overqualification, but they do not provide empirical evidence on the determinants of the duration of overqualification and do not examine the probability of leaving overqualification. Among these, Dolton and Vignoles [16] find that a majority of workers in the US who are overeducated in a given year are still overeducated six years later. For the US, Rubb [17] finds that the majority of individuals who are overqualified for their jobs in a given year remain overqualified the following year. For Sweden, Böhlmark [18] finds that 61% of younger graduates who were overqualified in 1981 remain overqualified in the following years. For Australia, McGuinness and Wooden [19] examine overskilling duration and conclude that only 25 percent of overskilled workers transition to a matched job within a period of three years. In Belgium, Schatteman and Verhaest [20] examine overeducated workers and find that a large proportion of graduates remain overeducated for more than seven years. Finally, de Grip and van Loo [21] look at the relationship between overeducation, skill obsolescence, and training. They suggest that the insufficient practice of skills during the overeducation may lead to atrophy of skills and that job-related training may contribute to the reduction in skills mismatch.

4. Data and Method

4.1. Data Source. In the literature on skills mismatch, skill requirement has been measured in three different ways: from job analysis, worker self-assessment, or realised matches. According to Hartog [22], the job analysis method is the most attractive one because of its objectivity, clear definitions, and detailed measurement instructions. Compared to the job analysis method, the worker self-assessment (WA) method has the advantage of drawing on all local, up-to-date information but lacks rigorous instructions. Consequently, WA measurement can easily be biased for individuals who cannot accurately describe the requirements for their job. Finally, realized matches (RM) use the mean (or mode of distribution) of required education derived from respondents' job or occupation as a measure of the demand. This measure is not precise enough to uncover the technological requirements of a job. In this paper, the approach we use to define overqualification is based on the job analysis method. Using the National Occupational Classification (NOC) matrix, we define a worker as over-qualified if the individual's level of education exceeds the education level required by the occupation at the end of 2002.

The data used in the analysis are drawn from the *Survey of Labour and Income Dynamics* (SLID panel 5, from 2002 to 2007). The SLID is a household survey that provides longitudinal followup on Canadian families and individuals' demographic background, income, education level, labour market activities, and financial situation. The SLID also collects information on workers by occupation at the four-digit level and with employer's industry code. This allows us to classify individuals by education and skill level and identify those who are overqualified and those who change jobs between occupations and industries over time. According to the NOC code obtained from each individual's current job, all workers in the sample are assigned a skill level in each given year. At the four-digit level, the 520 occupations can be reclassified within four skill levels (A, B, C, and D).

A: occupations usually requiring university education;

B: occupations usually requiring college education or apprenticeship training;

C: occupations requiring secondary school or occupation-specific training;

D: occupations requiring only on-the-job training.

Here, skill level is a job characteristic, while education is a characteristic of the individual. In our sample, 2882 prime-aged workers who were overqualified for their occupation in 2002 are followed over a 6-year period.

4.2. Survival Model. We estimate a proportional hazard [23] model using monthly data to analyse transitions from overqualification to a job match. The hazard rate measures the probability that an individual will transition out of overqualification in a period $(t, t + \Delta t)$, given that this individual remains overqualified at time t. The Cox model captures the impacts of training, immigration status, and tenure on the probability of transition. According to Frank [24], job immobility may be a potential cause of overqualification. In this model, we also include an indicator to measure if changing employer or industry can improve the chance of moving out of overqualification. Finally, $\lambda(t \mid X)$ denotes the hazard function and $\lambda_0(t)$ denotes the baseline hazard function at time t. The model in terms of the hazard function at time t is

$$\begin{aligned}\lambda(t \mid X) &= \lambda_0(t) \exp(\beta_1 \text{Tenure} + \beta_2 \text{Training} \\ &\quad + \beta_2 \text{Tenure} * I(t > \tau) + \beta_3 \text{Imm} \\ &\quad + \beta_4 \text{Age} + \beta_5 \text{Gender} + \beta_6 \text{Ci} + \beta_7 \text{Edu}). \end{aligned} \quad (5)$$

Table 1: Wage changes between 2002 and 2007.

	Remaining in overqualification		Transition to a matched occupation	
	Mean	Median	Mean	Median
Hourly wage, 2002	\$16.56	\$15.00	\$16.81	\$15.00
Hourly wage, 2007	\$19.71	\$17.68	\$23.72	\$21.12
Wage increase, 2002–2007	19.0%	17.9%	41.1%	40.8%

Source: authors' calculation from the SLID, panel 5, 2002–2007.

Explanatory variables are mentioned as follows.

(i) Tenure: the number of months of work in the current main job.

(ii) Training: 1 if individual takes job-related training or education, else 0.

(iii) $I(t > \tau)$: dummy variable for the specific time point.

(iv) Imm: set of dummy variables for the immigrant status: recent immigrant (less than 5 years), established immigrant (more than 5 years), and native born.

(v) Age: set of dummy variables for each age in the sample.

(vi) Gender: male = 1, else 0.

(vii) Educ_i: set of dummy variables for education level: postsecondary or university.

(viii) Ci: 1 if individual changes job between industry, else 0.

Under the assumption that the human capital of overqualified workers depreciates over time, the resulting probability of transitioning out of overqualification will decrease until time τ, the point where the individual becomes no longer attractive to the employers from the skilled sector. We therefore expect that the negative impact of tenure on the hazard rate will depend on time and violate the proportional assumption of the Cox model. We also identify the approximate time point τ by comparing Nelson-Aalen cumulative hazard estimates among workers with different tenures and then combine tenure and a time depending indicator $I(t > \tau)$ in the modeling process to compensate for the changing impacts.

5. Empirical Results

We first present some descriptive statistics, including wage changes associated with transitions and the results of the Kaplan-Meier failure function. This is followed by a presentation of the estimation results of the Cox model.

5.1. Wage Changes Associated with Transitions. Table 1 compares wage changes between 2002 and 2007 for overqualified workers who transition to a matched occupation and those who remain overqualified. As can be seen, wage increases associated with transition are substantial. For workers who transitioned to a matched occupation, nominal hourly wage increased by about 41 percent, compared to 19 percent for the mean hourly wage (and 17 percent for the median wage) for workers who remained overqualified. This clearly demonstrates that the wage loss associated with being overqualified is quite significant.

5.2. Transition Rates by Group. Table 2 summarizes the results of the failure function by individual and worker's characteristics. The failure function is presented at five different points in time (12, 24, 36, 48, and 60 months after the end of 2002). By gender, the probability for men of transitioning out of overqualification is about 8.5% within the first year, 13.5% after 24 months, 17.5% after 36 months, 20.5% after 48 months, and 22% after 60 months. The probability of transitioning to a matched occupation is about the same for overqualified women, reaching a little over 23% after 60 months.

This result clearly indicates that the probability of transition decreases quickly over time. It also suggests that the vast majority of overqualified workers remain in this situation throughout their career, which is in line with the assumption that overeducated individuals eventually become less attractive to employers.

Overqualified workers with post-secondary education and university degree also have a probability of transitioning out of overqualification that is similar at each point in time. However, when we look by age group and immigrant status, we find substantial variations in the probability of transitioning to a matched position. Workers aged 25–34 have the highest probability of transitioning, reaching 28% after 60 months, compared with 22% and 18% for age groups 35–44 and 45–54, respectively. By immigrant status, nonimmigrants record the highest transition rates for the whole period, reaching a probability of 23.8% after 60 months, followed by recent immigrants (18.6%) and established immigrants (13.4%).

As expected, overqualified workers who take job-related training record much higher transition rates, nearly twice the probability achieved for workers who do not take job-related training. This suggests that work-related training helps to transition out of overqualification. The results also reveal that changing industry of work is associated with a much higher probability of transition during the whole period (19.5% versus 5.6% after 12 months and 47.5% versus 19.5% after 60 months). In fact, nearly half of all transitions are associated with industry mobility.

5.3. Cut-Off Time Point τ. The use of the Kaplan-Meier failure function can help illustrate the overall transition patterns

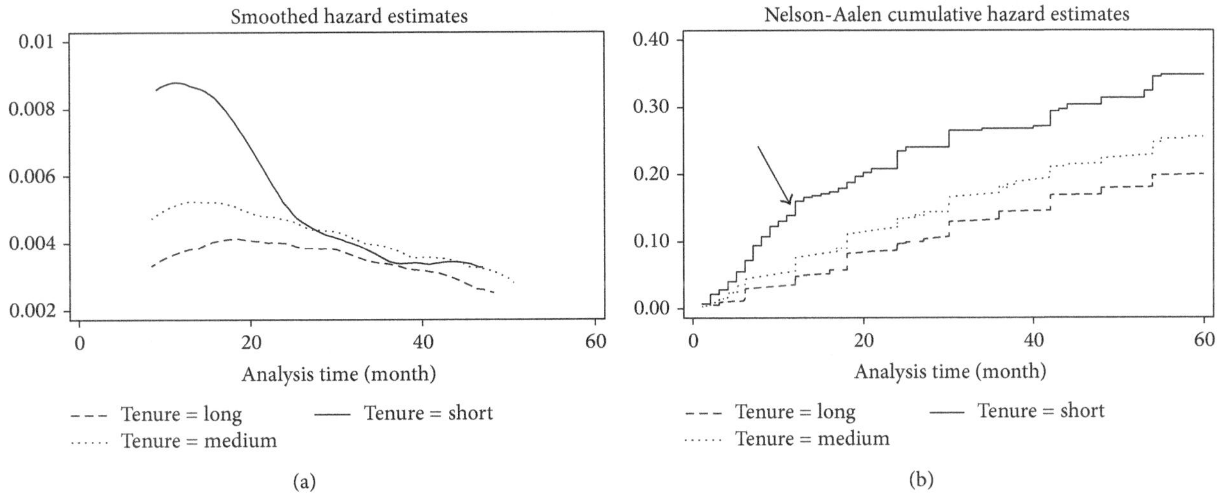

FIGURE 1: Estimated smoothed and cumulative hazard functions by tenure.

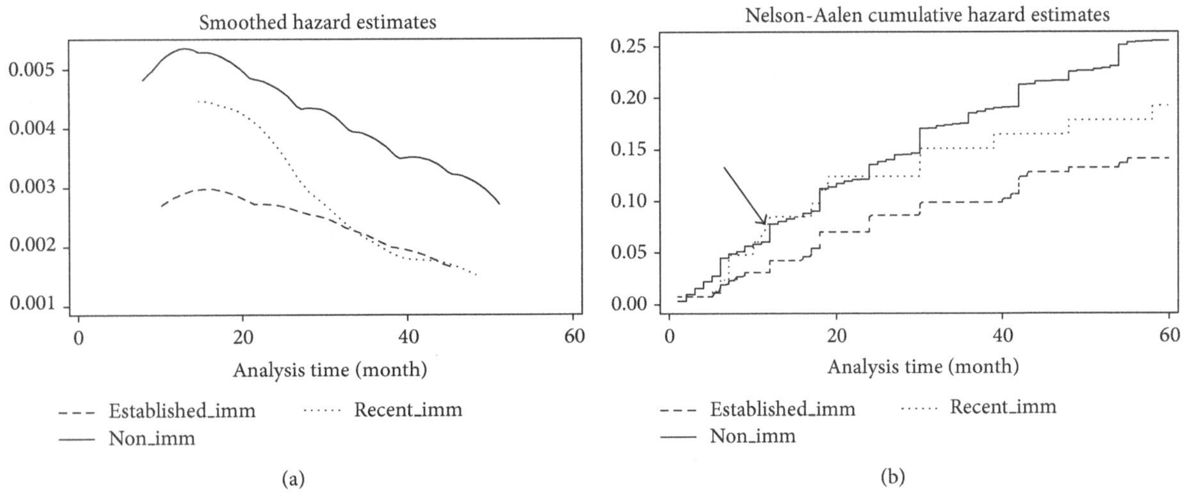

FIGURE 2: Estimated smoothed and cumulative hazard functions by immigrant status.

and variations by individual and job characteristics. However, these transition estimates are not precise enough to identify the time point τ, the approximate time after which the remaining human capital of an overqualified worker has fallen below the level required for a skilled job. We expect the hazard function of workers with short and medium tenure to converge after τ months. Both smooth hazard and Nelson-Aalen estimates can provide subjective and useful graphical assessments. Therefore, we use these plots to display the marginal effect of this potentially time-varying covariate, and diagnose τ.

Figure 1 presents the smooth hazard and Nelson-Aalen estimates stratified by tenure. The smoothed hazard function shows that compared to workers with medium (1 to 4 years) and long tenure (5 years or more), the hazard rate of overqualified workers with short tenure (less than 1 year) is much higher at the beginning and then drops quickly and converges with the other two groups after some time point τ. However, the smoothed hazard function is only one type of "moving average" statistic. We further the Nelson-Aalen estimate, an empirical cumulative hazard of transitioning to a job match as a function of the length of the overqualification spell, to identify τ in a more precise way.

From Nelson-Aalen estimate, it can be seen that within 12 months, the cumulative hazard function for individuals with short tenure is markedly larger than for the other two groups. However, after approximately 12 months, workers with short and medium tenure have roughly the same slope, suggesting that the hazard functions of these two groups are about the same. We therefore define $\tau = 12$ months after the end of 2002 in the sample (since the average job duration of the short tenure group is about 7 months, τ may be also considered as a 19-month period from the beginning of overqualification).

Among the variables, immigration status is also found to be a time-varying covariate. As shown in Figure 2, hazard rates of recent immigrants are much higher than for established immigrants at the beginning and then decrease quickly and converge with those of established immigrants

Table 2: Probability of transitioning to an occupation that correctly matches an individual's education level (Kaplan-Meier estimator).

	Transition to a matched occupation					Remaining in overqualification				
	12 months	24 months	36 months	48 months	60 months	12 months	24 months	36 months	48 months	60 months
Male	8.4%	13.5%	16.7%	20.0%	21.8%	91.6%	86.5%	83.3%	80.1%	78.2%
Female	8.5%	13.4%	17.8%	21.0%	23.3%	91.5%	86.6%	82.2%	79.0%	76.7%
Age: 25–34	11.1%	18.1%	21.9%	26.0%	28.4%	88.9%	81.9%	78.1%	74.0%	71.6%
Age: 35–44	8.0%	12.9%	17.0%	20.2%	22.0%	92.0%	87.1%	83.0%	79.8%	78.0%
Age: 45–54	6.7%	9.9%	13.4%	15.9%	18.1%	93.3%	90.2%	86.6%	84.1%	81.9%
Recent immigrants	7.0%	12.8%	15.1%	17.4%	18.6%	93.0%	87.2%	84.9%	82.6%	81.4%
Established immigrants	4.5%	8.7%	9.8%	12.8%	13.4%	95.5%	91.4%	90.2%	87.2%	86.7%
Nonimmigrants	8.9%	14.0%	18.2%	21.5%	23.8%	91.1%	86.0%	81.1%	78.5%	76.2%
Tenure: less than 1 year	14.9%	21.0%	23.7%	27.1%	29.6%	85.1%	79.0%	76.3%	72.9%	70.4%
Tenure: 1 to 4 years	9.6%	14.8%	18.7%	22.1%	24.5%	90.4%	85.2%	81.3%	77.9%	75.5%
Tenure: 5 or more years	5.6%	10.0%	14.2%	17.2%	19.0%	94.5%	90.0%	85.8%	82.8%	81.0%
Job-related training: yes	10.3%	16.7%	22.0%	26.9%	29.3%	89.7%	83.3%	78.0%	73.1%	70.7%
Job-related training: no	6.7%	10.1%	12.4%	13.9%	15.8%	93.4%	89.9%	87.6%	86.1%	84.2%
Changing industry: yes	19.5%	29.5%	36.7%	43.9%	47.1%	80.5%	70.5%	63.3%	56.1%	52.9%
Changing industry: no	5.6%	9.4%	13.4%	16.7%	19.5%	94.4%	90.6%	86.6%	83.3%	80.5%
Education: university	8.5%	12.9%	16.5%	18.9%	21.1%	91.5%	87.1%	83.6%	81.2%	78.9%
Education: postsecondary	8.5%	13.7%	17.6%	21.1%	23.2%	91.5%	86.3%	82.4%	78.9%	76.8%

Source: authors' calculation from the SLID, panel 5, 2002–2007.

after some period. Nelson-Aalen estimates show that the length of this period is about 12 months again. However, since the average period that recent immigrants have arrived in Canada at the end of 2002 is about 30 months, recent immigrants may be considered to have the same hazard rate as established immigrants after having arrived in Canada for 42 months.

5.4. Results from the Cox Model. Table 3 summarizes the estimation results of the Cox model fitted to the data. Overall, the model results from the Cox model are broadly in line with the descriptive findings. In particular, the results support the assumption for the existence of a cutoff point τ after which the remaining overqualified workers are no longer attractive to employers from the skilled sector and nearly have a zero probability of transition to a job match. As shown in Table 3, both short tenure and the covariate short tenure $* I(t > 12$ month) are statistically significant at a 99% degree of confidence. Furthermore, the positive regression coefficient of the covariate short tenure (2.58) is offset by the negative estimate of short tenure $* I(t > 12$ month) (−3.0). This suggests that compared with medium tenure, short tenure is associated with a higher hazard function for up to 12 months, after which there is no significant effect. We also find no evidence that medium and long tenure workers have a different transition probability.

As expected, job-related training positively influences the probability of transitioning out of overqualification and its impact is statistically significant. In addition, industry mobility is associated with higher hazard, suggesting that most overqualified workers who transition to a job match also changed employer and industry of work. Compared with established immigrants, nonimmigrants are more likely to move out of overqualification. Recent immigrants also have a much higher hazard than established immigrants for only the first 12 months, and then the effect quickly diminishes as the positive coefficient on recent immigrants (1.22) is offset by the negative coefficient on recent immigrants $* I(t > 12$ month) (−1.55).

There is no indication that the probabilities of transition over time are different between male and female workers or between university and college graduates. However, we find evidence that younger workers are more likely to transition out of a skills mismatch, compared with older working groups.

We also calculate marginal effects for the statistically significant variables. Table 4 shows that workers with short tenure transition out of overqualification in the first year 12

TABLE 3: Determinants of transition from overqualification (Cox model).

Variable	Coefficient	Standard error	Hazard ratio
Training	0.361	(0.093)***	1.428
Male	−0.018	(0.088)	0.982
University	−0.148	(0.153)	0.862
Short tenure	2.581	(0.196)***	13.186
Long tenure	−0.1555	(0.103)	0.856
Short tenure $* I$ (time > 12 months)	−3.015	(0.228)***	0.050
Recent immigrant	1.223	(0.511)**	3.246
Nonimmigrant	0.317	(0.189)*	1.373
Recent immigrant $* I$ (time > 12 months)	−1.559	(0.628)*	0.210
Change industry	0.948	(0.093)***	2.582
Age 25–34	0.264	(0.115)**	1.303
Age 35–44	0.121	(0.110)	1.128
Test of proportional hazard assumption	Chi-square	DF	Probability
Global test	13.65	12	0.3235

Estimates significant at a 99% (***), 95% (**), and 90% (*) degree of confidence, not significant otherwise.

TABLE 4: Marginal effect of statistically significant variables[4].

Variable	Marginal effect
Training (from no to yes)	43%
Short tenure and time < 12 months	1219%
Recent immigrant and time < 12	224%
Nonimmigrant	37%
Changing industry	158%
Age 25–34	30%
Age 35–44	13%

[4]Marginal effects represent the change in monthly transition hazard if the variable is altered from the baseline and all other variables are held constant. Baseline of the variables: no training, established immigrant, medium tenure, same industry, and age group 45–54.

times faster than workers with medium or long tenure. Similarly, the transition hazard associated with recent immigrants is 224 percent higher than for established immigrants, but only within the first 12 months, while nonimmigrants record a 37 percent higher hazard than established immigrants for the whole five-year period. The marginal effects of job-related training and industry mobility on the transition probability are also significantly large. Taking job-related training increases the transition hazard by 43 percent, while industry movers are 158 percent more likely to have a transition. The chance of an individual aged from 25 to 34 to transition to a job match is also 30 percent higher than that of individuals aged 45 and over, while the probability of transition for workers aged from 35 to 44 increases by only about 13 percent.

Overall, global test results indicate that the proportional hazard assumption of the Cox model is met. In addition, using the fitted Cox regression model, Figure 3 examines the model fit by comparing observed and estimated survival probability (the probability an individual remaining overqualified over time) for the selected variables. In general, the model performs quite well. The results for other variables are available upon request.

6. Summary and Conclusion

The extent to which overqualification persists over time determines the real economic costs of skills mismatch. However, there is very little work done in Canada on the persistence of skill mismatch. There is also very little known about how the depreciation of human capital induced by overqualification affects the probability of transitioning to a correct job match.

In this paper, we have investigated the duration of skills mismatch and found that a significant proportion of workers who are overqualified for their job persistently remain in such a state for a long time. Eventually the situation becomes permanent. We found that an overqualified worker has a 22 percent probability of transitioning to an occupation that matches the education level within a 5-year period. While the majority of individual spells of overqualification is permanent, the fact that the probability of transition quickly decreases over time confirms that overeducated individuals lose some of their skills and knowledge that are not used in their job and hence the probability of finding a job match decreases over time. Our findings support the assumption that unused skills and knowledge quickly depreciate over time and significantly reduce the transition probability of overeducated individuals.

While recent immigrants transition faster than established immigrants in the first 12 months, nonimmigrants have a higher probability of transition than established immigrants for the whole period. Changing industry of work doubles the chance of transition and workers have a better chance to transition out of overqualification when they are young.

Regression analyses provide evidence that recent overqualified workers (on average 7 months tenure) are more likely to transition than medium to long tenure workers, but

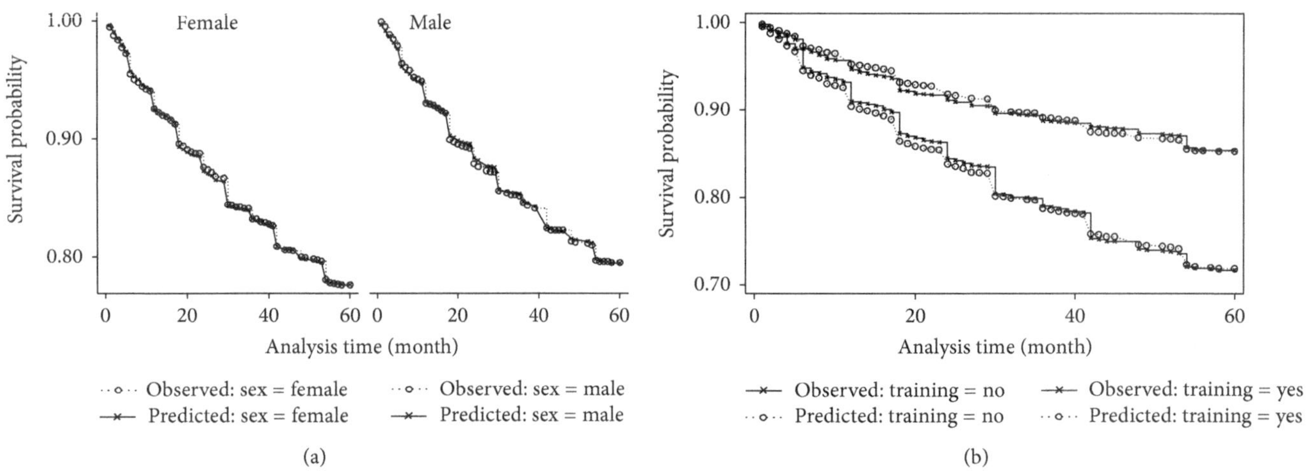

FIGURE 3: Model performance check.

only within the first year. These results also confirm the existence of the cut-off time point τ, after which the remaining overqualified workers become no longer attractive to employers from the skilled jobs.

Workers accepting job-related training are found to have a 43 percent higher monthly transition hazard, suggesting that job-related training is an effective way to restock human capital and improve the chance to work in a skilled job.

Typically, wage increases associated with transitions are substantial, suggesting that overeducated workers in low-skilled jobs prefer to work in high-skilled jobs because they can receive higher wages. However, once an overeducated individual works in a low-skilled job, the probability of transition quickly decreases over time. After a 19-month period, an overeducated individual no longer satisfies the skill requirement for level A or B occupations and overqualification spells becomes permanent. Finally, taking job-related training significantly raises the probability of transition.

Disclaimer

Views expressed herein are those of the authors and do not necessarily reflect those of HRSDC.

Conflict of Interests

The authors declare that there is no conflict of interests regarding the publication of this paper.

Acknowledgment

The authors wish to thank Gilles Bérubé, Mohsen Bouaissa, Jeff Carr, and two anonymous referees for useful comments. The authors are solely responsible for any errors remaining.

References

[1] J. Carr and X. Chen, *What is the Incidence of Occupation-Education mIsmatch in Canada and What are Its Consequences?* Policy research directorate, Human Resources and Skills Development Canada, 2011.

[2] Organisation for Economic Co-operation and Development (OECD 2011), *Right for the Job: Over-Qualified or Under-Skilled?* OECD Publishing, Paris, France.

[3] F. Green, S. McIntosh, and A. Vignoles, "Overeducation and Skills-Clarifying the concepts," Centre for Economic Performance, Discussion Paper 435, 1999.

[4] W. R. Johnson, "A theory of job shopping," *Quarterly Journal of Economics*, vol. 92, no. 2, pp. 261–278, 1978.

[5] B. Jovanovic, "Job matching and the theory of turnover," *Journal of Political Economy*, vol. 87, no. 5, pp. 972–990, 1979.

[6] M. Spence, "Job market signaling," *The Quarterly Journal of Economics*, vol. 87, no. 3, pp. 355–374, 1973.

[7] C. A. Pissarides, *Equilibrium Unemployment Theory*, Basil Blackwell Ltd, Cambridge, Mass, USA, 1990.

[8] B. Petrongolo and C. A. Pissarides, "Looking into the black box: a survey of the matching function," *Journal of Economic Literature*, vol. 39, no. 2, pp. 390–431, 2001.

[9] J. Muysken and B. T. Weel, *Overeducation and Crowding Out of Low- Skilled Workers*, Department of Economics and MERIT, Maastricht University, Maastricht, The Netherlands, 2000.

[10] C. A. Pissarides, "Loss of skill during unemployment and the persistence of employment shocks," *The Quarterly Journal of Economics*, vol. 107, no. 4, pp. 1371–1391, 1992.

[11] T. J. Devine and N. M. Kiefer, *Empirical Labor Economics: the Search Approach*, Oxford University Press, New York, NY, USA, 1991.

[12] J. J. Heckman and G. J. Borjas, "Does unemployment cause future unemployment? Definitions, questions and answers from a continuous time model of heterogeneity and state dependence," *Economica, London School of Economics and Political Science*, vol. 47, no. 187, pp. 247–283, 1980.

[13] M. Frenette, "Overqualified? Recent graduates and the needs of their employers," Education Quarterly Review, vol. 7, no. 1, Statistics Canada Catalogue no. 81-003-XIE, 2000.

[14] M. Frenette, "The overqualified Canadian graduate: the role of the academic program in the incidence, persistence, and economic returns to overqualification," *Economics of Education Review*, vol. 23, no. 1, pp. 29–45, 2004.

[15] R. Finnie, "'Graduates' earnings and the job skills-education match," *Education Quarterly Review*, vol. 7, Statistics Canada, no. 2, 2001.

[16] P. Dolton and A. Vignoles, "The incidence and effects of overeducation in the U.K. Graduate labour market," *Economics of Education Review*, vol. 19, no. 2, pp. 179–198, 2000.

[17] S. Rubb, "Overeducation: a short or long run phenomenon for individuals?" *Economics of Education Review*, vol. 22, no. 4, pp. 389–394, 2003.

[18] A. Böhlmark, *Over- and Undereducation in the Swedish Labour Market. Incidence, Wage Effects and Characteristics 1968–2000*, Swedish Institute for Social Research (SOFI), Stockholm University, 2003.

[19] S. McGuinness and M. Wooden, "Overskilling, job insecurity and career mobility," IZA Discussion Paper 2938, 2007.

[20] T. Schatteman and D. Verhaest, "Proceedings of the Overeducation in the early career: an analysis using sequence techniques," in *15th European Research Network on Transitions in Youth conference*, Ghent, Belgium, 2007.

[21] A. de Grip and J. van Loo, "The economics of skills obsolescence: a review," *Research in Labor Economics*, vol. 21, pp. 1–26, 2002.

[22] J. Hartog, "Over-education and earnings: where are we, where should we go?" *Economics of Education Review*, vol. 19, no. 2, pp. 131–147, 2000.

[23] D. R. Cox, "Regression models and life-tables," *Journal of the Royal Statistical Society B*, vol. 34, no. 2, pp. 187–220, 1972.

[24] R. H. Frank, "Why women earn less: the theory and estimation of differential overqualification," *American Economic Review*, vol. 68, no. 3, pp. 360–373, 1978.

5

Evolutionary Model of the City Size Distribution

Joachim Kaldasch

EBC Hochschule, Alexanderplatz 1, 10178 Berlin, Germany

Correspondence should be addressed to Joachim Kaldasch; joachim.kaldasch@international-business-school.de

Academic Editors: J. Le Gallo and E. Yeldan

An evolutionary model of the city size distribution is presented that explains the size of a city from the reproduction process and the migration of humans between cities. The model suggests that the city size distribution is a lognormal distribution with a power law tail in agreement with empirical results and computer simulations. The main idea of the model is that the competition between cities in the migration process is the origin of Gibrat's law. While growth rate fluctuations generate the lognormal branch of the size distribution, the power law tail for large cities is caused by a small mean growth rate.

1. Introduction

The paper aims at deriving the size distribution of cities from the idea that the evolution of a city is a self-organized process. The term city is used here very loosely to mean any human settlement not distinguishing between villages, towns, cities, or megacities. The size p is usually characterized by the urban area or human population. Ranking cities of a finite region, for example, a country, from largest to smallest, Zipf observed in 1949 that the probability to find the size of a city that is greater than some p_0 is given by $P(p > p_0) \sim p_0^{-z}$, with a Zipf exponent $z \approx 1$. This power law relationship is known as Zipf's law [1].

Using appropriate definitions of the city size the validity of Zipf law was confirmed by the investigation of large cities [2–10]. For smaller cities empirical investigations established considerable deviations from this law. Eeckhout [11, 12] showed that taking all settlements into account the size distribution for small cities can be rather described by a lognormal distribution. Empirical investigations suggest therefore that the size distribution is lognormal with a power law tail [13–15].

Several theoretical models have been established to understand these empirical facts [7, 16–22]. Since classic economic theories fail to explain the size distribution [23] the majority of models have in common to apply Gibrat's law of proportionate effects [24, 25] taking advantage of geographic and socioeconomic forces in their reasoning.

The presented evolutionary theory goes beyond previous research by deriving Gibrat's law from the main two processes governing the population size of a city: the reproduction of humans and their migration between cities. The key idea is to regard cites as entities of a self-organized system. The dynamics of self-organized systems is governed by positive feedback processes [26, 27]. Both the reproduction of humans and their migration are self-amplifying processes, while the migration flow is shown to be the result of an evolutionary competition between cities. Growth rate fluctuations of these processes are the origin of Gibrat's law in similarity to other competing social systems [28–30]. Gibrat's law together with a small mean growth rate generates the power law tail for large cities. A model of the self-organized evolution of cities is established in the next section. It allows the derivation of the empirically found city size distribution. The relation of the model to Zipf's law is discussed in the conclusion.

2. The Model

We want to study the city size evolution of a country in a time interval Δt. The size of a city is characterized by its population. The population of the ith city at time step t is denoted by $N_i(t)$ and the total population of a county $N(t)$ is the sum over all cities:

$$N(t) = \sum_{i=1}^{C(t)} N_i(t), \quad (1)$$

where $C(t) > 0$ indicates the total number of cities of the country. In order to establish a continuous model the size of a city is scaled by a large number Z such that

$$p_i(t) = \frac{N_i(t)}{Z} \tag{2}$$

is a positive real number and the total population $\tilde{p}(t)$ is determined by (the parameter Z can be interpreted as the total number of humans at the last time step of the time period Δt)

$$\tilde{p}(t) = \frac{N(t)}{Z} \leq 1. \tag{3}$$

Three processes changing the city population in time are taken into account:

(i) the reproduction process of the population of a city,

(ii) the migration flux of humans between cities,

(iii) the restructuring of existing cities (e.g., by mergers and the generation of new cities).

We want to take advantage of the fact that the restructuring process of cities (iii) is usually much slower than the first two processes (i) and (ii). We chose the time interval Δt such that the number of cities of a country can be regarded as constant:

$$\frac{\Delta C}{\Delta t} \cong 0. \tag{4}$$

The corresponding number of cities is denoted by C_0.

The reproduction process increases the population of a city by

$$\frac{dp_i}{dt} \sim \alpha_i p_i. \tag{5}$$

The effective growth rate of a city is determined by $\alpha_i = \alpha_i' - \alpha_i''$, while α_i' indicates the birth rate and α_i'' indicates the mortality rate of inhabitants of a city.

The evolution of the ith city size is further determined by the migration of humans between cities given by the following balance:

$$\frac{dp_i(t)}{dt} \sim y_i^{\text{in}}(t) - y_i^{\text{out}}(t) = y_i(t), \tag{6}$$

where $y_i^{\text{in}} \geq 0$ is the inflow rate and $y_i^{\text{out}} \geq 0$ is the outflow rate of humans. A positive y_i is related to an effective inflow and a negative to an effective outflow of inhabitants. Under the condition that migration takes place essentially within a country we obtain the following for this exchange process:

$$\sum_{i=1}^{C_0} y_i(t) = 0 \tag{7}$$

and hence $\sum y_i^{\text{in}} = \sum y_i^{\text{out}}$. Since both processes take place independently the growth of the population of a city is determined by

$$\frac{dp_i(t)}{dt} = \alpha_i(t)\,p_i(t) + y_i(t). \tag{8}$$

Taking advantage of (7) the growth of the total population of the country is determined by

$$\sum_{i=1}^{C_0} \frac{dp_i(t)}{dt} = \frac{d\tilde{p}(t)}{dt} = \langle \alpha(t) \rangle\,\tilde{p}(t) \tag{9}$$

with the mean growth rate as follows (the average over the population size is indicated by brackets):

$$\langle \alpha(t) \rangle = \frac{1}{\tilde{p}(t)} \sum_{i=1}^{C_0} \alpha_i(t)\,p_i(t). \tag{10}$$

2.1. The Migration Flow. In order to establish the growth dynamics caused by the migration of humans we have to specify the inflow and outflow rates of humans of a city. For this purpose we want to denote humans interested in relocation as potential movers. Their total number is indicated by the variable $X(t)$, respectively, by the real number $x(t) = X(t)/Z < 1$. As a first approximation we assume that potential movers occur randomly, independent of the city with a country mean generation rate $g(t)$. The number of potential movers generated per unit time in the ith city is therefore $g(t)p_i(t)$. The amount of potential movers at a given time step is then determined by the following balance:

$$\frac{dx_i(t)}{dt} = g(t)\,p_i(t) - y_i^{\text{out}}(t). \tag{11}$$

This relation means that the number of potential movers of a city increases with the generation rate $p_i g$ and decreases as a result of the migration outflow with y_i^{out}. Under the condition that x_i relaxes sufficiently fast, we obtain the following for the stationary solution:

$$y_i^{\text{out}}(t) = g(t)\,p_i(t) \tag{12}$$

which characterizes the outflow rate of inhabitants of a city.

The inflow rate y_i^{in} of humans of a city is determined by the number of decisions per unit time of potential movers to migrate to the ith city. This rate will be zero if there are no potential movers. Under the condition that migrants prefer existing cities, the decision rate will be also zero if the size of a city vanishes. Hence, the inflow rate of a city is a function of both parameters, the number of potential movers, and the size of a city, $y_i^{\text{in}} = y_i^{\text{in}}(x, p_i)$. As a first approximation the inflow rate can be expanded near $x = 0$ and $p = 0$ as a product of both variables. We obtain the following for the first nonzero contribution:

$$y_i^{\text{in}}(t) \cong \eta_i(t)\,x(t)\,p_i(t), \tag{13}$$

where the rate $\eta_i \geq 0$ characterizes the chance that potential movers prefer just the ith city for migration. It is therefore termed preference rate and can be regarded as a function of various location factors, not further specified here. From the constraint equation (7) we further demand that

$$\sum_{i=1}^{C_0} \left[y_i^{\text{in}}(t) - y_i^{\text{out}}(t)\right] = \sum_{i=1}^{C_0} \left[f_i(t)\,p_i(t) - g(t)\,p_i(t)\right] = 0, \tag{14}$$

where

$$f_i(t) = \eta_i(t)\, x(t). \quad (15)$$

From (14) it follows that

$$g(t) = \langle f(t) \rangle = \frac{1}{\tilde{p}(t)} \sum_{i=1}^{C_0} f_i(t)\, p_i(t) \quad (16)$$

and the migration flow of the ith city becomes

$$y_i(t) = y_i^{\text{in}}(t) - y_i^{\text{out}}(t) = \left(f_i(t) - \langle f(t) \rangle\right) p_i(t). \quad (17)$$

2.2. Evolutionary Dynamics. Taking advantage of (17) we obtain for the city growth dynamics given by (8) the following (note that both processes migration and reproduction are self-amplifying):

$$\frac{dp_i(t)}{dt} = \alpha_i(t)\, p_i(t) + \left(f_i - \langle f \rangle\right) p_i. \quad (18)$$

While the first term indicates population growth, the second term expresses a replicator dynamics. It suggests that the city evolution is governed by an evolutionary competition in the migration process. The preferential growth process of a city is determined by the parameter f. Since f is usually termed as fitness, we want to denote f given by (15) as city fitness. It is essentially characterized by the migration preference rate η_i.

The replicator dynamics implies that cities higher than the mean fitness increase their size in time at the expense of cities with a lower fitness. The effective city growth rate is determined by the fitness advantage as follows:

$$\Delta f_i(t) = f_i(t) - \langle f(t) \rangle. \quad (19)$$

2.3. The City Size Distribution. In this section we want to derive the city size distribution based on the dynamics of city growth given by (18). The size distribution of cities $P(p)$ is determined by the probability to find the population of a city p_i in the interval p and $p + dp$. The main idea to derive the city size distribution $P(p)$ is to regard both growth rates α and Δf as consisting of a mean growth rate averaged over the time interval Δt and growth rate fluctuations. Hence, we write the reproduction growth rate of a city as follows (for a simpler notation the subscription indicating the city is omitted. The average over the time interval Δt is indicated by brackets with index t):

$$\alpha(t) = \langle \alpha \rangle_t + \delta\alpha(t), \quad (20)$$

where the first term is the mean growth rate averaged over the time interval Δt and the growth rate fluctuations are indicated by $\delta\alpha(t)$. Equivalently we write the following for the fitness advantage:

$$\Delta f(t) = \langle \Delta f \rangle_t + \delta\Delta f(t). \quad (21)$$

The urban growth dynamics of cities given by (18) turns into

$$\frac{dp(t)}{dt} = \theta p(t) + \rho(t)\, p(t), \quad (22)$$

where the time average growth rates of the cities are

$$\theta = \langle \alpha \rangle_t + \langle \Delta f \rangle_t \quad (23)$$

and the fluctuating variable $\rho(t)$ is determined by

$$\rho(t) = \delta\alpha(t) + \delta\Delta f(t). \quad (24)$$

As a first approximation the fluctuating variable $\rho(t)$ is treated as an independent, identical distributed (iid), random function with mean value and time correlation:

$$\langle \rho(t) \rangle_t = 0, \qquad \langle \rho(t), \rho(t') \rangle_t = 2D\delta(t - t'), \quad (25)$$

where D is a white noise amplitude. The Dirac delta function $\delta(t - t')$ indicates that the fluctuating variable $\rho(t)$ is regarded as uncorrelated in time.

The evolution of the city size depends on the relation between the magnitudes of the mean growth rate θ and growth rate fluctuations $\rho(t)$. We can distinguish between two cases.

For the case $\theta \gg \rho$, the mean growth rate dominates over growth rate fluctuations in the considered time interval Δt. In this case it is shown in Appendix A that the growth dynamics of cities has the form of a Fisher-Eigen law [27]. The competition between cities leads to a rapid replacement process of cities accompanied by a concentration of inhabitants in the cities with the highest fitness advantage, while cities with lower fitness disappear. In this case the stationary distribution reduces to a single megacity. However, this evolution is in contradiction with (4), suggesting that the number of cities remains nearly constant in the time interval Δt.

Therefore we want to confine here the discussion to the other case $\theta \ll \rho$. This relation between the mean growth rate and growth rate fluctuations can be taken into account by regarding the mean city growth rate as a small quantity. Introducing a small parameter ε with $\varepsilon \ll 1$, we demand that the mean growth rates of the cities are of the order ε:

$$\theta \sim \varepsilon. \quad (26)$$

In this case, however, the city growth dynamics depends on the size of a city. This becomes clear when we consider (22) for small cities with a size $p(t) \le \varepsilon$. Equation (26) suggests that the first term in (22) is then of the order ε^2 and can be neglected compared to the second term. For small cities with $p(t) \le \varepsilon$ (22) reduces to

$$\frac{dp}{dt} \cong \rho(t)\, p(t). \quad (27)$$

Because $\rho(t)$ is a fluctuating variable, this relation describes a multiplicative stochastic growth process known as Gibrat's law of proportionate effects [24]. A consequence of the competition in the migration process between cities and fluctuations of the reproduction process is in this model. With (25) the central limit theorem claims that the size distribution is given by a time-dependent lognormal distribution of the following form:

$$P(p,t) = \frac{1}{\sqrt{2\pi t}\omega p} \exp\left(-\frac{(\ln(p/p_0) - ut)^2}{2\omega^2 t}\right), \quad (28)$$

where u and ω are free parameters and p/p_0 is the city size scaled by the size at $\Delta t = 0$.

For large cities with $p > \varepsilon$, however, the first term comes into play. As derived from Appendix B, (22) can be interpreted as a generalized Langevin equation [31]. It yields as a stationary solution a power law city size distribution of the following form:

$$P(p) \sim \frac{1}{p^{(1+z)}} \quad (29)$$

with a Zipf exponent $z = \langle\theta\rangle/D$. For large cities the city size distribution approaches therefore a power law (Pareto) distribution. At a given time step t in the city size evolution the size distribution separates into two branches, a lognormal distribution for small cities ($p \leq \varepsilon$) and a Pareto tail for large cities ($p > \varepsilon$).

3. Conclusion

In agreement with empirical results and numerical simulations the model suggests that the size distribution of cities is lognormal with a power law tail if the mean growth rate of cities can be regarded as small ($\theta \sim \varepsilon$). Neglecting restructuring processes of cities (e.g., by mergers) the stationary size distribution for all cities would be over a very long time interval a Pareto distribution. The size distribution separates at an intermediate time step into two branches because small cities ($p < \varepsilon$) approach this stationary Pareto distribution much slower than large cities ($p > \varepsilon$).

The lognormal contribution is in this theory essentially a consequence of a preferential growth process of cities. While the population size of small cities is mainly influenced by the competition between cities in the migration process, large cities benefit from their size and can grow faster due to the reproduction of their inhabitants. This prevents them from extinction and generates the Pareto tail in the size distribution. That large cities growth on average faster than small cities is confirmed empirically, for example, by Rosen and Resnick [32].

Gabaix discussed the stationary power law city size distribution and argued that the power law distribution has its origin in Gibrat's law [17]. He suggested that for a stationary city growth rate $\gamma = \langle p_{t+1}/p_t\rangle = 1$ the Zipf exponent must be $z = 1$. Empirical investigations found a Zipf exponent that is somewhat greater than one, depending on the various characteristics (these characteristics can be interpreted as the location factors mentioned above) [32]. The model suggests that the Zipf exponent $z = \langle\theta\rangle/D$ is determined by the relation between the mean growth rate and the magnitude of growth rate fluctuations. As shown in Appendix C the constraint that the mean growth rate $\langle\theta\rangle$ is small leads to $\gamma \approx 1$. Following Gabaix, the Pareto tail established in this model is therefore governed by Zipf's law.

Cities play in this approach the same role as species in the biological evolution. They adapt to the preferences of potential movers in a self-organized process. However, city preferences depend on a variety of location factors fluctuating in time [33]. Therefore the growth of small cities is dominated by growth rate fluctuations (Gibrat's law) generating the lognormal part of the city size distribution. As mentioned above large cities benefit from their size in the growth process. In the economic literature this effect is known as "economies of scale." Since only cities with $p > \varepsilon$ profit from their size, the parameter ε characterizes the minimum size of a city to exploit economies of scale. The Pareto tail of the city size distribution can be interpreted therefore to be the result of economies of scale.

The uneven shape of the city size distribution is in view of the presented evolutionary model universal and a direct consequence of the reproduction and migration of humans.

Appendices

A. Replacement Process

We want to discuss the case that the mean growth rate of cities is large compared to growth rate fluctuations $\theta_i \gg \rho_i$. Equation (22) suggests that in this case the growth of a city can be written as

$$\frac{dp_i(t)}{dt} = \theta_i p_i(t) + \rho_i(t)\, p_i(t) \cong \theta_i p_i(t). \quad (A.1)$$

Let us consider next to the city with index i an arbitrary second city with index j. The time evolution of the proportion of the two cities is determined by the quotient rule as follows:

$$\frac{d}{dt}\left(\frac{p_i}{p_j}\right) = \frac{1}{p_j^2}\left(p_j(t)\frac{dp_i(t)}{dt} - p_i(t)\frac{dp_j(t)}{dt}\right) = \frac{p_i}{p_j}\Delta\theta_{ij} \quad (A.2)$$

with

$$\Delta\theta_{ij} = \theta_i - \theta_j. \quad (A.3)$$

The time dependent solution is

$$\frac{p_i(t)}{p_j(t)} = \frac{p_i(0)}{p_j(0)} e^{\Delta\theta_{ij}t} = e^{\Delta\theta_{ij}t+\kappa_{ij}} \quad (A.4)$$

with the initial proportion of the city sizes at $\Delta t = 0$ as follows:

$$\kappa_{ij} = \ln\left(\frac{p_i(0)}{p_j(0)}\right). \quad (A.5)$$

Hence, if the ith city has a growth rate advantage $\Delta\theta ij > 0$, the other city is replaced in time. Introducing the population share of the ith city as:

$$m_i(t) = \frac{p_i(t)}{\tilde{p}(t)} \quad (A.6)$$

and taking the time derivative, we obtain the following:

$$\frac{dp_i(t)}{dt} = \frac{dm_i(t)}{dt}\tilde{p}(t) + \frac{d\tilde{p}(t)}{dt}m_i(t), \quad (A.7)$$

with

$$\frac{d\tilde{p}(t)}{dt} = \langle\theta\rangle\,\tilde{p}(t). \quad (A.8)$$

Applying (A.1) population shares are also governed by a replicator equation as follows:

$$\frac{dm_i(t)}{dt} = (\theta_i(t) - \langle\theta\rangle)\,m_i(t). \quad (A.9)$$

The stationary solution of the replacement process is determined by $dm_i/dt = 0$. This condition can be satisfied by setting either $m_i = 0$ or $\beta_i = \langle\beta\rangle$. Since $\sum m_i = 1$, the stationary solution is a megacity with $m_i = 1$; $\beta_1 = \langle\beta\rangle$ while $m_i = 0$, $\beta_i \neq \langle\beta\rangle$ for all other cities. Hence, the case of large mean growth rates of the cities $\theta_i \gg \rho_i$ during Δt corresponds to a rapid replacement process. It is associated with the disappearance of cities while a single megacity survives.

B. Power Law Distribution of the City Size

For $\rho \gg \theta$, (22) can be interpreted as a generalized Langevin equation of the following form:

$$\frac{dp}{dt} = F(p) + \rho G(p) \quad (B.1)$$

with $F(p) = \theta p$ and $G(p) = p$. Following Richmond and Solomon [31], this multiplicative stochastic relation can be transformed into a relation with additive noise by introducing the functions $h(p)$ and $V(p)$ as follows:

$$\frac{dh(p)}{dt} = \frac{1}{G(p)}\frac{dp}{dt} = \frac{1}{p}\frac{dp}{dt},$$
$$-\frac{dV(p)}{dh(p)} = \frac{F(p)}{G(p)} = \theta, \quad (B.1)$$

respectively. Inserting these relations into (B.1) we obtain a Langevin equation of the following form:

$$\frac{dh}{dt} = -\frac{dV}{dh} + \rho. \quad (B.2)$$

For uncorrelated fluctuations suggested by (25) this relation describes a random walk in the potential $V(p)$. For a sufficiently long time the probability distribution approaches the distribution as follows:

$$B(h)\,dh = \frac{1}{N'}\exp\left(-\frac{V(h)}{D}\right)dh, \quad (B.3)$$

where N' is a normalization constant. In terms of the original variable, we get

$$P(p)\,dp = B(h)\,dh = \frac{1}{N'}\exp\left(-\frac{1}{D}\int\frac{F(p')}{G(p')^2}dp'\right)\frac{dp}{G(p)} \quad (B.4)$$

which yields with the corresponding functions for $G(p)$ and $F(p)$ as follows:

$$P(p) \sim \frac{1}{p^{(1+\langle\theta\rangle/D)}}. \quad (B.5)$$

The stationary distribution of a multiplicative process is therefore a power law distribution.

C. Zipf's Law

Write the average growth rate γ of the cities as

$$\gamma \cong \left\langle\frac{p(t+\Delta t)}{p(t)}\right\rangle_t. \quad (C.1)$$

Using (25), we obtain by approximating (22) by a difference equation:

$$\left\langle\frac{p(t+\Delta t) - p(t)}{p(t)}\right\rangle_t \cong \langle\theta\rangle_t\Delta t = \gamma - 1. \quad (C.2)$$

It was shown by Gabaix [17] that for $\gamma = 1$ the stationary power law distribution has the form:

$$P(p) \sim \frac{1}{p^{(1+z)}} \quad (C.3)$$

with a Zipf exponent $z = 1$. Equation (26) implies, however, that $\langle\theta\rangle_t \sim \varepsilon$. Hence we can write (C.2) as

$$\gamma = 1 + \langle\theta\rangle_t\Delta t \approx 1 + \varepsilon\Delta t. \quad (C.4)$$

Taking the usual time interval $\Delta t \approx 1$ (year), we obtain for the average growth rate $\gamma \approx 1$ for sufficiently small ε. Following Gabaix, Zipf's law (with $z \approx 1$) applies to the Pareto tail of the city size distribution.

Conflict of Interests

The author declares that there is no conflict of interests regarding the publication of this paper.

References

[1] G. Zipf, *Human Behavior and the Principle of Last Effort*, Addison-Wesley, Reading, Mass, USA, 1949.

[2] G. R. Carroll, "National city-size distributions: what do we know after 67 years of research?" *Progress in Human Geography*, vol. 6, no. 1, pp. 1–43, 1982.

[3] H. A. Makse, S. Havlin, and H. E. Stanley, "Modelling urban growth patterns," *Nature*, vol. 377, no. 6550, pp. 608–612, 1995.

[4] Y. M. Ioannides and H. G. Overman, "Zipf's law for cities: an empirical examintion," *Regional Science and Urban Economics*, vol. 33, no. 2, pp. 127–137, 2003.

[5] A. S. Garmestani, C. R. Allen, and C. M. Gallagher, "Power laws, discontinuities and regional city size distributions," *Journal of Economic Behavior and Organization*, vol. 68, no. 1, pp. 209–216, 2008.

[6] K. Giesen, A. Zimmermann, and J. Suedekum, "The size distribution across all cities—double Pareto lognormal strikes," *Journal of Urban Economics*, vol. 68, no. 2, pp. 129–137, 2010.

[7] A. Saichev, D. Sornette, and Y. Malevergne, *Theory of Zipf's Law and Beyond*, Springer, Berlin, Germany, 2011.

[8] Q. Zhang and D. Sornette, "Empirical test of the origin of Zipf's law in growing social networks," *Physica A: Statistical Mechanics and Its Applications*, vol. 390, no. 23-24, pp. 4124–4130, 2011.

[9] H. D. Rozenfeld, D. Rybski, X. Gabaix, and H. A. Makse, "The area and population of cities: new insights from a different perspective on cities," *American Economic Review*, vol. 101, no. 5, pp. 2205–2225, 2011.

[10] Y. Ioannides and S. Skouras, "US city size distribution: robustly Pareto, but only in the tail," *Journal of Urban Economics*, vol. 73, pp. 18–29, 2013.

[11] J. Eeckhout, "Gibrat's law for (all) cities," *The American Economic Review*, vol. 94, no. 5, pp. 1429–1451, 2004.

[12] J. Eeckhout, "Gibrat's law for (all) cities: reply," *American Economic Review*, vol. 99, no. 4, pp. 1676–1683, 2009.

[13] E. H. Decker, A. J. Kerkhoff, and M. E. Moses, "Global patterns of city size distributions and their fundamental drivers," *PLoS ONE*, vol. 2, no. 9, article e934, 2007.

[14] Y. Malevergne, V. Pisarenko, and D. Sornette, "Testing the Pareto against the lognormal distributions with the uniformly most powerful unbiased test applied to the distribution of cities," *Physical Review E—Statistical, Nonlinear, and Soft Matter Physics*, vol. 83, no. 3, Article ID 036111, 2011.

[15] B. J. L. Berry and A. Okulicz-Kozaryn, "The city size distribution debate: resolution for US urban regions and megalopolitan areas," *Cities*, vol. 29, supplement 1, pp. S17–S23, 2012.

[16] H. Simon, "On a class of skew distribution functions," *Biometrika*, vol. 42, pp. 425–440, 1955.

[17] X. Gabaix, "Zipf's law for cities: an explanation," *Quarterly Journal of Economics*, vol. 114, no. 3, pp. 739–767, 1999.

[18] X. Gabaix, "Zipf's law and the growth of cities," *The American Economic Review*, vol. 89, no. 2, pp. 129–132, 1999.

[19] X. Gabaix and Y. Ioannides, "The evolution of city size distributions," in *Handbook of Regional and Urban Economics*, V. Henderson and J. Thisse, Eds., vol. 4, North-Holland, Amsterdam, The Netherlands, 2004.

[20] J. C. Córdoba, "A generalized Gibrat's Law for cities," *International Economics Review*, vol. 49, pp. 1463–1468, 2008.

[21] M. Levy, "Gibrat's law for (All) cities: comment," *The American Economic Review*, vol. 99, no. 4, pp. 1672–1675, 2009.

[22] S. Lee and Q. Li, "Uneven landscapes and city size distributions," *Journal of Urban Economics*, vol. 78, pp. 19–29, 2013.

[23] P. Krugman, "Confronting the mystery of urban hierarchy," *Journal of the Japanese and International Economies*, vol. 10, no. 4, pp. 399–418, 1996.

[24] R. Gibrat, *Les Inegalites Economiques*, Sirey, Paris, France, 1913.

[25] H. D. Rozenfeld, D. Rybski, J. S. Andrade Jr., M. Batty, H. E. Stanley, and H. A. Makse, "Laws of population growth," *Proceedings of the National Academy of Sciences of the United States of America*, vol. 105, no. 48, pp. 18702–18707, 2008.

[26] F. Schweitzer and G. Silverberg, Eds., *Evolution and Self-Organization in Economics*, Duncker & Humblot, Berlin, Germany, 1998.

[27] R. Feistel and W. Ebeling, *Physics of Self-Organization and Evolution*, Wiley-VCH, New York, NY, USA, 2011.

[28] J. Kaldasch, "Evolutionary model of the growth and size of firms," *Physica A: Statistical Mechanics and Its Applications*, vol. 391, no. 14, pp. 3751–3769, 2012.

[29] J. Kaldasch, "Evolutionary model of the personal income distribution," *Physica A: Statistical Mechanics and Its Applications*, vol. 391, no. 22, pp. 5628–5642, 2012.

[30] J. Kaldasch, "Evolutionary model of the bank size distribution," *Economics*, 2014.

[31] P. Richmond and S. Solomon, "Power-laws are Boltzmann laws in disguise," *International Journal of Modern Physics C*, vol. 12, no. 3, pp. 333–343, 2001.

[32] K. T. Rosen and M. Resnick, "The size distribution of cities: an examination of the Pareto law and primacy," *Journal of Urban Economics*, vol. 8, no. 2, pp. 165–186, 1980.

[33] S. Findeisen and J. Südekum, "Industry churning and the evolution of cities: evidence for Germany," *Journal of Urban Economics*, vol. 64, no. 2, pp. 326–339, 2008.

6

Technoeconomic and Policy Analysis for Corn Stover Biofuels

Ryan Petter and Wallace E. Tyner

Department of Agricultural Economics, Purdue University, 403 West State Street, West Lafayette, IN 47907-2056, USA

Correspondence should be addressed to Wallace E. Tyner; wtyner@purdue.edu

Academic Editors: J.-L. Hu, S. Managi, and J. Zarnikau

Conventional fossil fuels dominate the marketplace, and their prices are a direct competitor for drop-in biofuels. This paper examines the impact of fuel selling price uncertainty on investment risk in a fast pyrolysis derived biofuel production facility. Production cost specifications are gathered from previous research. Monte Carlo analysis is employed with uncertainty in fuel selling price, biomass cost, bio-oil yield, and hydrogen price parameters. Experiments reveal that fuel price has a large impact on investment risk. A reverse auction would shift risk from the private sector to the public sector and is shown to be more effective at encouraging private investment than capital subsidies for the same expected public cost.

1. Introduction

This study is a technoeconomic analysis of the fast pyrolysis process. The main objective is to evaluate the effect of fuel price and technical uncertainty on the economic feasibility of biofuels created by catalytic fast pyrolysis using a circulating fluidized bed reactor. Previous studies have focused on creating reliable estimates of the initial capital and operating costs of a biorefinery. This study analyzes the effect of uncertainty in capital cost, hydrogen price, bio-oil yield, feedstock cost, and final product selling price on the appeal of project investment to a private investor. It directly evaluates the effect of two policy instruments—a reverse auction, which effectively fixes the price of the biofuel over the life of the project, and a capital subsidy. This research provides policy makers with information on how these policies could affect biofuel investment decisions.

Supply of advanced biofuels is expected to be a growing part of future liquid supply. US government investment in renewable power and fuels was $36 billion in 2012 [1]. Total US investment in the clean energy sector was $268 billion in 2012, a 500% increase since 2004 [2]. Imported petroleum products as a percentage of US petroleum consumption have decreased from 60% to 40% between 2005 and 2012 [3]. Supply of advanced biofuels is expected to be a growing part of future liquid supply [4, 5]. Research and development of economically attractive alternative fuel sources are ongoing in many nations around the world.

Catalytic fast pyrolysis is a process used to convert biomass to a bio-oil. This process is chosen for this study because of the relatively low cost per gallon [6–9]. Pyrolysis oil can be refined to diesel, gasoline, or jet fuel. Detailed descriptions of the fast pyrolysis process are available in the previous literature [9–15]. In this study, we use corn stover (corn residue), but the process can handle most cellulosic feedstocks. The remaining char and off-gas are burned in the production of electricity. Excess electricity can be sold [6].

A review of literature found no strong naming convention for pyrolysis derived biofuels. Cellulosic biofuels, biomass derived liquids, hydrocarbon fuels, and "drop-in" fuels all refer to renewable fuel derived from biomass. We use the term "biofuels" to describe biofuels produced via fast pyrolysis, although it can have many different meanings.

Technoeconomic analysis of fast pyrolysis is a method of forecasting the potential returns to an investment in a fast-pyrolysis production facility. It has been used extensively for studying feasibility of biofuel production. The National Renewable Energy Laboratory and the Pacific Northwest National Laboratory have conducted a series of technoeconomic analyses on a range of advanced biofuels and production methods [6, 8, 14]. This research produced detailed projections of the total cost of large capital investments, although there is some variability in the results [15]. The result of technoeconomic analysis is a cost break-even selling fuel price at which the future sales of transportation liquids and byproducts are equal to the present value of capital and operating expenditures, that is, a minimum fuel selling price. Research has shown that pyrolysis derived biofuels could be produced competitively, with estimated fuel selling prices ranging from $2.00 to $2.71 per gallon ($0.53 to $0.72 per liter) [8, 9, 16]. These studies suggest that commercial production of biofuel via fast pyrolysis is a competitive method of increasing domestic supply of transportation fuels.

According to research by Brown and Brown (2013), 215 million gallons per year (814 million liters per year) of cellulosic biofuel facilities are expected to be produced in the US by 2014 [15]. KiOR, ClearFuels, and Sundrop Fuels are three of the nine companies with commercial-scale projects expected to begin production by 2014 [15]. Meier et al. (2013) summarized current research, interest, and production of biofuels from pyrolysis in the six member countries of the IEA Bioenergy Task 34 [17]. They highlight Envergent and KiOR as commercial interests in the United States.

Although this study focuses on the economics of biofuel production, there are environmental effects as well [18–22]. The impact of biofuel expansion on greenhouse gas emissions is debated. Snowden-Swan and Male found that GHG reduction estimates from the petroleum baseline range from 62 to 68% [23]. However, if dedicated energy crops are used as feedstock, increased demand for land might cause an overall increase in greenhouse gas emissions [24]. It is generally agreed that the corn stover to biofuels pathway has no land use change impacts. There are other societal and economic effects from constructing and managing large production facilities and from harvesting, storing, processing, and transporting large amounts of biomass.

This research focuses on the effect of reverse auctions on the variance of net present value and internal rate of return. The government has many options for affecting biofuel prices, but these are not discussed here because they are covered in the previous literature [25, 26]. In a reverse auction, biofuel suppliers bid against each other for the opportunity to supply a certain volume of biofuel [27]. The result is a long-term forward contract with a competitive known price. The winning (lowest) bidder would have the biofuel price fixed for the duration of the contract, which is here assumed to be 20 years. The government would decrease long-term risk and obtain a competitive long-term price. In addition to examining the risk reduction impacts of the reverse auction, we also compare it to a capital subsidy with the same expected cost to government as a reverse auction.

2. Methodology

The method of production of biofuel used in this study is based on a technoeconomic analysis done at Iowa State University [6]. That study analyzed the production of biofuel via catalytic fast pyrolysis and hydroprocessing, a similar process to the commercial implementation by KiOR [28]. This study uses the same assumptions to validate the base case but then uses financial and economic assumptions that more closely represent reality in the marketplace. Additionally, this report adds uncertainty distributions to some parameters.

Table 1: Economic assumptions.

Parameter	Input value	Units	Source
Real discount rate	10%	%	[6]
Nominal interest rate	7.5%	%	[6]
10 year depreciation	200%	%	[14]
Plant depreciable life	7	yrs	[14]
Equity	50%	%	[6]
Financing	50%	%	[6]
Loan term	10	yrs	[6]
Construction time	3	yrs	[14]
% spent in year 1	8%	%	[14]
% spent in year 2	60%	%	[14]
% spent in year 3	32%	%	[14]
Income taxes	35%	%	[14]

In this section, we first recreate the analysis done by Tristan Brown et al. [6]. We then detail the data used in our analysis and show how it differs from Tristan Brown et al. Next, we describe how uncertainty is modeled. Finally, we describe the eight experimental cases examined in this study.

Much of the research on fast pyrolysis has been done by chemists and engineers. In order to recreate the analysis done, we initially used the same spreadsheet model as some chemical engineers: a discounted cash flow rate of return analysis [14, 29]. Many economists employ a different treatment of inflation, debt repayment, taxes, and other factors. Of course, not all engineers use only the discounted case flow rate of return method, nor have all economists used the more complete economic and financial analysis. However, for simplicity in presentation, we will differentiate the two types of spreadsheets by labeling them as engineering analysis and economic analysis, respectively.

2.1. Engineering Analysis. To be certain that our spreadsheet was an accurate representation of the original Brown data, we first recreated the analysis by Tristan Brown et al. [6] using an engineering analysis. Some of the data needed to recreate the analysis was not available in that paper. For those parameters we assumed that they match those in a previous Iowa State University study [14].

The economic assumptions used by Wright et al. [14] or Tristan Brown et al. [6] are documented in Table 1.

Some of the key economic assumptions are a total project timeline of 23 years, 50% debt financing, a 10% discount rate, a loan payback period of 10 years, a tax rate of 35% of net income, and a construction time of 3 years. No inflation rate was specified in either analysis.

In addition to the economic variables, we used many of the technical variable values as Tristan Brown et al. [6]. The technical assumptions we used in our recreation are summarized in Table 2. More details, including the number and type of employees and other assumptions are available from the authors on request.

TABLE 2: Technical assumptions.

Parameter	Input value	Units	Source
Working capital	15%	%	[6]
Project contingency	$61,490,157	$	Calculated from data in [14]
Working capital expenditure	$55,341,142	$	Calculated from data in [14]
Total capital investment	$429,000,000	$	[6]
Land	$4,717,915	$	Calculated from data in [14]
Nominal fixed capital Investment	$394,799,061	$	Calculated from data in [14]
Plant operation/online time	329.5	days/yr	Calculated from data in [6]
Startup production rate	75%	%	[14]
Startup variable expense	87.5%	%	[14]
Input capacity	2,000	MT/day	[6]
Annual feedstock use	659,000	MT/yr	[6]
Bio-oil yield	63.00%	Mg/Mg	[6]
Gas conversion rate	21.0%	Mg/Mg bio-oil	[14]
Diesel conversion rate	21.0%	Mg/Mg bio-oil	[14]
Feedstock cost	83	$/MT	[6]
Catalyst replacement costs	1,767,000	$/yr	[14]
Electricity produced	223,000,000	kwh/yr	[6]
Electricity use	11,490	kw/hour	[14]
Electricity price	$0.0540	$/kwh	[14]
Hydrogen use	2,041	kg/hour	[14]
Hydrogen price	$1.33	$/kg	[6]

Besides technical parameters, financing assumptions also affect the analysis. Tristan Brown et al. [6] do not provide details, but we assume that their engineering spreadsheet is similar to work done by Humbird et al. [29]. Humbird et al. [29] assume that land is paid immediately with equity, interest is paid off during the first three construction years, and that tax benefits from losses on operations are claimed in the current year. Finally, Humbird et al. [29] do not include loan or interest payments when computing tax payments.

Using the engineering analysis and the above data, we found a facility fuel output of 58.6 millions of gallons per year (222 millions of liters). Wright et al. [14] reported a fuel yield of 58.2 MGY, and 57.4 MGY was reported by Tristan Brown et al. [6]. We found a minimum fuel selling price of $2.55 per gallon ($0.67 per liter) compared to $2.57 ($0.68 per liter) in Tristan Brown et al. [6]. Thus, we can be confident that we have accurately reconstructed the Tristan Brown et al. [6] assumptions and results.

The fuel price was determined using the goal seek add-in from Excel to set net present value equal to zero. Minimum fuel selling price is the price that makes the net present value with a 10% real discount rate equal to zero. The 10% discount rate is sometimes called a hurdle rate. We do not know what discount rate a private investor would require. However, choosing a different discount rate would not change the conclusions from this study. The conclusions from this study are based on variability not break-even fuel price. We have chosen to use the 10% real discount rate used in Tristan Brown et al. [6]. Thus, the term "minimum fuel selling price" is analogous to "break-even price."

2.2. Economic Spreadsheet Analysis. We did our economic analysis in an Excel spreadsheet using most of the same technical data values from Tristan Brown et al. [6]. This section provides details on changes made to the technical and economic parameters. First, we describe financing differences. Then, we describe the difference in assumed tax rate. Finally, we examine changes in parameter values and their effect on expected return.

In the previous section we described financing assumptions present in the engineering analysis. These were obtained from a report by Humbird et al. [29] and seem to be used in Table D-3 in Wright et al. [14]. We assume that they are also used in Tristan Brown et al. [6]. We chose different financing assumptions in our economic analysis which have material effects on the return on investment. For example, the engineering spreadsheets assumed the inflation rate to be zero. However, average inflation as shown in the US consumer price index has been 2.9% over the past 30 years (Bureau of Labor Statistics 2013a). We assumed a 2.5% inflation rate. The differences in financing assumptions are summarized in Table 3. Depreciation for tax purposes was the same in both the engineering and economic analyses.

The combined effect on investment return of the assumption differences was calculated to see the importance of the approach. As described previously, our recreation of the previous studies' assumptions found a 10.0% internal rate of return at a fuel price of $2.55 per gallon ($0.67 per liter). With our financing assumptions but not our price or tax assumptions, a fuel price of $2.55 per gallon ($0.67 per liter) results in a 12.0% return. Using the economic financing assumptions, we find a break-even fuel price of $2.40 per

TABLE 3: Differences in financing assumptions.

Engineering analysis	Economic analysis
Land paid with equity	Land included in capital investment and cost is divided between financing and equity
Tax benefits or losses carry over	Tax benefits or losses occur in the year they occur
Interest is paid with equity during construction	Interest is compounded annually during construction (interest is capitalized)
Loan and interest are not included in computing taxes	Loan interest is deductible for purposes of tax calculations
Inflation is assumed to be zero	Inflation is assumed to be 2.5%

gallon ($0.63 per liter). In other words, there is a 6.3% difference in the break-even price between the economic and engineering analyses and a 2.0% difference in the internal rate of return.

In addition to these financing assumption differences, three technical parameter values were changed: hydrogen price, feedstock price, and fuel yield. These variables have min, mode, and max values, which make up the Pert distribution input parameters for the stochastic analysis. Details on the changes to hydrogen price, feedstock price and fuel yield are explained in Section 2.3. However, for reference these changes are summarized in Table 4.

Hydrogen price, feedstock price, and fuel yield each have new mean values. Hydrogen has a much higher price, and fuel yield is slightly lower. The combined effect shifts the break-even fuel price from $2.40 to $2.65 per gallon ($0.63 to $0.70 per liter). Remember that our recreation of Tristan Brown et al. [6] had a break-even price of $2.55 per gallon ($0.67 per liter).

Besides the adjustments made to variables in Table 4, income tax was adjusted lower. The tax rate in Tristan Brown et al. [6] is 35%, which is the statutory corporate federal tax rate. Effective tax rates measure the proportion of taxes paid to economic income. For profitable firms filing a Schedule M-3, the effective federal tax rate was about 13% in 2010 [32]. Including foreign, state, and local taxes for all firms filing a Schedule M-3 raises the effective tax rate to about 23% [32]. Therefore, for this study, we assume a tax rate of 24% because it is closer to the tax rate paid by corporations.

The lower tax rate has a less severe effect than the previous changes. Lowering the tax rate from 35% to 24% in our recreation of the Tristan Brown et al. [6] study lowers the break-even price from $2.65 to $2.62 per gallon ($0.70 to $0.69 per liter). Table 5 summarizes the changes made and their effect on break-even price.

2.3. Technical Uncertainty. The uncertainty inherent in a biofuel production facility stems from a multitude of sources, but four are chosen because of their importance to project viability. The four parameters modeled as uncertain are grouped into technical uncertainty and fuel price uncertainty. The parameters labeled with technical uncertainty are the price of the feedstock, the bio-oil yield, and hydrogen purchase price. Table 6 shows the share in total cost of capital investment, feedstock, hydrogen, and other operating cost. Bio-oil yield clearly could have an important impact on economic viability, as the higher the yield, the lower the unit cost. Later, in one of the simulation cases, we will test the importance of the capital cost assumption.

In related studies, researchers conduct uncertainty analysis by showing the impact of changing certain variables one at a time and determining the maximum and minimum rate of return or fuel selling price [6, 14]. These analyses do not provide probability of the high or low values or the assessment of combined uncertainty. These studies use sensitivity analysis to identify the variables that are most critical to the cash flow. However, sensitivity analysis does not consider variable interaction, so it provides a less quantifiable measure of risk. These studies determine that two of the most important variables in terms of their expected effect on the break-even price are bio-oil and fuel yield and biomass cost. Other important parameters reported are electricity selling price, interest rate, and project investment cost.

This study uses Monte Carlo simulation, which uses input distributions rather than fixed values. The Palisades risk and decision analysis software, @Risk, is used to account for variability in the technical parameters: biomass cost, bio-oil yield, and hydrogen price. Monte Carlo simulation creates input distributions based on data from the literature, econometric estimates, or other sources. Common distributions that are used for input costs are the Triangular and Pert. Both of these distributions have as parameters the max, mode, and min values. Experts can more easily answer expected, maximum, and minimum parameter values than selecting a mean and standard deviation as for a normal distribution. The main difference between the two is that the Pert has more of the probability density closer to the mean, and the triangular has more towards the max and min values. Since Pert has more probability near the mean, it was chosen for this study.

The high, mode, and low values for bio-oil yield are the same as used by previous studies [6, 14]. Bio-oil yield varies depending on factors such as the type of catalyst and the rate of temperature change during the pyrolysis reaction. Yields are expressed as weight of oil as a percentage of the weight of starting biomass. Bio-oil yields of 70%, 63%, and 49% set out the max, mode, and min for a Pert distribution. The mean value for this Pert distribution, as reported earlier, is 61.8%. This changes the annual biofuel production from 58.6 MGY to 57.5 MGY, nearly the same as the 57.4 MGY reported in Tristan Brown et al. [6].

The feedstock price varies depending on material and the cost of preparing the material for pyrolysis. Prices of $110, $83, and $55/MT are reported in the same studies [6, 14]. We use these prices as the maximum, mode, and minimum for a Pert distribution. The mean value, as shown in Table 4, is $82.83/MT.

The other technical parameter modeled with uncertainty is hydrogen price. The National Research Council studied conventional and advanced hydrogen production related to their study of hydrogen fuel cell vehicles [30]. Using the H2A model, they found costs of $1.60 and $1.90 in 2005 dollars, respectively, for natural gas reforming and coal gasification.

Table 4: Differences in stochastic parameter estimates.

Parameter	Old value Tristan Brown et al. [6]	New value Min	New value Mode	New value Max	Mean value	Unit	Source
Hydrogen price	1.33	1.33	2.02	2.94	2.06	$/kg	[30, 31]
Feedstock price	83	55	83	110	82.83	$/MT	[6]
Fuel yield	63	49	63	70	61.8	%	[6]

Table 5: Alternative measures of break-even price.

Description of conditions	$ per gallon	$ per liter
As reported in Tristan Brown et al. [6]	$2.57	$0.68
Tristan Brown et al. [6] as recreated by authors with engineering financing assumptions, higher tax rate	$2.55	$0.67
Old variable values, economic financing assumptions, higher tax rate	$2.40	$0.63
New variable values, economic financing assumptions, higher tax rate	$2.65	$0.70
New variable values, economic financing assumptions, lower tax rate	$2.62	$0.69

Table 6: Cost shares for key cost components.

Item	NPV cost ($)	Cost share (%)
Capital cost (with working capital)	$303,129,655	30.3%
Feedstock	$344,499,049	34.4%
Hydrogen	$209,663,508	21.0%
Other operating cost	$142,824,530	14.3%
Total	$1,000,116,742	100.0%

Source: author's calculations.

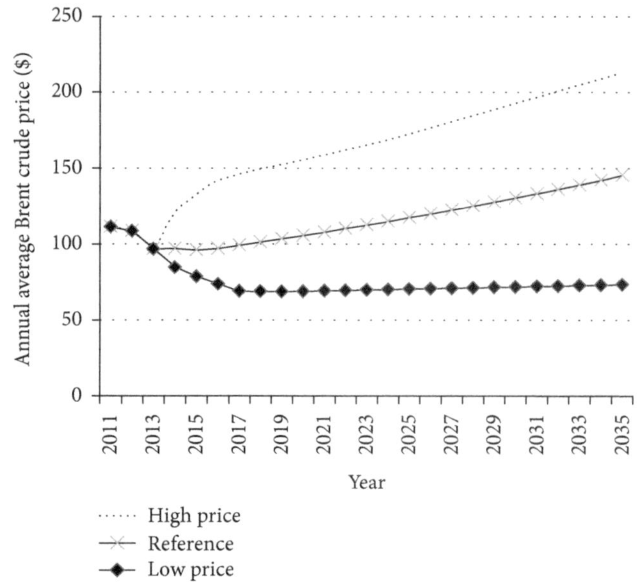

Figure 1: Projected Brent crude prices from Annual Energy Outlook 2013 [4].

Adjusted to 2011 dollars using the Producer Price Index for Industrial Commodities, the natural gas reforming cost increases to $2.02 [33]. A 2010 study conducted by Iowa State and Texas A&M summarized the cost estimates of various studies in the production of hydrogen [31]. They found coal gasification with current technology and carbon sequestration costing between $1.25 and $1.83 and natural gas steam methane reforming costing between $2.33 and $3.17, in 2007 dollars. The low estimate for steam methane reforming using natural gas was $2.33. Adjusted to 2011 dollars using the Producer Price Index for Industrial Commodities this cost increases to $2.94 [33]. We use a low price of $1.33, mode price of $2.02, and high price of $2.94 per kilogram. These three technical parameters were summarized in Table 4.

2.4. Fuel Price Uncertainty. Diesel and gasoline compete with biofuel, so the prices of those fuels directly impact the economic feasibility of biofuel production. The selling price of fuel in this study is assumed to be the same as wholesale gasoline and diesel prices [6]. The DOE projects real increases in the price of crude oil but with wide uncertainty as shown by the differences among the high, reference, and low price scenarios in Figure 1 [4]. Figure 1 displays projections from the 2013 Annual Energy Outlook for Brent crude spot prices from 1990 to 2040 in constant 2011 dollars per barrel.

To capture the uncertainty regarding fuel prices and the impact of selling price uncertainty on the expected return on investment, we employ three fuel price projections: (1) a fixed price, (2) a price that fluctuates but remains at about the same level on average over the time period, and (3) a price that fluctuates but increases at a rate similar to the DOE reference scenario.

In the first price projection, the fuel price is fixed in real terms. In nominal terms the price increases because of the 2.5% inflation rate. This fixed fuel price represents a reverse auction outcome. If the government created a long-term forward contract based on a reverse auction, from a private perspective the fuel selling price would be fixed.

The nondeterministic steady price is useful for understanding the importance of variability in fuel selling price on the economic profitability of investment in a biofuel refinery. It has about the same average price as the fixed price, but the uncertainty in fuel price is expected to increase the risk of investment.

The nondeterministic price with upward trend was created to be similar to DOE projections from 2013 to 2035. The starting gasoline price in our analysis is the DOE projection for 2013 (2011 dollars) but subtracting $0.70 per gallon ($0.18

per liter) to convert retail prices to wholesale prices [34]. This is the same starting price used for the fixed price. Our forecast for the uncertain price with upward trend also matches the DOE forecast less $0.70 per gallon ($0.18 per liter) for expected fuel price in 2035, which is the final project year.

We tested both mean reversion and Brownian motion with trend models. The Brownian motion with trend model had a lower standard deviation and did not follow the DOE projections as closely. Figure 2 compares the projections: static DOE projections, mean reversion, mean reversion with upward drift, and Brownian motion with upward drift. The three gasoline prices used in the experiments are static price, mean reversion with no upward trend, and mean reversion with upward trend.

Tristan Brown et al. [6] assume that half of the fuel output from the plant is gasoline and half is diesel. These fuels have different selling price, although their prices are highly correlated with each other. Regressing the historic wholesale prices of gasoline and diesel for 2004–2012, we found an R-square of 97%. We used the intercept and slope of this regression, which were −0.322 and 1.201, to find the diesel projected prices based on gas prices. This is shown in the following equation:

$$\text{Diesel price}_t = -0.322 + 1.201 * \text{Gasoline price}_t. \quad (1)$$

The fuel produced in this project is 50% each of diesel and gasoline. Therefore, we forecast a combined price by using the average of the diesel and gasoline price for each year. The cumulative results are fuel price forecasts for the next 23 years, from 2013 to 2035.

2.5. Experimental Cases. There is a high expected variance in gasoline and diesel prices over the time period. Thus, the experiments are chosen to help identify the effect of government intervention on the investment decision given that price uncertainty. Together, these cases provide an understanding of the impact of fuel price uncertainty on investment in a biofuel production facility.

(1) A base case with a fixed fuel price of $2.68 per gallon ($0.71 per liter) and no uncertain variables.

(2) A stochastic case (for all three technical uncertain variables) plus an uncertain fuel price that has *no* upward trend.

(3) A stochastic case (for all three technical uncertain variables) plus an uncertain fuel price that *has* an upward trend keyed to the DOE reference price forecast.

(4) A stochastic case (for all three technical uncertain variables) but with a break-even fuel price. The fuel price is fixed in real terms to provide the same expected net present value as in case two ($2.68 per gallon or $0.71 per liter). This price is a possible outcome of a reverse auction.

(5) A stochastic case (for all three technical uncertain variables) but with a fuel price fixed to provide the same expected economic net present value as in case three ($2.92 per gallon $0.77 per liter). This price is also a possible outcome of a reverse auction.

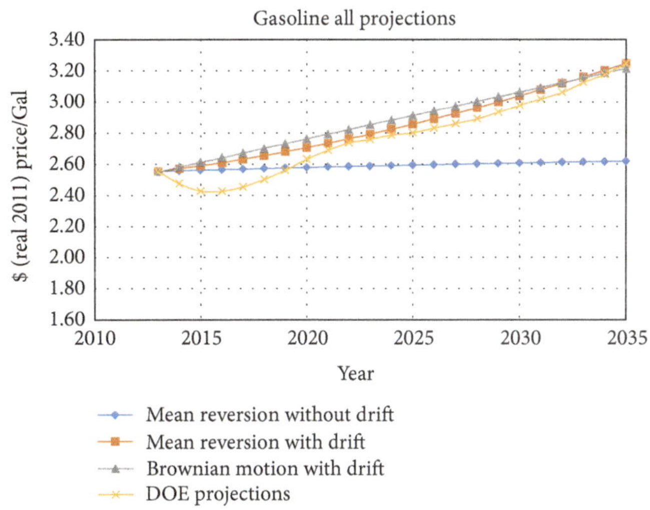

FIGURE 2: Comparison of all gasoline price projections.

(6) A stochastic case that matches case three but with 20% higher capital investment cost.

(7) A stochastic case that matches case three but with a fixed fuel selling price ($2.92 per gallon $0.77 per liter) for 45 million gallons (170 million liters) of fuel per year (for project years 5–23).

(8) A stochastic case that matches case three but with a $5 million capital subsidy. This is designed to compare public intervention in the form of a capital subsidy with a reverse auction. Cases (7) and (8) have the same expected government cost.

3. Results and Discussion

This section presents and summarizes the results of the analysis. The next section draws conclusions from these results.

3.1. Base Case. Case 1, the base case, is a completely deterministic model with the hydrogen price, bio-oil yield, feedstock price, and fuel selling price values fixed at their expected mean levels. It is the only case where the parameters are all deterministic. The values of the technical parameters are fixed at their mean levels which, for the Pert distribution, are calculated as shown in the following equation:

$$\text{Pert Mean} = \frac{\min + 4 * \text{mode} + \max}{6}. \quad (2)$$

The mean values are shown in Table 7.

Results are shown in net present value (NPV), internal rate of return (IRR), and benefit cost ratio (B/C). Net present value provides a discounted measure of project worth. The project is accepted when NPV is greater than zero. One problem with NPV is the large numbers that can come from

Table 7: Case 1 technical variable values.

Variable name	Input value
Hydrogen price	\$2.06/gal or \$0.71/liter
Feedstock price	\$82.83/MT
Fuel yield	61.8%

Table 8: Case 1 results.

	NPV	IRR (real)	*B/C*
Economic	\$0.00	10.0%	1.00
Financial	\$16,641,078	11.0%	1.09

large projects. Another problem is choosing an appropriate discount rate. IRR measures the rate of interest that makes the NPV equal zero. IRR assumes that profits can be reinvested at the IRR, but this may not be possible.

Table 8 summarizes the results from the base case.

Table 8 is separated into a financial analysis and an economic analysis. The economic analysis is before financing and taxes while the financial is after accounting for those. The economic analysis is also known in the financial literature as asset based analysis. There are two competing causes for differences in the financial and economic NPV and IRR. The first is that the nominal loan interest rate (7.5%) is lower than the real discount rate (10%). When the interest rate is lower than the discount rate, as the equity ratio decreases, the return increases. The rational private investor under these conditions would seek as much financing as possible for capital investments when the loan interest rate is below the discount rate. We assumed a 50% equity structure. Thus, including financing improves the project return.

Second, tax payments are included in financing, which lowers project return. All of the cases with positive expected IRR pay taxes during the project time period. When returns are higher, tax payments are greater. In some cases that follow, when returns are higher, the tax payment cost exceeds the benefit from financing. In those cases, the economic NPV will be higher than financial NPV. In Case 1, however, the benefit from financing exceeds the cost from tax payments.

In the base case, the project has an economic NPV of zero but a positive financial NPV. We chose to use an *economic* break-even fuel price for this case. At a price of \$2.68 (\$0.71 per liter), the financial IRR is 11.0% and the economic IRR is 10.0%. The financial break-even price is \$2.62 (\$0.69 per liter). The financial IRR at this price is 10%, and the economic is 9.2%. The economic break-even price is \$2.68 (\$0.71 per liter), higher than the \$2.57 (\$0.68 per liter) break-even price in the Tristan Brown et al. [6] study.

Investors are risk averse, so without knowing the riskiness of an investment one cannot discern its attractiveness. In the next scenario, we examine the impact of uncertainty.

3.2. Stochastic Steady Price Case. In Case 2, we employ Monte Carlo analysis to predict uncertainty in NPV given uncertainty in technical and market parameters. The break-even fuel selling price in the base case was \$2.68 per gallon

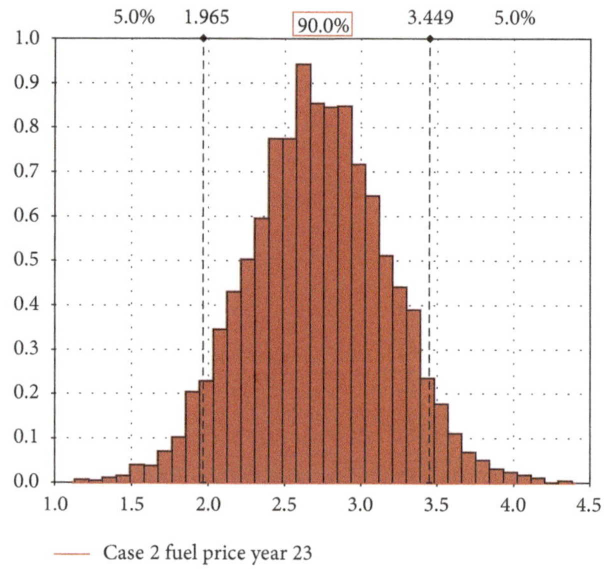

Minimum	1.1293
Maximum	4.3836
Mean	2.7178
Std dev	0.4533
Values	5000

Figure 3: steady fuel price distribution.

(\$0.71 per liter). This case has the same economic NPV as in Case 1 but adds uncertainty.

While the previous case could be shown in a small table, the results of Case 2 are better understood using graphs of input and output distributions. As noted earlier, the technical variables are assumed to have Pert probability distributions. The technical parameters for each year are considered to be independent of each other, so the distribution curves are nearly identical for each project year.

The fuel selling price is nondeterministic in a different way because of the mean reversion calculations. The fuel selling price distribution will have variance from year to year because of the mean reverting process. Figure 3 shows the outcome of a fuel price distribution in the final project year. There is an 80% probability that the ending price was between \$2.34 and \$3.10 per gallon (\$0.62 and \$0.82 per liter). The maximum fuel price in year 23 was \$4.38 (\$1.16 per liter) and the minimum was \$1.13 (\$0.30 per liter).

On average, the economic NPV was near zero. However, there was a total range of \$837 million for the economic case. Table 9 summarizes some of the key results from this experiment.

The financial case had a higher standard deviation for IRR but lower standard deviation for NPV. In calculating the economic IRR, there were 105 errors out of the 5,000 iterations during the simulation. The financial case IRR had 121 errors. Errors occur in the IRR because, under some combination of random draws from the input distributions, the flows are so skewed in the negative or positive direction (usually negative) that no IRR can be found. Under that condition, the IRR function returns an error, and the result is

TABLE 9: Case 2.

	Economic			Financial		
	NPV	IRR (nominal)	B/C	NPV	IRR (nominal)	B/C
Expected value	$0	10.0%	1.00	$16,641,078	11.0%	1.09
Standard deviation	$100,993,377	3.9%	0.29	$76,669,403	4.8%	0.40
Max	$427,930,098	22.8%	2.24	$339,121,179	26.9%	2.76
Min	**($408,886,573)**	−15.6%	−0.19	**($295,088,669)**	−13.6%	−0.53
Probability of loss	50.3%			40.8%		

reported as such in the Monte Carlo outputs. For example, for the financial case, the mean IRR is based on 4879 iterations instead of 5000. Errors are not found in NPV calculations. For this reason NPV is generally a better measure of risk distributions.

The economic case had a wider NPV distribution than the financial case, and this will remain true for all of the experiments. This is because of the tax payments which reduce gains in highly profitable iterations and reduce losses (due to negative taxes) in low profitability or loss iterations. One standard deviation in the financial case is $77 million, while it is $101 million in the economic case. These standard deviations are based on the input distributions from the uncertain variables. Since the underlying input distributions will not change in the stochastic cases, the standard deviations should be about the same from case to case except when uncertain variables are held constant. The financial NPV was slightly better than the economic NPV.

The economic NPV ranged from −$409 million to +$428 million. There was a 50% chance of a loss for the economic case, as the mean of the distribution was near zero. The financial NPV had an 80% probability of being between −$81 million and $113 million. The maximum was $339 million and the minimum was −$295 million. There was a 41% probability that the financial NPV was less than zero.

This case enforces the wide variability and high amount of risk inherent in an investment of this magnitude. Even if the expected IRR was 20% instead of 11%, the wide spread of possible outcomes would make investment risky. Remember, the initial capital investment is $429 million. In this result there is a spread in the financial NPV of $634 million. This experiment only had three technically uncertain variables. Including others would make the spread of possibilities even greater. The next case creates an increasing fuel selling price that more closely matches DOE projected fuel prices.

3.3. Stochastic Increasing Case. Case 3 has an uncertain fuel price that increases to, on average, meet DOE projections in 2035. It is the same as in the second case, except that it has a rising fuel selling price. The ending price is higher in Case 3, increasing to $3.41 per gallon ($0.90 per liter) of fuel on average in 2011 real dollars. One standard deviation is $0.40 ($0.11 per liter). Table 10 summarizes the results from this scenario.

The increasing fuel price had a positive effect on the expected NPV of the investment, but Case 3 still has a risk of loss. The economic NPV had a 21% probability of loss, while it was 50% in the second case. The financial NPV likelihood of loss decreased from 41% to 15%. Increasing the product selling price increased probability of having a positive NPV and increased the expected return.

While in Case 2 the economic NPV was greater than the financial NPV, in Case 3 the expected financial NPV of $81 million was lower than the expected economic NPV of $84 million. The higher fuel selling price results in higher profits from project investment. The negative cost of taxes had a larger impact than the benefit gained from the spread between debt and discount rate in the financing of capital debt. The NPV of taxes for case two was $18 million, but in Case 3 the NPV of taxes was $39 million.

At the same time, the financial IRR of 14% was slightly better than the economic IRR of 13%. This is because of the initial capital investment being financed through debt. The financial case had a lower initial equity investment. The IRR had a minimum return of −2% in this case, but the middle 80% of results were between 9% and 19%. The expected IRR increased by 3% from the second to the third case.

Cases 1 to 3 have shown a range of possibilities. The following cases will isolate the effect of changes in either the product selling price or the initial capital investment.

3.4. Forward Contract: Fixed Selling Price. Case 4 is the same as Case 2 except for the selling price of fuel. While Case 2 had a variable selling price, this case has a fixed fuel price. The fuel price in this scenario is set to $2.68 ($0.71 per liter) in real terms. This scenario isolates the uncertainty in return on investment caused by the technical variables. Table 11 shows the results.

The economic NPV is made to be zero by finding the break-even fuel price, while expected economic NPV did not change from Case 2. The expected economic NPV was equal to zero in both the second and the fourth scenarios, so although standard deviation decreased, half of the outcomes were positive and half were negative. Standard deviation decreased dramatically, from $101 million to $21 million. The probability of loss did not decrease.

The total range between the maximum and minimum financial NPV decreased from $634 million to $117 million from Case 2 to Case 4. One standard deviation decreased from $76 million to $15 million. The probability of a loss in NPV decreased from 41% to 13%. When risk is reduced to technical parameters, there is much less risk to the private investor.

TABLE 10: Case 3 results.

	Economic			Financial		
	NPV	IRR (nominal)	B/C	NPV	IRR (nominal)	B/C
Expected value	$84,252,474	12.6%	1.24	$80,672,958	14.2%	1.42
Standard deviation	$100,675,911	3.1%	0.29	$76,305,318	3.8%	0.40
Max	$447,048,535	22.7%	2.30	$349,991,319	26.4%	2.81
Min	**($268,437,824)**	−5.0%	0.22	**($190,303,825)**	−8.1%	0.01
Probability of loss	20.7%			14.5%		

TABLE 11: Case 4 results.

	Economic			Financial		
	NPV	IRR (nominal)	B/C	NPV	IRR (nominal)	B/C
Expected value	$0	10.0%	1.00	$16,641,078	11.0%	1.09
Standard deviation	$20,684,124	0.7%	0.06	$15,051,080	0.9%	0.08
Max	$79,292,123	12.9%	1.23	$73,091,401	14.5%	1.38
Min	**($86,537,333)**	6.8%	0.75	**($43,554,644)**	7.3%	0.77
Probability of loss	50.2%			13.2%		

If the government were to guarantee biofuel producers a minimum or a fixed price for their product, private investors would become more interested in this industry. Under these circumstances, it is apparent that reducing fuel price uncertainty would encourage investment.

3.5. Forward Contract: Increasing Selling Price. Case 5 is similar to Case 4 in that the fuel price is fixed while the technical parameters are still forecast with uncertainty. The fuel price in Case 5 is fixed to meet the financial NPV in Case 3. Fuel price is fixed to $2.92 ($0.77 per liter) in this case. It makes intuitive sense that the fixed fuel price is much higher in this scenario than in Cases 2 and 4 because of the higher product selling price. The results from this simulation are in Table 12.

Eliminating the fuel price uncertainty reduced the standard deviation in the financial NPV from $76 million to $16 million. The total range of financial NPVs decreased from $540 million in case three to $114 million in this case.

As in Case 3, the higher tax payments related to the higher fuel price result in a lower financial NPV than economic NPV. The financial IRR was better than the economic IRR because the financial IRR had a smaller initial investment cost.

Similar to our conclusion from Case 4, we can say that fuel price uncertainty comprised a large part of the uncertainty in these experiments. The government could employ reverse auctions to reduce private risk and encourage investment in this infant industry.

3.6. Stochastic with Higher Capital Cost. For Case 6, we test the impact of higher-than-expected capital costs. Capital costs with new technologies and unknown production costs are difficult to predict. There has been a history of cost overruns for new technologies. Also, much of the literature casts the estimated capital cost as being for the *n*th plant. We attempted to measure the impact on project investment with a 20% cost overrun.

Case 6 uses the scenario in Case 3 as its base. Total capital investment is modeled as deterministic in all cases. Total capital investment increased by 20% in this case, from $429 million to $514.8 million. Table 13 summarizes the results.

With an $86 million increase in upfront capital costs, the economic NPV changed by nearly the same amount, as would be expected. It was not exactly the same due to inflation. The financial NPV changed by about $60 million. This occurs because the increased capital investment was decreased by adding taxes and financing. Probability of a loss was more than twice as high as in Case 3. Financial NPV probability of loss increased from 15% to 34% with only the change in capital costs.

The standard deviation, middle 80% range, and total range remained about the same, because the shift occurred to a deterministic parameter. The economic NPV distribution is remarkably similar to Case 2, because the NPV loss from increased capital cost was about equal to the NPV of the benefit accrued from the higher selling price.

3.7. Stochastic with Forward Contract. Case 7 is a model of the impact of a realistic reverse auction outcome. We start with the assumptions used in Case 3. Then, we add a forward contract for 45 MGY for project years 5–23 at the fixed fuel price used in Case 5.

Project years 5–23 were chosen because this is the time period in which the facility is producing at full capacity. In project year four, the facility is starting up, so it has a 75% start-up production rate.

To determine the forward contract volume, we measured the minimum fuel output based on the input uncertainty during the project timeline. We assume that the biofuel producer is willing to contract for the minimum expected facility fuel output. The minimum facility fuel output is above 45 million gallons (170 million liters) per year. The expected volume is 57.5 MGY but changes each year. The remaining volume beyond 45 MGY is sold at the fuel price.

TABLE 12: Case 5 results.

	Economic			Financial		
	NPV	IRR (nominal)	B/C	NPV	IRR (nominal)	B/C
Expected value	$84,252,474	12.9%	1.24	$80,672,958	14.7%	1.42
Standard deviation	$21,955,577	0.8%	0.06	$15,980,391	1.0%	0.08
Max	$157,793,602	15.5%	1.46	$133,789,946	17.8%	1.69
Min	$3,099,769	10.1%	1.01	$19,716,164	11.1%	1.10
Probability of loss	0.0%			0.0%		

TABLE 13: Case 6.

	Economic			Financial		
	NPV	IRR (nominal)	B/C	NPV	IRR (nominal)	B/C
Expected value	$16,619,218	10.5%	1.04	$32,599,899	11.5%	1.14
Standard deviation	$101,765,400	2.9%	0.25	$77,252,890	3.5%	0.33
Max	$377,296,296	18.7%	1.91	$311,273,718	22.2%	2.34
Min	**($341,382,691)**	−8.9%	0.17	**($238,976,396)**	−11.8%	-0.03
Probability of loss	43.7%			34.0%		

The forecasted fuel price is nondeterministic and is the same as in Case 3.

The forward contract price used is $2.92 ($0.77 per liter). This is the price determined in Case 5 to provide the same expected return as in Case 3. $2.92 per gallon ($0.77 per liter) could be the estimated average price over the 20-year production period. The government benefits when the forward contract fuel price is below market fuel price. In other words, when the market fuel price is high, the government gains from a lower purchase price than what it could get on the open market. The opposite is also true. When the market fuel price falls below the contracted price, the government cannot choose to break the contract. It must purchase 45 MGY regardless of the market fuel price.

The total cost to government over the project timeline is expressed in NPV terms. Government cost is just the difference between the reverse auction contract price and the market price. The mean expected NPV is near zero because of the value of the forward contract fuel price. However, the variance of this cost is high. Case 7 shifts risk from the private sector to the public sector. The mean government cost is −$4.8 million and one standard deviation is $74 million. The government cost of the reverse auction could effectively range from −$260 million to $250 million.

Table 14 presents the results of this case. The expected NPV of this case is slightly lower than in Case 3, yet the variance is much lower. This is a result of the forward contract. In the first year—the startup year—of production, Case 3 had a fuel selling price of $2.92 ($0.77 per liter). The contract in Case 7 does not begin until the second year of production. The market price in the first year is on average much below this price so the benefit gained in the first production year of Case 3 is greater than in Case 7. The financial NPV probability of loss was reduced from 15% to 0%. The economic NPV probability of loss decreased from 21% to 1%.

This case quantifies how risk is transferred from the private to the public sectors through a reverse auction. Private investment in a biofuel production facility becomes much more appealing by having a forward contract. However, reverse auction is not commonly used in the United States. Much more common are tax breaks, low interest loans, or other capital subsidies.

3.8. Stochastic with Capital Subsidy. The government more often subsidizes the initial capital investment than it provides a forward contract. Case 8 uses the same expected public cost as in Case 7. However, while Case 7 had an uncertain public cost, the public cost in Case 8 is entirely deterministic: total capital investment is reduced in this case by $5 million. Therefore, Cases 7 and 8 have the same expected government cost. Table 15 summarizes the results of Case 8.

Although both cases have the same expected government cost, Case 8 has a specified cost while the government cost in Case 7 is uncertain. Case 8 has a slightly higher expected value than in Case 3 because of the lower capital cost. Still, the probability of loss is much higher than in Case 7: the probability of loss is 19% and 14% for the economic and financial cases, respectively.

4. Conclusions

The results reveal that product selling price uncertainty contributes greatly to the inherent risk of private investment in a biofuel production facility.

4.1. Cases 2 and 4. Cases 2 and 4 have the same expected economic NPV. Case 2 includes fuel price uncertainty, while Case 4 does not. Based on our estimates, it appears that private investment in biofuel production facilities could provide an expected 11% annual rate of return at a fuel

Table 14: Case 7.

	Economic			Financial		
	NPV	IRR (nominal)	B/C	NPV	IRR (nominal)	B/C
Expected value	$79,408,633	12.7%	1.23	$76,991,639	14.3%	1.40
Standard deviation	$33,119,073	1.1%	0.10	$24,732,466	1.4%	0.13
Max	$203,027,071	16.7%	1.59	$171,025,408	19.3%	1.89
Min	**($28,653,844)**	9.0%	0.92	**($4,140,055)**	9.8%	0.98
Probability of loss	0.73%			0.04%		

Table 15: Case 8.

	Economic			Financial		
	NPV	IRR (nominal)	B/C	NPV	IRR (nominal)	B/C
Expected value	$88,193,806	12.8%	1.26	$83,474,418	14.3%	1.44
Standard deviation	$101,965,463	3.2%	0.30	$77,349,466	3.9%	0.41
Max	$439,114,508	22.1%	2.29	$351,062,589	26.0%	2.84
Min	**($269,840,864)**	−5.9%	0.21	**($191,571,723)**	−11.1%	0.00
Probability of loss	19.3%			14.3%		

Table 16: Cases 2 and 4 comparison.

Financial measure	Case 2	Case 4
Expected NPV	$16,641,078	$16,641,078
Standard deviation of NPV	$76,669,403	$15,051,080
Probability of loss	40.8%	13.2%
Total range	$634,209,848	$116,646,045

price of $2.68 ($0.71 per liter), but including market price uncertainty makes this return rate highly uncertain. Case 2 had a 41% probability of loss even with an 11% expected IRR. The financial NPV ranged by $634 million. Table 16 compares these two scenarios.

4.2. Cases 3 and 5. Case 3 had both technical uncertainty and a fuel price that followed DOE projections. Case 5 had technical uncertainty but not fuel price uncertainty. Fuel selling price in Case 5 was fixed to $2.92 ($0.77 per liter), which provides the same expected NPV as in Case 3. The results of these two scenarios are compared in Table 17. Probability of a loss is greatly reduced from Case 3 to Case 5. Comparing the scenarios reveals the impact of fuel price uncertainty.

4.3. Cases 7 and 8. Case 7 forecasted the impact of a government originated reverse auction on profitability in investment. It had a forward contract for 45 MGY of fuel at a price of $2.92 ($0.77 per liter). The remaining facility fuel output was sold at wholesale gasoline and diesel prices. Under these conditions, the expected government cost was $4.8 million, with a standard deviation of $74 million.

Case 8 had a capital subsidy of $5 million, slightly higher than the expected government cost in Case 7. Cases 7 and 8 are compared in Table 18.

Table 17: Cases 3 and 5 comparison.

Financial measure	Case 3	Case 5
Expected NPV	$80,672,958	$80,672,958
Standard deviation of NPV	$76,305,318	$15,980,391
Probability of loss	14.5%	0.0%
Total range	$540,295,144	$114,073,782

Table 18: Cases 7 and 8 comparison.

Financial measure	Case 7	Case 8
Expected NPV	$76,991,639	$83,474,418
Standard deviation of NPV	$24,732,466	$77,349,466
Probability of loss	0.04%	14.33%
Total range	$175,165,462	$542,634,312

4.4. Policy Implications. Investment in a fast pyrolysis commercial biofuel facility carries a high amount of risk. Case 3 shows that, with a total capital investment of $429 million, the NPV could range from −$190 million to $350 million. Uncertainty arises directly from new technology and from market prices. This investment uncertainty arises from technical uncertainty and fuel price selling price uncertainty.

In our study, fuel price uncertainty was shown to have a large effect on investment risk. The government has many options for stimulating growth in biofuel production. However, to encourage private investment in biofuel production at the lowest public cost, the government should first look for ways to reduce private risk. Conventional fuels dominate the marketplace, and their prices are a direct competitor for drop-in biofuels. To reduce risk, the government may consider ways by which it can control fuel price fluctuations for biofuel producers. A reverse auction would provide a competitive long-term price and would shift risk from the private sector to the public sector. In our study, a reverse auction was shown to be more effective at encouraging private investment than capital subsidies for the same expected cost.

Conflict of Interests

The authors declare that there is no conflict of interests regarding the publication of this paper.

References

[1] A. McCrone, E. Usher, O. V. Sonntag-'Brien, U. Moslener, and C. Grüning, "Global Trends in Renewable Energy Investment," United Nations Environment Programme, 2013, http://www.unep.org/pdf/GTR-UNEP-FS-BNEF2.pdf.

[2] Energy Efficiency and Renewable Energy, FY 2014 Budget Rollout. U.S. Department of Energy, 2013, http://www1.eere.energy.gov/office_eere/pdfs/budget/fy2014_eere_congressional_budget_request.pdf.

[3] Bioenergy Technologies Office, "Replacing the Whole Barrel To Reduce U.S. Dependence on Oil," U.S. Department of Energy, 2013, https://www1.eere.energy.gov/bioenergy/pdfs/replacing_barrel_overview.pdf.

[4] U.S. Energy Information Administration, Annual Energy Outlook, 2013, http://www.eia.gov/aeo.

[5] Bioenergy Technologies Office, "US Billion-Ton Update: Biomass Supply for a Bioenergy and Bioproducts Industry," U.S. Department of Energy, http://www1.eere.energy.gov/bioenergy/pdfs/billion_ton_update.pdf.

[6] R. Tristan Brown, R. Thilakaratne, R. C. Brown, and G. Hu, "Techno-economic analysis of biomass to transportation fuels and electricity via fast pyrolysis and hydroprocessing," *Fuel*, vol. 106, pp. 463–469, 2013.

[7] S. B. Jones, C. Valkenburg, C. W. Walton et al., "Production of gasoline and diesel from biomass via fast pyrolysis, hydrotreating and hydrocracking: a design case," Pacific Northwest National Laboratory, http://www.pnl.gov/main/publications/external/technical_reports/PNNL-18284rev1.pdf.

[8] R. P. Anex, A. Aden, F. K. Kazi et al., "Techno-economic comparison of biomass-to-transportation fuels via pyrolysis, gasification, and biochemical pathways," *Fuel*, vol. 89, no. 1, supplement, pp. S29–S35, 2010.

[9] S. B. Jones and J. L. Male, "Production of Gasoline and Diesel from Biomass via Fast Pyrolysis, Hydrotreating and Hydrocracking: 2011 State of Technology and Projections to 2017," Pacific Northwest National Laboratory, http://www.pnnl.gov/main/publications/external/technical_reports/PNNL-22133.pdf.

[10] A. V. Bridgwater, "Review of fast pyrolysis of biomass and product upgrading," *Biomass and Bioenergy*, vol. 38, pp. 68–94, 2012.

[11] T. Bridgwater, "Biomass for energy," *Journal of the Science of Food and Agriculture*, vol. 86, no. 12, pp. 1755–1768, 2006.

[12] S. Czernik and A. V. Bridgwater, "Overview of applications of biomass fast pyrolysis oil," *Energy and Fuels*, vol. 18, no. 2, pp. 590–598, 2004.

[13] D. Mohan, C. U. Pittman Jr., and P. H. Steele, "Pyrolysis of wood/biomass for bio-oil: a critical review," *Energy and Fuels*, vol. 20, no. 3, pp. 848–889, 2006.

[14] M. M. Wright, D. E. Daugaard, J. A. Satrio, and R. C. Brown, "Techno-economic analysis of biomass fast pyrolysis to transportation fuels," *Fuel*, vol. 89, no. 1, supplement, pp. S2–S10, 2010.

[15] R. Tristan Brown and R. C. Brown, "Techno-economics of advanced biofuels pathways," *RSC Advances*, vol. 3, no. 17, pp. 5758–5764, 2013.

[16] T. Brown and G. Hu, "Technoeconomic sensitivity of biobased hydrocarbon production via fast pyrolysis to government incentive programs," *Journal of Energy Engineering*, vol. 138, no. 2, pp. 54–62, 2011.

[17] D. Meier, B. van de Beld, A. V. Bridgwaterorg et al., "State-of-the-art of fast pyrolysis in IEA bioenergy member countries," *Renewable and Sustainable Energy Reviews*, vol. 20, pp. 619–641, 2013.

[18] C. E. Ridley, C. M. Clark, S. D. Leduc et al., "Biofuels: network analysis of the literature reveals key environmental and economic unknowns," *Environmental Science and Technology*, vol. 46, no. 3, pp. 1309–1315, 2012.

[19] W. E. Tyner, "Biofuels and agriculture: a past perspective and uncertain future," *International Journal of Sustainable Development & World Ecology*, vol. 19, no. 5, pp. 389–394, 2012.

[20] D. Rajagopal and D. Zilberman, "Review of Environmental, Economic and Policy Aspects of Biofuels," Working Paper 4341, World Bank Policy Research, 2007.

[21] National Research Council, *Renewable Fuel Standard: Potential Economic and Environmental Effects of US Biofuel Policy*, National Academies Press, 2011.

[22] T. L. Richard, "Challenges in scaling up biofuels infrastructure," *Science*, vol. 329, no. 5993, pp. 793–796, 2010.

[23] L. J. Snowden-Swan and J. L. Male, "Summary of Fast Pyrolysis and Upgrading GHG Analyses," Pacific Northwest National Laboratory, 2012, http://www.pnnl.gov/main/publications/external/technical_reports/PNNL-22175.pdf.

[24] T. Searchinger, R. Heimlich, R. A. Houghton et al., "Use of U.S. croplands for biofuels increases greenhouse gases through emissions from land-use change," *Science*, vol. 319, no. 5867, pp. 1238–1240, 2008.

[25] W. E. Tyner, F. Taheripour, and D. Perkis, "Comparison of fixed versus variable biofuels incentives," *Energy Policy*, vol. 38, no. 10, pp. 5530–5540, 2010.

[26] W. Tyner, "Description of 2011 Biofuels Policy Alternatives," Policy Briefs 1, Global Policy Research Institute (GPRI), 2011.

[27] W. E. Tyner, "The US ethanol and biofuels boom: its origins, current status, and future prospects," *BioScience*, vol. 58, no. 7, pp. 646–653, 2008.

[28] KiOR, "Technology," 2013, http://www.kior.com/content/?s=11&t=Technology

[29] D. Humbird, R. Davis, L. Tao et al., "Process Design and Economics for Biochemical Conversion of Lignocellulosic Biomass to Ethanol: Dilute-Acid Pretreatment and Enzymatic Hydrolysis of Corn Stover," National Renewable Energy Laboratory, 2011, http://www.afdc.energy.gov/pdfs/47764.pdf.

[30] National Research Council, *Transitions to Alternative Transportation Technologies: A Focus on Hydrogen*, National Academies Press, 2008.

[31] J. R. Bartels, M. B. Pate, and N. K. Olson, "An economic survey of hydrogen production from conventional and alternative energy sources," *International Journal of Hydrogen Energy*, vol. 35, no. 16, pp. 8371–8384, 2010.

[32] U.S. Government Accountability Office, "Corporate Income Tax: Effective Tax Rates Can Differ Significantly from the Statutory Rate," 2013, http://www.gao.gov/products/gao-13-520.

[33] Bureau of Labor Statistics, "Producer Price Index-Commodities," U.S. Department of Labor, 2013, http://www.bls.gov/ppi.

[34] S. Irwin and D. Good, "Farmdocdaily: What Combination of Corn and RINs Prices Makes E85 Competitive?" University of Illinois, http://farmdocdaily.illinois.edu/2013/06/combination-corn-rins-prices-e85.html.

7

The Pricing of Portuguese Privatisation Second Initial Public Offerings

Rui Alpalhão

Department of Finance, ISCTE Business School, Avenida das Forças Armadas, 1649-026 Lisbon, Portugal

Correspondence should be addressed to Rui Alpalhão; rmaa@iscte.pt

Academic Editors: L. Grilli, D. Pick, A. Rodriguez-Alvarez, and J. Zarnikau

The paper studies the pricing of PSIPOs (privatization second initial public offerings) PIPOs of companies that had been public in the past. A dataset comprising all the Portuguese companies nationalized in 1975 and privatized in the late eighties and nineties is used. Findings on short- and long-run pricing of IPOs and PIPOs are summarized, and implications for the pricing of PSIPOs are discussed. Short- and long-run returns are computed, using three alternative methods (buy and hold abnormal returns, wealth relatives, and cumulative abnormal returns) in the long-run analysis. Short-run overpricing is identified, unlike the underpricing pattern revealed by most IPO research. This initial overpricing is essentially found to be corrected in the first trading month. In the long-run, no evidence of overpricing is found, again unlike the usual conclusion of the IPO literature, and more in line with empirical evidence on second IPOs. Results provide support to the conclusion that privatization IPOs tend to be less underpriced than standard IPOs and that firms coming back to the market for a second IPO tend to be less underpriced than pure IPOs and provide a good rating for the performance of the Portuguese Republic pricing stocks in the Portuguese privatization program.

1. Introduction

Initial public offerings (IPOs) are the first public offering of shares by a company. Although an IPO occurs, by definition, once in the life cycle of a company, it is possible that a firm reenters the public equity markets after an IPO and a subsequent delisting. In these cases, a "second" IPO takes place, termed a SIPO (second initial public offering). The privatization wave that swept the financial markets from the seventies on created a special category of IPO, the PIPO (privatization initial public offerings), IPOs where the offering firm is held by the State. Since privatized firms through PIPOs were, in some cases, listed firms when their nationalization took place, their PIPOs were, in reality, second IPOs. This paper studies the price performance of these twice special offerings, privatization second initial public offerings, or PSIPOs. Organization is as follows: Section 2 covers short-run underpricing, Section 3 discusses long-run returns, Section 4 addresses methodology, results are presented in Section 5, and Section 6 concludes.

2. Short-Run IPO and PIPO Underpricing

It is a well-established fact that IPOs are underpriced; that is, that a wealth transfer from original shareholders to new shareholders occurs when a firm's shares are offered to the public for the first time. This underpricing is a function of the offering price. By definition, a firm going public is previously unlisted, so its pre-IPO market price (P_{j0}^*) is unknown. Nevertheless, it can be inferred from the initial market price (P_{j1}) through

$$P_{j0}^* = \frac{P_{j1}N_{j1} - P_{j\,\mathrm{IPO}}\left(N_{j1} - N_{j0}\right)}{N_{j0}}, \tag{1}$$

where N_{j1} and N_{j0} represent, respectively, the number of shares outstanding before and after the IPO (if no shares are issued in the IPO, then $N_{j1} = N_{j0}$ and $P_{j0}^* = P_{j1}$) and $P_{j\,\mathrm{IPO}}$ is the IPO price. If the original shareholders place shares at a price below P_{j0}^*, wealth is transferred to the new shareholders, granting them abnormal returns which, from the old shareholders' point of view, are an additional cost of going public.

Several empirical studies, carried out in different markets and within various institutional frames, point to the fact that these implicit costs of going public are significant (Ritter [1] for the United States, Dawson [2] for Malaysia, Alpalhão [3], Vieira and Serra [4], Almeida and Duque [5], and Borges [6] for Portugal, Husson and Jacquillat [7] for France, Koh and Walter [8] for Singapore, Wethyavivorn and Koo-Smith [9] for Thailand, McGuiness [10] for Hong Kong, Kunz and Aggarwal [11] and Drobetz et al. [12] for Switzerland, Levis [13] for the United Kingdom, Rydqvist and Högholm [14] for Sweden, Lee et al. [15] for Australia, Krishnamurti and Kumar [16] for India, Engelen [17] for Belgium, Álvarez and González [18] for Spain, Günther and Rummer [19] for Germany, Aggarwal et al. [20] for Brazil, Chile, and Mexico, Loughran et al. [21] for a 25-country sample).

This generalized empirical evidence of underpricing is confirmed by the analysis of PIPO (Jenkinson and Mayer [22] for the United Kingdom and France, Menyah and Paudyal [23] for the United Kingdom, Paudyal et al. [24] for Malaysia, Su and Fleisher [25] for China, Jelic and Briston [26, 27] for Hungary and Poland, respectively, Jelic et al. [28] for Poland, Almeida and Duque [5] and Vieira and Serra [4] for Portugal, Omran [29] for Egypt, and Perotti and Guney [30], Dewenter and Malatesta [31], Choi and Nam [32], Jones et al. [33], Ljungqvist et al. [34], and Huang and Levich [35] for multicountry samples).

All these authors suggest, more or less assertively, that PIPO initial underpricing tends to exceed IPO underpricing. Some of these papers explicitly test and confirm this relation, namely, Jenkinson and Mayer [22], Menyah and Paudyal [23], Choi and Nam [32], Ljungqvist et al. [34], and Almeida and Duque [5]. On the contrary, both the papers on Poland of Aussenegg [36] and Jelic et al. [28] as well as the multicountry studies of Dewenter and Malatesta [31], Choi and Nam [32], and Huang and Levich [35] do not report significant differences. With the opposite findings, for example, lower PIPO underpricing relatively to IPO underpricing, one finds only the Vieira and Serra [4] results for Portugal.

Regarding SIPO samples, Muscarella and Vetsuypens [37] who have coined the acronym identify underpricing in their American sample, although significantly below the one posted by an IPO control sample. Derrien and Kecskés [38] find similar results in their sample of British IPO that were, before their so-called "initial" offer, the subject of an introduction to the public equity market. In their 119 AIM-listed company sample, Derrien and Kecskés [38] find underpricing for these quasi-initial offerings 10% to 33% below the one found in a "pure" IPO control sample.

Summing up, we have empirical evidence pointing to underpricing in IPOs generally speaking, larger underpricing in PIPOs than in IPOs unrelated to privatization programmes, and smaller underpricing in SIPOs than in truly initial IPOs.

Theories accounting for the generalized presence of underpricing are widely surveyed in the literature; Ljungqvist [39] is a very useful summary. The specific case of PIPO has received less attention. Nevertheless, Perotti [40] and, before, Bös [41] presented asymmetric information models (building on earlier research on IPO underpricing along the same lines, e.g., Allen and Faulhaber [42], Grinblatt and Hwang [43], and Welch [44]) in which the issuing State has an informational advantage over investors, as well as (contrary to what happens with corporate issuers in IPOs) the ability to transfer wealth from the to-be shareholders through policy decisions (e.g., regulation, barriers to entry, and taxation). In Perotti [40], the States signal their commitment to refrain from wealth transfers detrimental to postoffering shareholders by retaining a shareholding in the privatized company and by underpricing.

Generally speaking, one would expect to find, in asymmetric information models, underpricing varying with uncertainty over the offering. This being the case, and given that PIPOs are offerings of more mature companies than IPOs, a lower underpricing in PIPOs relatively to IPOs should be expected. Nevertheless, given the emerging nature of most of the capital markets in economies where privatizations are in the agenda, the hypothesis that potential PIPO underpricing in emerging markets should be lower than IPO underpricing in emerging markets but higher than IPO underpricing in mature markets should not be discarded.

Biais and Perotti [45] offer a different rationale for this apparent paradox, cunningly named "Machiavellian privatization," after the Italian Renaissance diplomat and writer Niccolò Machiavelli. In this model, the underpricing's rationale is the wish by right-wing governments to incentivize middle class voters to become shareholders and consequently align their interests with those of higher-income voters thus deepening support base and increasing reelection chances. In this mind frame, the issuing Government does not assess underpricing as a financially-minded corporate issuer would, but rather as a vote raising vehicle. Consequently, highly underpriced privatizations will be successes from the relevant point of view, even if far from revenue-maximizing.

Also relevant is the fact that the several goals, both economic and political, usually linked to privatization programmes give to policy-makers incentives to underprice which are significantly higher than the ones faced by a corporate issuer: underpricing can trigger popular support for a broad privatization programme, and underpricing helps popular capitalism. Given the fact that a Government pursuing a privatization programme will be a frequent issuer, unlike a corporation which taps the IPO market only once, Governments' investment in reputation built through underpricing tends to be more valuable and thus generates a greater appetite for underpricing.

Size of stock markets also matters. Frequently, privatization programmes are carried out in small, emerging markets. As the privatized companies are frequently the biggest in their home markets (Boutchkova and Megginson [46]), weak demands in small markets can trigger higher underpricing to allow the successful placing of relatively large offers, as is typically the case of a PIPO.

Jones et al. [33] offer an alternative explanation, suggesting that Governments deliberately underprice PIPO more than corporate issuer underprice their IPOs to bring the fees paid to book runners down, to compensate for the fact that they will hire them much more frequently than a corporate issuer.

For SIPOs in general, information asymmetry models should predict lower underpricing than for IPOs, since the previous track record of the company in the market should drive uncertainty down. This being the case, expected underpricing in PSIPOs should be lower than the ones posted by PIPOs.

The Portuguese IPO initial returns have been documented in previous research. Alpalhão [3], using a sample of 62 IPO, all of private issuers and all marketed in 1986 and 1987, that is, before the privatization program and during the only Portuguese IPO wave worthy of the name, reports a 54.4% initial return. Almeida and Duque [5] and Vieira and Serra [4] use samples collected after the start of the privatization program and comprising both PIPO (most of which PSIPO) and IPO launched by private issuers (the Vieira and Serra [4] sample also includes secondary offerings by privatized firms). A brief description of these papers' approaches is in Table 1.

Almeida and Duque [5] study a sample of 21 IPO marketed between 1992 and 1998, among which 11 PIPO, of which 9 PSIPO, and report initial returns between 4.74% (with equal weights (as in Alpalhão [3]) and 18.70% (value weighted). All PSIPO are part of our sample (Bonança, Mundial-Confiança, Império, Crédito Predial Português, União de Bancos Portugueses, in this case after the rebranding to Banco Mello following the takeover by José de Mello, Cimpor, Banco de Fomento e Exterior, Portucel Industrial and EDP). The two PIPO which are not PSIPO included are Portugal Telecom and Brisa. Portugal Telecom is a special case, because it absorbed one of the few firms which maintained a listing before and after the Exchange closure in 1974, Rádio Marconi, and thus had a part of its assets listed since the market reopened, in 1976. Brisa was, initially, a firm owned by private shareholders, founded by banker Jorge de Brito, the controlling shareholder of Banco Intercontinental Português, after whom the firm was named (Brito, SA) but was never listed before the IPO.

The Almeida and Duque [5] initial returns are substantially below the ones reported by Alpalhão [3], which is hardly surprising, given the market development and sophistication which occurred in the meantime, and specially the shortening of the interval between an initial public offer and the start of trading in the Exchange. The fall in underpricing relatively to the eighties IPO wave is confirmed by the underpricing found by the private issuer backed offers (13.33% with equal weights and 16.95% with value weights), but the relation between PIPO and IPO is ambiguous, since the PIPO initial returns are higher only with value weights.

Vieira and Serra [4] study 19 PIPO and report abnormal initial returns of 3.38%, statistically different from zero. The PIPO underpricing is found to be lower than contemporaneous IPO underpricing.

3. Long-Run Returns

It is well established in the literature that the generally applicable initial underpricing is reverted in the long-run in a similarly general way (Shaw [47] for Canada, Ritter [48] and, more recently, Carter et al. [49] for the United States, Keloharju [50] for Finland, Levis [51] for the United Kingdom, McGuiness [10] for Hong Kong, Lee et al. [15] for Australia, Kunz and Aggarwal [11] for Switzerland, Ljungqvist [52] for Germany, Cai and Wei [53] for Japan, Marisetty and Subrahmanyam [54] for India, Aggarwal et al. [20] for Brasil, Chile, and México). Posting dissenting conclusions, we find Kim et al. [55] for Korea, Brav and Gompers [56] and Gompers and Lerner [57] for the United States, and Degeorge and Derrien [58] for France. Stehle et al. [59], in their research of German IPO, Almeida and Duque [5] and Vieira and Serra [4] for Portugal, Aussenegg [36] for Poland, and Drobetz et al. [12] for Switzerland find long-run abnormal returns not significantly different from zero.

This pattern is not reported in most studies of PIPO buy-and-hold strategies (Levis [51] and Menyah et al. [60] for the United Kingdom, Jelic and Briston [26] for Hungary, Paudyal et al. [24] for Malaysia, Boardman and Laurin [61], Foerster and Karolyi [62], Dewenter and Malatesta [31], Perotti and Oijen [63], and Megginson et al. [64] for multicountry samples). With opposite results, and thus in line with IPO empirical evidence, we find Aggarwal et al. [20] for Chile, although with a sample of only 9 PIPO, Almeida and Duque [5] and Vieira and Serra [4] for Portugal, Bülent Aybar [65] for a multinational sample of American Depositary Receipts, Omran [29] for Egypt, and Choi et al. [66] for a multinational sample and using size-matched benchmarks.

The available SIPO research (Degeorge and Zeckhauser [67], Mian and Rosenfeld [68], and Holthausen and Larcker [69]) does not find the long-run overpricing pattern reported for IPO, and Mian and Rosenfeld [68], with an American sample from 1983 and 1988, even find positive and significant, abnormal returns.

To the best of our knowledge, no PSIPO research was ever produced (although the Almeida and Duque [5] and Vieira and Serra [4] samples also include PSIPOs). However, both the IPO empirical evidence and the SIPO literature point to the prevalence of positive abnormal returns.

Theories offering explanations for the generally found initial underpricing cannot account for the generally found long-run overpricing. The signalling theories would even point in the opposite direction. Although before Ritter [48] long-run overpricing was essentially absent from the literature, Miller [70] offered an interesting rationale, dropping the standard asset pricing assumption of homogeneous expectations. Without such homogeneous expectations and taking into account the usually small size of an IPO, a relatively small number of investors (the ones most bullish about the offer) will be enough to have the shares placed, making the initial price hardly an unbiased estimator of all publicly available information. The initial market price will, on the contrary, tend to be the most optimistic investors' appraisal, and these will tend to pump the prices up in the initial trades. As the divergence of opinion washes out, starting from the high levels registered after the start of trading, prices will tend to drop, even if the average investor's target price remains constant.

Table 1: Portuguese IPO research.

Period	Borges [6] 1987–2004	Almeida and Duque [5] 1992–1998	Vieira and Serra [4] 1989–2001	Alpalhão [3] 1986-1987
Offer category	57 IPO in 1987, 43 after 1987, the former either with the State or private shareholders as issuers, including Portugal Telecom, notwithstanding the Companhia Portuguesa Rádio Marconi previous listing	All IPO listed in the Lisbon Official Market, either with the State or private shareholders as issuers, including Portugal Telecom	All privatizations, both primary and secondary offers, including Portugal Telecom	All IPO
Sample size	100 (19 PIPO)	21 (11 PIPO)	42 (19 PIPO)	62 (0 PIPO)
Time frame	1 day, 36 months	1 year (247 days)	1, 7, 30 days; 6, 12, 18, 24, 30, and 36 months	30 days
Return definition	Daily, log	Daily, log	Daily, log	Daily, level
Performance measure	CAR	CAR, WR	CAR	CAR
Benchmark index	BTA (1987), PSI Geral (1988 on)	PSI Geral	PSI Geral, S&P500	BTA
Weightings	EW	EW, VW (weights formed with initial prices)	EW	EW

This table summarizes the results of Portuguese IPO research. IPO stands for initial public offers. PIPO means initial public offers which are privatizations. CAR are cumulative abnormal returns, with the market proxied by the benchmark index. WR means wealth relatives. EW means equal weights for each security and VW weights given by the initial prices of the shares offered in IPO.

Miller [70] does not claim that investors behave irrationally, only that their rational opinions diverge. Aggarwal and Rivoli [71] go farther, assuming that IPO investors might show, at least from time to time (Loughran et al. [21] would later term these times "windows of opportunity" for issuers) a tendency to overprice in the first trading days out of simple thoughtlessness. The long-term effects of such behaviour should not be significantly different from those implied by Miller [70]. Schultz [72] showed that, due to what he terms pseudo market timing meaning that companies tend to go ahead with their IPOs following high market prices (which is confirmed, e.g, by Pagano et al. [73] for Italy and by Loughran et al. [21] for 14 out of 15 countries included in their multicountry sample), the long-run IPO underperformance, if measured in event time, occurs even if issuers are unable to foresee future returns or identify "windows of opportunity".

To the best of our knowledge, the higher sustainability of the prices of privatization offers and of "second" initial offers has not generated rationalizations in the literature. However, the history of "second" initial offers, however remote in time, does suggest, at least, a lower divergence of opinion and, thus, a smaller reversion of returns as time goes by.

4. Methodology

4.1. Initial Returns. Alpalhão and Alves [74] show that the Portuguese PSIPOs have been floated at prices which implicitly show a return during the years between delisting and relisting significantly below the public market equivalent return. Analysis of the PSIPO initial market returns is required to shed light on the sustainability of privatization offer prices. To do so, we compute returns R_{jd} for every j company relatively to each of the first trading days following the PSIPO ($d = 1, 2, \ldots, 20$). We define $d = 1$ as the initial return, computed as the buy and hold return from the offer price to the first trading day closing price:

$$R_{j1} = \frac{P_{j1} - P_{j0}}{P_{j0}}, \quad (2)$$

where P_{j0} is the jth firm PSIPO price and P_{j1} is the first trading day closing price for the same firm.

For $d = 2, \ldots, 20$,

$$R_{jd} = \frac{P_{jd} - P_{jd-1}}{P_{jd-1}}. \quad (3)$$

Taking the average of N PSIPO, we define the portfolio average return as

$$RP_d = \frac{\sum_{n-1}^{N} R_{jd}}{N}. \quad (4)$$

We define the cumulative returns between day 1 and day s ($s = 1, \ldots, 20$) as the sum of average returns:

$$RPC_s = \sum_{d=1}^{s} RP_d. \quad (5)$$

We defer a discussion of the methodology for cumulating returns to the next section, since the short twenty-day horizon under analysis is adequately treated without need for more elaborate techniques.

We also define initial abnormal return, AR_{j1}, as

$$\text{AR}_{j1} = R_{j1} - R_{j\Psi}, \quad (6)$$

where $R_{j\Psi}$ is the return on the market portfolio, proxied by the PSI Geral index:

$$R_{j\Psi} = \frac{\Psi_{j1} - \Psi_{j0}}{\Psi_{j0}}, \quad (7)$$

where Ψ_{j1} is the value of the PSI Geral index for the first trading day of the jth PSIPO and Ψ_{j0} is the value of the same index on the jth PSIPO day.

For $d = 2, \ldots, 20$,

$$R_{\Psi d} = \frac{\Psi_d - \Psi_{d-1}}{\Psi_{d-1}}. \quad (8)$$

The average return of an equally weighted N PSIPO portfolio, for $d = 1, \ldots, 20$, is given by

$$\mathrm{AR}_d = \frac{\sum_{n=1}^{N} \mathrm{AR}_{jd}}{N}. \quad (9)$$

Finally, and as done with the gross returns, we define cumulative abnormal returns between day 1 and day s as the sum of average abnormal returns:

$$\mathrm{CAR}_s = \sum_{d=1}^{s} \mathrm{AR}_d. \quad (10)$$

For each security, the corresponding abnormal return is

$$\mathrm{CAR}_{js} = \sum_{d=1}^{s} \mathrm{AR}_{jd}. \quad (11)$$

To test the null hypothesis of zero CAR, we use the parametric test statistic (on the properties of this test statistic, see Kothari and Warner [75]):

$$t_{\mathrm{CAR},s} = \frac{\overline{\mathrm{CAR}_{js}}}{\sigma(\mathrm{CAR}_{js}) / \sqrt{N}}, \quad (12)$$

where $\overline{\mathrm{CAR}_{js}}$ is the sample mean and $\sigma(\mathrm{CAR}_{js})$ is the sample standard deviation of abnormal returns.

4.2. Long-Run Returns. The literature (Barber and Lyon [76], Kothari and Warner [77], and Lyon et al. [78]) makes available several alternative methods for the quantification of long-run returns, namely, buy and hold abnormal returns, wealth relatives, and cumulative abnormal returns, briefly described in the following sections.

4.2.1. Buy and Hold Abnormal Returns. One alternative, preferred by Barber and Lyon [76] and Lyon et al. [78] is the so-called buy and hold abnormal returns, BHAR for short, consisting in the capitalization of period (usually monthly) returns, from which returns earned on a benchmark portfolio, or on a control sample, chosen on the back of attributes (e.g., size, industry) of the stocks under analysis, are subtracted.

The daily returns of the jth PSIPO are defined as

$$R_{jd} = \frac{P_{jd} - P_{jd-1}}{P_{jd-1}}, \quad (13)$$

where P_{jd} is the closing price of stock j on d day. The corresponding return on month m (with k trading days and calculating monthly returns from monthly close prices) is similarly defined as

$$R_{jm} = \prod_{d=1}^{k} (1 + R_{jd}) - 1. \quad (14)$$

We continue to use the PSI Geral index as our benchmark portfolio, like we did when computing initial returns. Alternatives such as size-matching methods (as in, e.g., Loughran and Ritter [79]) are infeasible, taking into account the small size and lack of industrial diversity of the Portuguese Exchange, abundantly clear in the impossibility of finding a company of similar size to EDP (even with the standard convention of identical two-digit industry code and asset value with difference below 30%). Fortunately, these methods are also less relevant in the Portuguese case, given that their relative advantage comes from the fact that the initial offers are usually small, unlike the members of blue chip indices, which does not apply to PSIPO. On the other hand, what Barber and Lyon [76] and Lyon et al. [78] call new listing bias is particularly relevant in the Portuguese case, because the privatized companies are part of the benchmark portfolio and have significant weightings in it.

The PSI Geral daily return is defined as

$$R_{\psi d} = \frac{\Psi_d - \Psi_{d-1}}{\Psi_{d-1}}, \quad (15)$$

where Ψ_d designates the PSI Geral value on the dth day.

Like in (14), we define the monthly return on the benchmark portfolio as

$$R_{\psi m} = \prod_{d=1}^{k} (1 + R_{\psi d}) - 1. \quad (16)$$

When delisting generates absence of data for one of the sample constituents, we follow Gompers and Lerner [57], making both the missing stock return and the benchmark portfolio return equal to zero. The alternative—truncate the sample—would be feasible but would not deliver the average return earned by an investor carrying out an executable trading strategy, because the use of the proceeds from the delisting of the stocks taken private would remain undefined.

Each month m's average return, R_m, is obtained by taking the average of the various stocks:

$$R_m = \frac{1}{N} \sum_{n=1}^{N} R_{jm}, \quad (17)$$

where N is the sample size.

A security's return over an M-month period is given by

$$\mathrm{BHR}_{jM} = \prod_{m=1}^{\min(M,s)} (1 + R_{jm}) - 1, \quad (18)$$

where s stands for the month in which a security eventually ceases trading. This statistic measures the total return delivered by a strategy in which a stock is held for M months, or, in case the stock ceases trading before, until its exit from the market. The portfolio mean return is given by

$$\mathrm{BHR}_M = \frac{1}{N}\sum_{j=1}^{N} \mathrm{BHR}_{jM}. \quad (19)$$

The buy and hold return in our benchmark portfolio for the period M is similarly defined as

$$\mathrm{BHR}_{\psi M} = \prod_{m=1}^{\min(M,s)} \left(1 + R_{\psi m}\right) - 1. \quad (20)$$

With reference to $\mathrm{BHR}_{\Psi m}$, we can compute each security's BHAR, defined as

$$\mathrm{BHAR}_{jM} = \mathrm{BHR}_{jM} - \mathrm{BHR}_{\psi M}. \quad (21)$$

The portfolio mean return for the homologous period is

$$\mathrm{BHAR}_M = \frac{1}{N}\sum_{j=1}^{N} \mathrm{BHAR}_{jM}. \quad (22)$$

To test the hypothesis of zero BHAR in an N-stock sample, we use the parametric test statistic:

$$t_{\mathrm{BHAR}} = \frac{\overline{\mathrm{BHAR}_{jM}}}{\sigma\left(\mathrm{BHAR}_{jM}\right)/\sqrt{N}}, \quad (23)$$

where $\overline{\mathrm{BHAR}_{jM}}$ is the sample mean and $\sigma(\mathrm{BHAR}_{jM})$ is the abnormal returns sample standard deviation.

4.2.2. Wealth Relatives. Ritter [48] introduced wealth relatives as a method to interpret and adjust buy and hold returns. Wealth relatives are defined as

$$\mathrm{WR}_M = \frac{1 + \mathrm{BHR}_M}{1 + \mathrm{BHR}_{\psi M}}. \quad (24)$$

A WR above one indicates outperformance, whilst a WR below one means underperformance.

Fama [80] sees WR as more appropriate for the measurement of long-run returns than BHAR, due to the treatment given to the cumulation of returns (Fama [80] illustrates this point with a simple, yet clear, example, assuming, for the sake of simplicity, a single stock; imagine that, during the first year, its price increases by 10%, while the benchmark portfolio produces zero return. In the four following years, both the stock and the benchmark portfolio increase by 100%. The 5-year BHAR will be 20% (= 1.1 × 2 − 1.0 × 2), while the WR will produce a truthful outperformance of 10% (1.1 × 2 ÷ 1.0 × 2)).

4.2.3. Cumulative Abnormal Returns. The most common alternative to BHAR is the cumulative abnormal returns (CAR) preferred by Fama [80] and Mitchell and Stafford [81].

The choice of one method over the other, taking into consideration their respective pros and cons, is usually based on the assumed trading strategy and on the hypothesis meant to be tested. Specifically, a 12-month CAR allows testing if the abnormal monthly return of the sample companies for the year under appreciation is equal to zero, while annual BHAR allow testing if the annual mean abnormal return is equal to zero. On other words, CAR ignore the capitalization of returns, while BHAR include this factor.

We define the abnormal returns of the jth offering, always relatively to PSI Geral, for the m month as

$$\mathrm{AR}_{jm} = R_{jm} - R_{\Psi m}. \quad (25)$$

For the portfolio of N shares, the adjusted return for month m is the arithmetic mean of the adjusted returns for the relevant month:

$$\mathrm{AR}_m = \frac{1}{N}\sum_{j=1}^{N} \mathrm{AR}_{jm}. \quad (26)$$

The abnormal cumulative returns from month 1 to month s are the sum of the mean adjusted returns:

$$\mathrm{CAR}_s = \sum_{m=1}^{s} \mathrm{AR}_m. \quad (27)$$

For each security, the corresponding adjusted return is

$$\mathrm{CAR}_{js} = \sum_{m=1}^{s} \mathrm{AR}_{jm}. \quad (28)$$

As mentioned above, to test the null hypothesis of zero CAR, we use the parametric test statistic as follows:

$$t_{\mathrm{CAR},s} = \frac{\overline{\mathrm{CAR}_{js}}}{\sigma\left(\mathrm{CAR}_{js}\right)/\sqrt{N}}, \quad (29)$$

where $\overline{\mathrm{CAR}_{js}}$ is the sample mean and $\sigma(\mathrm{CAR}_{js})$ is the sample standard deviation of the abnormal returns.

When a company is delisted before the end of the period, the next month's portfolio return becomes the weighted average return of the remaining shares; that is, monthly portfolio rebalancing applies, with the proceeds from delisting(s) being allocated to the surviving offerings (this restriction can, as previously stated, be lifted using the computation of buy and hold returns).

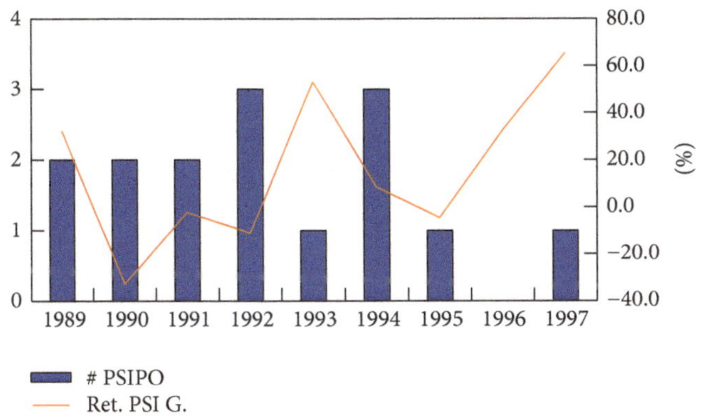

FIGURE 1: Time series of Portuguese PSIPO and annual returns of the PSI Geral index.

5. Results

5.1. Data and Sample Selection. The sample includes the 15 PSIPO made between 1989 and 1997 (Figure 1). From 1989 to 1995 offers took place in each and every year, and only twice (in 1993 and 1995) a single offer came to market. 1996 was the first PSIPOless year since the Portuguese privatization programme began, and 1997 saw the last PSIPO, with the EdP offer. After that, the Portuguese privatization programme comprised solely secondary offers of the large nonfinancial companies privatized in multiple stages. A significant relation between the number of PSIPO and the level of the market index is not visible, which suggests that analysing in event time is appropriate.

Given the time span covered, long-run performance is assessed over 12-, 36-, and 60-month intervals.

All companies in the sample have available aftermarkets of, at least, 12 months. The Banco de Fomento e Exterior return series is too short to allow the computation of 36-month returns (and, naturally, of 60-month returns), due to being taken private, after roughly 28 months in the market, following the acquisition offer placed by BPI in December 1996, after winning, in August 1996, the bid for the second stage of the Banco Fonsecas & Burnay privatization. This being the case, sample size drops to 14 for the 36-month time frame. Two additional offers—Bonança and UBP—produced return series of more than 36, but less than 60 months. Bonança, controlled by Banco Português do Atlântico after its privatization, was taken private in 1995 following the 1995 bid for Atlântico by BCP and Império, which made its free float minuscule. UBP also exited the market in 1996, for the same reason and following the same bid, which eventually put the bank under the influence of José de Mello SGPS, parent company of Império. Sample size for the 60-month time frame is thus reduced to 12.

5.2. Initial Returns. Table 2 shows the PSIPO portfolio initial returns, both gross and abnormal. Its time series is shown in Figure 2.

Initial returns, both gross and abnormal, are similar and significantly different from zero for a 5% significance level

TABLE 2: Initial returns.

	Equally weighted		Value-weighted	
	Gross	Abnormal	Gross	Abnormal
Mean	0,10%	−1,94%	24,31%	23,05%
T-statistic		−2,033**		14,236***
Median	0,16%	−0,10%		
Minimum	−24,14%	−27,26%		
Maximum	37,75%	37,84%		
Number of PSIPO with initial returns				
Positive	8	7		
Negative	7	8		
Total	**15**	**15**		

This table reports the fifteen privatization second initial public offerings (PSIPO) statistics. Asterisks show statistical significance: *** shows difference from zero with a 1% significance, and ** shows difference from zero for a 5% significance level. Equally weightedshows means computed with equal weights; value-weighted shows means weighted by the value of the initial privatization offer.

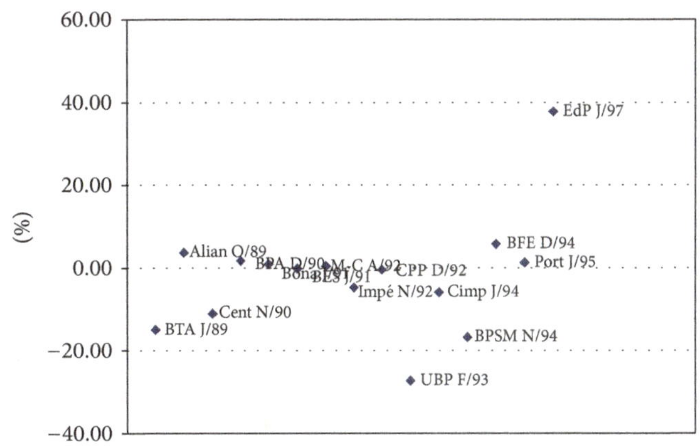

FIGURE 2: Initial abnormal returns (case by case, across time, 1989–97).

when adjusted for market movement. They vary between a highly adverse for the investor minimum of −24.14% gross and −27.26% after adjustment in the UBP offer and a maximum of 37.75% gross and 37.84% adjusted in the EDP offer. The high weight of the EDP offer, given the high underpricing posted, causes significantly positive mean value-weighted initial returns. We do not, however, grant this weighted mean particular relevance, both because its value is attributable essentially to a single offer and because an analysis based on equal weights shows the results of a strategy of investing equal amounts in every privatization offer, which we find to be more realistic than a value-weighted investment strategy.

Our PSIPO sample produces results which are different from available PIPO studies, with statistically different from zero overpricing. We fail to find evidence that the Portuguese Government behaved in a way consistent with the underpricing mode usually attributed to private issuers. Our results, although different from previous research results,

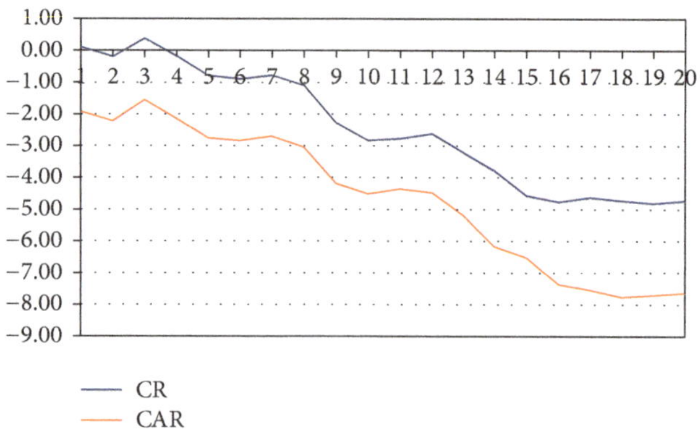

Figure 3: Short-run aftermarket of Portuguese PSIPO.

both Portuguese and international, are fully consistent with the expectation of lower PSIPO underpricing relative to PIPO underpricing and show that the negative return found for the investment in these companies while their capital remained private (Alpalhão and Alves [74]) was partially reverted with the initial market valuation of the shares. The Portuguese State proved to be more efficient pricing the privatization offers (which were not undervalued) than managing the assets of the companies floated (task in which beating the target of beating the market benchmark was not attained).

It is important to find out if this effect remained in the aftermarket. Figure 3 posts the evolution of cumulative mean return in the first twenty trading days, both before and after adjustment for market movements. Data are in Table 3.

The pattern of cumulative returns is similar, both before and after adjustment for market movement. The peak is registered on the third day, following a correction of the initial return in the second trading day. Abnormal cumulative returns are never positive, and cumulative raw returns are positive on the first and third day only. Cumulative raw returns are not significantly different from zero, for a 5% significance level, on the third day only, and are statistically different from zero, for a 1% significance level, for every day from the 13th on.

One can conclude that the initial overpricing, while being moderately reversed immediately after the initial trades, is not reverted in aftermarket. The negative abnormal returns earned by the Republic during the years in which companies remained private were partially corrected during the initial market trades of the shares. Evidence thus exists of wealth transfers

(1) from all Portuguese citizens to investors in privatization offers and

(2) among secondary market investors, from the slower to buy PSIPO to the faster.

In absolute terms, the identified abnormal return is of −6.128.368.014$71, calculated applying to the Republic's investment the average abnormal mean annual return of −28.25% for an average holding period of 19.4 years. This amount represents a wealth loss equivalent to 34.2% of the 1997 GDP, the process's final year, or 5.1% of the cumulative GDP from 1989 to 1997 or 140.7% of the proceeds of privatization offers between 1989 and 2003.

Table 3: Time series of short aftermarket returns.

Day	RP	RPC	AR	CAR	t-stat
1	0,10%	0,10%	−1,94%	−1,94%	−3,4223***
2	−0,29%	−0,20%	−0,30%	−2,24%	−2,79607***
3	0,57%	0,37%	0,66%	−1,58%	−1,61227*
4	−0,56%	−0,19%	−0,58%	−2,16%	−1,91131**
5	−0,61%	−0,80%	−0,64%	−2,80%	−2,21277**
6	−0,10%	−0,91%	−0,07%	−2,87%	−2,07011**
7	0,11%	−0,79%	0,14%	−2,73%	−1,82266**
8	−0,32%	−1,11%	−0,34%	−3,06%	−1,91544**
9	−1,19%	−2,29%	−1,15%	−4,21%	−2,48126**
10	−0,55%	−2,84%	−0,32%	−4,52%	−2,53021**
11	0,05%	−2,79%	0,14%	−4,39%	−2,33869**
12	0,16%	−2,63%	−0,11%	−4,49%	−2,29428**
13	−0,60%	−3,23%	−0,73%	−5,22%	−2,56099***
14	−0,56%	−3,79%	−0,98%	−6,20%	−2,92888***
15	−0,79%	−4,57%	−0,34%	−6,54%	−2,98669***
16	−0,20%	−4,78%	−0,86%	−7,40%	−3,27031***
17	0,13%	−4,64%	−0,17%	−7,57%	−3,24524***
18	−0,10%	−4,74%	−0,22%	−7,79%	−3,24546***
19	−0,08%	−4,82%	0,05%	−7,73%	−3,13736***
20	0,08%	−4,74%	0,07%	−7,66%	−3,02886***

The table reports values of average return of EW PSIPO portfolio, gross (RP and RPC) and abnormal (AR and CAR), period (RP and AR) and cumulative (RPC and CAR), for days 1 to 20. ∗∗∗, ∗∗, and ∗ denote, respectively, a return statistically different from zero for 1%, 5%, and 10% significance levels.

Alpalhão [82] reports a wealth transfer from the shareholders of nationalized companies to all Portuguese citizens of 0.15% of the 1978 GDP. Our results documented a second wealth transfer, this one from all Portuguese citizens to shareholders of privatized companies, of 5.1% of the cumulative GDP from 1989 to 1997. On aggregate, the balance is frankly negative for the Portuguese citizens as a whole.

The investors who benefited from this wealth transfer saw their holdings loose value during the securities' initial trades, making, in the short run, a PSIPO flipping strategy more profitable than a buy and hold strategy.

5.3. Long-Run Returns. The last section showed that the behaviour of the stock prices of Portuguese reprivatized companies generated negative abnormal returns. This section extends the analysis' time frame, to quantify possible wealth transfers between investors who purchased shares from the Republic in privatization offers and investors who, having been absent from the privatization offers, bought holdings in the privatized companies in the secondary market.

5.3.1. Buy and Hold Abnormal Returns. The sample's BHR and BHAR are posted in Table 4 and depicted in Figure 4.

We find negative and statistically different from zero returns in the first months, and we cannot reject, for a 10% significance level, the null hypothesis of zero returns from

Table 4: 1 to 12-, 36-, and 60-month BHR and BHAR.

Months		N	BHR	BHAR	# BHAR > 0	t_{BHAR}
Short-run Aftermarket	1	15	−5,4%	−7,1%	3	−3,20767***
	2	15	−9,9%	−12,1%	1	−3,91777***
	3	15	−7,2%	−10,1%	3	−3,631***
	4	15	−8,7%	−11,9%	3	−3,8785***
	5	15	−2,2%	−6,8%	2	−0,72954
	6	15	0,1%	−5,0%	4	−0,48288
	7	15	2,5%	−5,2%	4	−0,45987
	8	15	2,3%	−8,2%	4	−0,72498
	9	15	1,9%	−10,2%	2	−0,86628
	10	15	5,7%	−6,4%	6	−0,50836
	11	15	5,5%	−6,3%	5	−0,50836
	12	15	4,8%	−7,0%	4	−0,57442
	(· · ·)	(· · ·)	(· · ·)	(· · ·)	(· · ·)	(· · ·)
Aftermarket	36	14	56,5%	−4,8%	5	−0,27282
	(· · ·)	(· · ·)	(· · ·)	(· · ·)	(· · ·)	(· · ·)
	60	12	76,5%	−9,0%	5	−0,42775

The table reports returns earned with a buy and hold strategy of the equally weighted Portuguese PSIPO portfolio for 1 to 12, 36, and 60 months following the first (or only) public offer, both with (BHAR) and without (BHR) adjustment for market movements. ∗∗∗, ∗∗, and ∗ denote, respectively, a return statistically different from zero for a significance level of 1%, 5%, and 10%.

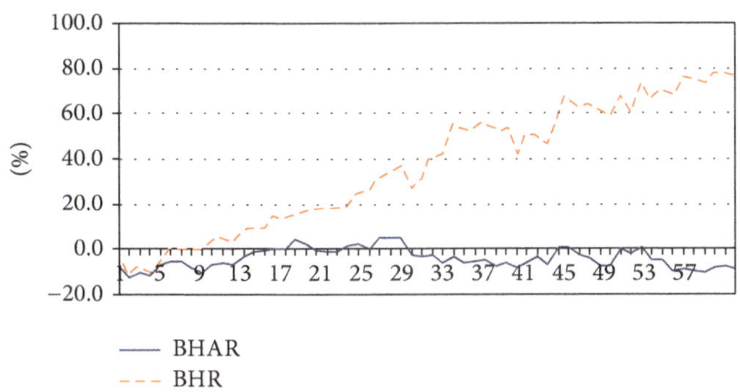

Figure 4: BHR and BHAR time series.

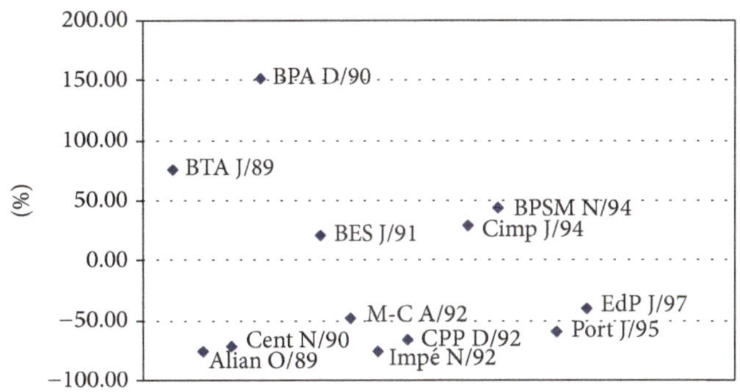

Figure 5: BHAR 60 months after the PSIPO held between July 1989 and June 1997 (for the 12 companies that remained listed for at least 60 months).

the 5th month on. The number of months with positive returns, with this methodology, is 13 (the 16th to the 19th, the 23th to the 28th, the 43rd, the 44th, and the 51th).

Figure 5 shows individual BHAR on the 60th month, organized by PSIPO date. The analysis of individual cases shows the scarcity of offers with very high abnormal returns and highlights the concentration of such offers in the early years of the privatization process. The two most successful cases on the long-run are shown to be one of the 1989 privatizations (Totta & Açores) and the Banco Português do Atlântico offer, two years later. The two last offers (Portucel in 1995 and EDP in 1997) both post negative abnormal returns in this time frame.

The individual analysis of offers suggests interesting patterns, the small sample size notwithstanding. The statistically not different from zero portfolio BHAR, when broken down offer by offer, reveals less positive BHAR (6) than negative ones (8). The time pattern suggests a trend shaped like a tunnel growing smaller, with the early offers generating both very and very low BHAR, and the latter offers showing a less scattered pattern, far from the earlier highs and lows.

The offer method used in PSIPO varied significantly and consistently over time. The eight first offers were auctions (all Dutch auctions, except for Mundial-Confiança, in which a single block was auctioned), followed by two fixed price offers and two bookbuilt offers. The eight auctions translated into only three positive BHAR (37.5%), while the (two) fixed price offers produced (two) positive BHAR and the (two) bookbuilt offers generated (two) negative BHAR. With the caution that the small sample size recommends, one is led to conclude that results match expectations, pointing to higher capacity of the offer methods which extract information from investors to generate pricings less prone to translate into positive long run abnormal returns. Curiously, this pattern is not present in initial returns: the relation between these and long-run returns is inverse, with a correlation coefficient

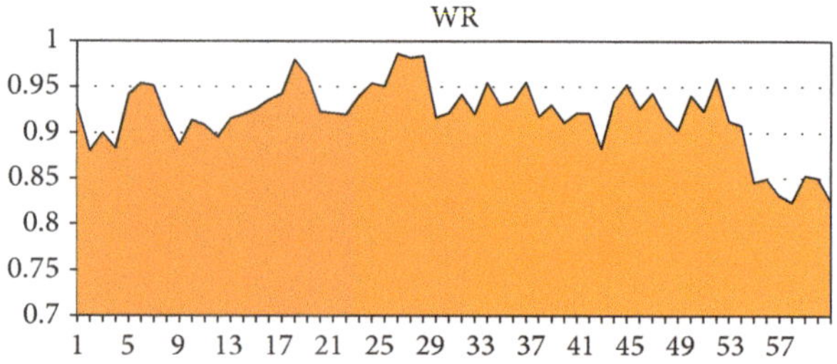

FIGURE 6: Wealth relatives over time.

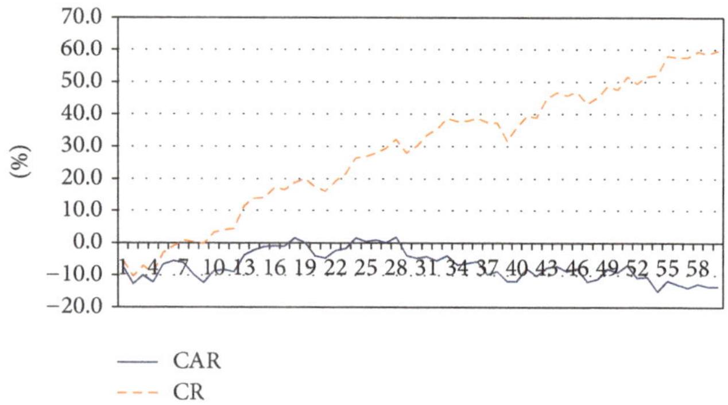

FIGURE 7: Time series of the cumulative monthly returns, gross and abnormal, on an equally weighted PSIPO portfolio.

TABLE 5: AR and CAR for 1 to 12, 36, and 60 months.

Months		N	AR	CAR	t_{CAR}
Short-run Aftermarket	1	15	−7,1%	−7,0%	−3,20767***
	2	15	−5,5%	−12,5%	−3,7942***
	3	15	2,4%	−10,1%	−3,5513***
	4	15	−2,0%	−12,1%	−3,7294***
	5	15	5,4%	−6,7%	−0,65324
	6	15	1,1%	−5,5%	−0,50533
	7	15	−0,7%	−6,2%	−0,53367
	8	15	−3,5%	−9,8%	−0,81478
	9	15	−2,5%	−12,2%	−0,96539
	10	15	3,1%	−9,1%	−0,6576
	11	15	0,4%	−8,7%	−0,62113
	12	15	−1,7%	−10,4%	−0,67213
	(⋯)	(⋯)	(⋯)	(⋯)	(⋯)
Long-run Aftermarket	36	14	0,6%	−5,7%	−0,31579
	(⋯)	(⋯)	(⋯)	(⋯)	(⋯)
	60	12	−0,02%	−13,5%	−0,54349

The table reports cumulative returns on the equally weighted Portuguese PSIPOportfolio for 1 to 12, 36, and 60 months after the first (or only) public offer (CAR) as well as the corresponding monthly returns (AR). ***, **, and * denote, respectively, a return statistically different from zero for 1%, 5%, and 10% significance levels.

of −0.196. Only in four cases (BPA, Centralcer, Império, and CPP) does one find returns sharing the same sign, positive in BPA's case and negative in the remaining ones. In the other eight offers, initial underpricing is matched by negative 5-year BHAR and vice versa, with the two fixed price offers posting initial overpricings and long-run positive BHAR and the two bookbuilt offers producing opposite results.

5.3.2. Wealth Relatives. The evolution of wealth relatives over time is depicted in Figure 6.

In the first month, the WR is 0.93, and although the maximum value (0.99) is posted in month 26, the unit value is never reached. After twelve months, the WR is 0.90, after 36 months 0.96, and after 60 months 0.82. The analysis of WR thus points to the underperformance of Portuguese PSIPO in the long run.

5.3.3. Cumulative Abnormal Returns. We have based our analysis of the Portuguese PSIPO's initial aftermarket, which, in the first twenty trading days, produced negative cumulative abnormal returns, in this method. To capture long-run patterns, we now turn to monthly periods for analysis. Computed monthly AR and CAR are posted in Table 5, and depicted in Figure 7, together with gross cumulative returns.

The long-run analysis does not reverse the results stemming from the analysis of short-run aftermarket. The pattern of negative, and significantly different from zero, returns is sustained initially, but immediately after the 5th month it is no longer possible to reject the null hypothesis of zero cumulative returns for a significance level of 10%. This pattern is upheld during the 60 months under scrutiny. Thus, the long-run analysis of PSIPO CAR, like the short-run results, produces negative returns (with only six exceptions in 60 months, in months 19, and 24 to 28, as depicted in Figures 4). However, in a long horizon the cumulative returns, although negative on average, are not statistically different from zero.

6. Conclusion

The analysis of Portuguese PSIPO's long-run returns generates robust conclusions, independent of the elected methodology. Abnormal returns are nonpositive, although not sufficiently negative to allow one to reject the hypothesis of zero returns.

These results are different from the ones made available by the IPO literature (no clear evidence of overpricing is found) and contrast even more with the results found for PIPO in international markets, since no evidence of long run underpricing is detected. On the contrary, our results are consistent with SIPO research, as well with the results of the Portuguese PIPO previous research, namely, Almeida and Duque [5] and Vieira and Serra [4], who use samples including some PIPO which are not PSIPO.

Our results show that no significant wealth transfer occurred between investors that participated in the share offers carried out by the Portuguese Republic and those who accepted exposure to privatized companies only in the secondary market. The former earned negative abnormal returns and the latter essentially zero abnormal returns. The price adjustment occurred in the first month of trading. Divergence of opinion or exaggerated optimism on the

PSIPO offers was eliminated relatively quickly; after all, the issuers, although coming to the market after long absences and under new names, were old acquaintances of investors.

Conflict of Interests

The author declares that there is no conflict of interests regarding the publication of this paper.

Acknowledgments

This paper draws upon the author's doctoral dissertation. The author acknowledges the support and helpful comments of the thesis supervisor, António Gomes Mota, and of thesis committee members António Nogueira Leite, Miguel Athayde Marques, Clara Raposo, and José Paulo Esperança. All remaining errors are the author's sole responsibility.

References

[1] J. R. Ritter, "The "hot issue" market of 1980," *Journal of Business*, vol. 57, no. 2, pp. 215–240, 1984.

[2] S. M. Dawson, "Secondary stock market performance of Initial Public Offers, Hong Kong, Singapore and Malaysia: 1978–84," *Journal of Business Finance and Accounting*, vol. 14, pp. 65–76, 1987.

[3] R. Alpalhão, *Ofertas Públicas Iniciais: o caso Português [M.S. thesis]*, Nova School of Business and Economics, 1988, (Portuguese).

[4] C. Vieira and A. P. Serra, "Abnormal returns in privatization public offerings: the case of Portuguese firms," *Notas Económicas*, vol. 22, pp. 1–35, 2005.

[5] J. M. Almeida and J. Duque, "Ownership structure and Initial Public Offerings in small economies: the case of Portugal," in *Initial Public Offerings: An International Perspective*, G. Gregoirou, Ed., Elsevier, New York, NY, USA, 2006.

[6] M. R. Borges, "Underpricing of Initial Public Offerings: the case of Portugal," *International Advances in Economic Research*, vol. 13, no. 1, pp. 65–80, 2007.

[7] B. Husson and B. Jacquillat, "French new issues, underpricing and alternative methods of distribution," in *A Reappraisal of the Efficiency of FInancial Markets*, R. M. C. Guimarães, B. G. Kingsman, and S. J. Taylor, Eds., pp. 349–368, Springer, Berlin, Germany, 1989.

[8] F. Koh and T. Walter, "A direct test of Rock's model of the pricing of unseasoned issues," *Journal of Financial Economics*, vol. 23, no. 2, pp. 251–272, 1989.

[9] K. Wethyavivorn and Y. Koo-Smith, "Initial Public Offerings in Thailand, 1988-89: price and return patterns," in *Pacific-Basin Capital Markets Research*, S. G. Rhee and R. P. Chang, Eds., vol. 2, North-Holland, Amsterdam, The Netherlands, 1991.

[10] P. McGuiness, "The post-listing return performance of unseasoned new issues of common stock in Hong Kong," *Journal of Business Finance and Accounting*, vol. 20, pp. 167–194, 1993.

[11] R. M. Kunz and R. Aggarwal, "Why Initial Public Offerings are underpriced: evidence from Switzerland," *Journal of Banking and Finance*, vol. 18, no. 4, pp. 705–723, 1994.

[12] W. Drobetz, M. Kammermann, and U. Wälchli, "Long-run performance of Initial Public Offerings: the evidence for Switzerland," *Schmalenbach Business Review*, vol. 57, pp. 253–275, 2005.

[13] M. Levis, "Seasoned equity offerings and the short term performance of Initial Public Offerings," *European Financial Management*, vol. 1, pp. 125–146, 1995.

[14] K. Rydqvist and K. Högholm, "Going public in the 1980s—evidence from Sweden," *European Financial Management*, vol. 1, no. 3, pp. 287–315, 1995.

[15] P. J. Lee, S. L. Taylor, and T. S. Walter, "Australian IPO pricing in the short and long run," *Journal of Banking and Finance*, vol. 20, no. 7, pp. 1189–1210, 1996.

[16] C. Krishnamurti and P. Kumar, "The initial listing performance of Indian IPOs," *Managerial Finance*, vol. 28, pp. 39–51, 2002.

[17] P.-J. Engelen, "Underpricing of IPOs—Belgian evidence," *European Review of Economics and Finance*, vol. 2, no. 1, pp. 53–69, 2003.

[18] S. Álvarez and V. M. González, "Signalling and the long-run performance of Spanish Initial Public Offerings (IPOs)," *Journal of Business Finance and Accounting*, vol. 32, no. 1-2, pp. 325–350, 2005.

[19] S. Günther and M. Rummer, "The hot-issue period in Germany: what factors drove IPO underpricing?" in *Initial Public Offerings: An International Perspective*, G. Gregoirou, Ed., pp. 215–245, Elsevier, New York, NY, USA, 2007.

[20] R. Aggarwal, R. Leal, and L. Hernández, "The aftermarket performance of Initial Public Offerings in Latin America," *Financial Management*, vol. 22, pp. 42–53, 1993.

[21] T. Loughran, J. R. Ritter, and K. Rydqvist, "Initial Public Offerings: international insights," *Pacific-Basin Finance Journal*, vol. 2, no. 2-3, pp. 165–199, 1994.

[22] T. Jenkinson and C. Mayer, "The privatisation process in France and the U.K," *European Economic Review*, vol. 32, no. 2-3, pp. 482–490, 1988.

[23] K. Menyah and K. Paudyal, "Share issue privatizations: the UK experience," in *Empirical Issues in Raising Equity Capital*, M. Levis, Ed., Elsevier, Amsterdam, The Netherlands, 1996.

[24] K. Paudyal, B. Saadouni, and R. J. Briston, "Privatisation Initial Public Offerings in Malaysia: initial premium and long-term performance," *Pacific Basin Finance Journal*, vol. 6, no. 5, pp. 427–451, 1998.

[25] D. Su and B. M. Fleisher, "An empirical investigation of underpricing in Chinese IPOs," *Pacific Basin Finance Journal*, vol. 7, no. 2, pp. 173–202, 1999.

[26] R. Jelic and R. Briston, "Hungarian privatisation strategy and financial performance of privatised companies," *Journal of Business Finance and Accounting*, vol. 26, no. 9-10, pp. 1319–1357, 1999.

[27] R. Jelic and R. Briston, "Privatisation Initial Public Offerings: the Polish experience," *European Financial Management*, vol. 9, no. 4, pp. 457–484, 2003.

[28] R. Jelic, R. Briston, and W. Aussenegg, "The choice of privatization method and the financial performance of newly privatized firms in transition economies," *Journal of Business Finance and Accounting*, vol. 30, no. 7-8, pp. 905–940, 2003.

[29] M. Omran, "Underpricing and long-run performance of share issue privatizations in the Egyptian stock market," *Journal of Financial Research*, vol. 28, no. 2, pp. 215–234, 2005.

[30] E. C. Perotti and S. E. Guney, "The structure of privatization plans," *Financial Management*, vol. 22, no. 1, pp. 84–98, 1993.

[31] K. L. Dewenter and P. H. Malatesta, "State-owned and privately owned firms: an empirical analysis of profitability, leverage, and

labor intensity," *American Economic Review*, vol. 91, no. 1, pp. 320–334, 2001.

[32] S. D. Choi and S. K. Nam, "The short-run performance of IPOs of privately- and publicly-owned firms: international evidence," *Multinational Finance Journal*, vol. 2, no. 3, pp. 225–244, 1998.

[33] S. L. Jones, W. L. Megginson, R. C. Nash, and J. M. Netter, "Share issue privatizations as financial means to political and economic ends," *Journal of Financial Economics*, vol. 53, no. 2, pp. 217–253, 1999.

[34] A. P. Ljungqvist, T. Jenkinson, and W. J. Wilhelm Jr., "Global integration in primary equity markets: the role of U.S. banks and U.S. investors," *Review of Financial Studies*, vol. 16, no. 1, pp. 63–99, 2003.

[35] Q. Huang and R. M. Levich, "Underpricing of new equity offerings by privatized firms: an international test," *International Journal of Theoretical and Applied Finance*, vol. 6, no. 1, pp. 1–30, 2003.

[36] W. Aussenegg, "Privatization versus private sector Initial Public Offerings in Poland," *Multinational Finance Journal*, vol. 4, no. 1-2, pp. 69–99, 2000.

[37] C. J. Muscarella and M. R. Vetsuypens, "The underpricing of "second" Initial Public Offerings," *Journal of Financial Research*, vol. 12, no. 3, pp. 183–192, 1989.

[38] F. Derrien and A. Kecskés, "The Initial Public Offerings of listed firms," *Journal of Finance*, vol. 62, no. 1, pp. 447–479, 2007.

[39] A. Ljungqvist, "IPO underpricing," in *Handbook of Corporate Finance: Empirical Corporate Finance*, B. Espen Eckbo, Ed., Elsevier, North Holland, 2007.

[40] E. C. Perotti, "Credible privatization," *American Economic Review*, vol. 85, no. 4, pp. 847–859, 1995.

[41] D. B. Bös, *Privatization: A Theoretical Treatment*, Oxford University Press, 1991.

[42] F. Allen and G. R. Faulhaber, "Signalling by underpricing in the IPO market," *Journal of Financial Economics*, vol. 23, no. 2, pp. 303–323, 1989.

[43] M. Grinblatt and C. Y. Hwang, "Signaling and the pricing of new issues," *Journal of Finance*, vol. 44, pp. 393–420, 1989.

[44] I. Welch, "Seasoned offerings, imitation costs, and the underpricing of Initial Public Offerings," *Journal of Finance*, vol. 44, pp. 421–449, 1989.

[45] B. Biais and E. Perotti, "Machiavellian privatization," *American Economic Review*, vol. 92, no. 1, pp. 240–258, 2002.

[46] M. K. Boutchkova and W. L. Megginson, "Privatization and the rise of global capital markets," *Financial Management*, vol. 29, no. 4, pp. 31–76, 2000.

[47] D. C. Shaw, "The performance of primary common stock offerings: a Canadian comparison," *Journal of Finance*, vol. 26, no. 5, pp. 1101–1113, 1971.

[48] J. R. Ritter, "The long-run performance of Initial Public Offerings," *Journal of Finance*, vol. 46, no. 1, pp. 3–27, 1991.

[49] R. B. Carter, F. H. Dark, and A. K. Singh, "Underwriter reputation, initial returns, and the long-run performance of IPO stocks," *Journal of Finance*, vol. 53, no. 1, pp. 285–311, 1998.

[50] M. Keloharju, "The winner's curse, legal liability, and the long-run price performance of Initial Public Offerings in Finland," *Journal of Financial Economics*, vol. 34, no. 2, pp. 251–277, 1993.

[51] M. Levis, "The long-run performance of Initial Public Offerings: the UK experience," *Financial Management*, vol. 22, pp. 28–41, 1993.

[52] A. P. Ljungqvist, "Pricing Initial Public Offerings: further evidence from Germany," *European Economic Review*, vol. 41, no. 7, pp. 1309–1320, 1997.

[53] J. Cai and K. C. J. Wei, "The investment and operating performance of Japanese Initial Public Offerings," *Pacific Basin Finance Journal*, vol. 5, no. 4, pp. 389–417, 1997.

[54] V. B. Marisetty and M. G. Subrahmanyam, "Group affiliation and the performance of IPOs in the Indian stock market," *Journal of Financial Markets*, vol. 13, no. 1, pp. 196–223, 2010.

[55] J.-B. Kim, I. Krinsky, and J. Lee, "The aftermarket performance of Initial Public Offerings in Korea," *Pacific-Basin Finance Journal*, vol. 3, no. 4, pp. 429–448, 1995.

[56] A. Brav and P. A. Gompers, "Myth or reality? The long-run underperformance of Initial Public Offerings: evidence from venture and nonventure capital-backed companies," *Journal of Finance*, vol. 52, no. 5, pp. 1791–1821, 1997.

[57] P. A. Gompers and J. Lerner, "The really long-run performance of Initial Public Offerings: the pre-nasdaq evidence," *Journal of Finance*, vol. 58, no. 4, pp. 1355–1392, 2003.

[58] F. Degeorge and F. Derrien, "Les déterminants de la performance à long terme des introductions en Bourse: le cas français," *Banque Et Marchés*, pp. 8–18, 2001 (French).

[59] R. Stehle, O. Ehrhardt, and R. Przyborowsky, "Long-run stock performance of German Initial Public Offerings and seasoned equity issues," *European Financial Management*, vol. 6, no. 2, pp. 173–196, 2000.

[60] K. Menyah, K. Paudyal, and C. G. Inyangete, "Subscriber return, underpricing, and long-term performance of U.K. privatization Initial Public Offers," *Journal of Economics and Business*, vol. 47, no. 5, pp. 473–495, 1995.

[61] A. E. Boardman and C. Laurin, "Factors affecting the stock price performance of share issued privatizations," *Applied Economics*, vol. 32, no. 11, pp. 1451–1464, 2000.

[62] S. R. Foerster and G. A. Karolyi, "The long-run performance of global equity offerings," *Journal of Financial and Quantitative Analysis*, vol. 35, no. 4, pp. 499–528, 2000.

[63] E. C. Perotti and P. van Oijen, "Privatization, political risk and stock market development in emerging economies," *Journal of International Money and Finance*, vol. 20, no. 1, pp. 43–69, 2001.

[64] W. L. Megginson, R. C. Nash, J. M. Netter, and A. L. Schwartz, "The long-run return to investors in share issue privatization," *Financial Management*, vol. 29, no. 1, pp. 67–77, 2000.

[65] C. Bülent Aybar, "The long-term performance of privatization-related ADR issues," *Emerging Markets Review*, vol. 3, no. 2, pp. 135–164, 2002.

[66] S.-D. Choi, I. Lee, and W. Megginson, "Do privatization ipos outperform in the long run?" *Financial Management*, vol. 39, no. 1, pp. 153–185, 2010.

[67] F. Degeorge and R. Zeckhauser, "The reverse LBO decision and firm performance: theory and evidence," *Journal of Finance*, vol. 48, no. 4, pp. 1323–1348, 1993.

[68] S. Mian and J. Rosenfeld, "Takeover activity and the long-run performance of reverse leveraged buyouts," *Financial Management*, vol. 22, no. 4, pp. 46–57, 1993.

[69] R. W. Holthausen and D. F. Larcker, "The financial performance of reverse leveraged buyouts," *Journal of Financial Economics*, vol. 42, no. 3, pp. 293–332, 1996.

[70] E. M. Miller, "Risk, uncertainty and divergence of opinion," *Journal of Finance*, vol. 32, pp. 1151–1168, 1977.

[71] R. Aggarwal and P. Rivoli, "Fads in the Initial Public Offering market?" *Financial Management*, vol. 19, pp. 45–57, 1990.

[72] P. Schultz, "Pseudo market timing and the long-run underperformance of IPOs," *Journal of Finance*, vol. 58, no. 2, pp. 483–517, 2003.

[73] M. Pagano, F. Panetta, and L. Zingales, "Why do companies go public? An empirical analysis," *Journal of Finance*, vol. 53, no. 1, pp. 27–64, 1998.

[74] R. Alpalhão and P. Alves, "States as LBO specialists: evidence from Portugal," *International Journal of Financial Research*, vol. 4, no. 2, pp. 68–76, 2013.

[75] S. P. Kothari and J. B. Warner, "Econometrics of event studies," in *Handbook of Corporate Finance: Empirical Corporate Finance*, B. Espen Eckbo, Ed., Elsevier, North Holland, 2007.

[76] B. M. Barber and J. D. Lyon, "Detecting abnormal operating performance: the empirical power and specification of test statistics," *Journal of Financial Economics*, vol. 41, no. 3, pp. 359–399, 1996.

[77] S. P. Kothari and J. B. Warner, "Measuring long-horizon security price performance," *Journal of Financial Economics*, vol. 43, no. 3, pp. 301–339, 1997.

[78] J. D. Lyon, B. M. Barber, and C.-L. Tsai, "Improved methods for tests of long-run abnormal stock returns," *Journal of Finance*, vol. 54, no. 1, pp. 165–201, 1999.

[79] T. Loughran and J. R. Ritter, "The new issues puzzle," *Journal of Finance*, vol. 50, pp. 23–51, 1995.

[80] E. F. Fama, "Market efficiency, long-term returns, and behavioral finance," *Journal of Financial Economics*, vol. 49, no. 3, pp. 283–306, 1998.

[81] M. L. Mitchell and E. Stafford, "Managerial decisions and long-term stock price performance," *Journal of Business*, vol. 73, no. 3, pp. 287–329, 2000.

[82] R. Alpalhão, "From market to state: wealth transfers in the Portuguese nationalisations of the 1970s1," *Financial History Review*, vol. 19, no. 1, pp. 49–74, 2012.

8

Evolutionary Model of Moore's Law

Joachim Kaldasch

EBC Hochschule Berlin, Alexanderplatz 1, 10178 Berlin, Germany

Correspondence should be addressed to Joachim Kaldasch; joachim.kaldasch@international-business-school.de

Academic Editors: L. Grilli and J.-L. Hu

Moore suggested an exponential growth of the number of transistors in integrated electronic circuits. In this paper, Moore's law is derived from a preferential growth model of successive production technology generations. The theory suggests that products manufactured with a new production technology generating lower costs per unit have a competitive advantage on the market. Therefore, previous technology generations are replaced according to a Fisher-Pry law. Discussed is the case that a production technology is governed by a cost relevant characteristic. If this characteristic is bounded by a technological or physical boundary, the presented evolutionary model predicts an asymptotic approach to this limit. The model discusses the wafer size evolution and the long term evolution of Moore's law for the case of a physical boundary of the lithographic production technology. It predicts that the miniaturization process of electronic devices will slow down considerably in the next two decades.

1. Introduction

The exponential growth of the number of transistors in integrated electronic circuits is known as Moore's Law [1]. In order to derive Moore's law, the paper develops an evolutionary model of successive production technologies. A large part of the evolutionary economic literature is devoted to the study of the economic consequences of innovation and technical change [2]. Initiated by Nelson and Winter [3], the Neo-Schumpeterian literature focusses on production technologies and routines, while the technological evolution is suggested to be governed by a fitness related to some sort of cost functions. It studies in particular technological and organizational opportunities [4, 5], while the impact of the market dynamics plays only a secondary role [6]. It is mediated by assuming a productivity-driven exogenous demand function or by postulating a population dynamics in evolutionary game theory. An attempt to take the market dynamics explicitly into account was based on the time evolution of firms [7].

In the presented evolutionary model, however, not firms but product variants manufactured with different production technologies are regarded to suffer from a preferential growth process. These product variants are the elementary units in a preferential growth process recognized independently by a number of researchers [8–13]. It is based on the idea that the demand side of a market is determined by the selection behaviour of potential buyers, while a key variable is the price. During the reproduction process, in order to make profit, the supply side responds on purchase decisions of the buyers and preferentially reproduces the best-selling products. Which means that manufacturers increase the output of the best-selling product variants and reduce, respectively, and terminate the production of the slow sellers. As a result, preferentially selected products increase their market shares in time, while less favoured variants are replaced.

Similar to the Neo(Post)-Schumpeterian literature, the presented evolutionary model suggests that as a result of this evolutionary adaptation process of products, also the production technologies suffer from a preferential growth process [14]. The presented model relates the market dynamics of products manufactured with different production technologies with the replacement evolution of successive technology generations. The theory further establishes the time evolution of a cost relevant characteristic of the production technology for the case that this characteristic is constrained by a technological limit. It is shown explicitly that in the technological evolution this limit is approached asymptotically.

The model is exemplified at empirical results of memory chips used in electronic consumer goods, the so-called

Dynamic Random Access Memory (DRAM). They find their main application in computers primarily in PCs and servers. There is an extensive literature available on the technological evolution of DRAMs [10, 15–19]. The production technology to create memory chips is quite complex. Moore discovered that the number of transistors in integrated electronic circuits had doubled approximately every two years. However, as already realized by Moore and other researchers, the miniaturization process must have a physical limit [20, 21]. Since Moore's law is taken as an empirical fact and is regarded as a key driver of the semiconductor industry, its economic impact was studied by a number of economic investigations [22, 23]. The presented evolutionary model, however, allows an explicit derivation of Moore's law for the case that the technological evolution of the DRAM production is constrained by a physical limit.

The paper is organized as follows. In the next section, a preferential growth model of production technology generations is established. It takes the case of a technological limit of a cost relevant characteristic into account. In order to test the theory, two examples of the technological evolution of the DRAM semiconductor industry are studied: the wafers size and Moore's law. The paper ends with a conclusion.

2. The Model

We want to consider a competitive commodity market. The market is characterized by product variants manufactured with production technologies. The commodity demand at time step t is determined by the total demand rate $d(t)$. It is the result of first and repurchases of buyers. We assume that the total unit sales $y(t)$ are (nearly) equal to the total demand rate:

$$y(t) \cong d(t). \tag{1}$$

We want to distinguish the unit sales of products of the commodity manufactured with different production technologies. For the ith generation of the production technology, the unit sales are indicated by $y_i(t)$. The total unit sales are determined by

$$y(t) = \sum_{i=1}^{N(t)} y_i(t), \tag{2}$$

where the number of different technological generations at a given time step is $N(t)$. The unit sales of products manufactured with the ith generation growths with

$$\frac{dy_i}{dt} = \theta_i y_i, \tag{3}$$

where θ_i is the growth rate of the corresponding generation. The growth process of products in a competitive market is not further discussed here (for details see, e.g., [13]). It is assumed that products manufactured with the ith production technology have costs per unit c_i. They decrease with increasing technological generation such that $c_i > c_{i+1}$. Since suppliers can offer the corresponding products for lower prices, the growth rates θ_i of the unit sales are different. Applying (3), the evolution of the total unit sales is given by

$$\frac{dy}{dt} = \sum_i \frac{dy_i}{dt} = \sum_i \theta_i y_i = \langle\theta\rangle\, y, \tag{4}$$

where $\langle\theta\rangle$ is the mean unit sales growth rate of the commodity market.

The market share m_i of sold units manufactured with the ith technological generation is defined as

$$m_i(t) = \frac{y_i(t)}{y(t)}. \tag{5}$$

The time derivative of this relation yields

$$\frac{dy_i(t)}{dt} = \frac{dm_i(t)}{dt} y(t) + \frac{dy(t)}{dt} m_i(t). \tag{6}$$

Using (3) and (4), this relation can be rearranged with (5):

$$\frac{dm_i(t)}{dt} = \left(\theta_i(t) - \langle\theta\rangle\right) m_i(t), \tag{7}$$

which is a replicator equation for the market shares of the technological generations. Since products manufactured with different technological generations have different growth rates, they suffer from a preferential growth process, while the growth rate θ_i represents the fitness of the ith generation. The sales dynamics of products are therefore governed by the fitness function θ_i which is regarded to be a function of the costs per unit $\theta_i = \theta_i(c_i)$.

Note that (7) can be rewritten as

$$\frac{d\ln(m_i(t))}{dt} = \theta_i - \langle\theta\rangle. \tag{8}$$

In order to derive the market share evolution of different generations, we diminish a second generation with index j from (8) and obtain

$$\frac{d\ln(m_i(t))}{dt} - \frac{d\ln(m_j(t))}{dt} = \theta_i(t) - \theta_j(t) = \Delta\theta_{ij}(t), \tag{9}$$

where $\Delta\theta_{ij}(t)$ is termed fitness (competitive) advantage. The relation between two market shares becomes as follows:

$$\frac{m_i(t)}{m_j(t)} = \frac{m_i(t_0)}{m_j(t_0)} \exp\left(\int_{t_0}^{t} \Delta\theta_{ij}(t')\,dt'\right). \tag{10}$$

In order to simplify this relation, we rewrite the fitness advantage as a mean fitness advantage and time dependent fluctuations:

$$\Delta\theta_{ij}(t) = \left\langle\Delta\theta_{ij}\right\rangle_{\Delta t} + \delta\theta_{ij}(t), \tag{11}$$

where the mean fitness advantage is the average over a time period Δt:

$$\left\langle\Delta\theta_{ij}\right\rangle_{\Delta t} = \frac{1}{\Delta t}\int_{t_0}^{t_0+\Delta t} \left(\theta_i(t) - \theta_j(t)\right) dt. \tag{12}$$

The integral in (12) yields $\Delta t = t - t_0$:

$$\int_{t_0}^{t} \Delta\theta_{ij}(t')\,dt' = \langle \Delta\theta_{ij} \rangle_{\Delta t}(t - t_0) + \Xi_{ij}(t), \tag{13}$$

while the time dependent function $\Xi_{ij}(t)$ is obtained from the integration over the fluctuations $\delta\theta_{ij}(t)$. With identity [24],

$$m_i(t) = \frac{m_i(t)}{\sum_j m_j(t)} = \frac{1}{1 + \sum_{j\neq i}(m_j(t)/m_i(t))}, \tag{14}$$

we formally obtain the time evolution of the ith market share:

$$m_i(t) \cong \frac{1}{1 + \sum_{j\neq i} e^{-\langle \Delta\theta_{ij}\rangle_{\Delta t} t + \kappa_{ij} + \Xi_{ij}(t)}}, \tag{15}$$

with the coefficients $\kappa_{ij} = t_0 \langle \Delta\theta_{ij} \rangle_{\Delta t}$. For the case where the impact of the time-dependent fluctuations $\Xi_{ij}(t)$ is sufficiently small to be neglected, we obtain for the two generation case the well-known Fisher-Pry substitution relation [25]:

$$m_i(t) = \frac{1}{1 + e^{-\langle \Delta\theta_{ij}\rangle_{\Delta t} t + \kappa_{ij}}}; \qquad m_j(t) = \frac{1}{1 + e^{-\langle \Delta\theta_{ji}\rangle_{\Delta t} t + \kappa_{ji}}}. \tag{16}$$

Applying (1) and (5), the unit sales of products of successive technological generations become

$$y_i(t) \cong \frac{d(t)}{1 + \sum_{j\neq i} e^{-\langle \Delta\theta_{ij}\rangle_{\Delta t} t + \kappa_{ij}}}. \tag{17}$$

The sales evolution of products manufactured with different production technologies is essentially determined by their fitness advantage. Products with lower unit costs have a fitness advantage, since they can be sold for a lower price. Those product generations generating higher costs per unit are therefore replaced in time by those with lower costs per unit according to a logistic law of the unit sales given by (17).

2.1. Constrained Technological Evolution. Implementing a new production technology with lower costs per unit gives manufacturers a competitive advantage. We want to discuss the technological evolution for the case that this advantage is related to a cost relevant characteristic Γ of the production technology. That means that the fitness is regarded to be as a function of a technological or physical characteristic $\theta_i = \theta_i(\Gamma_i)$. The unit costs of a product of the ith generation depend on the magnitude of Γ_i such that its increase (or decrease) reduces the costs per unit significantly. The mean magnitude of the characteristic at a given time step can be obtained by taking the average over the sold number of products manufactured with current technologies:

$$\langle \Gamma \rangle = \frac{1}{y} \sum_i \Gamma_i y_i. \tag{18}$$

In the run of time successive generations of the production technology are replaced as described by (17). This leads to a slow shift of the characteristic $\langle \Gamma \rangle$ and simultaneously to a lowering of the mean costs per unit. In order to quantify this slow technological evolution, we introduce a separation of the time scales. On the short time scale t the change of the mean characteristic can be neglected as follows:

$$\frac{d\langle \Gamma \rangle}{dt} \sim \varepsilon \approx 0, \tag{19}$$

where $\varepsilon \ll 1$. The long time scale T, however, is chosen such that the replacement of successive production technology generations can be regarded as a continuous process with

$$\frac{d\langle \Gamma \rangle}{\varepsilon\, dt} = \frac{d\langle \Gamma \rangle}{dT} \neq 0. \tag{20}$$

Hence, the time scales are related by $T = \varepsilon t$. In order to establish this evolution, we take advantage from the definition of $\langle \Gamma \rangle$ in a continuous form:

$$\langle \Gamma \rangle = \int_0^\infty P(\Gamma)\,\Gamma\, d\Gamma, \tag{21}$$

where $P(\Gamma)$ is the probability density distribution characterizing the relative abundance of products manufactured with different production technologies. The time derivative of the mean characteristic becomes

$$\frac{d\langle \Gamma \rangle}{dt} = \int_0^\infty \frac{dP(\Gamma)}{dt} \Gamma\, d\Gamma. \tag{22}$$

For the time evolution of the relative abundance $P(\Gamma)$, we take advantage from the evolution of the unit sales market shares. They are governed by the replicator equation (7). We can therefore write

$$\frac{d\langle \Gamma \rangle}{dt} = \int_0^\infty P(\Gamma)(\theta(\Gamma) - \langle \theta(\Gamma) \rangle)\,\Gamma\, d\Gamma \tag{23}$$

and further evaluate

$$\frac{d\langle \Gamma \rangle}{dt} = \int_0^\infty \Gamma\theta(\Gamma) P(\Gamma)\, d\Gamma - \langle \Gamma \rangle \langle \theta \rangle. \tag{24}$$

For the case that the distribution $P(\Gamma)$ is located around the mean value, the fitness function can be expanded around $\langle \Gamma \rangle$ as

$$\theta(\Gamma) = \theta(\langle \Gamma \rangle + \delta\Gamma) = \theta(\langle \Gamma \rangle) + \left.\frac{\partial\theta(\Gamma)}{\partial\Gamma}\right|_{\langle \Gamma \rangle} \delta\Gamma, \tag{25}$$

with the small deviation $\delta\Gamma = \Gamma - \langle \Gamma \rangle$. Inserting this relation in (24), we obtain for the evolution of the characteristic on the long time scale,

$$\frac{d\langle \Gamma \rangle}{dT} = \left.\frac{d\theta(\Gamma)}{\varepsilon\, d\Gamma}\right|_{\langle \Gamma \rangle} \mathrm{Var}(P(\Gamma)), \tag{26}$$

where $\langle \theta \rangle = \theta(\langle \Gamma \rangle)$ and the variance is defined as

$$\mathrm{Var}(P(\Gamma)) = \int P(\Gamma)\Gamma^2 d\Gamma - \left(\int P(\Gamma)\,\Gamma\, d\Gamma\right)^2. \tag{27}$$

This result suggests that the mean characteristic will change in time as long as the fitness can be increased by a variation of Γ, since in this case the variance is nonzero. The velocity by which the mean technological characteristic varies depends on the selection pressure given by $d\theta(\Gamma)/d\Gamma$. In order to determine the selection pressure, the function $\theta(\Gamma)$ has to be known.

We want to confine the model to the special case that Γ has a technological limit at Γ^*, such that Γ cannot have a magnitude beyond this limit. Since a variation of Γ reduces the unit costs, the function $c(\Gamma)$ must have a minimum at Γ^*. Because the costs per unit have an overall minimum at Γ^*, the long term fitness function $\theta(\Gamma)$ must have a maximum there. Expanding the fitness function sufficiently close to Γ^*, we can write

$$\theta(\Gamma) \cong \theta^{\max} - \theta_0(\Gamma - \Gamma^*)^2, \tag{28}$$

where we consider the case that the technological characteristic Γ must decrease in order to decrease the costs per unit. In this relation, $\theta^{\max}$ indicates the maximum fitness at minimum costs per unit and θ_0 is a free parameter. Taking advantage form (26), we obtain, with this approximation,

$$\frac{d\langle\Gamma\rangle}{dT} = -\frac{2}{\varepsilon}\operatorname{Var}(P(\Gamma))\,\theta_0\left(\langle\Gamma\rangle - \Gamma^*\right) = -a^{\Gamma}\left(\langle\Gamma\rangle - \Gamma^*\right), \tag{29}$$

where the parameter a^{Γ} is denoted as decline rate of Γ. Treating the decline rate in a first approximation as constant, we finally get

$$\langle\Gamma(T)\rangle \cong \Gamma_0 \exp\left(-a^{\Gamma}T\right) + \Gamma^*, \tag{30}$$

where Γ_0 is as a free parameter related to Γ at introduction of the technology. This result suggests that after sufficient time, the mean magnitude $\langle\Gamma(T)\rangle$ approaches the technological limit at Γ^* asymptotically in time. It is a result of the replacement process of successive technologies with different production costs.

2.2. Moore's Law. We want to apply the model describing the evolution of successive production technologies to the semiconductor industry in order to establish Moore's law. As mentioned above, Moore's Law is related to the number of transistors in integrated electronic circuits. The production technology to create transistors on a wafer is essentially determined by the lithographic method. The number of transistors and hence the memory size depends on the minimum feature size fs. The increase of the density of electronic devices on a microelectronic chip leads to faster switching times and to lower cost per bit [10]. The presented evolutionary model can be applied by regarding the minimum feature size fs as the cost relevant technological characteristic Γ.

In order to bring electronic units on a chip, the circuits need to be delineated with a finer and finer brush. Applying optical lithography, the size of this brush, respectively, the resolution, is defined by [26]:

$$\mathrm{fs} = k_1 \frac{\lambda_{\text{light}}}{\mathrm{NA}}, \tag{31}$$

where λ_{light} is the wavelength of the light source used, NA is the numerical aperture of the lens applied to image the circuit patterns, and k_1 (known as k-factor) is a factor describing the ability of the recording process to resolve small features.

In order to increase the memory size, more and more transistors are placed on a given surface. Applying the lithographic method, the number of transistors Nt must increase proportional to the inverse of the minimum feature size:

$$\mathrm{Nt}(T) \sim \frac{1}{\mathrm{fs}(T)^{di}}, \tag{32}$$

where di is a dimension. Since the lithographic method is based on the exposure of light on a surface, it could be expected that the dimension is that of a surface $di = 2$. However, lithographic methods take advantage from several stacked electronic layers. Therefore, the dimension will deviate from that of a surface. Instead, the dimension must be higher than a surface but less than the spatial dimension: $2 < di < 3$. Since fs has the dimension of a length, we introduce the length fs_c as a proportionality factor and establish a relation between the number of transistors and the minimum feature size of the form:

$$\mathrm{Nt}(T) \cong \left(\frac{\mathrm{fs}_c}{\mathrm{fs}(T)}\right)^{di}. \tag{33}$$

Note that such relations are known in statistical physics as scaling relations [27]. It is suggested that transitions are arranged in some sort of a self-similar structure.

Increasing the number of transitions per chip decreases the costs per memory unit (bit). In order to increase Nt, the minimum feature size must be decreased. In the evolution of the lithographic method this takes place mainly by decreasing the wavelength of the applied light source [26]. However, the minimum feature size is bounded by the shortest wavelength of light. It determines the technological limit of the minimum feature size fs^*. The technological evolution of the number of transistors can be understood in terms of the presented evolutionary model as an adaptation process towards this limit. Applying (30) with $\Gamma = \mathrm{fs}$, the mean minimum feature size evolution is expected to have the form:

$$\mathrm{fs}(T) = \mathrm{fs}_0 e^{-a^{\mathrm{fs}}T} + \mathrm{fs}^*, \tag{34}$$

where fs_0 is related to the minimum feature size at introduction, fs^* is the technological limit, and a^{fs} is the corresponding decline rate. Note that this relation is only valid on the long time scale sufficiently close to fs^*. It expresses the fact that the costs per bit cannot decrease below fs^* with the standard lithographic technology.

Applying this time evolution of the feature size in (33), we obtain Moore's law in the form:

$$\mathrm{Nt}(T) = \left(\frac{\mathrm{fs}_c}{\mathrm{fs}_0 e^{-a^{\mathrm{fs}}T} + \mathrm{fs}^*}\right)^{di}. \tag{35}$$

The miniaturization process increases the number Nt of electronic devices on a chip. For small T and sufficiently far from the limit fs*, the relation suggests that the number of transistors increases exponentially with $\mathrm{Nt}(T) \sim \exp(a^{\mathrm{fs}} T)$ in agreement to Moore's law, while Moore estimated the growth rate a^{fs} to be equivalent to an eighteen month doubling of Nt. However, the number of transistors cannot increase to infinity but must be limited by the minimum feature size that can be physically achieved. This effect is included in (35). It describes therefore the long term technological evolution of Moore's law even close to the technological limit.

3. Comparison with Empirical Results

The presented evolutionary model suggests a logistic replacement of successive production technologies when they can be related to a reduction of the production costs per unit. In the case that the main competition is between neighbouring generations, the replacement takes place according to a Fisher-Pry-law in terms of the unit sales market shares. If the production technology is constraint by a physical or technological limit, then the technological evolution evolves such that the mean value of a characteristic parameter $\langle \Gamma \rangle$ related to the costs per unit approaches the technological limit Γ^* asymptotically as given by (30). We want to compare the theory with empirical results of two characteristics of the production technology of DRAM chips. We first study the wafer size as a cost relevant characteristic. Then, the evolution of Moore's law is predicted under the condition of a technological limit.

3.1. Wafer Size Evolution. We want to consider the wafer size as a cost relevant technological characteristic Γ of the DRAM production technology. A wafer serves as the substrate for microelectronic devices characterized by its diameter. The increase of the waver diameter increases the number of units that can be obtained from a single waver. Therefore, the costs per unit decrease with increasing wafer size. The model suggests that the replacement process of different waver sizes must be governed by the Fisher-Pry law for the case that competition takes place essentially between neighbouring generations. Displayed in Figure 1 is the evolution of the wafer size market shares in a Fisher-Pry plot using the empirical data from La Fontaine [26]. Shown are the empirical market shares m_i for the 5, 6, 8, and 12 inch wafer diameters. The solid lines obtained from a linear regression fit indicate a constant evolutionary advantage (disadvantage) of the corresponding production technology. The latest transition from eight inch to twelve inch diameter wafers provides 125% more chips and thus reduces the costs by about 20% [28]. Since increasing wafer sizes decrease the costs per unit, Figure 1 exhibits the replacement dynamics of successive production technologies as suggested by the model.

3.2. Moore's Law. In order to test Moore's law, we take advantage form empirical data of the minimum feature size. They are displayed in Figure 2 [28, 29]. The empirical data (squares) show the expected exponential decline of the minimum feature size fs in nm [30]. The solid line is a fit of (34) with $\mathrm{fs}_0 = 8100\,\mathrm{nm}$ and $a^{\mathrm{fs}} = 0.16$ per year, and

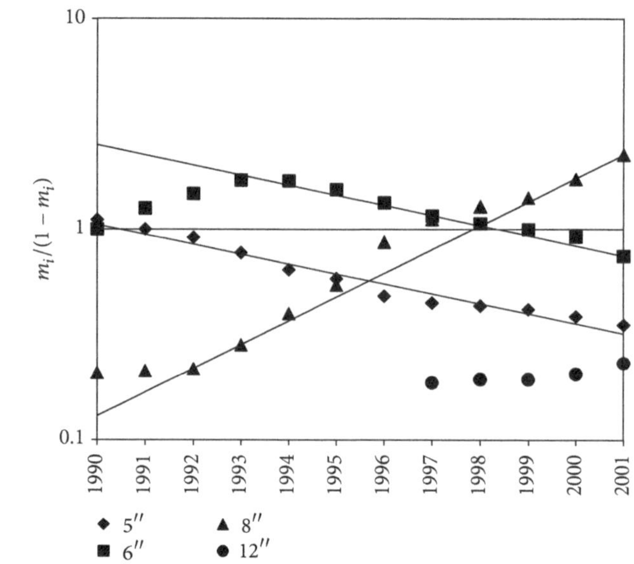

FIGURE 1: The wafer size market shares m_i of the production technology with different diameters in a Fisher-Pry plot.

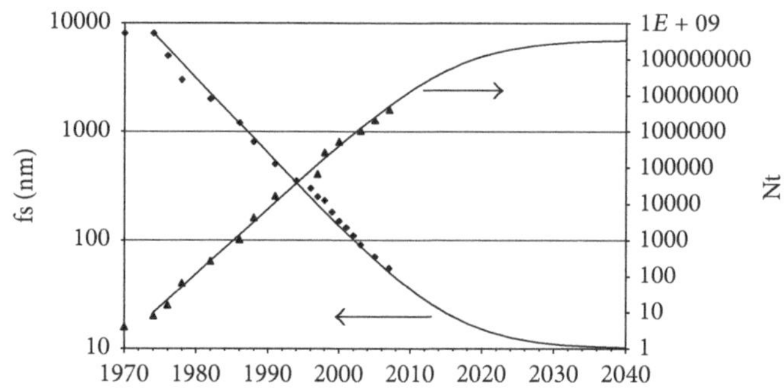

FIGURE 2: Minimum feature size fs (triangles) and Moore's law in terms of the number of transistors per chip Nt (squares) for DRAM's as a function of time. The solid lines represent a fit with the evolutionary model.

the technological limit can be estimated to be of the order of the minimum wavelength of UV light $\mathrm{fs}^* \approx 10\,\mathrm{nm}$.

From the evolution of the minimum feature size follows Moore's law given by the number of transistors per chip Nf also displayed in Figure 2. While triangles indicate the empirical data of transistors per chip and the solid line is a fit of (35) with $di = 2.6$ and $\mathrm{fs}_c = 19.3\,\mu\mathrm{m}$. (It is remarkable that fs_c is equivalent to the minimum device width in order to avoid performance loss in a pure poly-Si word line [31] (Neumueller et al. (1997)).) As expected, the dimension is higher than a surface but not space filling. The fit suggests that the growth of the number of transistors per chip will slow down considerably in next two decades.

4. Conclusion

Since the costs per unit of a good are governed by the production technology, the presented evolutionary model suggests that manufacturers have a competitive advantage when they apply new generations of the production technology. If the main competition is confined to neighbouring generations, the unit sales market shares of sold products are expected to evolve according to a Fisher-Pry-plot law. Also, derived is the case that a process technology is governed by a cost relevant characteristic that is constrained by a technological or physical boundary. The model suggests that in this case the limit is approached asymptotically in time.

In order to test the model two characteristics of the DRAM semiconductor production technology are studied. The wafer size is a cost relevant characteristic of the production technology because the costs per unit decrease with an increasing wafer size. The model suggests that different wafer sizes replace each other according to a Fisher-Pry law. Empirical data confirm this replacement process of successive generations of the wafer size. Note that similar replacement processes are known from other technologies [9, 32–34].

Another cost relevant characteristic of the DRAM production technology is related to the minimum feature size of electronic elements on a chip. It determines the number of transistors per chip and governs therefore Moore's law. Applying the lithographic method, the minimum feature size is bounded by the minimum wavelength that can be applied. This limit restricts the density of transistors. While Moore's law suggests an exponential increase of the number of transistors per chip, the model agrees with this statement far from the technological limit but suggests a deviation from Moore's law in the run of time. It predicts that the miniaturization process will slow down considerably in the next two decades (Figure 2).

Note that the evolution of the production technology can be regarded as a learning process. It is a search for decreasing costs per unit in the production process. However, we have to distinguish this "evolutionary learning process" from the "learning by doing". The technological learning process described here is driven by the commodity market. It is in fact an evolutionary adaptation process of the suppliers to the demands of the buyers. Since, the demand side prefers a lower price for a unit of the commodity, production technologies with lower costs per unit have an evolutionary advantage. As a consequence, cost reducing technologies replace each other in time leading to a decrease of the mean price for a unit of this commodity. Moore's law is a prominent example of this process. The ability to increase the number of transistors per chip by improvements of the lithographic method not only increases the performance of a computer chip but also decreases its mean price considerably in the run of time [10].

The two learning processes can be distinguished by the costs for variations of the production technology. If the costs for a change of the production process are low, the variation can be applied easily within short time periods. This effect can be regarded as learning by doing process. In the semiconductor industry, the fast decrease of the lead time in the production process of computer chips can be regarded as learning by doing [35]. However, if a technology variation requires considerably investments, manufacturers will try to apply the old technology as long as possible. In this case, the replacement process of successive production technologies takes place by a preferential growth process and is governed by the costs per unit, respectively, the product price. The evolutionary learning process discussed here is therefore confined to production technologies associated with high investments.

Production technologies are bounded by physical constrains. Learning processes aim at approaching these limits. The prediction of the time evolution of Moore's law in Figure 2 is based on the application of the lithographic method. The learning process implies, however, that manufacturers may apply alternative techniques in order to circumvent this limit. But even so, new physical boundaries will appear. As soon as the corresponding production technology will lead to an increase of the costs per unit, the model suggests that the miniaturization process will come to an end.

Conflict of Interests

The author declares that there is no conflict of interests regarding the publication of this paper.

References

[1] G. E. Moore, "Cramming more components onto integrated circuits," *Electronics*, vol. 38, no. 8, pp. 114–117, 1965.

[2] K. Dopfer, *The Evolutionary Foundation of Economics*, Cambridge University Press, Cambridge, UK, 2005.

[3] R. R. Nelson and S. G. Winter, *An Evolutionary Theory of Economic Change*, Harvard University Press, Cambridge, Mass, USA, 1982.

[4] G. Dosi and S. Winter, "Interpreting economic change: evolution, structures and games," LEM Working Paper 2000-08, Laboratory of Economics and Management, Pisa, Italy, 2000.

[5] U. Witt, "What is specific about evolutionary economics?" *Journal of Evolutionary Economics*, vol. 18, no. 5, pp. 547–575, 2008.

[6] J. S. Metcalfe, "Accounting for economic evolution: fitness and the population method," *Journal of Bioeconomics*, vol. 10, no. 1, pp. 23–49, 2008.

[7] S. Winter, Y. Kaniovski, and G. Dosi, "A baseline model of industry evolution," *Journal of Evolutionary Economics*, vol. 13, no. 4, pp. 355–383, 2003.

[8] G. J. Tellis and C. M. Crawford, "An evolutionary approach to product growth theory," *Journal of Marketing*, vol. 45, no. 4, pp. 125–132, 1981.

[9] T. Modis, *Predictions*, Simon & Schuster, New York, NY, USA, 1992.

[10] N. M. Victor and J. H. Ausubel, "DRAMs as model organisms for study of technological evolution," *Technological Forecasting and Social Change*, vol. 69, no. 3, pp. 243–262, 2002.

[11] E. D. Beinhocker, *The Origin of Wealth*, Harvard Business School Press, Boston, Mass, USA, 2006.

[12] U. Cantner, J. J. Krüger, and R. Söllner, "Product quality, product price, and share dynamics in the German compact car market," Jena Economic Research Papers 24, 2010.

[13] J. Kaldasch, "Evolutionary model of an anonymous consumer durable market," *Physica A*, vol. 390, no. 14, pp. 2692–2715, 2011.

[14] P. P. Saviotti and G. S. Mani, "Competition, variety and technological evolution: a replicator dynamics model," *Journal of Evolutionary Economics*, vol. 5, no. 4, pp. 369–392, 1995.

[15] C. Versluis, "DRAMs, fiber and energy compared with three, models of market penetration," *Technological Forecasting and Social Change*, vol. 69, no. 3, pp. 263–286, 2002.

[16] R. Siebert, "Learning by doing and multiproduction effects over the life cycle: evidence from the semiconductor industry," CEPR Discussion Paper 3734, 2003.

[17] W. Kim and J.-D. Lee, "Measuring the role of technology-push and demand-pull in the dynamic development of the semiconductor industry: the case of the global DRAM market," *Journal of Applied Economics*, vol. 12, no. 1, pp. 83–108, 2009.

[18] S. Park, "An empirical evaluation of the 1986 Semiconductor Trade Arrangement," *Japan and the World Economy*, vol. 21, no. 4, pp. 349–357, 2009.

[19] R. Kapoor and R. Adner, "What firms make vs. what they know: how firms' production and knowledge boundaries affect competitive advantage in the face of technological change," *Organization Science*, vol. 23, no. 5, pp. 1227–1248, 2012.

[20] S. Lloyd, "Ultimate physical limits to computation," *Nature*, vol. 406, no. 6799, pp. 1047–1054, 2000.

[21] M. J. Bowden, "Moore's law and the Technology S-Curve," *Stevens Alliance for Technology Management*, vol. 8, no. 1, pp. 1–4, 2004.

[22] A. Aizcorbe and S. Kortum, "Moore's law and the semiconductor industry: a vintage model," *The Scandinavian Journal of Economics*, vol. 107, no. 4, pp. 603–630, 2005.

[23] G. D. Hutcheson, "The economic implications of Moore's law," in *Into the Nano Era*, H. Huff, Ed., vol. 106, pp. 11–38, Springer, Berlin, Germany, 2009.

[24] V. Peterka, "Macrodynamics of technological change: market penetration by new technologies," IIASA Research Report RR-77-022, International Institute for Applied Systems Analysis (IIASA), Laxenburg, Austria, 1977.

[25] J. C. Fisher and H. R. Pry, "A simple substitution model of technological change," *Technological Forecasting and Social Change*, vol. 3, pp. 75–88, 1971.

[26] B. la Fontaine, "Lasers and Moore's law," *SPIE Professional*, 2010.

[27] D. Sornette, *Critical Phenomena in Natural Sciences*, Springer, Berlin, Germany, 2006.

[28] D. Ma and J. Mark, "The DRAM market structure: the rise and fall in concentration," in *Proceedings of the 8th Annual Cambridge International Manufacturing Symposium*, M. Gregory and Y. Shi, Eds., Exploiting the Potential of International Supply Networks, Cambridge, UK, September 2003.

[29] T. K. Choon, "The World DRAM Market," in *Proceedings of the VIA Technology Forum (VTF '04)*, Taipei, Taiwan, June 2004.

[30] A. I. Kingon, J.-P. Maria, and S. K. Streiffer, "Alternative dielectrics to silicon dioxide for memory and logic devices," *Nature*, vol. 406, no. 6799, pp. 1032–1038, 2000.

[31] W. Neumueller, J. Alsmeier, G. Bronner, S. Ishibashi, and H. Klose, "DRAM technology for today's market and future DRAM generations," in *Proceeding of the 27th European Solid-State Device Research Conference (ESSDERC '97)*, pp. 49–56, Stuttgart, Germany, September 1997.

[32] C. Marchetti, "Primary energy substitution models: on the interaction between energy and society," *Technological Forecasting and Social Change*, vol. 10, no. 4, pp. 345–356, 1977.

[33] A. Gruebler, *The Rise and Fall of Infrastructures*, Physica, Heidelberg, Germany, 1990.

[34] A. Gruebler, *Technology and Global Change*, Cambridge University, Cambridge UK, 1998.

[35] C. Hiroyuki and H. Norikazu, "Moore's law, increasing complexity and the limits of organization: the modern significance of Japanese chipmakers' DRAM business," RETI Discussion Papers 08-E-001, Research Institute of Economy, Trade and Industry (RIETI), Tokyo, Japan, 2008.

Exchange Rate Volatility and Aggregate Exports: Evidence from Two Small Countries

Dimitrios Serenis[1] and Nicholas Tsounis[1,2]

[1] *Department of International Trade, Technological Institute of Western Macedonia Kastoria Campus, 52100 Kastoria, Greece*
[2] *Adjunct Faculty, Hellenic Open University, Greece*

Correspondence should be addressed to Dimitrios Serenis; dseren01@yahoo.com

Academic Editors: J. M. Labeaga and K. P. Upadhyaya

This paper examines the effect of exchange rate volatility for two small countries, Croatia and Cyprus, on aggregate exports during the period of first quarter of 1990 to first quarter of 2012. It is claimed by some researchers that exchange rate volatility causes a reduction on the overall level of trade. Empirical researchers often utilize the standard deviation of the moving average of the logarithm of the exchange rate as a measure of exchange rate fluctuation. In this study, we propose a new measure for volatility. Overall, our results suggest that there is a positive effect of volatility on exports of Croatia and Cyprus.

1. Introduction

The relationship between exchange rate volatility and export flows has been studied in a large number of theoretical and empirical papers. The main notion, suggested by some theoretical models, is that a rise in exchange rate volatility increases uncertainty of profits on contracts denominated in foreign currency and force risk averse agents to redirect their activity to the lower risk home market. Other models suggest that higher levels of exchange rate movements offer greater opportunity for profit and therefore might lead to an increase in exports. Alternatively, some researchers have suggested that it is possible to offset potential unexpected movements of the exchange rate by investing at the forward market causing producers to be unaffected by movements of the exchange rate. These different ranges of results have been supported by a large variety of empirical studies causing the effects of exchange rate volatility on exports to be one of the most controversial topics of international trade.

This paper aims to model the effects of exchange rate volatility for Croatia and Cyprus for which empirical evidence is both limited and ambiguous and to utilize a new measure of volatility which captures unexpected movements of the exchange rate. Overall, our results contribute to the existing literature in the following ways: first, our investigation has attempted to shed some light on a topic for which the empirical literature is ambiguous. Second, our investigation examines a sample which is comprised of two countries, Croatia and Cyprus, for which the empirical literature is limited. Third, we model the effects of exchange rate volatility on exports taking into account data sample properties such as unit roots and cointegration and estimate the results with the use of a recently developed method: the ARDL methodology. Fourth, in addition to the common measure of volatility (logarithm of the moving average of the exchange rate), we will also examine a second new measure which allows us to capture high and low values of the exchange rate.

The results suggest that exchange rate volatility does produce a mixed and significant long-run effect, when measured as a moving average. However, when an alternative measure is used which captures high and low values of the exchange rate, the long-run effect of volatility to exports is significant for one of the sample countries, Croatia, and with a negative coefficient. This finding indicates that extremely high and low values of the exchange rate do effect the level of exports for some countries.

The paper is organised as follows: first, the existing literature is analyzed; second, the model is presented; third, various measurement issues of exchange rate volatility are discussed; fourth, the data is presented; fifth, the methodological framework is discussed; sixth, the results of the utilised statistical tests, the estimated equations, and an analysis of the main empirical findings are discussed. Finally, the last section addresses the issue of policy implications and presents a brief summary as well as the main conclusions.

2. Literature Review

The literature on the issue is quite large. Both theoretical as well as empirical studies provide ambiguous effects of volatility on exports. An extensive review of both theoretical and empirical literature is well surveyed in McKenzie [1]. However in this section the main arguments are survived with an emphasis on key aspects pertaining to this study. Early empirical work, utilising the OLS methodology, favoured the negative hypothesis of Clark [2] as well as an insignificant relationship between export quantity and volatility [3]. Hooper and Kohlhagen [3] investigated bilateral and multilateral trade among developed countries using the standard error of nominal exchange rate fluctuations as their volatility measure.

In the 1980s' the empirical evidence continues to be mixed and often differs with samples and estimation methods. Therefore, there is no consistent pattern when the same method is applied to different countries. While many suggest that the exchange rate uncertainties depress trade, (e.g. J. Thursby and M. Thursby [4]), others provide evidence they affect international trade positively [5]. In an attempt to explain these different ranges of results, some researchers have turned to the measure of exchange rate volatility. Cushman [6] used the moving average of the real exchange rate as his volatility measure and found a negative relationship between volatility and exports. In his 1988 study, Cushman added the absolute difference between spot, forward, and current rates as an alternative measure of volatility and found mixed effects of volatility on exports. Akhtar and Hilton [7] concluded that exchange rate uncertainty is detrimental to the international trade. P. de Grauwe [8] captured the ambiguity of the debate by modelling a producer who must decide selling in the domestic or the foreign market. By providing some basic assumptions, his model assumes that the only source affecting the exporter's behaviour is the local currency price of exports as well as his risk preferences. In his model, exchange rate volatility is measured as a percentage change of the exchange rate. Following de Grauwe's study, Perée and Steinherr [9] proposed the average absolute difference between the previous forward rate and the current spot rate as better indicator of exchange rate volatility to bilateral exports.

Even though new empirical statistical techniques are applied in the 1990s' ambiguity of the estimated relationships continues to dominate the empirical literature. Several authors used the ARCH-GARCH method in order to model and measure exchange rate volatility [10, 11]. Others follow the VAR and VECM methodology allowing them to examine and model the properties of the samples such as unit roots and cointegration [12]. Asseery and Peel [13] emphasized the importance of examining the characteristics of the data being used and examined for stationarity as well as seasonality. Chowdhury [14] investigated the impact of exchange rate trade volatility on trade flows for the G-7 countries utilizing an error correction model. His study found exchange rate volatility measure as an eight-period moving sample standard deviation of the growth rate of the real exchange rate and found a significant negative impact. Despite all these developments, the traditional measure of exchange rate still remains the moving average of the standard deviation.

Recent empirical studies have confirmed that exchange rate volatility has a negative effect on exports, especially for developing economies [15, 16]. However, in addition to the literature which suggests a negative [17] relationship there are studies that have suggested a positive [18] or no effects at all [19]. The literature, however, for the most part, continues to overlook additional measures of volatility. Awokuse and Yuan [20] tried to apply three measures of volatility which included the variance of the spot exchange rate around the preferred trend to sectorial exports and revealed mixed effects.

Overall, three conclusions can be drawn from the literature. First, some studies rely mainly on the OLS methodology which proves to be inadequate to cope and account with some of the statistical properties that the samples often may contain, such as unit roots and cointegration [21, 22]. As a result, inadequate estimates might be obtained. Second, the empirical research has provided limited or no evidence of the effects of exchange rate volatility on exports for Croatia and Cyprus. Thirdly, for the most part the empirical research uses the standard deviation of the moving average of the logarithm of the exchange rate as a measure of exchange rate volatility.

3. Methodology for the Measurement of the Exchange Rate Volatility

3.1. The Model. The model underling the empirical analysis is that of Goldstein and Khan [23] which has been extended in such a way to account for volatility as well as seasonality effects. The model can be summarised by

$$\ln X_t = \lambda_0 + \lambda_1 \ln \left(\frac{P_X}{P_w}\right)_t + \lambda_2 \ln \text{GDP}_t + \lambda_3 V_t + \lambda_4 D_1 + \lambda_5 D_3 + \lambda_6 D_4 + \lambda_7 T + \omega_t, \quad (1)$$

where X is real exports; P_X and P_w are the relative prices; GDP is real world GDP; V is volatility (defined as the standard deviation of the moving average of the logarithm of real exchange rate), as well as a dummy capturing the amount of times the exchange rate moves above and below the average values of the real effective exchange rate in predetermined intervals, D_1, D_3 and D_4 are seasonal dummies; T is a time trend, and ω is an error term.

The real export value is created using the unit value method. The first explanatory variable is the relative prices and it is constructed by the division of the export price of each sector to an index comprised of world export prices for each corresponding sector. The second right-hand variable is real world GDP, and the third right-hand variable is volatility which is measured in two ways. Firstly, as a measure of time varying exchange rate volatility, the standard deviation of the moving average of the logarithm of real effective exchange rate is used. Secondly, we utilize a dummy variable capturing

TABLE 1: Phillips-Peron unit root test results.

Croatia				Cyprus			
ln VEX	−7.1141*	−12.275*	−14.542*	ln VEX	−7.1775*	−10.358*	−11.259*
ln GDP	−2.8248	−7.7070*	−14.233*	ln GDP	−2.869	−7.5172*	−13.571*
$V1$	−9.1703*	−20.558*	−31.843*	$V1$	−6.075*	−13.327*	−21.997*
ln P	−3.0787	−8.4785*	−18.235*	ln P	−2.1747	−8.788*	−20.660*
ln $V2$	−0.3383	−4.4482*	−11.305*	ln $V2$	−2.2604	−7.2409*	−11.305*

Note: all tests are performed using the 5% level of significance; VEX is the logarithm of export quantity, GDP represents the logarithm of the real gross domestic product, $V1$ is volatility measured as the moving average of the standard deviation of the exchange rate, P is the logarithm of relative prices of each country to the world price, and $V2$ is the amount of times the value of the exchange rate moves above and below its average value at predetermined intervals. All tests are performed to a maximum of three lags. The null hypothesis of a unit root is tested against the alternative. The asterisk denotes significance at least at 5% level.
Source: authors' calculations.

the amount of times which the exchange rate moves above and below the average value of the real effective exchange rate for each sectoral trade flow at predetermined intervals [22]. Our estimation of each of the reduced form export equations for each country will be consistent with the autoregressive distributed lags (ARDL) methodology.

3.2. Exchange Rate Volatility Measurement. One of the most fundamental issues of the topic in question is volatility measure. Exchange rate volatility is a measure that is not directly observable; thus, there is no clear, right, or wrong, measure of volatility. Most empirical studies have utilized the standard deviation of the moving average of the logarithm of the exchange rate:

$$V_{t+m} = \left(\frac{1}{m}\sum_{i=1}^{m}\left(R_{t+i-1} - R_{t+i-2}\right)^2\right)^{1/2}, \quad (2)$$

where: R is the nominal or real effective exchange rate and M is the number of periods which usually ranges between 4 and 12.

The main criticism for the application of the standard deviation of the moving average of the logarithm of the exchange rate is that it fails to capture the potential effects of high and low peak values of the exchange rate. According to some economic models, these high and low values refer to the unpredictable factor which affects exports. Our investigation will be comprised of two measures of volatility: the first is the standard deviation of the moving average of the logarithm of real effective exchange rate, while the second is comprised of a dummy variable capturing the unexpected variation of the exchange rate. This dummy variable is constructed in the following way: first, the values of the exchange rate are divided by the average value in an attempt to capture the amount of times where each variable exceeds the average value; second, with the use of a dummy variable we capture only the previously calculated values which correspond to the cases for which the exchange rate falls above and below 4%–7% of its average value. This calculation is to determine the amount of times that the exchange rate moves above and below its average value as a measure of unexpected fluctuation. However, since for each country different values above and below the average value (of the exchange rate) affect exporter's behavior, various cases are examined for which the exchange rate fluctuates above and below its average value from 4% to 7%. Since these ranges might be different for each country, therefore only the first significant cases obtained irrespective of the percentage used will be reported.

4. Estimating Methodology and Results

This study examines the effects of exchange rate volatility for two countries, Cyprus and Croatia. All the data are derived from Eurostat with the exception of GDP and real effective exchange rate figures which are derived from the IFS (International Financial Statistics). All the data are collected quarterly and extend from 1990: q1 to 2012: q1.

Before examining the existence of a long-run relationship (cointegration) between the variables, we must analyse first, the order of integration of the variables considered. This analysis is usually done using the ADF [24] or the P-P [25] unit root test. The P-P unit root test was used to test the series for stationarity.

The values of the P-P test are presented in Table 1. The bandwidth length is four lags; both a trend and an intercept were used in the test equation and the critical values were determined using the Bartlett Kernel estimation method.

From Table 1, it is seen that the ln VEX and the $V1$ series for both countries is $I(0)$, while the remaining variables are $I(1)$ in both countries examined here. As one would expect, the null hypothesis of a unit root is rejected for volatility when measured as the moving average, partly due to the fact that it is already differenced. When there are $I(1)$ variables, the maximum likelihood approach of Johansen and Juselius [26] can be used. However, the requirement is that all the variables are $I(1)$. In our case, the system contains variables with different orders of integration and therefore the autoregressive distributed lag modeling (ARDL) suggested by Pesaran et al. [27, 28] will be used. The ARDL method can be applied on a time series data irrespective of whether the variables are $I(0)$ or $I(1)$ [29], and it generally provides unbiased estimates of the long-run model and validates the t-statistics even when some of the regressors are endogenous [30]. However, it is necessary to check that the variables are not $I(2)$ because, in this case, ARDL would produce spurious results [31]. In our case, none of the variables are $I(2)$.

Following [27, 28], the ARDL representation of (1) can be formulated as follows:

$$\Delta \ln X_t = a_0 + \vartheta \ln X_{t-1} + \sum_{i=1}^{\mu} \theta_i G_{i,t-1} + \sum_{j=1}^{p} a_j \Delta \ln X_{t-j} + \sum_{i=1}^{\mu}\sum_{j=0}^{p} \beta_{ij} \Delta G_{i,t-j} + \tau T + \delta_1 D_1 + \delta_3 D_3 + \delta_4 D_4 + \omega_t, \quad (3)$$

where Δ is the first-difference operator, X is export quantities, and $G = (\ln P, \ln \text{GDP}, V1)$ is the vector with the explanatory variables; P is the relative prices, GDP is the real domestic GDP, $V1$ and $V2$ represent the first and second measure of exchange rate volatility, D_1, D_3, and D_4 are seasonal dummies, T is a time trend, ω is a white noise error term, $\mu = 3$ is the number of explanatory variables, ϑ , θ_i are the coefficients that represent the long-run relationship, α_j, β_{ij} are the coefficients that represent the short-run dynamics of the model, and p is the number of lag length. The ARDL method to co-integration requires the following steps:

Step 1. Equation (3) is estimated after establishing that all the variables are either $I(0)$ or $I(1)$ and not $I(2)$. The lag order of the ARDL was determined using the appropriate lag selection criterion. In the literature, three criteria are alternatively used. In our case, the Akaike information criterion (AIC) will be used.

Step 2. After finding, in Step 1, the order of the ARDL model, a test was conducted that the errors in (3) are serially independent. The Lagrange multiplier (LM) test was used to test the null hypothesis that the errors in (3) are serially independent against the alternative that there are autoregressive or moving average relationships in the errors.

Step 3. When a model has autoregressive (AR) terms, it will be stationary (i.e., dynamically stable) when the inverse roots of the AR polynomials lie strictly inside the unit circle. In our case, after finding the AR order of the ARDL model, in Step 1, the plot of the inverse roots of the AR polynomial was made.

Step 4. From (3) a test for the existence of long-run relationship was made. This is called the "bounds testing" approach to cointegration and it is associated with the hypothesis testing $H_0 : \vartheta = \theta_1 = \cdots = \theta_i = 0$; i is the number of explanatory variables; that is, the long-run relationship does not exist against the alternative $H_1 : \vartheta \neq \theta_1 \neq \cdots \neq \theta_i \neq 0$; that is, the long-run relationship exists. This hypothesis is tested by the use of the F-statistic. However, the distribution of the F-statistic is nonstandard and the critical values are available in Pesaran et al. [28]. In our case, a Wald test was computed in the E-views programme and the F-statistic was compared to that given by the appropriate upper bound critical value.

Step 5. Assuming that the bound test in Step 5 is conclusive and there is a cointegrating relationship, the coefficient and its statistical significance of the error correction term (ECT) can be found by estimating

$$\Delta \ln X_t = a_0 + \sum_{j=1}^{p} a_j \Delta \ln X_{t-j} + \sum_{i=1}^{\mu}\sum_{j=0}^{p} \beta_{ij} \Delta G_{i,t-j} + e\text{ECT}_{t-1} + \omega_t. \quad (4)$$

Step 6. Once the model is obtained in Step 2, the long-run impact of the explanatory variables to the dependent variable is calculated using the expression [32]:

$$\widehat{\gamma}_i = -\frac{\widehat{\theta}_i}{\widehat{\vartheta}}, \quad (5)$$

where $\widehat{\theta}_i$ and $\widehat{\vartheta}$ are the estimated long-run coefficients in (3). However, the $\widehat{\gamma}_i$s provide a single value to quantify the long-run effect and they do not provide any information about the degree of variability associated to them [33]. Following Efron and Tibshirani [34], the bootstrap method, which is a nonparametric method, can be used in order to calculate empirically confidence intervals without assuming a specific distribution of the γ_is. The calculation of the confidence intervals for each $\widehat{\gamma}_i$ was made with the use of the STATA programme for 95% level of statistical significance. If the zero is contained in the interval, then the effect of the explanatory variable will not be statistically significant.

The estimation results of the ARDL model are presented in Table 2; dependent variable is export quantity (VEX). The order of the ARDL model, the F-statistic for the LM test of serial correlation, the F-statistic Wald bound test, the long-run impact of the explanatory variables to the dependent variable $\widehat{\gamma}_i$, the coefficient of the error correction term e, and the confidence intervals of the $\widehat{\gamma}_i$s calculated using the bootstrap method are presented. The test for dynamic stability is presented in the Appendix.

The lag order of the ARDL model is presented in second column of Table 2. It was determined using the Akaike selection criterion. The F-statistic of the Wald "bound" test of cointegration is presented in the fifth column of the same Table. As it can be seen, the F-statistic is higher than the upper bound critical value (5.119 and 5.872 for the ER volatility measure 1 and the ER volatility measure 2 model, resp.) indicating a long-run relationship between exports (ln VEX) and the explanatory variables (ln P, ln GDP and $V1$). Further, the LM test was used to test the null hypothesis that the errors in (3) are serially independent against the alternative that there are autoregressive or moving average relationships in the errors. The F-statistic from the LM test is presented in the sixth column. Serial correlation is not detected in all cases.

The results from the examination of the effects of exchange rate volatility (measures 1 and 2) on exports are shown in Table 2. The fourth column shows the long-run impact of the exchange rate on the dependent variable and it is statistically significant. The results show that the effects of exchange rate volatility on sectoral exports are mostly positive

TABLE 2: ARDL results for the effects of ER volatility (measures 1 and 2) on exports of Croatia and Cyprus.

Country, Sector	ARDL order	Regressor, coefficient	$\widehat{\gamma}_i$	F-statistic, Wald bound test	F-statistic LM test	$\widehat{e}$	Confidence intervals for $\widehat{\gamma}_i$	Dynamic stability
Croatia—ER volatility measure 1	(7, 4, 6, 6)	ln VEX (−1): −0.134 ln P (−1): −1.428* ln GDP (−1): −0.466 $V1$ (−1): −62.532* Δ (ln (VEX (−1))): −0.725* Δ (ln (VEX (−2))): −0.530* Δ (ln (VEX (−3))): −0.469+ Δ (ln (VEX (−4))): −0.425+ Δ (ln (VEX (−5))): −0.493* Δ (ln (VEX (−6))): −0.092 Δ (ln (VEX (−7))): −0.307 Δ (ln (P)): −1.303 Δ (ln (P (−1))): 0.652 Δ (ln (P (−2))): 0.712 Δ (ln (P (−3))): 2.265* Δ (ln (P (−4))): −0.406 Δ (ln (GDP)): 2.400* Δ (ln (GDP (−1))): 1.260 Δ (ln (GDP (−2))): 2.358+ Δ (ln (GDP (−3))): 2.457* Δ (ln (GDP (−4))): 1.222 Δ (ln (GDP (−5))): 1.918+ Δ (ln (GDP (−6))): 1.786 Δ ($V1$): −7.827 Δ ($V1$ (−1)): 49.049* Δ ($V1$ (−2)): 50.896* Δ ($V1$ (−3)): 45.363* Δ ($V1$ (−4)): 36.609* Δ ($V1$ (−5)): 25.189* Δ ($V1$ (−6)): 16.707*	ln P: −10.65773* ln GDP: −3.47714 $V1$: −466.39183*	5.5103*	0.66372	−0.2343*	**[−17.4177, −3.8978]** [−8.4090, 1.4547] **[−818.935, −113.851]**	Yes

TABLE 2: Continued.

Country, Sector	ARDL order	Regressor, coefficient	$\hat{\gamma}_i$	F-statistic, Wald bound test	F-statistic LM test	$\hat{e}$	Confidence intervals for $\hat{\gamma}_i$	Dynamic stability
Cyprus—ER volatility measure 1	(1, 4, 6, 0)	ln VEX (−1): −1.033337* ln P (−1): −0.415671* ln GDP (−1): 0.485851 $V1$ (−1): 15.78140* Δ (ln (VEX (−1))): 0.183368 Δ (ln (P)): 0.150960 Δ (ln (P (−1))): 0.759289^{+} Δ (ln (P (−2))): 0.706178 Δ (ln (P (−3))): 0.616798 Δ (ln (P (−4))): 0.710739^{+} Δ (ln (GDP)): 3.480582* Δ (ln (GDP (−1))): 0.983846 Δ (ln (GDP (−2))): 3.100975^{+} Δ (ln (GDP (−3))): −0.797226 Δ (ln (GDP (−4))): 2.530708 Δ (ln (GDP (−5))): 1.420947 Δ (ln (GDP (−6))): 4.071522* Δ ($V1$): 13.62624*	ln P: −0.402260* ln GDP: 0.470177 $V1$: 15.272268*	9.4420*	1.4896	−0.433*	**[−0.64803, −0.15649]** [−1.0730, 2.0134] **[1.7265, 28.818]**	Yes
Croatia—ER volatility measure 2	(1, 2, 4, 0)	ln VEX (−1): −1.817775* ln P (−1): 117.8602* ln GDP (−1): 5.340606* ln $V2$ (−1): −1.468365* Δ (ln (VEX (−1))): 0.685608* Δ (ln (P)): 33.34486* Δ (ln (P (−1))): 8.323432* Δ (ln (P (−2))): 23.46942^{+} Δ (ln (GDP)): 3.586092* Δ (ln (GDP (−1))): −4.255792* Δ (ln (GDP (−2))): 1.802907^{+} Δ (ln (GDP (−3))): 0.801685 Δ (ln (GDP (−4))): −0.283179 Δ ($V1$): −0.451535	ln P: 64.83765* ln GDP: 2.93799* ln $V2$: 0.80778*	168.678*	2.1006	−1.1017	**[35.2047, 94.4705]** **[2.6029, 3.2731]** **[0.2792, 1.3365]**	Yes

Table 2: Continued.

Country, Sector	ARDL order	Regressor, coefficient	$\widehat{\gamma}_i$	F-statistic, Wald bound test	F-statistic LM test	$\widehat{e}$	Confidence intervals for $\widehat{\gamma}_i$	Dynamic stability
Cyprus—ER volatility measure 2	(1, 4, 2, 0)	ln VEX (−1): −1.131485* ln P (−1): −0.585692* ln GDP (−1): 2.275066* ln $V2$ (−1): 0.386714 Δ (ln (VEX (−1))): 0.150424 Δ (ln (P)): 0.838574+ Δ (ln (P (−1))): 0.731348+ Δ (ln (P (−2))): 0.391101 Δ (ln (P (−3))): 0.524350 Δ (ln (P (−4))): 0.889837+ Δ (ln (GDP)): −2.046932 Δ (ln (GDP (−1))): 1.149470 Δ (ln (GDP (−2))): 2.460438 Δ (ln ($V2$)): 0.352926	ln P: −0.517631* ln GDP: 2.01069* ln $V2$: 0.341775	8.6375*	0.7455	−0.6401*	**[−0.5395, −0.4958]** **[1.1367, 2.8847]** [−1.3772, 2.0608]	Yes

Notes: the asterisk and the cross denote at least 5% level of statistical significance and 10% level of statistical significance, respectively. Confidence intervals indicating statistically significant long-run coefficients ($\widehat{\gamma}_i$s) are presented in bold. The plot of the inverse roots of the AR polynomials for examining the dynamic stability of the model is presented in the Appendix.

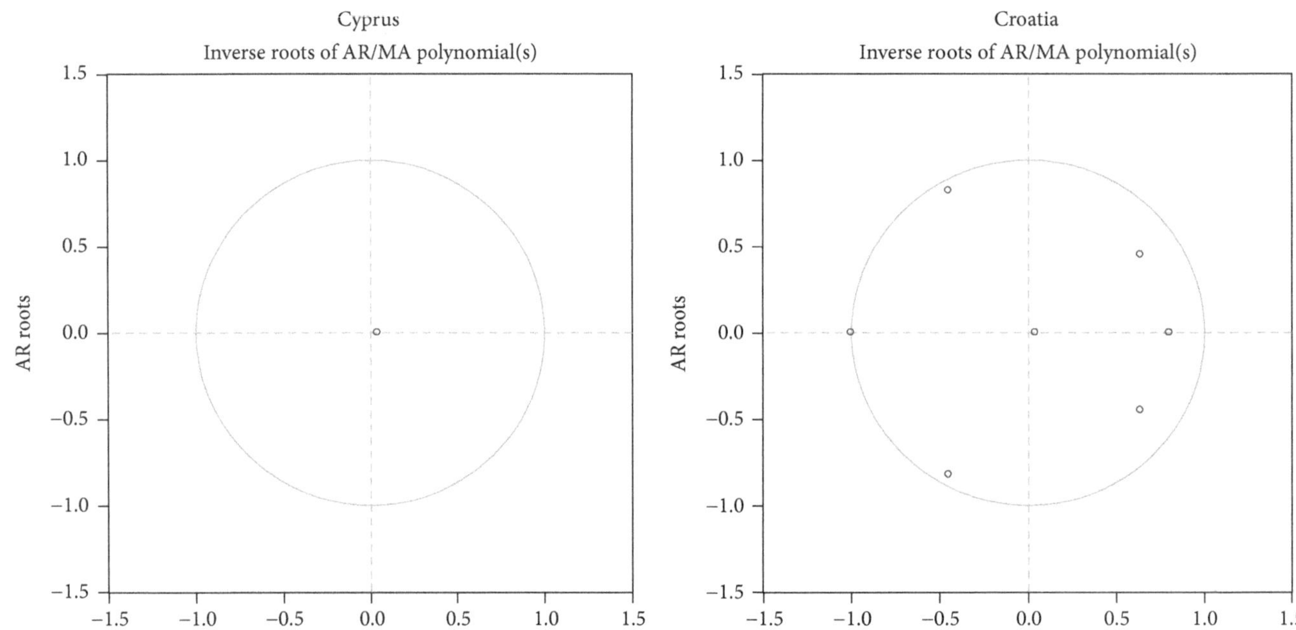

FIGURE 1: Measure 1.

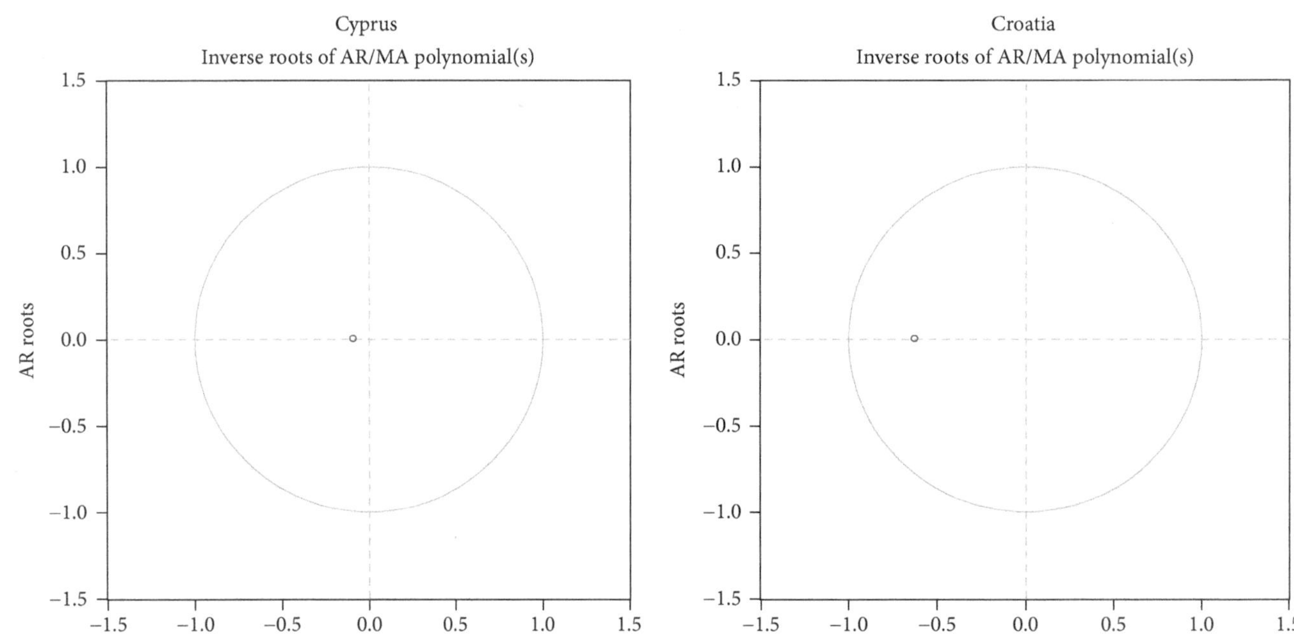

FIGURE 2: Measure 2.

(except for Croatia when measure 1 was used). They indicate that exchange rate volatility has statistically significant effects for both exports of Croatia and Cyrus.

The relative price variable is, for the most part, negatively related with the export volume and it has a larger value in Croatia when measure 2 is used. The relative prices are statistically significant in all of the four cases examined here.

The GDP variable, in the cases that it is statistically significant, presents a more mixed effect than relative prices. The estimated coefficient is significant for all of the cases examined here with the exception of Cyprus when measure 2 is used and ranges from −4.255792 to 4.071522 showing that it may affect export volume either positively or negatively.

The coefficients of the error correction term were estimated using (4) and they are shown in the seventh column of Table 2. They are negative and statistically significant for all cases indicating that there is a cointegration between the dependent and the explanatory variables. The coefficient of the error correction term (in absolute value) ranges from approximately 0.2343 in Croatia when measure 1 is used and

Croatia when measure 2 is used to a high of 1.1017. This results shows that any disequilibrium between the exports and the explanatory variables is corrected in a year or less. For the most part, the error correction term (in absolute value) seems to be larger for the cases where measure 2 is used, compared to the cases where measure 1 is used for each country. This indicates that for measure 1 any deviation in exports resulting from the selected variables takes longer time to fine tune back to its long-run equilibrium when compared with the results of measure 2.

The results of this paper add to the literature in several ways. First, there is a limited amount of empirical studies concentrating on the effects of volatility on exports. Second, in addition to the ambiguity as to samples, time periods, and variables, there is also an ambiguity with regard to the exchange rate volatility measure. Third, in addition to the common measure of volatility we calculated a new measure capturing fluctuations between 4% and 7% of the average value of the exchange rate. This new measure was constructed in order to examine the effects of high and low exchange rate fluctuations on export volume.

5. Conclusions and Policy Implications

In this study, an explicit account of nonstationarity has been taken into account and a multivariate cointegration error correction model has been applied for Cyprus and Croatia and two different measures of volatility. Each model satisfies several commonly utilised econometric tests in the analysis of time-series data such as cointegration and unit roots. Our empirical analysis suggests that exchange rate volatility when measured as the simple standard deviation of the log effective exchange has an effect on the level of exports for both Croatia and Cyprus. However, when an alternative measure is used, there is also an indication of an effect from movements of the exchange rate to the level of exports. As a result, a mixed statistical significant relationship is estimated, for both countries in our sample. Overall, the empirical findings are quite important. First, they suggest that additional measures of volatility can be used to model the effects of exchange rate volatility to exports, thus indicating that there is no specific way of measuring volatility. Second, the results prove that high and low fluctuation produce a significant negative long-run effect on the real exports for some countries. These high and low values can be attributed to the unexpected factor which, as suggested by some models, to the extent that it cannot be hedged, it effects the exporter behavior. From a policy prospective, the results are important: they suggest that policy makers should consider volatility for some but not all countries when applying economic policy, especially, for those like Cyprus and Croatia, that it was found that the exchange rate volatility had a positive impact on exports.

Appendix

Dynamic Stability Test

For more details see Figures 1 and 2.

Conflict of Interests

The authors declare that there is no conflict of interests regarding the publication of this article.

References

[1] M. D. McKenzie, "The impact of exchange rate volatility of international trade flows," *Journal of Economic Surveys*, vol. 13, no. 1, pp. 71–106, 1999.

[2] P. Clark, "Uncertainty, exchange rate risk, and the level of international trade," *Western Economic Journal*, vol. 11, pp. 302–313, 1973.

[3] P. Hooper and S. W. Kohlhagen, "The effect of exchange rate uncertainty on the prices and volume of international trade," *Journal of International Economics*, vol. 8, no. 4, pp. 483–511, 1978.

[4] J. Thursby and M. Thursby, "Bilateral trade flows, the linder hypothesis and exchange risk," *Review of Economics and Statistics*, vol. 69, pp. 488–495, 1987.

[5] M. D. McKenzie and R. D. Brooks, "The impact of exchange rate volatility on German-US trade flows," *Journal of International Financial Markets, Institutions and Money*, vol. 7, no. 1, pp. 73–87, 1997.

[6] D. O. Cushman, "The effects of real exchange rate risk on international trade," *Journal of International Economics*, vol. 15, no. 1-2, pp. 45–63, 1983.

[7] M. Akhtar and S. R. Hilton, "Effects of exchange rate uncertainty on German and U.S. Trade," *Federal Reserve Bank of New York, Quarterly Review*, vol. 9, pp. 7–16, 1984.

[8] P. de Grauwe, "Exchange rate variability and the slowdown in growth of international trade," *Staff Papers*, vol. 35, pp. 63–83, 1988.

[9] E. Perée and A. Steinherr, "Exchange rate uncertainty and foreign trade," *European Economic Review*, vol. 33, no. 6, pp. 1241–1264, 1989.

[10] K. F. Kroner and W. D. Lastrapes, "The impact of exchange rate volatility on international trade: reduced form estimates using the GARCH-in-mean model," *Journal of International Money and Finance*, vol. 12, no. 3, pp. 298–318, 1993.

[11] S. Pozo, "Conditional exchange rate volatility and the volume of international trade: evidence from the early 1900s," *The Review of Economics and Statistics*, vol. 75, pp. 325–329, 1992.

[12] A. C. Arize, "Trade flows and real exchange-rate volatility: an application of cointegration and error-correction modeling," *North American Journal of Economics and Finance*, vol. 6, no. 1, pp. 37–51, 1995.

[13] A. Asseery and D. A. Peel, "The effects of exchange rate volatility on exports," *Economics Letters*, vol. 37, no. 2, pp. 173–177, 1991.

[14] A. R. Chowdhury, "Does exchange rate volatility depress trade flows? Evidence from error-correction models," *The Review of Economics & Statistics*, vol. 75, no. 4, pp. 700–706, 1993.

[15] A. C. Arize, T. Osang, and D. J. Slottje, "Exchange-rate volatility and foreign trade: evidence from thirteen LDC's," *Journal of Business and Economic Statistics*, vol. 18, no. 1, pp. 10–17, 2000.

[16] M. Doğanlar, "Estimating the impact of exchange rate volatility on exports: evidence from Asian countries," *Applied Economics Letters*, vol. 9, no. 13, pp. 859–863, 2002.

[17] Z. Javed and M. Farooq, "Economic growth and exchange rate volatility in the case of Pakistan," *Pakistan Journal of Life and Social Sciencees*, vol. 7, no. 2, pp. 112–118, 2009.

[18] A. Shehu and Z. Youtang, "Exchange rate volatility, trade flows and economic growth in a small economy," *International Review of Business Papers*, vol. 8, no. 2, pp. 118–131, 2012.

[19] S. Hall, G. Hondroyiannis, P. A. V. B. Swamy, G. Tavlas, and M. Ulan, "Exchange-rate volatility and export performance: do emerging market economies resemble industrial countries or other developing countries?" *Economic Modelling*, vol. 27, no. 6, pp. 1514–1521, 2010.

[20] T. Awokuse and Y. Yuan, "The impact of exchange rate volatility on U.S. poultry exports," *Agribusiness*, vol. 22, no. 2, pp. 233–245, 2006.

[21] D. Serenis, N. Tsounis, and P. Serenis, "Exchange rate volatility, and sectoral exports is there a relationship? New evidence from the EU," in *Proceedings of the International Conference on Applied Economics (ICOAE '11)*, pp. 579–588, 2011.

[22] D. Serenis and N. Tsounis, "A new approach for measuring volatility of the exchange rate," *Procedia Economics and Finance*, vol. 1, pp. 374–382, 2012.

[23] M. Goldstein and M. Khan, "The supply and demand for exports: a simultaneous approach," *The Review of Economics and Statistics*, vol. 60, no. 2, pp. 275–286, 1978.

[24] D. A. Dickey and W. Fuller, "Likelihood ratio statistics for autoregressive time series with unit root," *Econometrica*, vol. 49, no. 4, pp. 1057–1072, 1981.

[25] P. C. Phillips and P. Perron, "Testing for a unit root in time series regrassion," *Biometrica*, vol. 75, no. 2, pp. 335–346, 1988.

[26] S. Johansen and K. Juselius, "Maximum likelihood estimation and inference on co-integration—with applications to the demand for money," *Oxford Bulletin of Economics and Statistics*, vol. 52, no. 2, pp. 169–210, 1990.

[27] M. H. Pesaran and Y. Shin, "An autoregressive distributed lag modelling approach to cointegration analysis," in *Econometrics and Economic Theory in the 20th Century: The Ragnar Frisch-Centennial Symposium*, S. Strom and P. Diamond, Eds., Cambridge University Press, Cambridge, UK, 1999.

[28] M. H. Pesaran, Y. Shin, and R. J. Smith, "Bounds testing approaches to the analysis of level relationships," *Journal of Applied Econometrics*, vol. 16, no. 3, pp. 289–326, 2001.

[29] M. H. Pesaran and B. Persaran, *Working with Microfit 4.0: Interactive Econometric Analysis*, Oxford University Press, Oxford, UK, 1997.

[30] J. Laurenceson and J. C. H. Chai, *Financial Reform and Economic Development in China*, Edward Elgar, Northampton, Mass, USA, 2003.

[31] E. Oteng-Abayie and J. Frimpong, "Bound testing approach to cointegration: an examination of foreign direct investment trade and growth relationships," *The Americal Journal of Applied Sciences*, vol. 11, no. 3, pp. 2079–2085, 2006.

[32] G. Bardsen, "Estimation of long run coefficients in error correction models," *Oxford Bulletin of Economics and Statistics*, vol. 51, no. 3, pp. 345–350, 1989.

[33] M. Gonzalez-Gomez, M. Alvarez-Diaz, and M. Otero-Giraldez, "Modeling domestic tourism demand in Galicia using the ARDL approach," *Tourism and Management Studies*, vol. 7, pp. 54–61, 2011.

[34] B. Efron and R. Tibshirani, *An Introduction to the Bootstrap*, Chapman & Hall, New York, NY, USA, 1998.

10

Endogenous Technical Progress in the Theory of Economic Growth

Vladimir N. Pokrovskii

Moscow State University of Economics, Statistics and Informatics, Moscow 119501, Russia

Correspondence should be addressed to Vladimir N. Pokrovskii; vpok@comtv.ru

Academic Editors: T. Kuosmanen and M. Tsionas

It is shown that substitutive work, which can be defined as work of production equipment (capital stock) replacing the efforts of workers in production processes, can be considered as a measure of technical progress. The methods of estimation of substitutive work are discussed. The theoretical results are illustrated on the data for the US. economy.

1. Introduction

The theory of economic growth tries to connect the magnitude of gross domestic product (GDP), which is a measure of current achievements of an economy as a whole—a money measure of a multitude of things and services—created by society for unit of time [1], with some universal, basic factors, called production factors. In other words, one can say that the aim of the theory is to separate original sources of wealth.

The most important production factor is labour, which, in our days, is considered as the sum of the efforts of all workers, participating in the production of things and services. The labour theory of value, due to Adam Smith, Karl Marx, and David Ricardo, considered labour as the only production factor, but it has appeared that, to account for the effect of the enlargement of output with introduction of production equipment, about which we think as a collection of animals, machines, buildings, roads, harbours, pipelines, and so on, something else ought to be added into the theory. In the beginning of the last century, it was a fundamental problem of economic theory, which has required a generalisation of labour theory of value. A hypothesis was declared: the amount of capital stock itself is a source of enlargement, so that output Y can be considered as a function of two variables: labour L and capital K:

$$Y = Y(K, L). \qquad (1)$$

This simple approach appears to be a foundation of the conventional neoclassical interpretation of economic development [2, 3]. Capital stock K is measured in money units, whereas labour L is measured as a number of workers or a number of working hours per year. Having an energy estimate of efforts, which are spent by a worker for a unit of time, it is possible and convenient to count labour L in energy units per year. The fundamental property of the approach (1) is that the two production factors: labour L and capital K, can substitute for each other without limit during the development of production system.

To the middle of the last century it was recognised that the theory in the simple classic form, independent of the specific form of the function (1), leaves no place for technical progress, which, nevertheless, was believed to be the ultimate source of economic growth in developed countries in recent centuries. In other words, the hypothesis about productive force of capital does not correspond to the reality. To incorporate the technical progress into the theory and save the neoclassical approach, it was suggested by different investigators [4] to modify the variables K and L in function (1) to allow for time-dependent changes in the quality or effectiveness of production factors:

$$Y = Y\left(K', L'\right). \qquad (2)$$

The new variables $K' = A_K(t)K$ and $L' = A_L(t)L$ are called capital and labour services, which are connected with the measurable quantities of capital stock K and labour L, but are somewhat different from them. The time-dependent multipliers $A_K(t)$ and $A_L(t)$ reduce capital stock K and labour L to two arguments of a suitable dimensionality: it is convenient to think that K' and L' are measured in energy units.

The specific form of the function (2) may be presented in different ways [4] due to different choice of multipliers. In one of the simple cases, for example, the production function can be written in the conventional Cobb-Douglas form

$$Y = Y_0 A(t) \frac{L}{L_0} \left(\frac{L_0}{L} \frac{K}{K_0} \right)^{\alpha}, \quad 0 < \alpha < 1, \tag{3}$$

where the only time-dependent multiplier $A(t)$ has appeared to describe overall technical progress, so called exogenous technical progress.

The concepts of labour and capital services appeared to be necessary and very useful to explain the observed growth of output, but time-dependent multiplier $A(t)$ itself remains to be uncertain. It is a mere fitting device that remains unexplained, despite various reinterpretations and modifications of the production function [2, 3]. In this way, a complete description of economic growth is achieved, but we do not know what technical progress is actually, and the problem of endogenous technical progress remains.

In this paper, based on the generalised labour theory of value [5], it will be shown that a new production factor—substitutive work can be introduced, as a characteristic of capital stock, and considered as a driver of technical progress. An expression for multiplier $A(t)$ in (3) will be given in terms of production factors. I hope that the short and concise exposition of the theory in the first sections of the paper could be helpful.

2. The Concept of Substitutive Work

The complexity of the concept of neoclassical capital was analysed by Robinson [6], who noted that capital can be characterised not only by the money estimate of production equipment: the collection of industry buildings, roads, production tools, instruments, rather sophisticated machines, animals, and so on, but also by other quantities. Apparently, as a collection of equipment, capital is not "productive" in the physical sense; it is dead [7]. The production equipment is needed to do some actions, to perform some work, and one needs in another characteristic of the existing capital stock to describe the activity. The neoclassical variable "capital" unites two functions of production equipment: both static and dynamic. One can think that it would be more appropriate if we would ascribe a separate independent variable to each of the two distinct roles of the variable "capital" in (1) to separate the functional roles of capital in production: its quantity and its activity.

These statements can be reformulated as a special generalisation of the labour theory of value, which ought to be completed with the law of substitution: the workers' efforts are substituted with work of equipment in production processes. Indeed, it is not so important how much of equipment we have, as how much work can be done by the equipment. To quantify the phenomenon, we have to introduce a variable P, work of production equipment (including animals), which produces, in all relations, the same effect as the workers' efforts. So, the production of value Y can be considered as a function of the two production factors:

$$Y = Y(L, P). \tag{4}$$

The quantity P substitutes for workers' efforts in production, and this allows to dub it as *substitutive work*, which is genuine work of production equipment, which fulfils the same operations as working people, but with help of external sources of energy. Human work is substituted by useful work (in the thermodynamic sense) of the production equipment. Simultaneously, production of value can be related to the magnitude of capital stock K, so that we can write

$$Y = Y(K). \tag{5}$$

One can note that the above speculations are nothing more than reinterpretation of neoclassical theory. The only change we have made is a separation of the two distinct roles of the variable "capital" in (1): instead of the only neoclassical variable "capital," we have to introduce two variables to describe the functional roles of capital in production: its quantity and its activity. The total capital stock K is monetary value of all cumulative investment (after depreciation), while capital service P is a substitute of human labour. Substitutive work P can be identified with capital service $K' = A_K(t)K$ in (2). Such interpretation of neoclassical theory corresponds to understanding of the concept of capital by Robinson [6].

3. Three-Factor Production Function

Due to the previous speculations, production of value Y can be considered as a function of the three production factors:

$$Y = Y(K, L, P). \tag{6}$$

We consider aggregate capital stock K to be the various means of attracting both labour L and capital service P to the production, so that K ought to be considered as a complement to both L and P, which are substitutes to each other. These properties of the production factors allow us to specify the production function for output Y. In a simple, one-sector approximation, an expression for production of value is presented by two alternative relations [5, 8]:

$$Y = \begin{cases} \xi K, & \xi > 0 \\ Y_0 \dfrac{L}{L_0} \left(\dfrac{L_0}{L} \dfrac{P}{P_0} \right)^{\alpha}, & 0 < \alpha < 1. \end{cases} \tag{7}$$

The quantity ξ represents marginal productivity of aggregate capital K. The time-dependent quantities α and ξ are interconnected internal characteristics of the production system itself.

The production function ought to be completed with equations for production factors. The total capital stock K is determined as a monetary value of all cumulative investment (after depreciation). The two other production factors, L and P in (6) and (7), are determined by investment I and technological characteristics of capital stock, $\bar{\lambda}$ and $\bar{\varepsilon}$:

$$\frac{dK}{dt} = I - \mu K, \qquad \frac{dL}{dt} = \left(\bar{\lambda}\frac{I}{K} - \mu\right)L,$$
$$\frac{dP}{dt} = \left(\bar{\varepsilon}\frac{I}{K} - \mu\right)P, \tag{8}$$

where μ is a coefficient of depreciation.

It can be easily found that the growth rates of production factors are connected by the relation

$$\frac{1}{K}\frac{dK}{dt} = \frac{1}{L}\frac{dL}{dt} + \alpha\left(\frac{1}{P}\frac{dP}{dt} - \frac{1}{L}\frac{dL}{dt}\right), \qquad \alpha = \frac{1-\bar{\lambda}}{\bar{\varepsilon}-\bar{\lambda}}. \tag{9}$$

It can be demonstrated that the index α in (7) is the same quantity as α in (9).

4. Substitutive Work as a Measure of Technical Progress

The comparison of the two generalisations of labour theory of value, presented by (3) and (7), allows us to give interpretation of the neoclassical technical progress. One can note that capital service $K' = A_K(t)K$ in (2) presents the active role of production equipment and can be considered as an independent variable, that is, a direct substitute for labour, and one can identify capital service with substitutive work, $K' = P$. Labour services $L' = L$ are regarded just as estimation of workers' effort (in energy units) to have a standard reference. The comparison of (3) with the second line of (7) allows us to connect the neoclassical technical progress with the (time-dependent) ratio of production factors P/K:

$$A(t) = \left(\frac{K_0}{K}\frac{P}{P_0}\right)^{\alpha}, \qquad 0 < \alpha < 1. \tag{10}$$

For simplicity, we assume here that the indexes in (3) and (6) are equal. In the considered simple case, the exogenous technical progress in neoclassical sense appears to be a function of the ratio of substitutive work to stock of capital P/K. In other cases, the situation can be more complex, but the ratio P/K itself can considered as a measure of technological progress, independent of the interpretations made in the neoclassical theory. The nondimensional ratio of substitutive work to labour efforts P/L can also be a convenient characteristic of technical progress.

5. A Method of Calculation of Substitutive Work

The definition of index of technical progress as the ratio of production factors P/K or P/L could be useful, if one has methods to measure the quantity P. This is a problem which has been considered elsewhere [9, 10]. The direct estimations of substitutive work P, as work of production equipment, are possible and, for sure, will be in use in the future, though at the moment direct methods of estimations do not determine good numbers. Luckily, there is a method of calculating the quantity (simultaneously with calculating the technological index α) in the case, when empirical time series for output Y, capital K, and labour L are known [5].

At given values of K and L, the growth rate of substitutive work, due to (9), can be presented as function of α:

$$\frac{1}{P}\frac{dP}{dt} = \frac{1}{\alpha}\left(\frac{1}{K}\frac{dK}{dt} - (1-\alpha)\frac{1}{L}\frac{dL}{dt}\right). \tag{11}$$

The technological index α can be exposed, due to the second line of (7), as

$$\alpha = \frac{\ln(L_0 Y / L Y_0)}{\ln(L_0 P / L P_0)}. \tag{12}$$

One can introduce a symbol for logarithm of substitutive work

$$Z = \ln\frac{P}{P_0} \tag{13}$$

and see that, when the technological index α is excluded from (11) and (12), this quantity obeys the differential equation

$$\frac{dZ}{dt} = \left[\ln\left(\frac{L_0 Y}{L Y_0}\right)\right]^{-1}\left(\ln\frac{L_0}{L} + Z\right) \times \left(\frac{1}{K}\frac{dK}{dt} - \frac{1}{L}\frac{dL}{dt}\right) + \frac{1}{L}\frac{dL}{dt}. \tag{14}$$

This equation can be solved numerically to obtain the substitutive work corresponding to the given values of Y, K, and L. The value of P_0 ought to be estimated empirically. Simultaneously, values of the technological index α, according to (12), can be found.

6. Estimates for the US Economy

The method of description of economic growth, discussed in this paper, has been developed and tested through analysis of empirical data for the US economy [8–10]. It was shown that the proposed theory, in contrast to the neoclassical generalisation of labour theory of value, allows us to explain the main fact of industrial development; that is, output expansion has outpaced population growth, due to the technical progress. Here we are presenting some results to illustrate the situation.

To test the theory, the empirical time series of output Y, capital stock K, and labour L were used. The compatibility of data, a collection of which can be found in [9], or in [5], was investigated. The results for important quantities, values of the substitutive work P and technological index α, are demonstrated in Figures 1 and 2. In the first of the figures, one can see the calculated values of substitutive work (the lower solid line in Figure 1) in comparison with total consumption of energy carries E (the upper solid line in Figure 1). The running of production equipment is obviously impossible without attraction of great amounts of energy to the production. However, one can see that the magnitude and

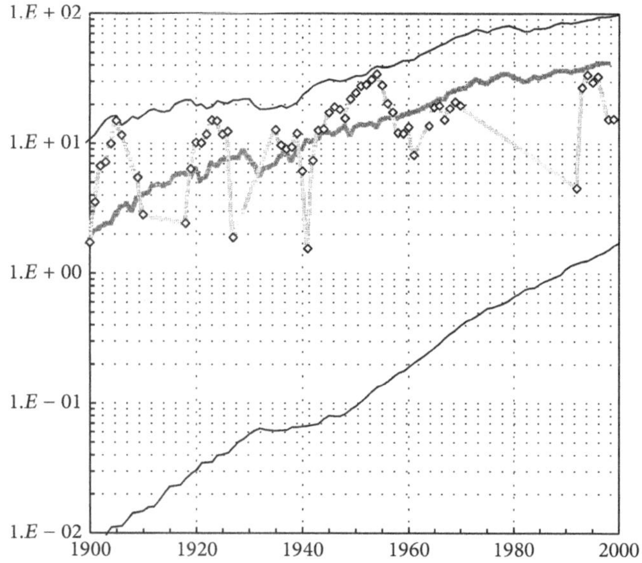

Figure 1: Total energy and substitutive work in the US economy. The solid lines represent consumption of energy careers (primary energy, top curve) and productive consumption of energy (substitutive work, bottom curve). The dashed line depicts primary energy needed for work of production equipment, estimated directly on the basis of empirical data. Primary substitutive energy is also calculated (and depicted by symbol ◇) as a part of primary energy, which is anticorrelated with labour. All quantities are estimated in quads per year (1 quad $= 10^{15}$ Btu $\approx 10^{18}$ joules). According to Figure 1 of [10].

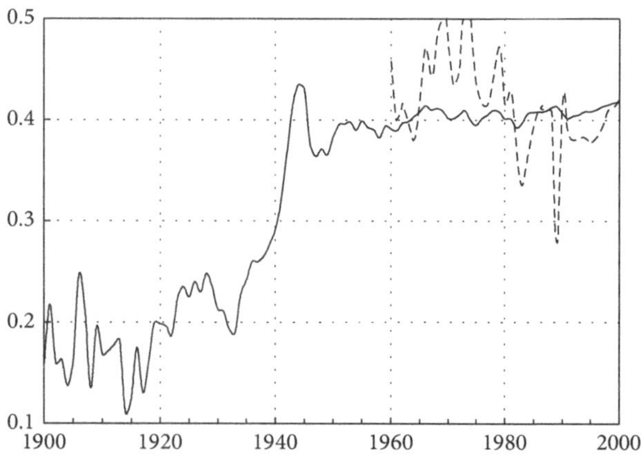

Figure 2: Technological index. Solid line represents values of the technological index α found according to (12)–(15). The dashed line represents values calculated as the fraction of expenses, necessary for maintenance of the production equipment. According to Figure 2 of [9].

the growth rate of substitutive work are, generally speaking, different from the growth rate of total consumption of energy carries. The difference is connected, first, with the fact that only part of the total energy is directed to do work with the help of production equipment; this part—primary substitutive work was estimated by two different methods and shown in Figure 1 by points and rhombi. Then, the amount

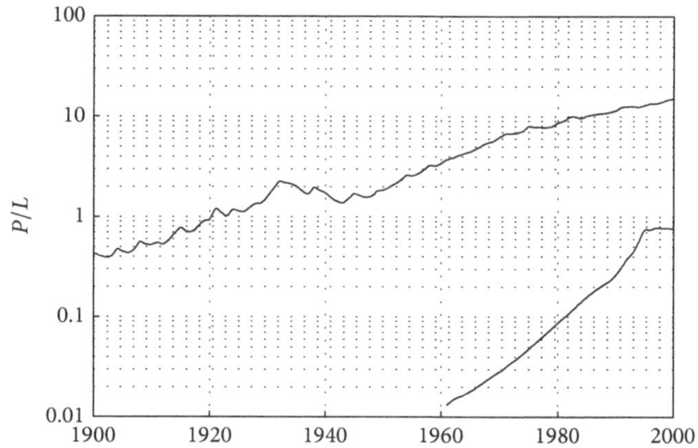

Figure 3: The ratio of substitutive work to workers' efforts. The ratio of substitutive work to energy estimates of workers' efforts for the US economy (the upper curve) and for the Russian economy (the lower shorter curve). According to Figure 1 of [8].

of substitutive work depends on the efficiency of conversion, the growth rate of which is increasing with time due to the technical innovation.

A number of authors in the past and recent times have emphasized the importance of energy in economic activity. There were some hopes that introduction of characteristics of usage of energy into the theory of economic growth could help to solve the problem of technical progress, and some attempts were made to introduce total consumption of energy E as a production factor in line with neoclassical factors L and K, so that production function could be written in the form

$$Y = Y(K, L, E). \tag{15}$$

However, it has appeared that relation (15) does not reflect the proper role of capital and energy in production, and attempts to expand the neoclassical theory of economic growth by introducing "consumed" energy as a production factor led to unresolved contradictions and were unsuccessful [11].

Simultaneously, with substitutive work, values of the technological index α are estimated and shown in Figure 2. The value of the technological index α can be also calculated by another method; the technological index represents the fraction of expenses, necessary for maintenance of the production equipment, in the full expenses for the production factors [9].

It is important that, in contrast to the exogenous neoclassical technical progress, values of substitutive work P, which is responsible for "endogenous" technical progress, can be estimated with different methods. One can use the ratio P/K or P/L as a measure of technical progress: for this aim, it is convenient to use the nondimensional quantity P/L, values of which are shown in Figure 3 for two countries. The quantity shows the level of development: at the end of the last century, every worker in the US was accompanied by more than ten automatic people, whereas in Russia it was only one, who accompanied the worker.

7. The Concluding Remarks

Production equipment is an essential part of modern production processes, but capital stock, as collection of machines, is not productive; productivity is provided with work that is fulfilled with capital stock [7]. Thus, to construct a proper and consistent description of economic growth, one has to leave the neoclassical interpretation, return to the labour theory of value, and expand it in the different direction. The theory has to be completed with the substitution law: the new and very important production factor appears to be *substitutive work*. This approach allows us to change the *"exogenous"* technical progress of the neoclassical approach into *"endogenous"* one, that is, to demonstrate that substitutive work is the underlying driver of technical progress. The two production factors: labour and substitutive work, appear to be the only original sources of wealth and drivers of economic growth.

Conflict of Interests

The author declares that there is no conflict of interests regarding the publication of this paper.

References

[1] P. Studenski, *The Income of Nations. Theory, Measurement and Analysis: Past and Present*, New York University Press, Washington, DC, USA, 1961.

[2] P. Aghion and P. W. Howitt, *Endogenous Growth Theory*, The MIT Press, Cambridge, Mass, USA, 1998.

[3] P. Aghion and P. W. Howitt, *The Economics of Growth*, MIT Press, Cambridge, Mass, USA, 2009.

[4] R. Solow, "Technical change and the aggregate production function," *Review of Economic Studies*, vol. 39, pp. 312–330, 1957.

[5] V. N. Pokrovskii, *Econodynamics. The Theory of Social Production*, Springer, London, UK, 2011, http://www.springer.com/physics/complexity/book/978-94-007-2095-4.

[6] J. Robinson, "The production function and the theory of capital," *The Review of Economic Studies*, vol. 21, no. 2, pp. 81–106, 1953-1954.

[7] B. C. Beaudreau, *Energy and Organization: Growth and Distribution Re-Examined*, Greenwood Press, Westport, Conn, USA, 1998.

[8] B. C. Beaudreau and V. N. Pokrovskii, "On the energy content of a money unit," *Physica A: Statistical Mechanics and its Applications*, vol. 389, no. 13, pp. 2597–2606, 2010.

[9] V. N. Pokrovskii, "Energy in the theory of production," *Energy*, vol. 28, no. 8, pp. 769–788, 2003.

[10] V. N. Pokrovskii, "Productive energy in the US economy," *Energy*, vol. 32, no. 5, pp. 816–822, 2007.

[11] R. U. Ayres, J. C. J. M. van den Bergh, D. Lindenberger, and B. Warr, "The underestimated contribution of energy to economic growth," *Structural Change and Economic Dynamics*, vol. 27, pp. 79–88, 2013.

11

Dynamics of Housing Price: Foreclosure Rate Interactions

John F. McDonald and Houston H. Stokes

Department of Economics, University of Illinois at Chicago, Chicago, IL 60680, USA

Correspondence should be addressed to John F. McDonald; mcdonald@uic.edu

Academic Editors: D. M. Hanink, A. Rodriguez-Alvarez, and B. M. Tabak

The dynamic impacts of the federal funds rate and the foreclosure rate on the log of the S&P/Case-Shiller aggregate 10-city monthly housing price index are investigated using VMA modeling techniques in the period 2000(1)–2011(3). The findings are consistent with the view that the interest rate policy of the Federal Reserve in that period that kept rates artificially low contributed to the housing bubble. Positive shocks in the foreclosure rate are shown to be associated with declines in the change in the housing price index after a lag. In addition, negative shocks in the change in the housing price index are associated with a higher foreclosure rate. The results suggest that both the change in the housing price index and the foreclosure rate create a negative externality that is dynamic.

1. Introduction

Recent studies have documented the negative impact of foreclosures on housing prices. The most recent studies employ data that pertain to the period after the collapse of the housing price bubble in the US. As this paper is being written, the effects of the boom and bust of housing prices are still playing out over seven years after the peak in housing prices. The research strategy that has been followed in most of the previous studies is to examine the effect of nearby foreclosures in a recent prior time period on the selling prices of individual houses. However, most of these studies do not examine the effect of a decline in housing prices on foreclosure rates (An exception is the recent study by Capozza and Van Order [1], which finds that worsening economic conditions (i.e., declining house prices) are associated with much of the increase in mortgage defaults.). It is generally understood that a drop in the value of a house increases the incentive to default of the mortgage loan, especially if the fall in house value puts the owner "under water." The remaining balance on the loan is greater than the value of the house. A foreclosed house adds one more house to the supply of houses but does not increase demand since the credit rating of the prior owners is usually lower, limiting their demand in the housing market. The net effect is a further downward pressure on housing prices, usually with a lag.

The basic hypothesis to be investigated in this paper is that house prices and foreclosure rates interact over time conditional on the log federal funds rate. The results of the study show that the housing market generates dynamic negative externalities that at this time seem to have no end point. An increase in foreclosures begets declines in house prices, which may lead to further increases in foreclosures and further declines in housing prices, and on and on. These effects may operate with complex time lags that differ across cities. Furthermore, housing prices react to lag housing prices (the bubble and crash phenomena), and the same may be true for foreclosures as well. Due to the dynamics of the relationship and the possibility of feedback, the study of these ideas requires the use of time-series data and time-series econometric methods. It is not possible to detect these possible effects using cross-section analysis or annual data. As a result, this study employs monthly data for thirteen metropolitan areas on single-family housing prices and home mortgage foreclosure rates and builds on McDonald and Stokes [2] a time-series study of monetary policy and housing prices in those metropolitan areas over a longer period (Other recent studies of the impact of monetary policy on housing prices and other variables using time-series analysis include Jarociński and Smets [3] and Vargas-Silva [4]. Vargas-Silva provides a useful summary of previous studies of monetary policy and housing. However, these studies did not examine foreclosures.). Data for the US are also studied.

The general topic to which this paper contributes is of critical importance, and recent research has included special issues in major journals, such as Green et al. [6] and Sanders and Van Order [7]. This paper is the first to employ modern time-series methods to study the interactions between housing prices and foreclosure rates.

2. Review of the Literature

Four strands of housing literature are relevant to this study:

(i) research on mortgage default,

(ii) studies of the impact of mortgage default and foreclosure on the price of the house and losses suffered,

(iii) studies of the spillover effect of foreclosures on neighboring property selling prices,

(iv) studies of housing price dynamics (i.e., price bubbles).

Mortgage default is the topic of a great deal of research. Vandell [8] provided an early survey, and LaCour-Little [9] is a more recent survey article. Mortgage default is considered to be a function of (changes in) the borrower's ability to pay and/or the borrower's equity (the put option model). Deng et al. [10] show that negative equity is a necessary condition for default, but studies conducted prior to the financial crisis (Vandell [8] and Deng et al. [10]) show that negative equity is not enough to trigger default. Foote et al. [11] found that subprime loans with adjustable interest rates are sensitive to declining housing prices and Capozza and Van Order [1] found that declining economic conditions caused defaults. Research by Deng et al. [10] and others shows that shocks such as unemployment, divorce, and health problems are factors that lead to default, and Deng et al. [12] found that the desire to move when there is negative equity generates defaults. All of these forces have been at work in the financial crisis that began in 2007. The declines in housing prices that began in 2006 wiped out the equity of millions of home owners and put them "under water," and the resulting recession reduced their ability to pay and motivated households to move to rental housing. One lesson from the previous research is that a decline in housing prices alone does not necessarily lead to foreclosures. Indeed, it is now well documented by the Financial Crisis Inquiry Commission [13, page 217] and many others that foreclosures were concentrated among the subprime and adjustable-rate mortgages. As discussed below, most of these mortgages were structured to cause default if borrowers were unable to refinance after two or three years at more favorable terms. The recent study by deRitis et al. [14] finds that both "teaser" rate shocks and market rate shocks increased the mortgage delinquency, and Archer and Smith [15] find that the put option is an important factor in default.

The extensive literature on mortgage default and foreclosure on selling price includes Clauretie and Herzog [16], Shilling et al. [17], Forgey et al. [18], Hardin and Wolverton [19], Springer [20], Carroll et al. [21], Pennington-Cross [22], Clauretie and Daneshvary [23], and Campbell et al. [24]. These studies document the sizable price discount that can vary from 7% to 27%, depending upon location. The details of the foreclosure process and the mortgage insurance contract matter. The price discount and loss suffered by the lender and/or mortgage insurer are larger in states with judicial foreclosure compared to states with power-of-sale foreclosure. Clauretie and Herzog [16] showed that losses for mortgage insurers are greater if the entire loss is covered by insurance (i.e., FHA insurance) compared to coinsurance contracts that are typical with private mortgage insurance. Losses generally are lower if the foreclosure process can be completed quickly. States with power-of-sale foreclosure, deficiency judgments permitted, and no statutory right of redemption have more expeditious foreclosures and smaller losses. Goodman and Smith [25] found lower default rates in states in which default is more costly to lenders. Mian et al. [26] find that while loan delinquency rates are similar, foreclosure rates are lower in states with judicial foreclosure procedures (rather than power-of-sale procedures) because costs of foreclosure are greater. Their findings are an important part of the puzzle but due to the fact that they use annual data and only two periods, 2008 and 2009, cannot because of research design effectively study the dynamics of adjustment that is the focus of our paper.

Studies of the spillover effect of foreclosures on the selling prices of neighboring properties are reviewed by Daneshvary et al. [27], and include Immergluck and Smith [28], Lin et al. [29], Schuetz et al. [30], Harding et al. [31], Leonard and Murdoch [32], Rogers and Winter [33], Campbell et al. [24], and Mian et al. [26]. With the exception of Campbell et al. [24], Daneshvary et al. [27], and Mian et al. [26], all of the previous studies were based on samples of sales of nondistressed houses during a time period of stability in the housing market. Except for Lin et al. [29], these studies found relatively small effects of 1% or less of one or more nearby foreclosed properties on the selling price of a non-distressed property. Lin et al. [29] found that a foreclosure within two years and 300 feet was associated with a price discount of 8.7%. The time lag assumed between foreclosure and sale of the non-distressed property varied from study to study.

Daneshvary et al. [27] studied the spillover effect in Las Vegas during 2008, a year in which the number of distressed sales was extraordinarily large (Nevada uses a power-of-sale foreclosure process in which the foreclosure sale can take place three months after the notice of default has been issued by the lender to the property owner. There is no statutory right of redemption in Nevada (right of owner to regain the property after the foreclosure sale) and deficiency judgments are permitted—but not often sought.). During the 13 months covered by the study, there were a total of 22,532 sales of single-family houses, of which 7,017 were regular sales, 12,270 were sales of repossessed houses (REO sales), 2,185 were short sales, and 1,060 were sales of properties in the process of foreclosure (A short sale is a sale in which the lender agrees to permit the owner to arrange the sale of the property for less than the outstanding balance on the loan. This can be done either before or after the notice of default has been issued by the lender. A sale in process of foreclosure means that at the foreclosure sale that is conducted by the lender, a buyer other than the lender has purchased the property. The lender normally will bid the amount of the remaining loan balance plus costs. A basic distinction therefore is between a sale arranged by the owner (short sale) versus a sale conducted by the lender (sale in process of foreclosure or sale of REO property).). The study examines the spillover effects on non-distressed and distressed sales and controls for numerous features of the property, the neighborhood, and the general trend in housing prices. The results for the own-price discounts are that properties sold as short sales had a discount of about 9%, while properties in the process of foreclosure or lender-owned (REO) properties were discounted about 15%. These results are consistent with previous studies. The estimated spillover effects for sales of REO properties and properties in process of foreclosure are large and highly statistically significant. The estimated spillover effect of one such distressed sale is about 1% within 0.1 miles and three months after the transaction and increases with the number of these nearby distressed sales up to a maximum effect of about 8% at 20 distressed sales. Estimated spillover effects for such distressed sales within a six-month time window are about 20% lower than for the three-month window. However, no spillover effects of short sales were detected. Daneshvary et al. [27] conclude that short sales appear to be in the interest of the lender and in the public interest compared to sales that take place at the conclusion of the foreclosure process.

The large-scale study by Mian et al. [26] examined the effect of foreclosures on housing prices indices at the state, core based statistical area (CBSA), and zip code levels during 2007–2009 annual data. Mian et al. [26, page 2] began their study with the observation that a study seeking to estimate the effect of foreclosures on house prices is confounded by concerns of unobserved shocks and reverse causality. For example, an unobserved negative shock can drive down house prices and increase delinquencies and foreclosures at the same time.

Cross-section data on foreclosure rates, housing price indices, and other variables for this period are employed (Data on housing prices pertain to 2007–2009 or 2010ql, and foreclosure rate data pertain to 2008-2009.). Because the foreclosure rate and housing price data pertain approximately to the same time period and it is reasonable to presume that these two variables are simultaneously determined, an instrumental variable for the foreclosure rate was constructed. That instrumental variable is based on whether the state law requires a judicial foreclosure procedure. The study finds evidence that the contemporaneous foreclosure rate (i.e., within the same two-year time interval) has a large negative impact on housing prices at the state, CBSA, and zip code levels. The zip code samples are drawn from the border areas of two states that have different foreclosure procedure requirements—judicial versus power of sale. The study did not estimate the effect of housing prices on the foreclosure rate.

Evidence is accumulating in support of bubbles in the housing market. Shiller [34] believes that the housing price bubble in the US. began as early as 1997, while Zandi [35] dates the beginning of the bubble back to 2003. Econometric tests for the presence of asset price bubbles usually involve testing for a divorce of asset prices from fundamental determinants of value such as rent, real interest rates, risk premia, and changes in tax laws. A basic reference is Hamilton [36], who concluded that whether the data violate the hypothesis that value is function of fundamentals depends upon the validity of the restrictions assumed for the dynamics of those fundamentals. Recent econometric studies that find housing market bubbles include Mikhed and Zemčík [37], a study that finds breakdowns in the relationship between an index of housing prices and rent levels in 23 US metropolitan areas.

This brief review of the literature leads us to expect that foreclosures lead to declines in housing prices, and that there is momentum in housing prices. A decline in housing prices may lead to foreclosures, but this expectation is less certain unless combined with other factors that reduce the household's ability to pay debt service. The results of our study confirm that larger declines in housing prices are causally prior to higher foreclosure rates.

3. The Data

This study makes use of three monthly time-series data sets from January 1998 to March 2011: the S&P/Case-Shiller Home Price Indices for 13 metropolitan areas, the foreclosure rate series provided by Zillow for these same metropolitan areas, and the federal funds rate. The Zillow foreclosure rate series is a weighted average of the current and past two months for the percentage of all homes foreclosed on in the given month (with the heaviest weight in the most recent month). Foreclosures include those sold at a sheriff's sale or forfeited to the bank. The metropolitan areas included in the study are Cleveland, Dallas, Denver, Las Vegas, Los Angeles, Minneapolis, New York, Phoenix, Portland, San Diego, San Francisco, Seattle, and Washington DC. These are the metropolitan areas for which both the S&P/Case-Shiller and Zillow data are available. Graphical presentations of the home price indices and the federal funds rate are included in McDonald and Stokes study [2]. These graphs show that all thirteen metropolitan areas experienced home price declines beginning either in 2006 or 2007. The sharpest declines took place in Las Vegas, Los Angeles, Minneapolis, Phoenix, San Diego, and San Francisco, and the smallest decline occurred in Denver. The others fall somewhere in between. The federal funds rate increased from 4.07% to 6.60% in the period from 1998 to 2000. The Federal Reserve lowered the rate to 1.54% in December 2001, and to 1.00% in August 2003. The rate was held at 1.00% till June 2004, and then began its steady rise to 5.25% in June 2006, where it remained until July 2007. The rate was dropped sharply in response to the financial crisis, reaching 0.10% in December 2008, and it remains at or below 0.20%.

Data on log housing price index and the foreclosure rate for the US as a whole are shown in Figure 1. One issue is whether to use logs of the 10-city Case-Shiller series or the 20-city Case-Shiller series. The left-hand plot in Exhibit 1 shows that both housing series move closely together, although the 10-city series is in general somewhat higher. The middle plot shows the Case-Shiller 10-city series indexed on the left of the plot and the foreclosure rate indexed on the right of the plot. It is clear from the plot that there is a negative relationship

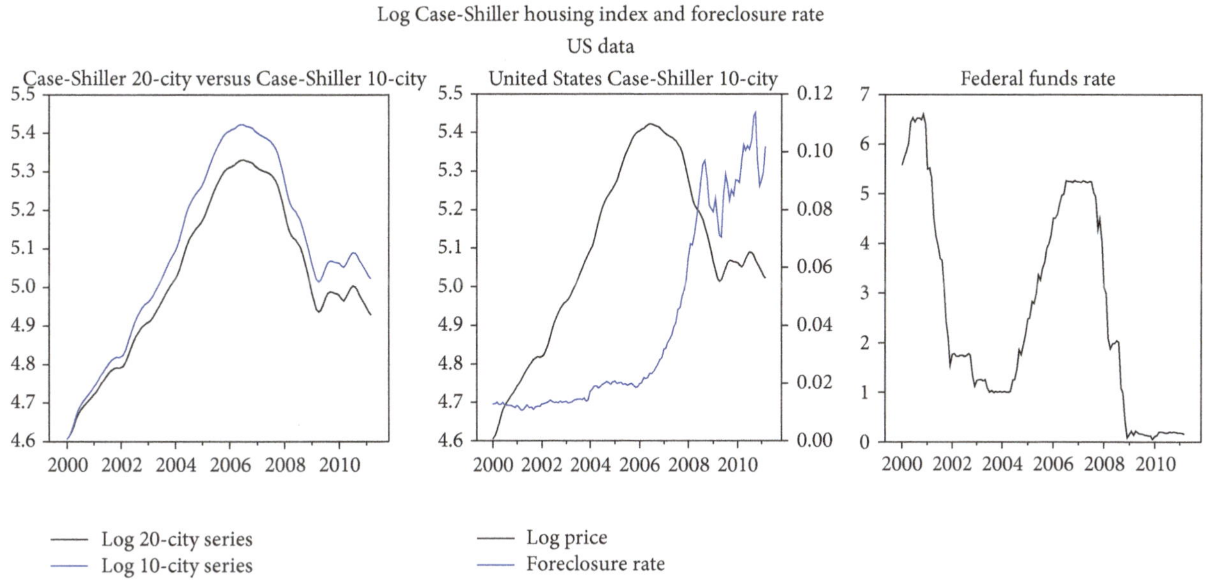

FIGURE 1

TABLE 1: Foreclosure systems.

Metropolitan area	Method of foreclosure	Typical months to foreclosure sale	Statutory right of redemption
Cleveland	Judicial	8	None
Dallas	Power of sale	1	None
Denver	Power of sale	2	2.5 months
Las Vegas	Power of sale	5	None
Los Angeles	Power of sale	5	None
Minneapolis	Power of sale	3	6 months
New York	Judicial	8	None
Phoenix	Power of sale	4	None
Portland	Power of sale	9	None
San Diego	Power of sale	5	None
San Francisco	Power of sale	5	None
Seattle	Power of sale	1	None
Washington DC	Power of sale	2	None

Source: Clauretie and Sirmans [5, p. 313].

between the two series after the peak of the housing series when the foreclosure rate started to pick up. What cannot be seen from the graph is the dynamics of the relationship between the two series.

While Figure 1 shows the national data, Figures 2 and 3 show the data for 13 cities. Cleveland, Las Vegas, New York, Los Angeles, Phoenix, Portland, Minneapolis, San Diego, Seattle, San Francisco, and Washington DC all follow the national pattern, except that the foreclosure rates in some of these metropolitan areas have declined somewhat from peak. Dallas, and to some extent Denver, did not experience a large decline in housing prices.

As noted above, the nature of the foreclosure process matters both for the propensity of foreclosures to occur and for the timing of any relationships between foreclosures and housing prices. Recent studies include Ghent and Kudlyak study [38], which examined the impact of deficiency judgments on defaults, and the Pennington-Cross [39] study of the effect of the statutory right of redemption. For these reasons, each metropolitan area is examined separately. The basic nature of the foreclosure process in each of these metropolitan areas is shown in Table 1.

Table 1 shows that the predominant method of foreclosure is power of sale, the procedure in which the lender can declare the borrower to be in default and schedule a foreclosure sale in accordance with the governing statute. Statutory right of redemption, in which the borrower has the opportunity to regain the property after the foreclosure sale, exists in only in two of the metropolitan areas.

Most of the foreclosure sales actually involve the lender assuming ownership (REO) rather than sheriff's sales. The foreclosure rate in any month is a small number; the overall

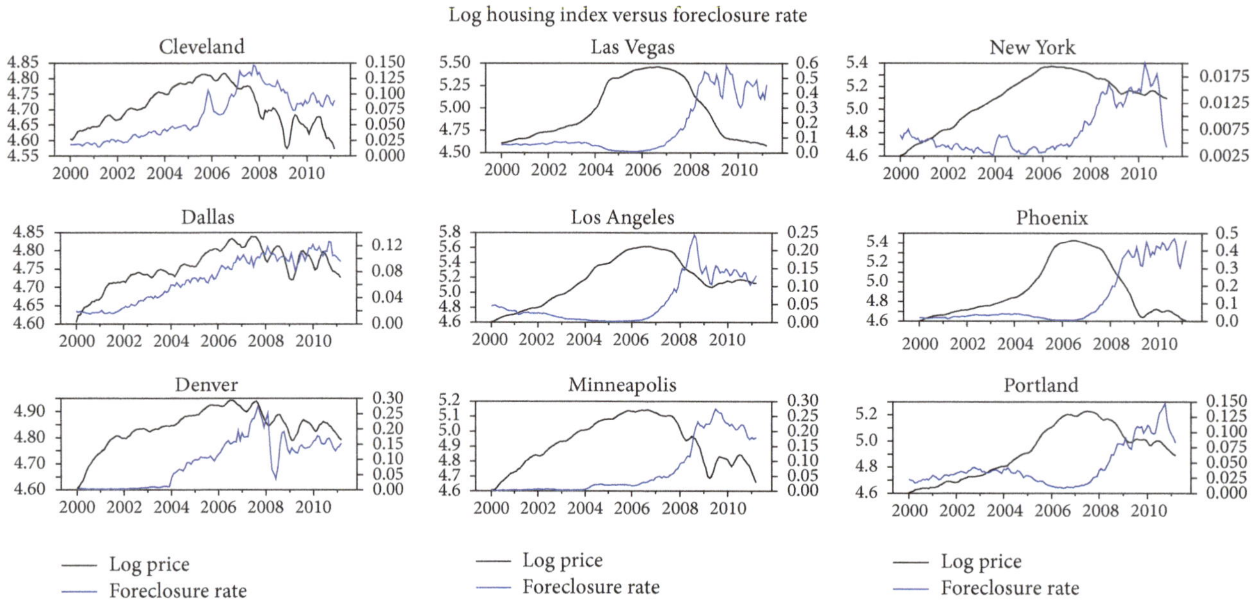

FIGURE 2

TABLE 2: Foreclosure Rates per Month: 2000 to 2011.

Metropolitan Area	Mean	Standard Deviation	Minimum	Maximum
Cleveland	0.0577%	.0394	0.0128%	0.1458%
Dallas	0.0609	.0366	0.0147	0.1259
Denver	0.0782	.0771	0.0014	0.2745
Las Vegas	0.1488	.1759	0.0056	0.5815
Los Angeles	0.0604	.0582	0.0021	0.2437
Minneapolis	0.0592	.0845	0.0011	0.2727
New York	0.0071	.0043	0.0026	0.0200
Phoenix	0.1132	.1550	0.0038	0.4675
Portland	0.0389	.0335	0.0060	0.1473
San Diego	0.0591	.0767	0.0010	0.2976
San Francisco	0.0511	.0695	0.0024	0.2641
Seattle	0.0353	.0348	0.0092	0.1568
Washington, DC	0.0397	.0429	0.0029	0.1677
United States	0.03621	.03179	.01060	.11340

Source: Zillow web site.

mean rate for the nation for the 1998–2011 period as recorded by Zillow is 0.0362% per month (with standard deviation of 0.03179). This foreclosure rate for the nation varies from a low rate of 0.0106% to a high rate of 0.1134% during these years. A summary of the foreclosure rate data for the 13 metropolitan areas is presented in Table 2.

Table 2 shows that the mean foreclosure rate varies from a low rate of 0.0071% in New York metropolitan area to a high rate of 0.1488% in the metropolitan area of Las Vegas. Metropolitan area of Phoenix has the next-highest mean foreclosure rate at 0.1132%. Note that the mean foreclosure rates for the three California metropolitan areas are very similar at 0.05% to 0.06%. Foreclosures in these three metropolitan areas are governed by the same state statute, of course. The figures for the minimum and maximum foreclosure rates demonstrate the great changes that took place as the financial crisis has proceeded. Foreclosure sales went from being a rarity (less than 0.015% per month) to a commonplace occurrence—as much as 0.5% per month in Las Vegas and Phoenix and 0.25% per month in Denver, Los Angeles, Minneapolis, San Diego, and San Francisco. The foreclosure rates in Denver, Las Vegas, Los Angeles, Minneapolis, Phoenix, San Diego, and San Francisco increased by factors that exceed 100. Metropolitan area of New York is the one place in which foreclosure sales never reached a relatively large number. The maximum is only 0.02%.

4. Model Estimation, Discussion, and Testing

While the plots in Figures 1–3 are instructive, they do not allow us to measure the dynamic relationship between

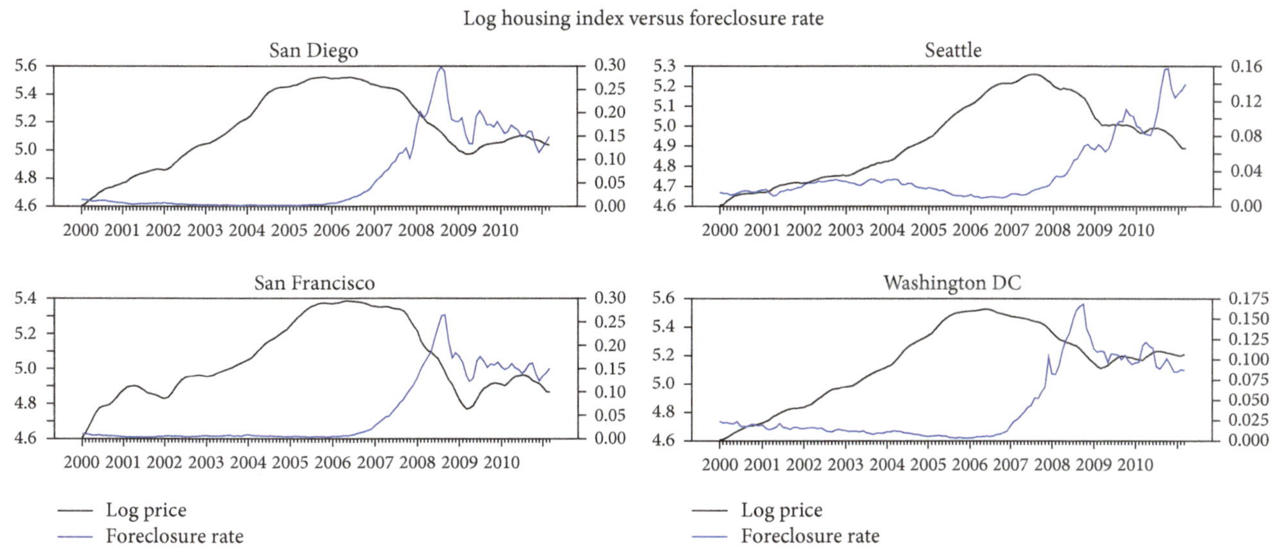

FIGURE 3

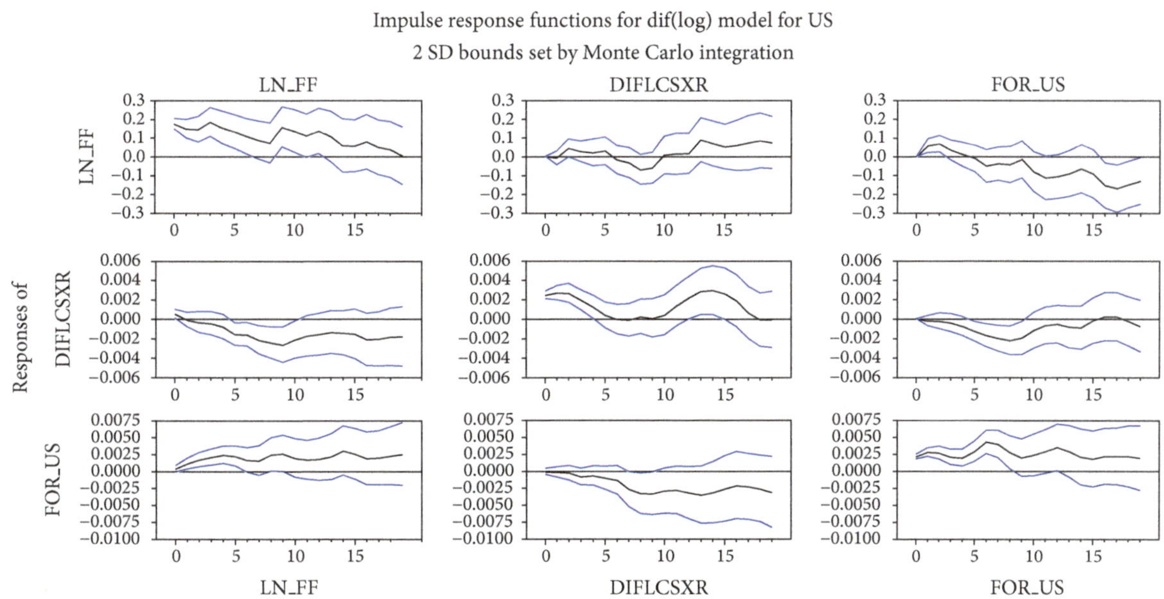

FIGURE 4

the three series. For this, we need a model. This section begins with a short discussion of one-way Granger causality but quickly moves on to the vector autoregressive model (VAR) that includes feedback effects and complex lag structures. The data used in this study are monthly time-series data that have been assembled to permit use of the VAR method.

Given that y_t = the change in the log of composite housing price index in period t, x_{1t} = the log federal funds rate, and x_{2t} = the foreclosure rate, then x_{jt} will Granger-cause y_t [40] if a model

$$y_t = a + \sum_{i=1}^{m}\gamma_i B^i y_t + \sum_{j=1}^{2}\sum_{i=1}^{m}\delta_{ji}B^i x_{jt} + e_t \qquad (1)$$

has a significantly lower error sum of squares than a model that restricts $\delta_{ji} = 0$, for $i = 1, \ldots, m$, where B is the lag operator defined such as $B^i x_{jt} \equiv x_{j,t-i}$ as in Greene [41, page 699]. In order to use (1) to test for Granger causality, let the lag m be set sufficiently long so as to remove all the significant autocorrelations in the error term e_t.

Given that housing prices and foreclosures are interrelated, the more satisfactory method is to use a VAR model that includes the possibility of feedback from y to x of the form

$$\Phi(B)\begin{bmatrix}x_{1t}\\ x_{2t}\\ y_t\end{bmatrix} = \begin{bmatrix}e_{1t}\\ e_{2t}\\ e_{3t}\end{bmatrix}, \qquad (2)$$

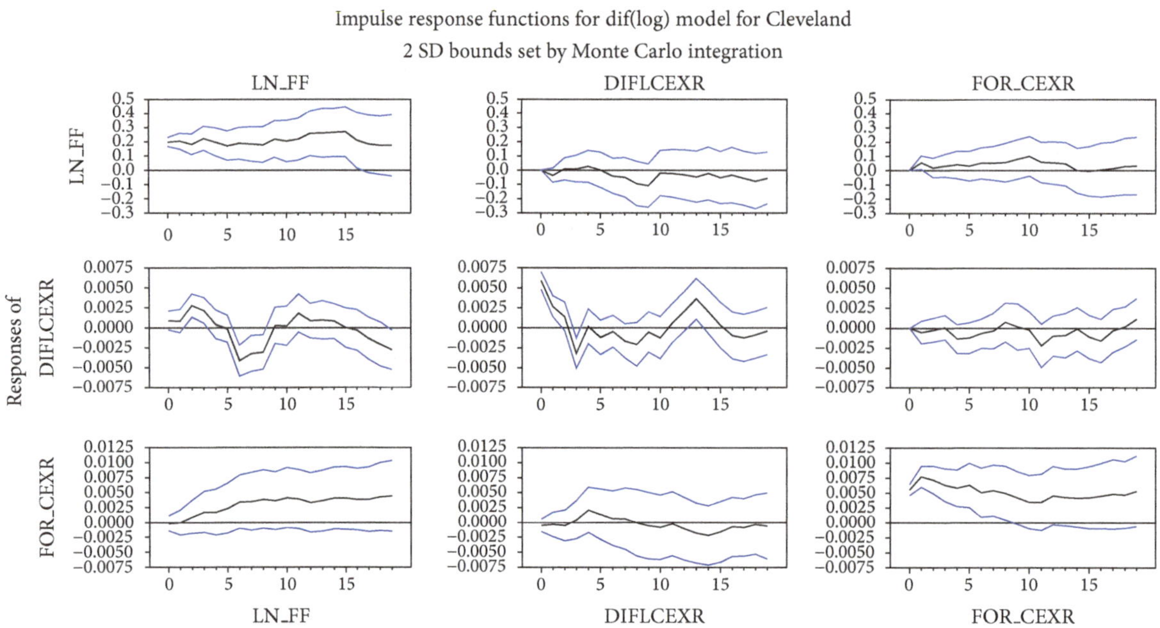

Figure 5

which can be written as

$$\begin{bmatrix} \phi_{11}(B) & \phi_{12}(B) & \phi_{13}(B) \\ \phi_{21}(B) & \phi_{22}(B) & \phi_{23}(B) \\ \phi_{31}(B) & \phi_{32}(B) & \phi_{33}(B) \end{bmatrix} \begin{bmatrix} x_{1t} \\ x_{2t} \\ y_t \end{bmatrix} = \begin{bmatrix} e_{1t} \\ e_{2t} \\ e_{3t} \end{bmatrix}, \tag{3}$$

where, for example, Granger causality from x_{it} to y_t implies that $\phi_{3i}(B) \neq 0$, where $\phi_{ij}(B)$ is a polynomial in the lag operator B with m terms. It should be noted that such a VAR model is a reduced form in which each dependent variable is a function of its own past values and past values of the other dependent variables. The empirical work in this paper is in the Sims [42] tradition. Zellner and Palm [43] have a detailed discussion of the relationship between these alternative models, both of which have their uses. For example, (1) can be written as

$$\left(1 - \sum_{i=1}^{m} \gamma_i B^i\right) y_t = a + \sum_{i=1}^{m} \delta_{1i} B^i x_{1t} + \sum_{i=1}^{m} \delta_{2t} B^i x_{2t} + e_t, \tag{4}$$

which can be simplified to

$$\gamma(B)\, y_t = \delta_1(B)\, x_{1t} + \delta_2(B)\, x_{2t} + e_t. \tag{5}$$

Provided that $\gamma(B)$ is invertible ($\sum_{j=1}^{\infty} |\gamma_i| < \infty$), (5) can be expressed as a rational distributed lag or transfer function, as in Box et al. [44]; that is,

$$y_t = \frac{\delta_1(B)}{\gamma(B)} x_{1t} + \frac{\delta_2(B)}{\gamma(B)} x_{2t} + \frac{1}{\gamma(B)} e_t. \tag{6}$$

The term $\delta_i(B)/\gamma(B)$ measures the effect of x_{it} on y_t taking into account both the effect of lags of x_{it} on lags of y_t and the direct effects of lags of x_{it} on y_t and is called the impulse response function by Box et al. [44, page 13]. It is important to stress that (6) implies that there is no feedback from y_t to x_{it} or that $\phi_{ij}(B) \equiv 0$ for $i < j$ in (3). Since McDonald and Stokes [2] found feedback from the log housing price, y_t, to the federal funds rate, x_{1t}, the specification in (6) is not appropriate for the research design in this current paper that adds another variable, the foreclosure rate, to the analysis.

An alternative estimation approach that does not restrict feedback to zero by assumption is to invert the VAR model in (2) and form the vector moving average (VMA) form of the model which will allow measurement of shocks coming from one equation to impact another equation. A VAR model can be transformed to a VMA model, given $\Phi(B)$ is invertible, or

$$\begin{bmatrix} x_{1t} \\ x_{2t} \\ y_t \end{bmatrix} = \Theta(B) \begin{bmatrix} e_{1t} \\ e_{2t} \\ e_{3t} \end{bmatrix}, \tag{7}$$

where $\Theta(B) \equiv [\Phi(B)]^{-1}$. The terms in $\Theta(B)$ measure the dynamic responses of each of the potentially endogenous variables to shock the system. Equation (7) can be expanded to

$$\begin{bmatrix} x_{1t} \\ x_{2t} \\ y_t \end{bmatrix} = \begin{bmatrix} \theta_{11}(B) & \theta_{12}(B) & \theta_{13}(B) \\ \theta_{21}(B) & \theta_{22}(B) & \theta_{23}(B) \\ \theta_{31}(B) & \theta_{32}(B) & \theta_{33}(B) \end{bmatrix} \begin{bmatrix} e_{1t} \\ e_{2t} \\ e_{3t} \end{bmatrix}. \tag{8}$$

Significance bounds on the VMA coefficients can be obtained using Monte Carlo integration (RATS software version 8.1 routine @mcgraphirf, Doan [44, page 495], is used to calculate using Monte Carlo integration the 95% bounds for $\theta_{ij}(B)$ for all nine possible cases. In general, the number of lags in VAR model m is not the number of lags in $\theta_{ij}(B)$ which we will call q. In the results reported later, $m = 12$ and $q = 20$. The lag length m was selected using both the M statistic suggested by Tiao and Box as in [45] and inspection of

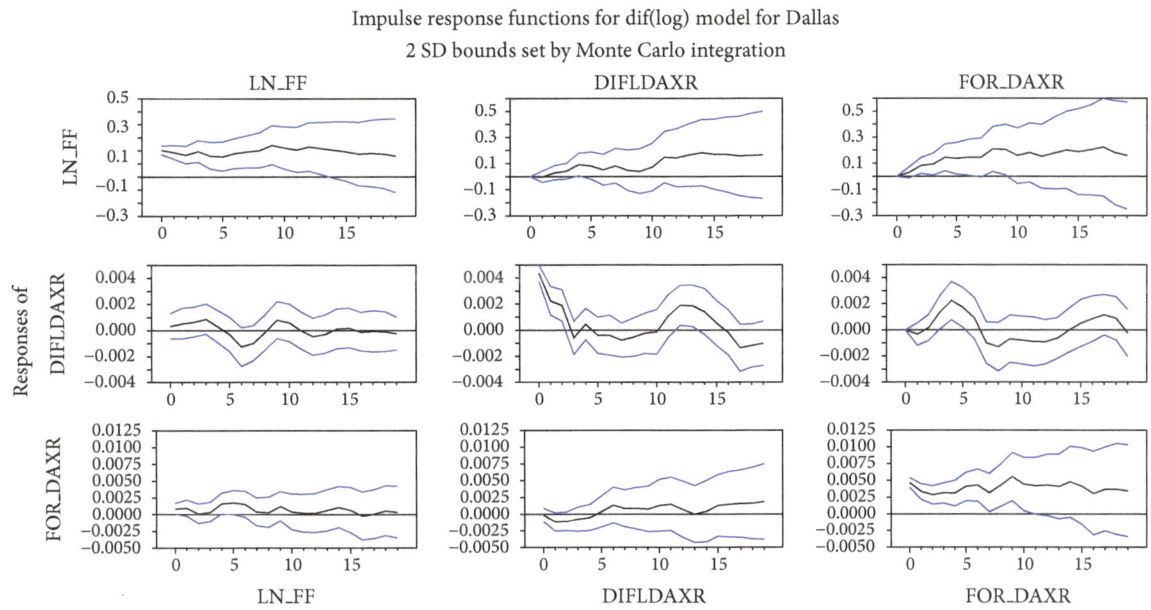

FIGURE 6

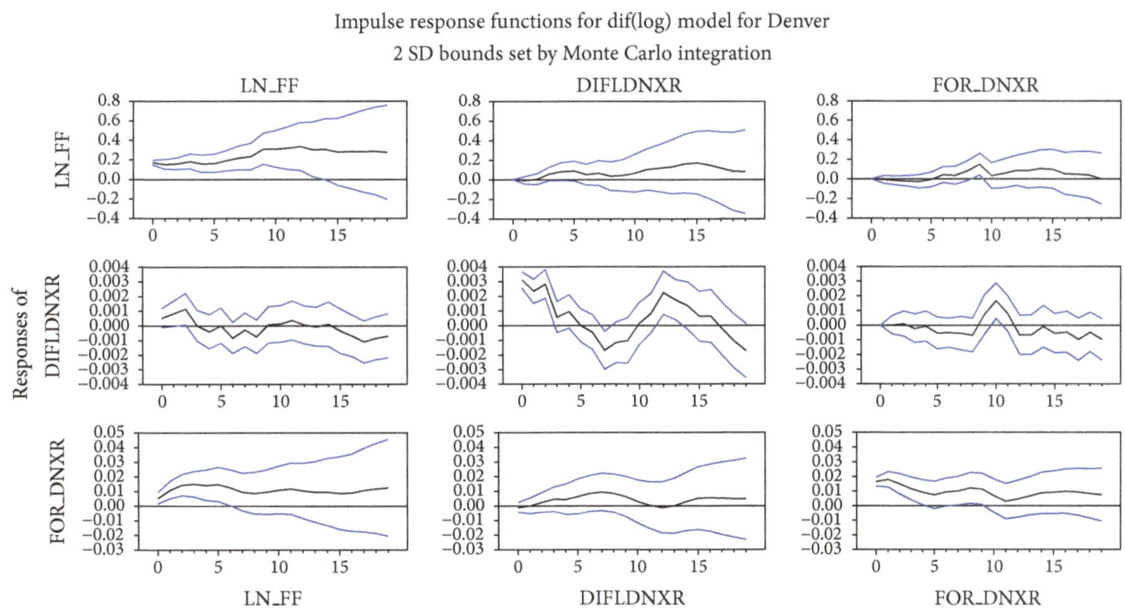

FIGURE 7

the cross-correlations. B34S version 8.11F was used to calculate these tests reported in the paper. The results reported later are about the effects of normalized residuals.). The covariance matrix of the residuals Σ is in general not diagonal since contemporaneous correlation between x_{1t}, x_{2t}, and y_t cannot be ruled out. The effect of this possible endogeneity will be that the innovations $e_{1t}, \ldots, e_{3t}$ will not be orthogonal. The Cholesky factorization has been used to normalize the innovations using the lower triangular matrix G defined such that $G\Sigma G' = I$ which can be calculated as $G = F^{-1}$, where $FF' = \Sigma$. F and G are lower triangular matrices. The new orthogonal innovations $[v_{1t}, \ldots, v_{3t}]' = G[e_{1t}, \ldots, e_{3t}]'$, however, are not invariant to the ordering of the series if there are contemporaneous effects resulting in G not being diagonal. A finding that the results are substantially the same for different ordering of x_{1t}, x_{2t}, and y_t is inconsistent with contemporaneous effects between the series.

If x_{1t} is the log of the federal funds rate, x_{2t} is the foreclosure rate, and y_t is the change in the log of the housing price series, then the term $\theta_{31}(B)$ measures the effect of shocks in the log federal funds market on the log housing price variable, $\theta_{23}(B)$ measures the effect of shocks in the housing price series on the foreclosure rate, and $\theta_{32}(B)$ measures the effect of shocks in the foreclosure market on the log housing

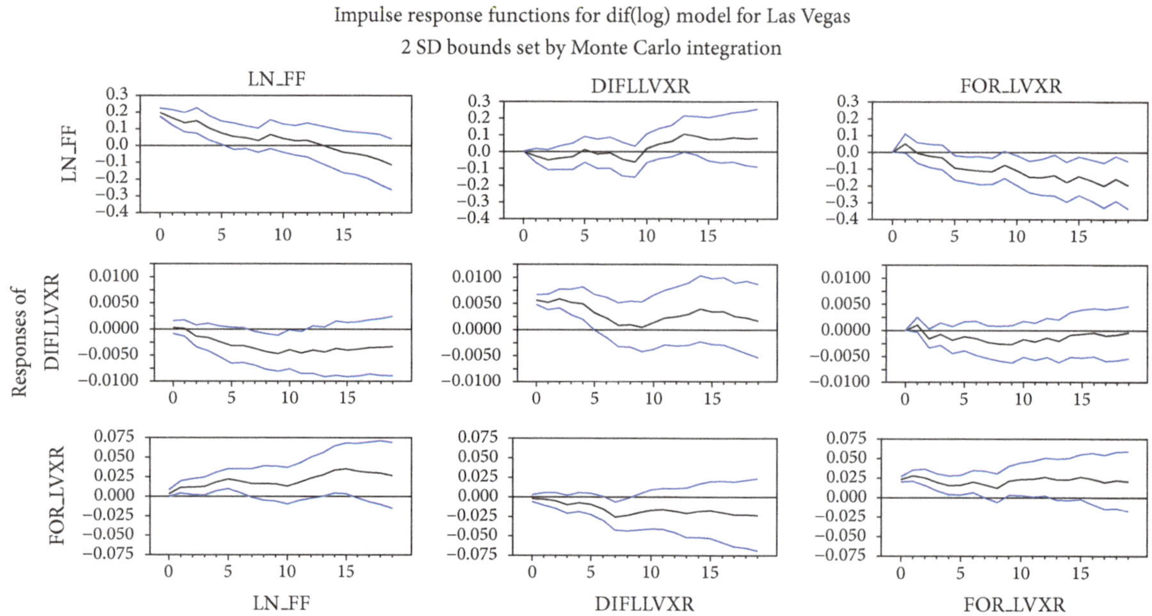

FIGURE 8

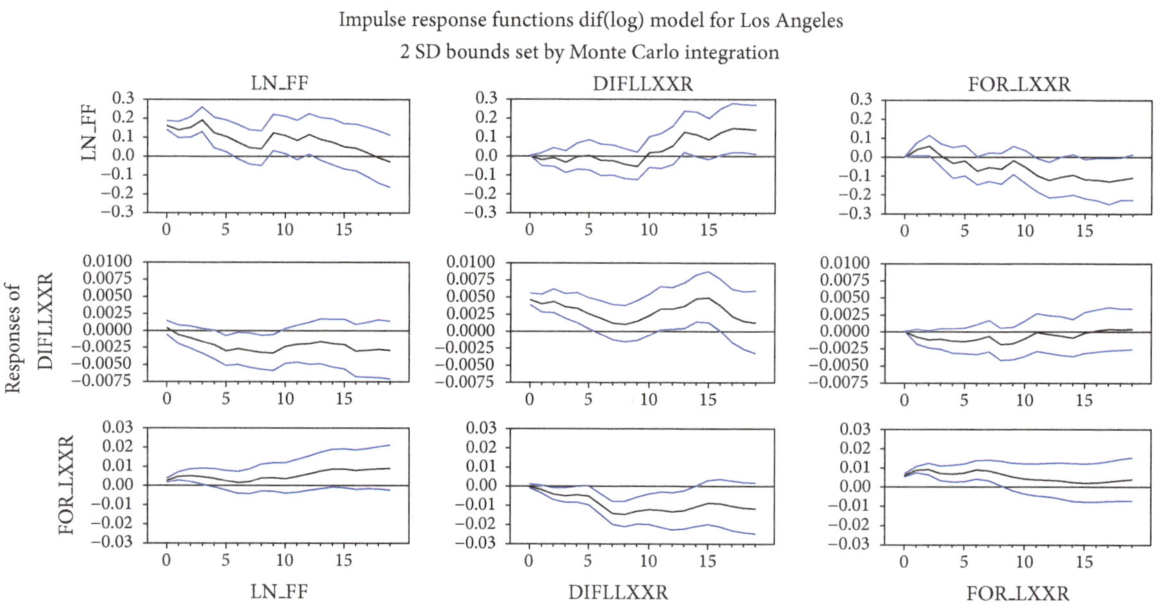

FIGURE 9

price variable. If $\theta_{ij}(B) = 0$ for $i \neq j$, then each endogenous variable is not impacted from shocks coming from the other endogenous variables.

Theory would suggest that shocks from the interest side would have a negative effect on housing prices, resulting in $\theta_{31}(B) < 0$, but positive shocks coming from the housing market would tend to have the Fed increase the federal funds rate, resulting in $\theta_{13}(B) > 0$. Theory suggests both $\theta_{23}(B)$ and $\theta_{32}(B) < 0$: the housing price change variable and the foreclosure rate interact. These hypotheses will be investigated in the Results Section of this paper.

5. Results

The VAR model with three variables (natural log of federal funds rate, the foreclosure rate, and the change in the natural log of the house price index) was estimated for the US and for each of the 13 metropolitan areas using the software described by Stokes [46]. Interest centers on the interactions between two dependent variables, the foreclosure rate and the change in the log of the Case-Shiller housing price index. The best method for examining those interactions is to compute impulse response functions, which show

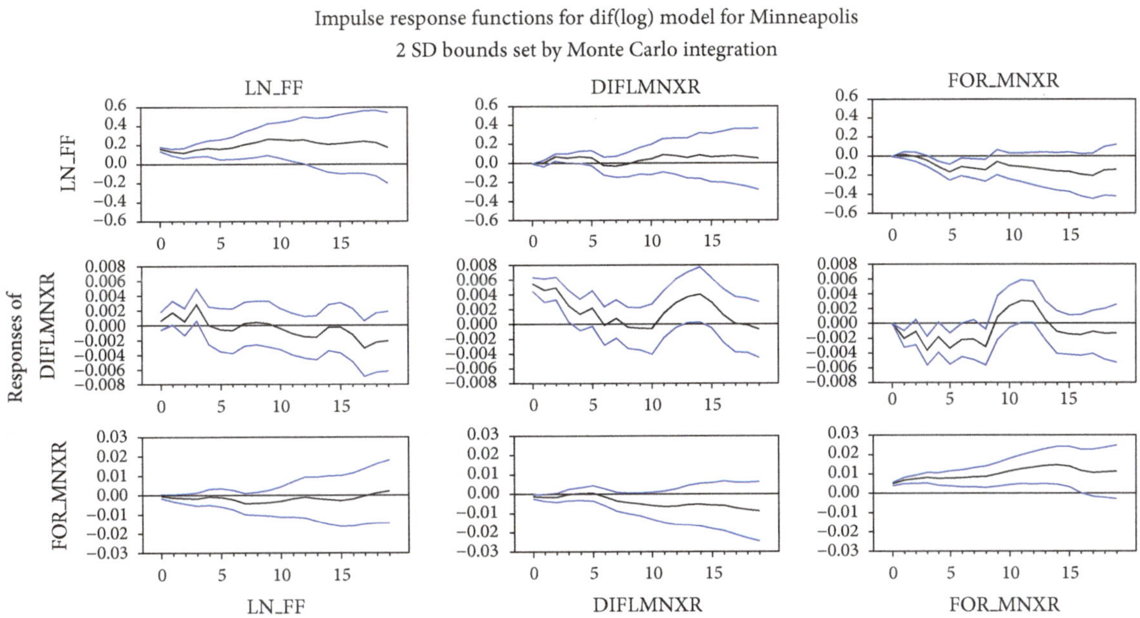

Figure 10

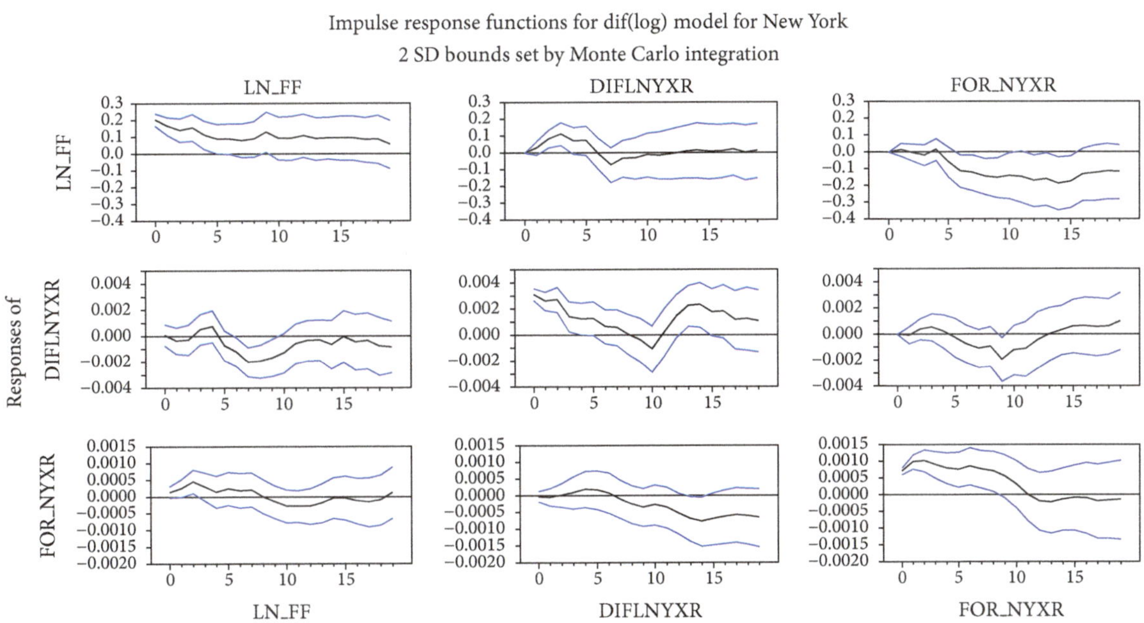

Figure 11

the computed distributions of the θ_{ij} terms from (8) based on 10,000 draws from the estimated distributions of error terms e_{1t}, e_{2t}, and e_{3t}. The Monte Carlo procedure in RATS software version 8.1, as explained by Doan [45, 47], is used to obtain estimates of the 95% confidence intervals for the effects of shocks in each of the three variables on equilibrium in the system. As discussed earlier, the Cholesky method was used to form orthogonal innovations. The lowest and highest 2.5% confidence intervals of the responses are excluded to produce the 95% confidence intervals. The results are presented in graphical form.

We hypothesized that the foreclosure rate might be interrelated with *changes* in the natural log of the housing price index. The change in the housing price index is generally positive prior to the peak and generally negative after the peak of the price bubble. Experts in time-series analysis such as Sims [42] and Enders [48, page 270] advise the researcher not to use the first differences in variables in VAR models because of the possibility that vital information will be discarded. However, in this case, the first difference in the housing price series provides vital information. When housing prices decline (increase), the foreclosure rate is apt

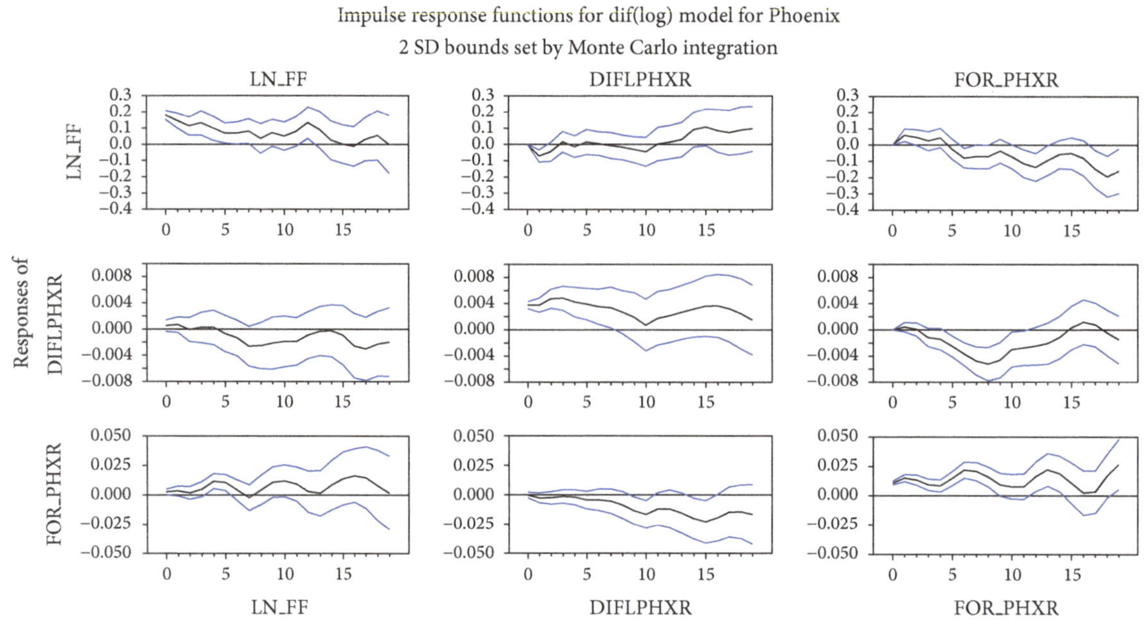

Figure 12

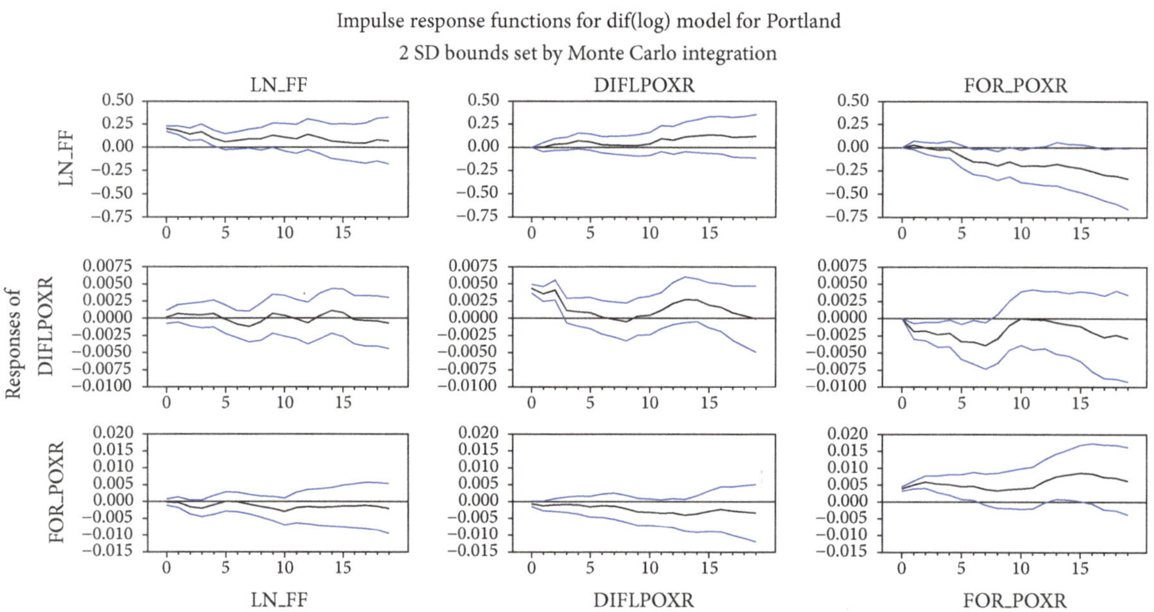

Figure 13

to rise (fall) because equity is lost (gained). And the larger the price decline the greater the loss in equity and the larger the foreclosure rate.

A summary of the impulse response function results is provided in Table 3. Graphs of the impulse response functions are shown in Figures 4, 5, 6, 7, 8, 9, 10, 11, 12, 13, 14, 15, 16, and 17. This table notes the instances in which six of the effects of shocks are different from zero with 95% confidence. Those six effects, together with their position (row and column) on the 3 by 3 graphs, are as follows:

(i) effect of the change in the natural log of house price (LnP) index on foreclosure rate (Foreclose) in position $\theta_{23}(B)$,

(ii) effect of foreclosure rate on the change in the natural log of house price in position $\theta_{32}(B)$,

(iii) effect of the change in the natural log of house price on itself in position $\theta_{33}(B)$,

(iv) effect of foreclosure rate on itself in position $\theta_{22}(B)$,

(v) effect of natural log of the federal funds rate (LnFF) on the change in the natural log of house price in position $\theta_{31}(B)$,

(vi) effect of natural log of the federal funds rate on foreclosure rate in position $\theta_{21}(B)$.

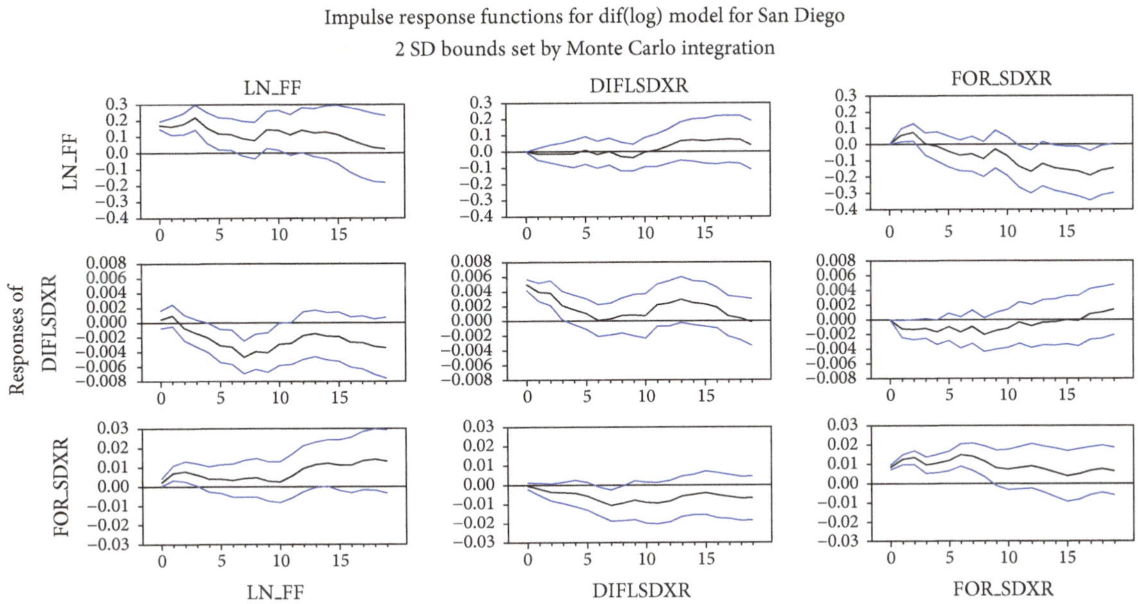

FIGURE 14

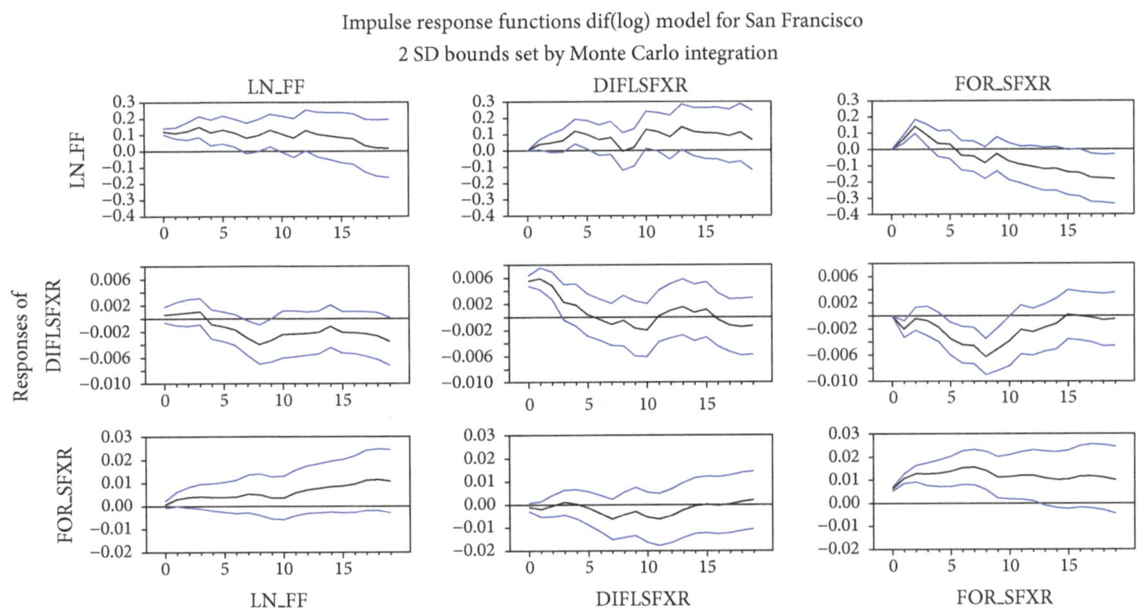

FIGURE 15

Table 3 shows the maximum effect and the month lag in which maximum effect is estimated to have taken place. The model estimated using the national data has effects that are significant at the 95% level with the expected signs. The impulse response functions show negative effects of the foreclosure rate on the change in the log of the price index that are significant at the 95% level in 11 out of 13 metropolitan areas (and two positive and significant results—Dallas and Denver). The effect of the change in the log of the price index on the foreclosure rate is negative and significant at the 95% level in 10 out of 13 metropolitan areas (with one additional result that is negative and very close to being significant and two that are zero). The effects of the change in the log of the price index on itself and the foreclosure rate on itself both are positive and significant at the 95% level in all 13 metropolitan areas. The effect of the federal funds rate on the log of the change in the housing price series is negative and significant at the 95% level in 11 out of 13 cases (with one significant result with a positive sign and one with no effect). And the effect of the federal funds rate on the foreclosure rate is positive and significant at the 95% level in 9 out of 13 cases (with three zero effects and one significant negative effect). In summary, of 84 impulse response results in Table 3, 73 are significant at the 95% level with the expected sign (and one is very close

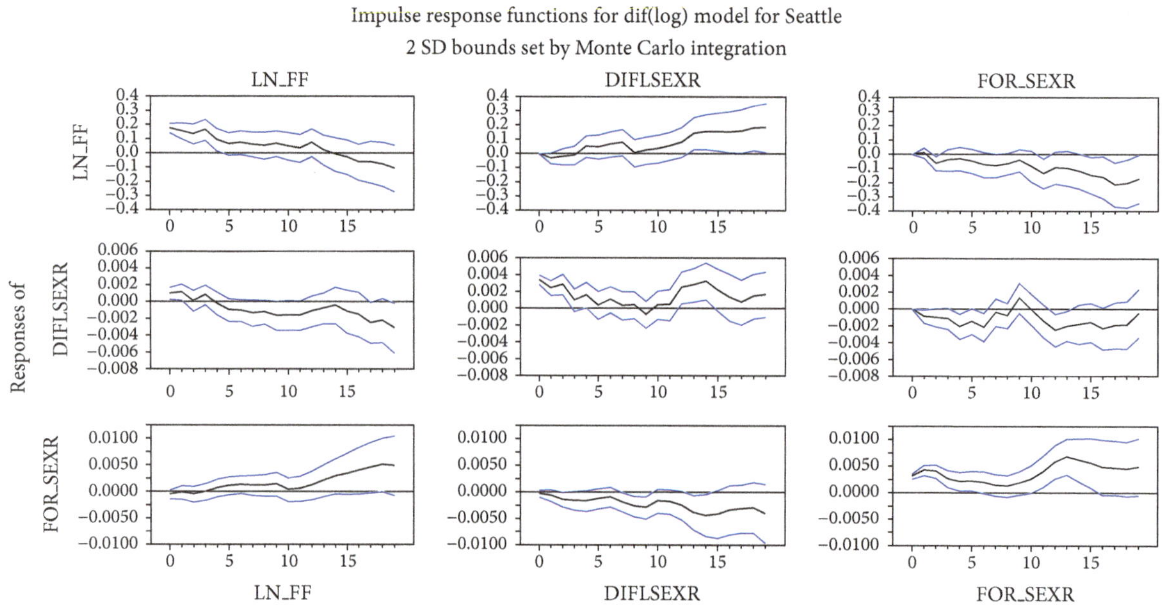

FIGURE 16

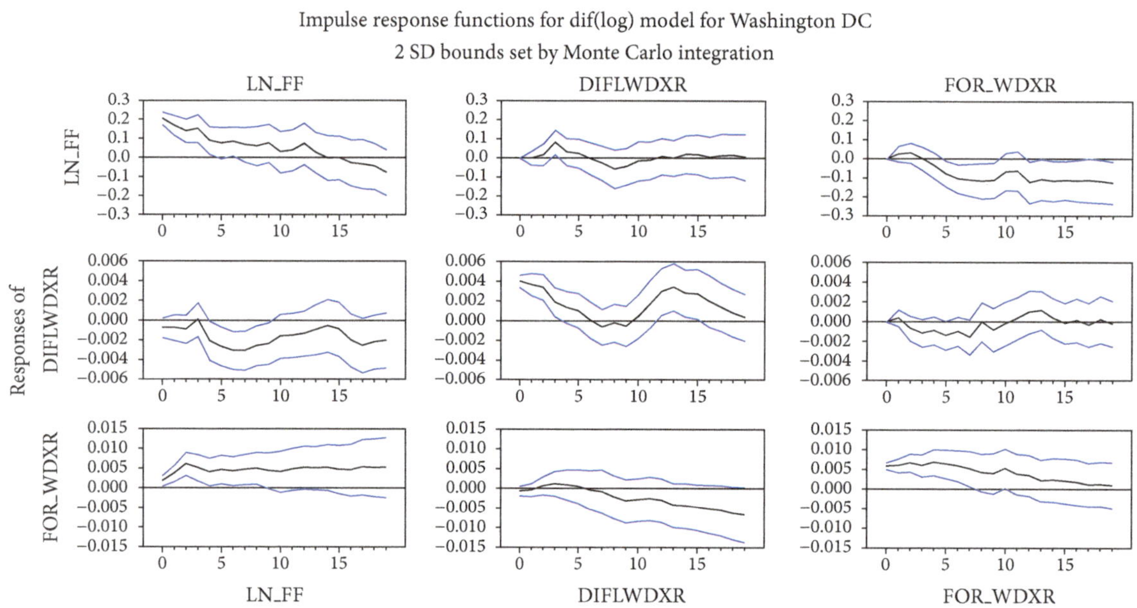

FIGURE 17

to 95% significance), 4 are significant not with the expected sign, and 7 show no effect. The expected sign is obtained in 88% of the cases.

The estimated models and Monte Carlo results suggest a basic story of the dynamics of the crisis in the housing market. An upward shock in the foreclosure rate triggers a decline in housing prices and a further increase in the foreclosure rate. The decline in housing prices generates further declines in housing prices and those declines in housing prices result in increases in foreclosures. In short, foreclosures and declines in housing prices result in both declines in housing prices (and loss of wealth) and in more foreclosures. Furthermore, an increase in the federal funds rate tended to generate more foreclosures and larger declines in housing prices.

This basic story is consistent with the hypothesis that the foreclosure crisis began with subprime mortgage loans. Subprime loans are loans to borrowers with relatively weak credentials. Zandi [35, page 38] shows that the subprime loans that were securitized in 2006 had an average loan-to-value ratio of 95% and 90.6% had adjustable interest rates (87.1% adjusted within three years or less). Adjustable-rate loans were used because subprime borrowers were charged an initial nonadjustable interest rate that was greater than the standard mortgage loans. As Gorton [49] suggests, these

TABLE 3: Magnitude and Lag Length of Maximum Significant 95% Shocks.

Metropolitan Area Exp. Sign	ΔLnP on Foreclose −	Foreclose on ΔlnP −	ΔLnP on Itself +	Foreclose on Itself +	LnFF on ΔLnP −	LnFF on Foreclose +
Cleveland		−0.0015 (4)	0.003 (1,13) −0.003 (3)	0.0075 (1)	−0.0045 (6)	
Dallas	−0.001 (1)	0.002 (4)	0.002 (1) 0.001 (12)	0.004 (6)	−0.001 (6)	0.001 (1)
Denver		0.0013 (10)	−0.0017 (7) 0.002 (12)	0.017 (1)	0.001 (2) −0.001 (17)	0.015 (5)
Las Vegas	−0.025 (7)	−0.002 (2)	0.0055 (2)	0.025 (1,12)	−0.005 (8)	0.030 (14)
Los Angeles	−0.017 (7)	−0.002 (8)	0.004 (2,15)	0.008 (7)	−0.0035 (9)	
Minneapolis	−0.001 (2)	−0.0045 (3) 0.0025 (12)	0.005 (2) 0.004 (9)	0.011 (14)	0.0025 (3)	
New York	−0.0009 (14)	−0.002 (9)	0.0023 (2,13)	0.0008 (2)	−0.002 (7,17)	0.004 (2)
Phoenix	−0.025 (15)	−0.0045 (8)	0.004 (3)	0.020 (6,13)	−0.030 (7)	0.010 (10)
Portland	−0.001 (1) *−0.004 (13)*	−0.004 (7)	0.0037 (2)	0.007 (14)		−0.002 (3)
San Diego	−0.011 (7)	−0.002 (4)	0.004 (1)	0.012 (2,6)	−0.005 (7)	0.014 (18)
San Fran.	*−0.006 (8)*	−0.006 (8)	0.0055 (1)	0.015 (7)	−0.004 (8)	0.002 (1)
Seattle	−0.005 (14)	−0.003 (12)	0.0025 (2,14)	0.0063 (13)	−0.002 (9)	0.005 (18)
Washington	−0.008 (19)	−0.002 (7)	0.0037 (2,13)	0.006 (4)	−0.0035 (6)	0.005 (8)
U. S.	−0.0035 (8)	−0.002 (8)	0.0023 (2,14)	0.0025 (12)	−0.003 (9)	0.002 (9)

Effects close to significant 95% shocks in italics.

ARMs were designed to force the borrower to refinance into a lower-cost loan after two or three years—after the value of the house (and the borrower's equity stake) had increased—because the interest rate on the original loan would increase by a large amount at the time of adjustment. Lenders are safe only if house prices rise. The decline of house prices triggered the default of many of these loans. A chart provided by the Financial Crisis Inquiry Commission [13, page 217] illustrates the sharp increase in delinquencies of adjustable-rate subprime loans that began in the middle of 2006, the point at which house prices stopped increasing and began to fall. This same chart shows that the increases of delinquencies of other types of mortgage loans lagged behind the increase of delinquencies of subprime ARMs. The Commission states [13, page 217] that "Serious delinquencies started earlier and were substantially higher among subprime adjustable-rate loans, compared to other types of loans." According to our results a shocks both in the change in housing prices and in foreclosures result in more foreclosures and larger declines in housing prices as well.

The impulse response function results in Table 3 that are contrary to expectations are few in number (four). The effect of foreclosures on the change in the log of the price index is positive for Dallas and Denver. As shown in Figure 6, Dallas had a relatively small increase in housing prices and suffered virtually no subsequent housing price decline. These outcomes perhaps can be attributed to Texas mortgage lending laws that are different from those in other states and are designed to prevent some of the worst mortgage lending abuses. For example, both loans with negative amortization and high-cost loans with balloon payments are prohibited. Mortgage brokers that are licensed must conform to strict disclosure rules and can face fines and imprisonment for providing false information to borrowers. Denver also experienced a relatively modest increase and subsequent decline in housing prices, but Figure 7 shows a large decline in the foreclosure rate after the housing price peak. This decline can be explained by the change in the Colorado foreclosure law in 2008, that extended the time between the commencement of the foreclosure process and the foreclosure sale from 60 to 125 days. Other provisions prevented foreclosure sales in March and April of 2008 and delayed foreclosure filings. The effect of the federal funds rate on the change in the log of housing prices was positive in Minneapolis perhaps because the largest decline in housing prices took place during the last half of 2008 and early 2009, when the Fed was dropping the federal funds rate dramatically. The effect of the federal funds rate on foreclosures in Portland and Oregon was negative perhaps because the foreclosure rate spiked upwards in late 2010—after the federal funds rate had been reduced to its lowest level. A possible explanation is that Oregon experienced the recession later than did most states. These specific outcomes can be topics for further research.

6. Conclusion

This study makes use of monthly time-series data on housing prices and foreclosure rates at the metropolitan level in the period from 2000(1) to 2011(3) to estimate models of the interactions between these two endogenous variables, contingent on the federal funds rate. The results are that, at the level of the metropolitan area, increases in the foreclosure rate lead to declines in house prices (with a lag) and further increases in the foreclosure rate. A larger decline in housing prices results in an increase in foreclosures and an even larger decline in housing prices. Only the cross-section study by Mian et al. [26] tested for and found a negative (contemporaneous) effect of foreclosures on house prices at the level of the metropolitan area (CBSA), but it did not test for the effect of housing prices on foreclosures due to the research design of their study. The estimated lags in the effects vary by metropolitan area. Tests of the model at the national level find that all four of these effects are statistically significant with the expected signs.

The basic findings of the study are consistent with the view that the financial crisis of the late 2000–2010 decade originated in the portion of the home mortgage market that was dominated by especially risky subprime home loans that seem almost designed to fail unless housing prices continued to rise. The sharp increases in delinquencies and subsequent foreclosures on these loans set off declines in house prices (and loss of wealth) and further increases in foreclosures, which produced huge losses in the values of the mortgage-backed securities and other assets that were based on these loans. The existence of what appear to be strong dynamic negative externalities between housing prices and foreclosure rates suggests stronger policy responses than have been attempted thus far.

Conflict of Interests

There exists no financial interest (direct or indirect) with any commercial entity mentioned that might lead to a conflict of interests for any of the authors.

References

[1] D. R. Capozza and R. Van Order, "The great surge in mortgage defaults 2006–2009: the comparative roles of economic conditions, underwriting and moral hazard," *Journal of Housing Economics*, vol. 20, no. 2, pp. 141–151, 2011.

[2] J. F. McDonald and H. H. Stokes, "Monetary policy and the housing bubble," *Journal of Real Estate Finance and Economics*, vol. 46, pp. 437–451, 2013.

[3] M. Jarociński and F. R. Smets, "House prices and the stance of monetary policy," *Federal Reserve Bank of St. Louis Review*, vol. 90, no. 4, pp. 339–365, 2008.

[4] C. Vargas-Silva, "Monetary policy and the US housing market: a VAR analysis imposing sign restrictions," *Journal of Macroeconomics*, vol. 30, no. 3, pp. 977–990, 2008.

[5] T. Clauretie and G. Sirmans, *Real Estate Finance*, Cengage, Mason, Ohio, USA, 6th edition, 2010.

[6] R. Green, A. B. Sanders, and S. Wachter, "Special issue on subprime mortgage lending," *Journal of Housing Economics*, vol. 17, no. 4, p. 253, 2008.

[7] A. B. Sanders and R. Van Order, "Introduction to the special issue on housing and the credit crunch," *Journal of Housing Economics*, vol. 20, no. 2, pp. 66–67, 2011.

[8] K. Vandell, "How ruthless is mortgage default? A review and synthesis of the evidence," *Journal of Housing Research*, vol. 62, pp. 245–264, 1995.

[9] M. LaCour-Little, "Mortgage termination risk: a review of the recent literature," *Journal of Real Estate Literature*, vol. 16, no. 3, pp. 297–326, 2008.

[10] Y. Deng, J. M. Quigley, and R. Van Order, "Mortgage terminations, heterogeneity and the exercise of mortgage options," *Econometrica*, vol. 68, no. 2, pp. 275–307, 2000.

[11] C. L. Foote, K. Gerardi, L. Goette, and P. S. Willen, "Just the facts: an initial analysis of subprime's role in the housing crisis," *Journal of Housing Economics*, vol. 17, no. 4, pp. 291–305, 2008.

[12] Y. Deng, A. D. Pavlov, and L. Yang, "Spatial heterogeneity in mortgage terminations by refinance, sale and default," *Real Estate Economics*, vol. 33, no. 4, pp. 739–764, 2005.

[13] Financial Crisis Inquiry Commission, *The Financial Crisis Inquiry Report*, Public Affairs, Perseus Books, New York, NY, USA, 2011.

[14] C. deRitis, C. Kuo, and Y. Liang, "Payment shock and mortgage performance," *Journal of Housing Economics*, vol. 19, no. 4, pp. 295–314, 2010.

[15] W. R. Archer and B. C. Smith, "Residential mortgage default: the roles of house price volatility, euphoria and the borrower's put option," *Journal of Real Estate Finance and Economics*, vol. 46, pp. 355–378, 2013.

[16] T. Clauretie and T. Herzog, "The effect of state foreclosure laws on loan losses: evidence from the mortgage insurance industry," *Journal of Money, Credit, and Banking*, vol. 22, pp. 221–233, 1990.

[17] J. Shilling, J. Benjamin, and C. F. Sirmans, "Estimating net realizable value for distressed real estate," *Journal of Real Estate Research*, vol. 5, pp. 129–139, 1990.

[18] F. Forgey, R. Rutherford, and M. VanBuskirk, "Effect of foreclosure status on residential selling price," *Journal of Real Estate Research*, vol. 9, pp. 313–318, 1994.

[19] W. Hardin and M. Wolverton, "The relationship between foreclosure status and apartment price," *Journal of Real Estate Research*, vol. 12, pp. 101–109, 1996.

[20] T. M. Springer, "Single-family housing transactions: seller motivations, price, and marketing time," *Journal of Real Estate Finance and Economics*, vol. 13, no. 3, pp. 237–254, 1996.

[21] T. Carroll, T. Clauretie, and H. Neill, "Effect of foreclosure status on residential selling price: comment," *Journal of Real Estate Research*, vol. 13, pp. 95–102, 1997.

[22] A. Pennington-Cross, "The value of foreclosed property," *Journal of Real Estate Research*, vol. 28, no. 2, pp. 193–214, 2006.

[23] T. M. Clauretie and N. Daneshvary, "Estimating the house foreclosure discount corrected for spatial price interdependence and endogeneity of marketing time," *Real Estate Economics*, vol. 37, no. 1, pp. 43–67, 2009.

[24] J. Y. Campbell, S. Giglio, and P. Pathak, "Forced sales and house prices," *American Economic Review*, vol. 101, no. 5, pp. 2108–2131, 2011.

[25] A. C. Goodman and B. C. Smith, "Residential mortgage default: theory works and so does policy," *Journal of Housing Economics*, vol. 19, no. 4, pp. 280–294, 2010.

[26] A. Mian, A. Sufi, and F. Trebbi, "Foreclosures, house prices, and the real economy," Working Paper 16685, National Bureau of Economic Research, 2011.

[27] N. Daneshvary, T. M. Clauretie, and A. Kader, "Short-term own-price and spillover effects of distressed residential properties: the case of a housing crash," *Journal of Real Estate Research*, vol. 33, no. 2, pp. 179–208, 2011.

[28] D. Immergluck and G. Smith, "The external costs of foreclosure: the impact of single-family mortgage foreclosures on property values," *Housing Policy Debate*, vol. 17, no. 1, pp. 57–79, 2006.

[29] Z. Lin, E. Rosenblatt, and V. W. Yao, "Spillover effects of foreclosures on neighborhood property values," *Journal of Real Estate Finance and Economics*, vol. 38, no. 4, pp. 387–407, 2009.

[30] J. Schuetz, V. Been, and I. G. Ellen, "Neighborhood effects of concentrated mortgage foreclosures," *Journal of Housing Economics*, vol. 17, no. 4, pp. 306–319, 2008.

[31] J. P. Harding, E. Rosenblatt, and V. W. Yao, "The contagion effect of foreclosed properties," *Journal of Urban Economics*, vol. 66, no. 3, pp. 164–178, 2009.

[32] T. Leonard and J. C. Murdoch, "The neighborhood effects of foreclosure," *Journal of Geographical Systems*, vol. 11, no. 4, pp. 317–332, 2009.

[33] W. H. Rogers and W. Winter, "The impact of foreclosures on neighboring housing sales," *Journal of Real Estate Research*, vol. 31, no. 4, pp. 455–479, 2009.

[34] R. Shiller, *The Subprime Solution*, Princeton University Press, Princeton, NJ, USA, 2009.

[35] M. Zandi, *Financial Shock*, FT Press, Upper Saddle River, NJ, USA, 2009.

[36] J. Hamilton, "On testing for self-fulfilling speculative price bubbles," *International Economic Review*, vol. 27, pp. 545–552, 1986.

[37] V. Mikhed and P. Zemčík, "Testing for bubbles in housing markets: a panel data approach," *Journal of Real Estate Finance and Economics*, vol. 38, no. 4, pp. 366–386, 2009.

[38] A. C. Ghent and M. Kudlyak, "Recourse and residential mortgage default: evidence from US states," *Review of Financial Studies*, vol. 24, no. 9, pp. 3139–3186, 2011.

[39] A. Pennington-Cross, "The duration of foreclosures in the subprime mortgage market: a competing risks model with mixing," *Journal of Real Estate Finance and Economics*, vol. 40, no. 2, pp. 109–129, 2010.

[40] C. Granger, "Investigating causal relations by econometric models and cross-spectral models," *Econometrica*, vol. 37, pp. 424–438, 1969.

[41] W. Greene, *Econometric Analysis*, Pearson/Prentice Hall, Upper Saddle River, NJ, USA, 6th edition, 2008.

[42] C. Sims, "Macroeconomics and reality," *Econometrica*, vol. 48, pp. 1–49, 1980.

[43] A. Zellner and F. Palm, "Time series analysis and simultaneous equation econometric models," *Journal of Econometrics*, vol. 2, no. 1, pp. 17–54, 1974.

[44] G. Box, G. Jenkins, and G. Reinsel, *Time Series Analysis: Forecasting and Control*, John Wiley & Sons, Hoboken, NJ, USA, 4th edition, 2008.

[45] T. Doan, *RatS USer'S Manual: VerSion 8.0*, Evanston, Ill, USA, 2010.

[46] H. Stokes, *Specifying and Diagnostically Testing Econometric Models*, Quorum Books, New York, NY, USA, 3rd edition, 2011.

[47] T. Doan, *Rats Reference Manual: Version 8.0*, Evanston, Ill, USA, 2010.

[48] W. Enders, *Applied Econometric Time Series*, John Wiley & Sons, Hoboken, NJ, USA, 2nd edition, 2004.

[49] G. Gorton, *Slapped by the Invisible Hand*, Oxford University Press, New York, NY, USA, 2010.

Fund-Raising Games Played on a Network

Alison Watts

Department of Economics, Southern Illinois University, Carbondale, IL 62901, USA

Correspondence should be addressed to Alison Watts; wattsa@siu.edu

Academic Editors: D. Dave, D. Mitra, and E. Silva

It is well known among fund-raisers that many people contribute to charities or organizations only when asked and that large donations are more likely to occur as a fund-raiser increases the time spent soliciting and/or researching a potential donor. As fund-raisers can only spend time with research donors that they are aware of, the relationship (or links) between fund-raisers and donors is quite important. We model a fund-raising game where fund-raisers can only solicit donors whom they are tied to and analyze how this network influences donation requests. We show that if this network is incomplete and if donors experience extreme donor fatigue, then fund-raisers will spend more time soliciting donors that other fund-raisers are also tied to and less time soliciting donors that they are the only fund-raiser tied to. If instead donors experience mild donor fatigue, then fund-raisers prefer donors that they are the only fund-raiser tied to over donors that are shared with other fund-raisers. If donors are potential givers with no donor fatigue, then multiple equilibria may exist. Stochastic stability is used to refine the number of equilibria in this case, and conditions are given under which the unique stochastically stable equilibrium is efficient.

1. Introduction

In 2005, seventy percent of all US households gave to charity donations totalling over $200 billion; see Andreoni [1]. In Canada, private donations to charity represent approximately two percent of GDP (this figure includes volunteer time; private monetary donations to charity represent approximately one percent of GDP.); see Hall et al. [2]. This high charitable contribution rate is due in part to the "power of the ask" as most people contribute to charities or organizations only when asked; see Yörük [3], Yörük [4], Andreoni [5], Andreoni and Payne [6], and Keegan [7]. Large donations are more likely to occur as a fund-raiser increases the time spent with the potential donor and/or increases the time spent researching the potential donor. (For instance, Dellavigna et al. [8] compare donation rates from a door to door fund-raising drive to donations received via the mail or the Internet. They find that the mail and Internet donation rate is around 0.0001 percent while the face to face donation rate is over 6 percent. Thus, fund-raisers can greatly increase donations by using the more time consuming face to face solicitation technique.) However, a fund-raiser can only research or solicit a donor that he is aware of or has some sort of tie to; for instance, a fund-raiser may research or solicit a donor who has responded in the past to a mail out campaign. Thus, the relationship or ties between fund-raisers and donors is quite important. However, the network of ties between fund-raisers and donors and this network's influence on donations has not been explored in the fund-raising literature. We analyze such a network and examine how this network influences "the ask" or donation requests.

In particular, we show that if the fund-raiser donor network is incomplete, then whether or not a fund-raiser shares a donor tie with other fund-raisers becomes important and will influence donation requests. For instance, if donors experience extreme "donor fatigue," then fund-raisers prefer shared donor ties, while if donors experience mild "donor fatigue" then fund-raisers prefer unshared donor ties. Additionally, if donors are identified as potential givers with no "donor fatigue," then multiple equilibria may exist. We use stochastic stability to refine the number of equilibria and give conditions under which the unique stochastically stable state is efficient.

The basic model and results are as follows. Fund-raisers are tied to donors in a network, and fund-raisers may only ask donors whom they are tied to for donations. (Some companies sell donor information; thus, a fund-raiser may learn of a donor in this fashion and may decide to research and solicit him. We model this as just an existing tie between the fund-raiser and donor. Thus, we assume a fixed network for tractability purposes and discuss the endogenous network case in the conclusion.) If multiple fund-raisers are tied to the same donor, then they compete with each other for donations in an average donation sharing game. In such a game, a donor's total donation increases as the total time all fund-raisers spend with the donor increases and donations are split among fund-raisers in proportion to the time each fund-raiser spends soliciting or researching the donor. (Note that we assume that donors are homogeneous or that a donor's donation to a particular fund-raiser depends only on time spent with the donor by each fund-raiser and does not depend on the identity of the donor. We make this assumption because our focus is on how the fund-raiser donor network affects solicitation time and assuming homogeneous donors allows us to concentrate on this network effect.) If there is a monopoly fund-raiser who is tied to all donors, then this fund-raiser splits his solicitation efforts evenly among all donors if donors experience "donor fatigue" or if donations increase at a decreasing rate with solicitation time, and thus donors become less and less responsive to solicitation appeals. The monopoly fund-raiser picks a single donor and spends all his time soliciting this donor if donors are thought of as potential givers with no donor fatigue whose donations increase at an increasing rate with solicitation time. These results are echoed if multiple fund-raisers compete on the complete network where every fund-raiser is tied to every donor. Here, fund-raisers split their solicitation efforts evenly among donors if donor fatigue is present or if the returns to solicitation time are increasing at a decreasing rate, while all fund-raisers spend all their time soliciting the same donor if the returns to solicitation time are increasing at an increasing rate.

The results change if the fund-raiser donor network is incomplete or if not all donors are tied to all fund-raisers. For instance, alumni donors are tied to colleges and/or universities that they attended and not to all institutions, religious donors are tied to religious organizations of which they are members, and charities in general have lists of donors who have responded to past mail out campaigns where again not all donors will respond to all campaigns.

First, we assume that donors experience donor fatigue or that donations are increasing at a decreasing rate with time spent soliciting donations. (Donor fatigue as defined in Yörük [4] occurs when a donor is solicited repeatedly and eventually stops giving or gives less than he gave previously. In our model, donors are not asked to give repeatedly instead fund-raisers decide how much effort or time to spend with a donor and donations occur at the end of this time. Thus, in our model donor fatigue occurs when each unit of time spent by the fund-raiser with a particular donor results in a smaller marginal donation than the previous unit. Note that one can reinterpret our model as allowing donations to flow to the fund-raiser after each unit of time spent soliciting a particular donor. Donations would then decrease with repeated solicitation, and the two definitions of donor fatigue would coincide.) Here, fund-raisers will no longer split their time evenly among donors. In an incomplete network, some fund-raisers may have access to donors that others do not while other donors may be tied to multiple fund-raisers. If donors experience extreme donor fatigue or if the donation-solicitation function is fairly curved, then as a fund-raiser spends extra time with a donor although the total donation does not increase much the fund-raiser's share of the donation increases quite a bit. Thus, the fund-raiser spends more time soliciting donors that other fund-raisers are also tied to and less time soliciting donors that he is the only fund-raiser tied to. Although one might expect fund-raisers to prefer shared donor ties for any concave donor-solicitation function, we find that this is not the case. If donors experience mild donor fatigue or if the donation-solicitation function is not as curved, then the fund-raiser prefers un-shared donor ties and the fund-raiser will spend more time soliciting donors that other fund-raisers are not tied to and less time soliciting donors that other fund-raisers are also tied to.

Next, we consider donors who experience no donor fatigue, and we allow donations to increase in solicitation time at an increasing rate. Here all fund-raisers would prefer to solicit the same donor. If the network is incomplete, then this may not be possible. Even if there exists a donor who all fund-raisers are tied to, not all fund-raisers will have access to every other donor and multiple equilibria will exist. At most equilibria, multiple donors will be solicited since once a fund-raiser solicits a potential donor, the incompleteness of the network may not allow other fund-raisers also to solicit this same donor; there can exist a large number of these inefficient equilibria. As the number of equilibria may be quite large, stochastic stability is used in order to refine the number of equilibria. Trembles or mistakes are allowed to occur where after a fund-raiser has decided how much time to spend with a donor, there is a positive probability that a mistake occurs and that his solicitation decisions are reallocated. If the network is such that there is a donor whom all fund-raisers are tied to, then at the unique stochastically stable state all fund-raisers will solicit this donor which coincides with the efficient Nash equilibrium.

Our paper contributes to several literatures. First, it contributes to the literature on the strategic analysis of fund-raising. Andreoni [5] offers an excellent literature review on this topic. This literature answers questions such as how fund-raisers react to government grants (see Andreoni and Payne [6]) as well as how competition among charities can result in too many or too few solicitations (see Mungan and Yörük [9] and Yörük [4]). Our paper adds to this literature by allowing fund-raisers to behave strategically while competing for donations on a network. Other fund-raising literatures analyze the strategic behavior of donors in a public good context. (For simplicity, we do not model the strategic behavior of donors explicitly but focus instead on competition between fund-raisers on a network. Similarly, in models of Cournot competition firms are modeled as strategic players and the strategic behavior of consumers is not modeled explicitly, but instead consumers are assumed to follow a demand function. In our model, donors follow a donation function based on the time fund-raisers spend soliciting donations which is similar in spirit to the assumption of Andreoni and Payne [6] that donors only donate if asked.) See Marx and Matthews [10], Bagnoli and Lipman [11], and Andreoni [5] for a literature review. Recent empirical studies show that fund-raising behavior is crucial to donations; see Yörük [3], Yörük [4], and Dellavigna et al. [8]. Additionally, Meer and Rosen [12] document the importance of personal solicitations in fund-raising, van Diepen et al. [13] document the effect of direct mailings on donations, and Andreoni and Rao [14] show experimentally the importance of asking for a donation.

Second, our paper contributes to the literature on economic and social networks; a literature review is given by Jackson [15], and Jackson and Wolinsky [16] is a founding paper of this literature. Specifically, our model adds to the literature on applications of social and economic networks. In our model, donations or money can only flow along social links. Previous papers have looked at the flow of information regarding coauthors or job prospects along links (see Jackson and Wolinsky [16] and Calvó-Armengol and Jackson [17]) as well as the flow of financial help along social links in developing countries (see Bramoullé and Kranton [18] and Fafchamps and Lund [19]) and the flow of bids or money in bipartite buyer-seller networks (see Kranton and Minehart [20, 21]); for further examples of network applications, see Jackson [15]. Additionally, we employ stochastic stability in a network context as does Jackson and Watts [22, 23].

Lastly, we assume donations are divided among fund-raisers in proportion to the time spent by the fund-raiser with the donor. Thus, our paper is related to the literature on productive rent-seeking games of Skaperdas [24] as well as to the literature on average surplus and average cost sharing games of Moulin [25], Moulin and Watts [26], and Watts [27]. (In fact, our model can be interpreted as a model where people have rights (or ties) to multiple common use resources. For instance, consider a group of fisherman where each fisherman has rights to fish on a subset of shared pools and must decide how much time to spend fishing on each pool given the decisions of the other fishermen.) The current paper differs from these previous papers in that the average surplus sharing or rent-seeking game is played on a network and each fund-raiser may solicit multiple donors.

The paper proceeds as follows. The basic model and monopoly fund-raiser results are presented in Sections 2 and 3. In Section 4, fund-raisers compete on the complete network. While the incomplete network results are presented in Section 5, and concluding remarks are presented in Section 6.

2. Basic Model

There are $N = \{1, 2, \dots, n\}$ potential donors. Let $M = \{1, 2, \dots, m\}$ represent the set of fund-raisers. Each $i \in M$ has total time $T = 1$ to spend asking for donations. Fund-raiser i can divide T among the set N where t^i_j is the time i spends with donor $j \in N$ to solicit his donation and $\sum_{j=1}^n t^i_j \le 1$. Let $t^i \equiv \{t^i_1, t^i_2, \dots, t^i_n\}$, $t_j \equiv \{t^1_j, t^2_j, \dots, t^m_j\}$, and $t \equiv \{t^1; t^2; \dots; t^m\}$. Let $t^{-i} \equiv \{t^1; t^2; \dots, t^{i-1}, t^{i+1}, \dots, t^m\}$ and $t^{-i}_j \equiv \{t^1_j, t^2_j, \dots t^{i-1}_j, t^{i+1}_j, \dots, t^m_j\}$.

The profit $i \in M$ receives equals his donations net fund-raising costs, where we assume a constant marginal cost of fund-raising equal to c. The donation i receives from $j \in N$ depends on the time all fund-raisers spend with j and is represented by $y(t^i_j, t^{-i}_j)$, while the profit i receives from j is represented by $\pi^i_j(t_j) = y(t^i_j, t^{-i}_j) - ct^i_j$. We assume $\partial y/\partial t^i_j > 0$ and $y(0, t^{-i}_j) = 0$. Additionally, we assume that if $\tilde{t}^{-i}_j$ is any permutation of t^{-i}_j, then $y(t^i_j; \tilde{t}^{-i}_j) = y(t^i_j; t^{-i}_j)$. Let the total profits that i receives be represented by $\pi^i(t) = \sum_{j=1}^n \pi^i_j(t_j)$. For brevity, we will often abbreviate $\pi^i_j(t_j)$ by π^i_j and $\pi^i(t)$ by π^i.

We assume that c is small enough so that in all of the following results each fund-raiser will select t^i such that $\sum_{j=1}^n t^i_j = 1$. Thus, for simplicity we will ignore fund-raising costs in what follows.

3. Monopoly Fund-Raiser

As a benchmark, we first consider the case where there is no competition for donors by fund-raisers, or where $m = 1$. We assume here that the monopoly fund-raiser has ties or links to all n donors and thus that the fund-raiser donor network is complete. (Of course, if the fund-raiser were tied to less than n donors, then the results below could easily be adjusted.)

The monopoly fund-raiser $i \in M$ wants to choose t^i to maximize his total expected profits $\pi^i = \sum_{j=1}^n y(t^i_j)$. In the first proposition, we assume donor fatigue is present or that the donation function, y, is concave.

Proposition 1. *Let $m = 1$ and assume $y'' < 0$. Then $i \in M$ maximizes total expected profits by setting $t^i_j = 1/n$ for all $j \in N$.*

Proof. As $y' > 0$, agent i will always choose to use all of his time or to set $\sum_{j=1}^n t^i_j = 1$. Agent i wants to maximize π^i or $\max_{t^i_1,\dots,t^i_n} \sum_{j=1}^n y(t^i_j)$ subject to $\sum_{j=1}^n t^i_j = 1$. First order conditions yield $y'(t^i_j) = y'(1 - t^i_1 - t^i_2 - \cdots - t^i_n)$ for all $j \in \{1, 2, \dots, n-1\}$. Given $y' > 0$ and $y'' < 0$, these first order conditions are only met if $t^i_1 = t^i_2 = \cdots t^i_n$ or if $t^i_j = 1/n$ for all $j \in N$. Since $y'' < 0$, the corresponding bordered Hessian has leading principal minors which alternate in sign. Thus, π^i is negative definite on $\sum_{j=1}^n t^i_j = 1$ and our solution is a maximum. □

In the second proposition, it is assumed that there is no donor fatigue or that the donation function is convex.

Proposition 2. *Let $m = 1$ and assume $y'' > 0$. Then $i \in M$ maximizes total expected profits by setting $t^i_j = 1$ for some $j \in N$ and $t^i_k = 0$ for all $k \neq j$, $k \in N$.*

Proof. Agent i wants to maximize π^i or to $\max_{t^i_1,\dots,t^i_n} \sum_{j=1}^n y(t^i_j)$ such that $\sum_{j=1}^n t^i_j \le 1$. It is easy to check that given $y' > 0$ and

$y'' > 0$, the solution to the maximization problem is a corner solution where $t_j^i = 1$ for some $j \in N$. □

4. Fund-Raisers Competing on the Complete Network

Next we consider the case where the number of fund-raisers $m > 1$. In this section, we assume that each fund-raiser has access to every donor. If we consider a fund-raiser's access to a donor as a link between a fund-raiser and a donor, then every fund-raiser is linked to every donor and the fund-raiser donor network is complete. The case of an incomplete network is considered in Section 5.

4.1. Average Donation Sharing Model on the Complete Network. Fund-raisers compete against each other in an average donation sharing game for each agent $j \in N$'s donation. Fund-raisers simultaneously choose time spent with donors and if multiple fund-raisers solicit the same donor, then the donation is split among fund-raisers in proportion to the time spent with the donor. Formally, the donation $i \in M$ expects from $j \in N$ equals

$$\pi_j^i = y\left(t_j^i; t_j^{-i}\right) = \frac{t_j^i}{\sum_{k=1}^m t_j^k} f\left(\sum_{k=1}^m t_j^k\right) \quad (1)$$

for some function f such that $f(0) = 0$ and $f' > 0$. Here, $f(\sum_{k=1}^m t_j^k)$ represents the total donations that donor j will make given the total time all fund-raisers spend soliciting j's donation. For simplicity, we assume this function is the same for all donors. Additionally, note that we use the convention that if $t_j^i = 0$ for all $i \in M$, then $\pi_j^i = 0$.

We show next that allowing multiple fund-raisers to compete on the complete network generates results similar to those found in the monopoly fund-raiser case.

4.2. Average Donation Sharing Results on the Complete Network

Proposition 3. *Let $m > 1$, $f'' < 0$, and assume fund-raisers compete in an average donation sharing game. At the symmetric Nash equilibrium of the average donation sharing game, $t_j^i = 1/n$ for all $j \in N$ and $i \in M$.*

Proof. We find $i \in M$'s best response to $t_j^k = 1/n$ for all $k \neq i$, $k \in M$, and $j \in N$. Since $\pi_j^i = (t_j^i / \sum_{k=1}^m t_j^k) f(\sum_{k=1}^m t_j^k)$ we know that $\pi^i = \sum_{j=1}^n ((t_j^i / \sum_{k=1}^m t_j^k) f(\sum_{k=1}^m t_j^k))$. Thus i's maximization problem is

$$\max_{t_1^i, t_2^i, \ldots, t_n^i} \quad \pi^i \qquad \text{such that} \quad \sum_{j=1}^n t_j^i = 1 \quad (2)$$

with Lagrangian $\mathscr{L}^i = \pi^i - \lambda(\sum_{j=1}^n t_j^i - 1)$ and first order conditions

$$\begin{aligned} \frac{\partial \mathscr{L}^i}{\partial t_j^i} = & \left(\frac{\sum_{k\neq i} t_j^k}{\left(t_j^i + \sum_{k\neq i} t_j^k\right)^2}\right) f\left(t_j^i + \sum_{k\neq i} t_j^k\right) \\ & + \left(\frac{t_j^i}{\left(t_j^i + \sum_{k\neq i} t_j^k\right)}\right) f'\left(t_j^i + \sum_{k\neq i} t_j^k\right) \\ & - \lambda = 0 \quad \forall j \in N, \\ \frac{\partial \mathscr{L}^i}{\partial \lambda} = & -\sum_{j=1}^n t_j^i + 1 = 0. \end{aligned} \quad (3)$$

If $t_j^k = 1/n$ for all $k \neq i$, $k \in M$, and $j \in N$, then $\sum_{k\neq i} t_j^k = (m-1)/n$ for all $j \in N$ and the solution to the above first order conditions is $t_j^i = 1/n$ for all $j \in N$. To check the second order conditions, let $O_j^i((m-1)/n) = p(t_j^i/(t_j^i + (m-1)/n)) f(t_j^i + (m-1)/n)$ represent i's opportunity set for donations from j given $t_j^k = 1/n$ for all $k \neq i$, $k \in M$. Thus, $\pi^i(t^i, (m-1)/n) = \sum_{j=1}^n O_j^i((m-1)/n)$. It is easy to check that $\partial O_j^i / \partial t_j^i > 0$ and $\partial^2 O_j^i / \partial (t_j^i)^2 < 0$ for all $0 < t_j^i \leq 1$. Thus, $\pi^i(t^i, (m-1)/n)$ is negative definite on $\sum_{j=1}^n t_j^i = 1$. So $t_j^i = 1/n$ for all $j \in N$ is i's best response to $t_j^k = 1/n$ for all $k \neq i$, $k \in M$, and $j \in N$, and our solution is a Nash equilibrium. □

Note that we focus on only the symmetric Nash equilibrium in this proposition and in the first part of Section 5 where the donation function is concave. The reason is threefold. First, we want to compare the Nash equilibria of the game played on the complete network to the game played on the incomplete network. Concentrating on the symmetric Nash in each situation facilitates this comparison. Second, focusing on the symmetric Nash simplifies our calculations. The first order conditions of our maximization problem are quite complex making it extremely difficult to compute other possible equilibria. Lastly, we hypothesize that in many cases the symmetric Nash is the unique Nash, although proving this is quite difficult and is beyond the scope of the current paper.

Proposition 4. *Let $m > 1$, $f'' > 0$, and assume fund-raisers compete in an average donation sharing game. At all Nash equilibria there exists $k \in N$ such that $t_k^i = 1$ for all $i \in M$.*

Proof. Assume that there exists $k \in N$ such that $t_k^\ell = 1$ for all $\ell \neq i$, $\ell \in M$. We find $i \in M$'s best response. Here, $\pi^i = \sum_{j\in N, j\neq k} (t_j^i/(t_j^i)) f(t_j^i) + (t_k^i/(t_k^i + (m-1))) f(t_k^i + (m-1))$ with $\sum_{j=1}^n t_j^i = 1$. Since $f' > 0$ and $f'' > 0$, i does best by choosing $t_k^i = 1$ and $t_j^i = 0$ for all $j \in N$, $j \neq k$. Next we show that all Nash equilibria are of this type. Consider i's best response to a fixed t^{-i}. Here i's best response is to set $t_k^i = 1$ for some k such that $k \in \arg\max_j \sum_{\ell \in M, \ell \neq i} t_j^\ell$. Given that this is true for all $i \in M$, all Nash equilibria must be as described. □

5. Competition on an Incomplete Network

Let g represent a network of connections between fund-raisers and donors. If $i \in M$ and $j \in N$, then $ij \in g$ if i and j are linked. Note that for all links, ij, we will use the convention that the fund-raiser is always listed first.

Let $B(j,g) = \{i \mid ij \in g, i \in M\}$; thus, $B(j,g)$ represents the set of fund-raisers that $j \in N$ is directly linked with in graph g. Let $|S|$ represent the cardinality of set $S \subset \mathbb{Z}$. Let $A_z(i,g) = \{j \mid ij \in g, j \in N \text{ and } |B(j,g)| = z\}$; thus, $A_z(i,g)$ represents the set of donors that i is linked to in g such that each donor in the set has exactly z direct links.

Let fund-raisers compete in an average donation sharing game and assume g is fixed. Here

$$\pi^i = \sum_{j\in A_1(i,g)} f\left(t_j^i\right) + \sum_{j\in A_2(i,g)} \frac{t_j^i}{t_j^i + t_j^{k(j)}} f\left(t_j^i + t_j^{k(j)}\right) + \cdots + \sum_{j\in A_m(i,g)} \frac{t_j^i}{\sum_{\ell=1}^m t_j^\ell} f\left(\sum_{\ell=1}^m t_j^\ell\right), \quad (4)$$

where $k(j) \in M$ such that $kj \in g$.

5.1. Competition on an Incomplete Network with Donor Fatigue. In this section, donor fatigue is present or the donation function is assumed to be concave. Thus, every unit of time a fund-raiser spends with a donor increases his total donation less than does the previous unit of time.

The following example illustrates how the results for the incomplete network are quite different from those found for the complete network. The example shows that time spent soliciting donations depends on both the network configuration and on the degree of donor fatigue or on the curvature of $f(t)$.

Example 5 (Illustrating the effects of severe versus mild donor fatigue). Let $M = \{1,2\}$ and $N = \{1,2,3\}$. Let $f(t) = t^{1/2}$. Let $g_1 = \{11,12,21,22\}$ and $g_2 = \{11,12,22,23\}$. Notice that in network g_1 each fund-raiser is tied to the same two donors. In network g_2 each fund-raiser again has two ties, but this time only one donor is common to both fund-raisers while each fund-raiser also has one tie to a donor that the other has no ties to. By Proposition 3, the symmetric Nash equilibrium of the average donation sharing game with network g_1 is $t_j^i = 1/2$ for all $i \in M$, $j \in N$. Next, we consider the symmetric Nash equilibrium of the average donation sharing game with network g_2. Here $\pi^1 = (t_1^1)^{1/2} + (t_2^1/(t_2^1 + t_2^2))(t_2^1 + t_2^2)^{1/2}$ and π^2 is similar. First order conditions for fund-raiser 1 yield $(1/2)(t_1^1)^{-1/2} = (t_2^2/(t_2^1+t_2^2)^2)(t_2^1+t_2^2)^{1/2} + ((1/2)t_2^1/(t_2^1+t_2^2))(t_2^1+t_2^2)^{-1/2}$ and $t_1^1 + t_2^1 = 1$, with fund-raiser 2 having similar first order conditions. At the symmetric Nash equilibrium $t_1^1 = t_3^2 = .47$ and $t_2^1 = t_2^2 = .53$. Thus, if donor fatigue is severe or if the donation function is fairly curved, then fund-raisers spend more time with the shared donor than they do in network g_1 and less time with the unshared donor. However, if we decrease the level of donor fatigue or change $f(t)$ so that $f(t) = t^{.7}$, then at the symmetric Nash of the game with g_2, $t_1^1 = t_3^2 = .502$ and $t_2^1 = t_2^2 = .498$. Now fund-raisers spend less time with the shared donor and more time with the unshared donor.

Next, we generalize the mild versus severe donor fatigue results of these examples. Consider the general case of any concave donation function, f, and compare two symmetric networks: one where all fund-raisers are linked to the same set of donors, and one where each fund-raiser has the same number of un-shared ties and has the same set of shared ties.

Specifically, let $M = \{1,2\}$ and $N = \{1,2,\ldots,2a+b\}$ for $a, b \in \mathbb{Z}$, $a \ge 1$ and $b \ge 1$. Let $g^{(a+b)} = \{11,12,\ldots,1(a+b),21,22,\ldots,2(a+b)\}$. Here each donor has $(a+b)$ shared links. Let $g^{a,b} = \{11,12,\ldots,1(a+b),2(a+1),2(a+2),\ldots,2(2a+b)\}$. Here each donor has a un-shared ties and b shared ties.

Proposition 6. *Let $m = 2$ and $n = 2a+b$. At the symmetric Nash equilibrium of the average donation sharing game with $g^{(a+b)}$, $t_j^i = 1/(a+b)$ for all $j \in N$, $i \in M$. At the symmetric Nash equilibrium of the average donation sharing game with $g^{a,b}$,*

(1) *if $f'(t) < f(2t)/4t + f'(2t)/2$ for all $0 \le t \le m$, then*

(a) *$t_j^i < 1/(a+b)$ for all $i \in M$ and $j \in \{1,2,\ldots,a,a+b+1,a+b+2,\ldots,2a+b\}$ and*

(b) *$t_j^i > 1/(a+b)$ for all $i \in M$ and $j \in \{a+1,a+2,\ldots,a+b\}$, and*

(2) *if $f'(t) > f(2t)/4t + f'(2t)/2$ for all $0 \le t \le m$, then*

(a) *$t_j^i > 1/(a+b)$ for all $i \in M$ and $j \in \{1,2,\ldots,a,a+b+1,a+b+2,\ldots,2a+b\}$ and*

(b) *$t_j^i < 1/(a+b)$ for all $i \in M$ and $j \in \{a+1,a+2,\ldots,a+b\}$.*

Proof. The statement regarding the symmetric Nash equilibrium for the game with $g^{(a+b)}$ is proven true by Proposition 3. Next we find the symmetric Nash equilibrium for the average donation sharing game with $g^{a,b}$. Here $\pi^1 = \sum_{j=1}^a f(t_j^1) + \sum_{k=a+1}^{a+b} (t_k^1/(t_k^1+t_k^2)) f(t_k^1+t_k^2)$ while π^2 is similar. The first order conditions for the Nash equilibrium require that $f'(t_j^1) = (t_k^2/(t_k^1+t_k^2)^2) f(t_k^1+t_k^2) + (t_k^1/(t_k^1+t_k^2)) f'(t_k^1+t_k^2)$ for all $j \in \{1,2,\ldots,a\}$ and $k \in \{a+1,a+2,\ldots,a+b\}$. At the symmetric Nash equilibrium, $t_1 \equiv t_j^1 = t_\ell^2$ for all $j \in \{1,2,\ldots,a\}$ and $\ell \in \{a+b+1,a+b+2,\ldots,2a+b\}$ and $t_{a+1} \equiv t_k^1 = t_k^2$ for all $k \in \{a+1,a+2,\ldots,a+b\}$. In addition we know that $\sum_{j=1}^{a+b} t_j^1 = 1$. Thus, we can rewrite the first order conditions as

$$f'(t_1) = \frac{t_{a+1}}{(2t_{a+1})^2} f(2t_{a+1}) + \frac{t_{a+1}}{2t_{a+1}} f'(2t_{a+1}) \quad \text{where } at_1 + bt_{a+1} = 1. \quad (5)$$

If to the contrary we let $t_1 = t_{a+1} = 1/(a+b)$, then the first order conditions simplify to $f'(1/(a+b)) = (1/2)(f(2/(a+b))/(2/(a+b))) + (1/2)f'(2/(a+b))$. If $f'(t) < f(2t)/4t + f'(2t)/2$ for all $0 \le t \le m$, then our first order condition will not be met. Fund-raiser 1 must increase the left hand side of (5) and decrease the right hand side. Since $f' > 0$ and $f'' < 0$, we know that t_1 must be decreased and thus t_{a+b} increased. Thus, at the Nash equilibrium $t_1 < 1/(a+b)$ and $t_{a+1} > 1/(a+b)$. If instead $f'(t) > f(2t)/4t + f'(2t)/2$ for all $0 \le t \le m$, then in order to meet (5) we must increase t_1 and so at the Nash $t_1 > 1/(a+b)$ and $t_{a+1} < 1/(a+b)$. □

Notice that our condition $f'(t) < f(2t)/4t + f'(2t)/2$ and our assumptions $f' > 0$, $f'' < 0$, and $f(0) = 0$ together imply that $f(t)/t$ is significantly larger than $f'(t)$ which is true when f is fairly curved. For the function $f(t) = t^\alpha$, the condition $f'(t) < f(2t)/4t + f'(2t)/2$ is met when $0 < \alpha \le .63$, while the condition $f'(t) > f(2t)/4t + f'(2t)/2$ is met when $f(t) = t^\alpha$ for $.64 \le \alpha < 1$.

Proposition 6 says that if donor fatigue is severe or if the donation function, $f(t)$, is fairly curved, then fund-raisers spend more time with shared ties and less time with un-shared ties. While if donor fatigue is mild or if the donation function is straighter, then fund-raisers spend more time with un-shared donors and less time with shared donors. Intuitively, if donor fatigue is severe, then when a fund-raiser spends more time with a donor, the donor's total donation does not increase much. Thus, the benefit from increasing time spent with an un-shared donor tie is not very large. However, if a fund-raiser spends more time with a shared donor tie, then although this donor's total donation may not increase much the fund-raiser's share of this donation does increase. Thus, it is worthwhile for the fund-raiser to increase time spent with shared ties in order to steal donations from other fund-raisers. If donor fatigue is mild, then as the fund-raiser increases the time spent with a donor, his total donation increases more than in the severe donor fatigue case making it worthwhile for the fund-raiser to spend extra time with un-shared donors.

Next we consider an example with extreme donor fatigue and compare three networks; in all three networks each fund-raiser is tied to $z \in \mathbb{Z}^+$ donors. In the first network, g^z, all fund-raisers are linked to the same set of donors. In network $g^{z-1,1}$, each fund-raiser has only one shared tie and $(z-1)$ un-shared ties. In $g^{1,z-1}$, each fund-raiser has only one un-shared tie and $(z-1)$ shared ties.

Example 7 (Severe donor fatigue and the number of shared ties). Let $M = \{1, 2\}$ and $N = \{1, 2, 3, \ldots, 2z-1\}$ for $z \ge 2$ and $z \in \mathbb{Z}$. Let $f(t) = t^{1/2}$. Let $g^z = \{11, 12, \ldots, 1z, 21, 22, \ldots, 2z\}$, $g^{z-1,1} = \{11, 12, \ldots, 1z, 2z, 2(z+1), \ldots, 2(2z-1)\}$, and $g^{1,z-1} = \{11, 12, \ldots, 1z, 22, 23, \ldots, 2(z+1)\}$. By Proposition 3, the symmetric Nash equilibrium of the average donation sharing game with network g^z is $t_j^i = 1/z$ for all $i \in M$, $j \in N$. For $g^{z-1,1}$ at the symmetric Nash $t_k^1 = t_j^2 = 1/(z + .125)$ for $k \in \{1, \ldots, z-1\}$, $j \in \{z+1, \ldots, 2z-1\}$ and $t_z^1 = t_z^2 = 1.125/(z + .125)$. While at the symmetric Nash for $g^{1,z-1}$, $t_1^1 = t_{z+1}^2 = 1/(1.125z - .125)$ and $t_k^1 = t_j^2 = 1.125/(1.125z - .125)$ for $k, j \in \{2, \ldots, z\}$. Again if donor fatigue is severe, then the fund-raisers spend more time with the shared donors and less time with the un-shared donors. Notice that fund-raisers spend more time per link with both un-shared and shared links in the network with fewer shared ties ($g^{z-1,1}$) than in $g^{1,z-1}$, but the ratio of time spent with un-shared to shared links (t_1^1/t_z^1) is the same for these two networks. Thus, as the number of shared ties increases, a fund-raiser's time per donor decreases since a fund-raiser with severe donor fatigue now has more of the time-consuming shared ties.

Next we generalize the results of Proposition 6 to the case of $m \ge 2$ fund-raisers. Let there be m fund-raisers and n donors. Let g^{sym} be a symmetric network such that each fund-raiser has a_1 ties to donors shared with no one, a_2 ties to donors shared with one other fund-raiser, a_3 ties to donors shared with two other fund-raisers,. . ., and a_m ties to donors shared with all other fund-raisers, where $a_k \in \mathbb{Z}_+$ for all $k \in \{1, 2, \ldots, m\}$. Let g^C, be a complete network where each fund-raiser is tied to each $j \in \{1, 2, \ldots, \sum_{i=1}^m a_i\}$ and $j \in N$. Note that in network g^C each fund-raiser has the same number of links as he does in g^{sym}.

At the symmetric Nash equilibrium of the average donation sharing game with any g^{sym} we define t_{α_k} as the time $i \in M$ spends with each of his a_k ties.

Proposition 8. *If* $((k-1)/k)(f(kt)/kt) + (1/k)f'(kt) > (k/(k+1))(f((k+1)t)/(k+1)t) + (1/(k+1))f'((k+1)t)$ *for all* $0 \le t \le 1$ *and* $k \in \{1, 2, \ldots, m-1\}$, *then at the symmetric Nash equilibrium of the average donation sharing game with any* g^{sym}, $t_{\alpha_k} > t_{\alpha_{k+1}}$. *At the symmetric Nash equilibrium of the game with* g^C, $t_j^i = 1/\sum_{\ell=1}^m a_\ell$ *for all* $i \in M$, $j \in N$.

Thus, Proposition 8 says that if donor fatigue is mild, then fund-raisers spend the most time soliciting donors that they are the only fund-raiser tied to and the least time soliciting donors that all fund-raisers are tied to.

Essentially the condition $((k-1)/k)(f(kt)/kt) + (1/k)f'(kt) > (k/(k+1))(f((k+1)t)/(k+1)t) + (1/(k+1))f'((k+1)t)$ requires that $f((k+1)t)/(k+1)t$ is not too big or that the average of f is not too much bigger than the slope of f. If $f(t) = t^\beta$, then the condition $((k-1)/k)(f(kt)/kt) + (1/k)f'(kt) > (k/(k+1))(f((k+1)t)/(k+1)t) + (1/(k+1))f'((k+1)t)$ is equivalent to requiring $((k-1+\beta)/(k+\beta)) > ((k+1)/k)^{\beta-2}$ and is true for all $.64 \le \beta < 1$ but does not hold true for $0 < \beta \le .63$.

Proof. The results regarding the complete network g^C are proved true by Proposition 3. Consider any fixed network g^{sym}. Let $A_j \subseteq N$ represent the set of donors each having j ties in g^{sym}, $j \in \{1, 2, \ldots, m\}$. Thus, $A_j = \cup_{i=1}^m A_j(i, g^{\text{sym}})$. Let $\alpha_j \in A_j$ represent an element of this set. Profits for fund-raiser 1 are represented as

$$\pi^1 = \sum_{\alpha_1 \in A_1; 1\alpha_1 \in g^{\text{sym}}} f\left(t_{\alpha_1}^1\right) + \sum_{\alpha_2 \in A_2; 1\alpha_2 \in g^{\text{sym}}, \ell\alpha_2 \in g^{\text{sym}}} \frac{t_{\alpha_2}^1}{t_{\alpha_2}^1 + t_{\alpha_2}^\ell} f\left(t_{\alpha_2}^1 + t_{\alpha_2}^\ell\right) + \cdots + \sum_{\alpha_m \in A_m; 1\alpha_m \in g^{\text{sym}}} \frac{t_{\alpha_m}^1}{\sum_{i=1}^m t_{\alpha_m}^i} f\left(\sum_{i=1}^m t_{\alpha_m}^i\right) \quad (6)$$

with $\ell \in M$ and $\ell \neq 1$. First order conditions require

$$f'\left(t_{\alpha_1}^1\right) = \frac{t_{\alpha_2}^{\ell}}{\left(t_{\alpha_2}^1 + t_{\alpha_2}^{\ell}\right)^2} f\left(t_{\alpha_2}^1 + t_{\alpha_2}^{\ell}\right) + \frac{t_{\alpha_2}^1}{t_{\alpha_2}^1 + t_{\alpha_2}^{\ell}} f'\left(t_{\alpha_2}^1 + t_{\alpha_2}^{\ell}\right) = \cdots$$
$$= \frac{t_{\alpha_m}^2 + t_{\alpha_m}^3 + \cdots + t_{\alpha_m}^m}{\left(t_{\alpha_n}^1 + t_{\alpha_n}^2 + \cdots + t_{\alpha_n}^n\right)^2} f\left(t_{\alpha_m}^1 + t_{\alpha_m}^2 + \cdots + t_{\alpha_m}^m\right) + \frac{t_{\alpha_m}^1}{t_{\alpha_m}^1 + t_{\alpha_m}^2 + \cdots + t_{\alpha_m}^m} f'\left(t_{\alpha_m}^1 + t_{\alpha_m}^2 + \cdots + t_{\alpha_m}^m\right) \quad (7)$$

and $\sum_{j=1}^m a_j t_{\alpha_j}^1 = 1$, where $\alpha_i \in A_i$, $1\alpha_i \in g^{\text{sym}}$, $\ell\alpha_i \in g^{\text{sym}}$ for $i \in \{1, 2, \ldots, m\}$, $\ell \neq 1$, $\ell \in M$. The first order conditions for $i \neq 1$, $i \in M$ are similar.

At the symmetric Nash equilibrium $t_{\alpha_j} \equiv t_{\alpha_j}^i = t_{\alpha_j}^{\ell}$ for all $i \neq \ell$, $i, \ell \in M, \alpha_j \in A_j$, $i\alpha_j \in g^{\text{sym}}$, $\ell\alpha_j \in g^{\text{sym}}$ and $j \in \{1, 2, \ldots, m\}$. We can rewrite the first order conditions as

$$f'\left(t_{\alpha_1}\right) = \frac{1}{4t_{\alpha_2}} f\left(2t_{\alpha_2}\right) + \frac{1}{2} f'\left(2t_{\alpha_2}\right) = \frac{2}{9t_{\alpha_3}} f\left(3t_{\alpha_3}\right) + \frac{1}{3} f'\left(3t_{\alpha_3}\right) = \cdots = \frac{(m-1)}{m^2 t_{\alpha_m}} f\left(mt_{\alpha_m}\right) + \frac{1}{m} f'\left(mt_{\alpha_m}\right), \quad (8)$$

where $\sum_{j=1}^m a_j t_{\alpha_j} = 1$.

Assume to the contrary that $t_{\alpha_k} = 1/\sum_{j=1}^m a_j \equiv \bar{t}$ for all $k \in \{1, 2, \ldots, m\}$. Then, by assumption

$$f'(\bar{t}) > \frac{1}{2}\frac{f(2\bar{t})}{2\bar{t}} + \frac{1}{2} f'(2\bar{t}) > \frac{2}{3}\frac{f(3\bar{t})}{3\bar{t}} + \frac{1}{3} f'(3\bar{t}) > \cdots > \frac{(m-1)}{m}\frac{f(m\bar{t})}{m\bar{t}} + \frac{1}{m} f'(m\bar{t}) \quad (9)$$

and the first order conditions are not met. In order to meet the first order conditions, we must decrease $f'(t_{\alpha_1})$ in comparison to $(1/4t_{\alpha_2})f(2t_{\alpha_2}) + (1/2)f'(2t_{\alpha_2})$ and decrease $(1/4t_{\alpha_2})f(2t_{\alpha_2}) + (1/2)f'(2t_{\alpha_2})$ in comparison to $(2/9t_{\alpha_3})f(3t_{\alpha_3}) + (1/3)f'(3t_{\alpha_3})$, and so forth. Since $f' > 0$, $f'' < 0$, we know that t_{α_i} must be increased in comparison to $t_{\alpha_{i+1}}$ for all $i \in \{1, 2, \ldots, m-1\}$. Thus, in equilibrium $t_{\alpha_1} > t_{\alpha_2} > \cdots > t_{\alpha_m}$. □

Proposition 9. *If $f'(t) < ((k-1)/k)(f(kt)/kt) + (1/k)f'(kt)$ for $k \in \{2, 3, \ldots, m\}$, then at the symmetric Nash equilibrium of the average donation sharing game with any g^{sym}, $t_{\alpha_k} > t_{\alpha_1}$.*

Corollary 10. *If $f'(t) < (1/2)(f(2t)/2t) + (1/2)f'(2t)$, then at the symmetric Nash equilibrium of the average donation sharing game with any g^{sym}, $t_{\alpha_2} < t_{\alpha_1}$.*

Proof. The following is a proof of Corollary 10 as the proof of Proposition 9 is similar. Profits for fund-raiser 1 are as given by (6) and first order conditions are as given by (7). Thus, in equilibrium we must have $f'(t_{\alpha_1}^1) = (t_{\alpha_2}^j/(t_{\alpha_2}^1 + t_{\alpha_2}^j)^2)f(t_{\alpha_2}^1 + t_{\alpha_2}^j) + (t_{\alpha_2}^1/(t_{\alpha_2}^1 + t_{\alpha_2}^j))f'(t_{\alpha_2}^1 + t_{\alpha_2}^j)$ for $\alpha_1 \in A_1$, $\alpha_2 \in A_2$, $1\alpha_1 \in g^{\text{sym}}$, $j\alpha_2 \in g^{\text{sym}}$, $j \neq 1$, and $j \in M$. Assume to the contrary that $t_{\alpha_1} = t_{\alpha_2} = \bar{t}$. Then, by assumption $f'(\bar{t}) < (1/2)(f(2\bar{t})/2\bar{t}) + (1/2)f'(2\bar{t})$. In order to meet our first order conditions, we must increase the left hand side of this inequality and decrease the right hand side. Since $f' > 0$ and $f'' < 0$, this requires that we decrease t_{α_1} and increase t_{α_2} and so in equilibrium $t_{\alpha_1} < t_{\alpha_2}$. □

Proposition 9 says that if donor fatigue is severe, then fund-raisers spend more time soliciting donors that at least one other fund-raiser is also tied to over donors that they are the only fund-raiser tied to. We additionally provide Corollary 10 as it is fairly easy to meet the conditions of Proposition 9 for $k = 2$, but as k increases the conditions are only met as donor fatigue becomes more severe. For instance if $f(t) = t^{\beta}$ and $k = 2$, then the conditions of Proposition 9 are met for $0 < \beta \leq .63$. For $k = 3$, the conditions are met if $0 < \beta \leq .43$ and if $k = 10$, the conditions are met if $0 < \beta \leq .12$. (We stop our calculations at $k = 10$ as k represents the number of fund-raisers who are tied to a particular donor and in a fund-raising network one would expect for this number not to be too large.) Thus, if donor fatigue is severe enough, then t_{α_1} is the smallest t_{α_k} for $k \in \{1, 2, \ldots, m\}$. As the following example illustrates if donor fatigue is not as severe it is possible for $t_{\alpha_1} < t_{\alpha_2}$ but $t_{\alpha_1} > t_{\alpha_3}$.

Example 11 (Donor fatigue and the relationship between t_{α_1}, t_{α_2}, and t_{α_3}). Let $M = \{1, 2, 3\}$ and $N = \{1, 2, 3, 4, 5, 6, 7\}$. Let $g_1 = \{11, 12, 13, 14, 21, 22, 23, 24, 31, 32, 33, 34\}$ and let $g_2 = \{11, 12, 13, 14, 22, 24, 25, 26, 33, 34, 35, 37\}$. A graph of g_2 is provided in Figure 1. In network g_2 each fund-raiser has one tie to an un-shared donor, two ties to donors shared with one other fund-raiser, and one tie to donor 4, while in network g_1 all fund-raisers are tied to the same set of four donors. By Proposition 3, the symmetric Nash equilibrium of the average donation sharing game with network g_1 is $t_j^i = 1/4$ for all $i \in M$, $j \in N$. Next we consider the symmetric Nash equilibrium of the game with network g_2. Here $\pi^1 = f(t_1^1) + \sum_{j \in \{2,3\}}(t_j^j/(t_j^1 + t_j^j))f(t_j^1 + t_j^j) + (t_4^1/(t_4^1 + t_4^2 + t_4^3))f(t_4^1 + t_4^2 + t_4^3)$ and π^2 and π^3 are similar. First we consider a case of extreme donor fatigue. Let $f(t) = t^{.5}$; then at the symmetric Nash equilibrium $t_1^1 = t_6^2 = t_7^3 = .24$, $t_j^i = .27$, and $t_4^i = .22$ for $i \in M$, $j \in \{2, 3, 5\}$. Thus, $t_{\alpha_2} > t_{\alpha_1} > t_{\alpha_3}$ or the tie to donor 4 who is tied to all fund-raisers is weighted least while the ties to donors shared among two fund-raisers are weighted most. Next we allow the extreme donor fatigue to be more severe. Let $f(t) = t^{.1}$, then at the symmetric Nash equilibrium $t_1^1 = t_6^2 = t_7^3 = .09$, $t_j^i = .32$, and $t_4^i = .27$ for $i \in M$, $j \in \{2, 3, 5\}$. Here $t_{\alpha_2} > t_{\alpha_3} > t_{\alpha_1}$ and the tie to the donor shared with no one is weighted least while the ties to donors shared among two fund-raisers are weighted most. Finally, we

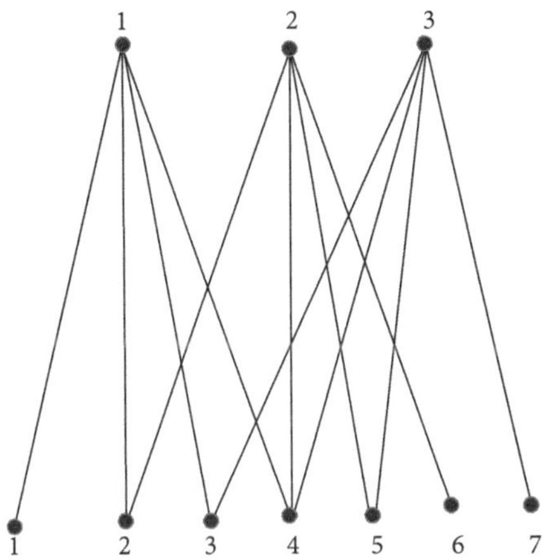

FIGURE 1: Fund-raisers $\{1, 2, 3\}$ are on top and donors $\{1, 2, 3, 4, 5, 6, 7\}$ are on bottom.

consider a case of mild donor fatigue. Let $f(t) = t^{.9}$, then at the symmetric Nash equilibrium $t_1^1 = t_6^2 = t_7^3 = .29$, $t_j^i = .25$, and $t_4^i = .20$ for $i \in M$, $j \in \{2, 3, 5\}$. Just as predicted in Proposition 8, $t_{\alpha_1} > t_{\alpha_2} > t_{\alpha_3}$ and the tie to donor 4 who is tied to all fund-raisers is weighted least while the tie to the donor shared with no one is weighted most.

5.2. Competition on an Incomplete Network with No Donor Fatigue. Next we consider a case of no donor fatigue where the donation function is convex or where all of the time spent with a donor significantly increases donations. Here agents want to spend time with donors that others are soliciting. However, the network may not allow all fund-raisers to solicit a popular donor; this can create multiple equilibria where several donors are solicited at the same time as can be seen in the following example.

Example 12 (Multiple equilibria with no donor fatigue). Let $M = \{1, 2, 3\}$ and $N = \{1, 2, 3, 4, 5, 6, 7\}$. Let $f' > 0$ and $f'' > 0$. Let $g = \{11, 12, 13, 14, 22, 24, 25, 26, 33, 34, 35, 37\}$. A graph of g is provided in Figure 1. Each fund-raiser has one tie to a donor untied to other fund-raisers, two ties to donors shared with one other fund-raiser, and one tie to a donor (donor 4) shared with all fund-raisers. As $f' > 0$ and $f'' > 0$, each fund-raiser wants to solicit only one donor and prefers to solicit a donor who is already being solicited by others. In this example, there are 14 pure Nash equilibrium: (1) $t_1^1 = t_6^2 = t_7^3 = 1$, all other $t_j^i = 0$; (2) $t_4^1 = t_4^2 = t_4^3 = 1$, all other $t_j^i = 0$; (3) $t_2^1 = t_2^2 = t_3^3 = 1$, all other $t_j^1 = 0$; (4) $t_2^1 = t_2^2 = t_4^3 = 1$, all other $t_j^1 = 0$; (5) $t_2^1 = t_2^2 = t_7^3 = 1$, all other $t_j^1 = 0$. There are 9 other Nash equilibria similar to those described in (3), (4), and (5) above where two fund-raisers put all their weight on a shared tie and the third fund-raiser is left to put all his weight on a donor shared with no other fund-raisers. There are also several mixed Nash. For instance there is a mixed Nash where $t_2^1 = t_2^2 = t_7^3 = 1$ each with probability 1/2 and $t_3^1 = t_6^2 = t_5^3 = 1$ each with probability 1/2 and all other $t_j^1 = 0$. There are also a number of mixed Nash similar to the following one where $t_2^1 = t_2^2 = 1$ and fund-raiser 3 plays $t_3^3 = 1, t_4^3 = 1, t_7^3 = 1$ all with positive probability. Note that pure Nash (2) above where all fund-raisers solicit donor 4 generates the highest payoff for the fund-raisers. However, at all of the other Nash equilibria, donor 4 is either unsolicited or solicited by only one fund-raiser.

As the above example shows the number of Nash equilibria can be quite large for the case where $f'' > 0$. Next, we try to refine the number of Nash equilibria using stochastic stability.

Dynamics. Let time be discrete and represented as $\{0, 1, 2, \ldots, \tau, \ldots\}$. Let $t(\tau - 1)$ be a vector representing the time $t(\tau - 1) \equiv \{t^1(\tau - 1), t^2(\tau - 1), \ldots, t^m(\tau - 1)\}$ the fund-raisers spend soliciting donations in period $(\tau - 1)$. At each period τ, one fund-raiser i is chosen at random to update his strategy, t^i. Fund-raiser i will choose a myopic best response to $t^{-i}(\tau - 1)$. After this choice is made, there is a small probability $1 > \varepsilon > 0$ that another strategy is chosen instead. Thus, with probability ε there is a mistake and the strategy $t^i(\tau)$ is chosen at random with each possible t^i receiving positive probability.

Stochastic Stability. This process determines a finite state, irreducible, aperiodic Markov chain and has a unique invariant probability distribution μ^ε over strategy configurations. A strategy t is *stochastically stable* if it is in the support of $\mu = \lim_{\varepsilon \to 0} \mu^\varepsilon$. (See Freidlin and Wentzell [28] or Young [29] for further discussion of stochastic stability.)

Let g^1 represent a network such that there is exactly one donor, say donor 1, that all fund-raisers are tied to; all other donors have strictly less than m ties.

Proposition 13. *Assume $f' > 0$ and $f'' > 0$. At the unique stochastically stable equilibrium of the average donation sharing game with any g^1, $t_1^i = 1$ for all $i \in M$, $m \geq 2$.*

Proof. First we show that setting $t_1^i = 1$ for all $i \in M$ is a Nash equilibrium. Given all $k \neq i$, $k \in M$ set $t_1^k = 1$, we show that i's best response is to set $t_1^i = 1$. Assume to the contrary that $t_1^i = a$ such that $0 \leq a < 1$ and that $t_j^i = 1 - a$ for some $j \in N$. Then $\pi^i = f(1-a) + (a/(n-1+a)) f(n-1+a)$. Since $f' > 0$ and $f'' > 0$, $f(1-a) + (a/(n-1+a)) f(n-1+a) < (1/n) f(n)$, which is i's payoff if $t_1^i = 1$. Similarly, for any other $t^i \neq (1, 0, \ldots, 0)$, i's payoff will be smaller than $(1/n) f(n)$. Thus, i sets $t_1^i = 1$ and our proposed strategy is a Nash equilibrium. (Note that at all Nash equilibrium each fund-raiser i sets $t_j^i = 1$ for some $j \in N$ since i's payoff, $(t/(t + a)) f(t + a)$, from soliciting a donor who others are soliciting with total time $a \geq 0$, is increasing in both t and a; thus i would like to spend all his time soliciting the donor with the largest such a.)

Let t^* represent the equilibrium where $t_1^i = 1$ for all $i \in M$. If t^* is the unique Nash equilibrium of the game, then it is trivially stochastically stable. Next, we assume that there is at least one other Nash equilibrium say $\tilde{t} = (\tilde{t}^1, \tilde{t}^2, \ldots, \tilde{t}^m)$. Let $m \geq 3$, we will consider the case of $m = 2$ below. To leave state t^* and move to state $\tilde{t}$ takes at least $\lceil m/2 \rceil$ trembles (where $\lceil a \rceil$, $a \in \mathbb{R}$, represents the integer $z \in \mathbb{Z}$ closest to a such that $z \geq a$). To see this note that if $\lceil m/2 - 1 \rceil$ trembles occur, then the largest payoff a trembling agent could have is if all trembling fund-raisers solicit the same new donor resulting in a payoff for each trembling agent of $(1/\lceil m/2 - 1 \rceil) f(\lceil m/2 - 1 \rceil)$; this is because $(1/t) f(t)$ is strictly increasing in t whenever $f' > 0$ and $f'' > 0$. If the trembling agent goes back to his t^* strategy his payoff would be $(1/(m+1-\lceil m/2-1 \rceil)) f(m+1- \lceil m/2-1 \rceil)$ which is larger than $(1/\lceil m/2-1 \rceil) f(\lceil m/2-1 \rceil)$. Thus, $\lceil m/2-1 \rceil$ trembles are not enough to leave state t^*.

However, to go from state $\tilde{t}$ to state t^* takes at most $\lceil m/2 - 1 \rceil$ trembles for $m \geq 3$. To see this notice that at the $\tilde{t}$ equilibrium not all fund-raisers are soliciting the same donor, since in g^1 there is only one donor who is linked to all fund-raisers and this donor is solicited by all fund-raisers at the t^* equilibrium. Thus, at the $\tilde{t}$ equilibrium, there exists a donor, say 2, such that the number of fund-raisers soliciting 2 is less than or equal to $m/2$. First, assume that the number of fund-raisers soliciting 2 is less than $m/2$. Let $\lceil m/2 - 1 \rceil$ fund-raisers not soliciting 2 tremble to the t^* equilibrium. Then any fund-raiser soliciting 2 has incentive to move to the t^* equilibrium as his payoff will increase from at most $(1/\lceil m/2-1 \rceil) f(\lceil m/2-1 \rceil)$ to $(1/(\lceil m/2-1 \rceil+1)) f(\lceil m/2-1 \rceil+1)$. Similarly, all remaining fund-raisers will move to the t^* equilibrium. Second, let the number of fund-raisers soliciting 2 equal $m/2$. Again let $\lceil m/2 - 1 \rceil$ other fund-raisers tremble to the t^* equilibrium. Next, the remaining fund-raiser who is also not soliciting donor 2 will move to the t^* equilibrium as his payoff will increase from $f(1)$ to $(1/(\lceil m/2 - 1 \rceil + 1)) f(\lceil m/2-1 \rceil + 1)$. Similarly, all remaining fund-raisers will move to t^*. Thus, $\lceil m/2-1 \rceil$ trembles are enough to move from state $\tilde{t}$ to state t^*.

Lastly, consider the case where $m = 2$ and where an alternative Nash, $\tilde{t}$, exists. To move from t^* to $\tilde{t}$ takes two trembles, since if either fund-raiser is soliciting donor 1, then the other fund-raiser has incentive to also solicit donor 1. However, to leave $\tilde{t}$ and move to t^* takes just one tremble. Here if one fund-raiser trembles to his t^* strategy, then the other fund-raiser will also switch to solicit donor 1. By Young [30] only states with the minimum resistance are stochastically stable; so t^* is stochastically stable while $\tilde{t}$ is not. □

Notice here that the unique stochastically stable state coincides with the efficient Nash equilibrium, since all players are better off soliciting the same donor when the donation function is increasing and convex.

Remark 14. If the network has multiple donors each of whom are linked to all fund-raisers, then the above proof can be modified to show that there will be multiple stochastically stable states. At each stochastically stable state, each fund-raiser spends all his time soliciting the same donor.

6. Conclusion

We showed that donation requests are influenced by the fund-raiser donor network and in particular by whether or not a fund-raiser shares a donor tie with other fund-raisers. For instance, in an incomplete network with extreme donor fatigue fund-raisers spend more time soliciting donors shared with other fund-raisers as compared with un-shared donor ties. If donors experience instead mild donor fatigue, then fund-raisers prefer to solicit donors un-shared with other fund-raisers. Additionally, we examined the case of no donor fatigue and showed that multiple equilibria may exist; stochastic stability was used to refine the number of equilibria.

A policy implication for fund-raisers is that fund-raisers should examine the fund-raiser donor network and the level of donor fatigue and use this information when deciding how much time to spend soliciting particular donors. Fund-raisers can learn the fund-raiser donor network by joining pools in which many fund-raisers share information about donors; we know such pools are quite prevalent from the popular press, see Kadet [31]. Additionally, if a fund-raiser is spending a lot of time with a donor in order to secure a large donation, then the fund-raiser will probably learn from the donor whether or not he is also being solicited by others. Fund-raisers can learn the level of donor fatigue by observing a donor's donation history; since donor fatigue occurs when an increase in solicitation efforts results in a smaller marginal donation, the level of donor fatigue could be learned by analyzing past and present donor databases. If a fund-raiser learns that donor fatigue is mild, then he may be better off not joining pools where he must share information about his donors with other fund-raisers, while if donor fatigue is severe, then joining such pools would be beneficial.

If a fund-raiser learns of a set of donors who are solicited by only a few or no other fund-raisers and if donor fatigue is mild, then the fund-raiser may want to focus his efforts on this set of donors. If a fund-raiser learns of a set of donors who are solicited by numerous other fund-raisers and if donor fatigue is severe, then the fund-raiser may actually want to spend time soliciting these donors as although doing so may not increase these donors' total donations to all fund-raisers much it may instead allow this fund-raiser to "steal" donations that would otherwise go to someone else.

The model may be extended in several ways. For instance, we could allow heterogeneous donors to exist on the same network where some donors are more willing to donate money than others. It would be interesting to see how the placement of such a donor onto the network would influence donation requests. As the current model is already quite complicated, solving this issue is beyond the scope of the current paper and is left for future research.

Additionally, we have assumed for simplicity that the network is exogenous; however, it would be interesting to allow the network to be endogenous. For instance, perhaps every period fund-raisers could learn of new donors and have a chance to add these new links as well as a chance to sever existing links. Here, if donor fatigue is mild, then fund-raisers may prefer to sever links shared with others and attempt to find new unlinked donors to link to by purchasing donor lists or through mail out campaigns or by sponsoring fund-raising events where existing donors are encouraged to bring their friends. If donor fatigue is extreme, then fund-raisers may want to buy or share information about potential donors and add ties to donors who are already linked to other fund-raisers.

Acknowledgments

The author thanks Chi-ang Lin, Maria Arbatskaya, Philip Grossman, Laura Kalambokidis, and David Yi for valuable comments and criticisms.

References

[1] J. Andreoni, "Charitable giving," in *The New Palgrave Dictionary of Economics*, S. Durlauf and L. Blume, Eds., Palgrave Macmillan, 2nd edition, 2008.

[2] M. Hall, C. W. Barr, M. Easwaramoorthy, S. W. Sokolowski, and L. M. Salamon, *The Canadian Nonprofit and Volunteer Sector in Comparative Perspective*, Imagine Canada, Toronto, Canada, 2005.

[3] B. K. Yörük, "How responsive are charitable donors to requests to give?" *Journal of Public Economics*, vol. 93, no. 9-10, pp. 1111–1117, 2009.

[4] B. K. Yörük, "How responsive are charitable donors to requests to give?" Working Paper Version, Boston College, 2007.

[5] J. Andreoni, "Philanthropy," in *Handbook of Giving, Reciprocity and Altruism*, S. C. Kolm and J. Mercier Ythier, Eds., pp. 1201–1269, North Holland, Amsterdam, The Netherlands, 2006.

[6] J. Andreoni and A. A. Payne, "Do government grants to private charities crowd out giving or fund-raising?" *American Economic Review*, vol. 93, no. 3, pp. 792–812, 2003.

[7] B. Keegan, *Fundraising for Non-Profits: How to Build a Community Partnership*, Harper Collins, New York, NY, USA, 1994.

[8] S. Dellavigna, J. A. List, and U. Malmendier, "Testing for altruism and social pressure in charitable giving," *The Quarterly Journal of Economics*, vol. 127, no. 1, pp. 1–56, 2012.

[9] M. Mungan and B. K. Yörük, "Fundraising and optimal policy rules," Mimeo, University at Albany, SUNY, 2009.

[10] L. M. Marx and S. A. Matthews, "Dynamic voluntary contribution to a public project," *Review of Economic Studies*, vol. 67, no. 2, pp. 327–358, 2000.

[11] M. Bagnoli and B. L. Lipman, "Provision of public goods: fully implementing the core through private contributions," *Review of Economic Studies*, vol. 56, no. 4, pp. 583–601, 1989.

[12] J. Meer and H. S. Rosen, "The ABCs of charitable solicitation," *Journal of Public Economics*, vol. 95, no. 5-6, pp. 363–371, 2011.

[13] M. van Diepen, B. Donkers, and P. H. Franses, "Dynamic and competitive effects of direct mailings: a charitable giving application," *Journal of Marketing Research*, vol. 46, no. 1, pp. 120–133, 2009.

[14] J. Andreoni and J. M. Rao, "The power of asking: how communication affects selfishness, empathy, and altruism," *Journal of Public Economics*, vol. 95, no. 7-8, pp. 513–520, 2011.

[15] M. O. Jackson, "An overview of social networks and economic applications," in *Forthcoming in the Handbook of Social Economics*, J. Benhabib, A. Bisin, and M. O. Jackson, Eds., Elsevier, 2009.

[16] M. O. Jackson and A. Wolinsky, "A strategic model of social and economic networks," *Journal of Economic Theory*, vol. 71, no. 1, pp. 44–74, 1996.

[17] A. Calvó-Armengol and M. O. Jackson, "The effects of social networks on employment and inequality," *American Economic Review*, vol. 94, no. 3, pp. 426–454, 2004.

[18] Y. Bramoullé and R. Kranton, "Risk-sharing networks," *Journal of Economic Behavior and Organization*, vol. 64, no. 3-4, pp. 275–294, 2007.

[19] M. Fafchamps and S. Lund, "Risk-sharing networks in rural Philippines," *Journal of Development Economics*, vol. 71, no. 2, pp. 261–287, 2003.

[20] R. E. Kranton and D. F. Minehart, "Competition for goods in buyer-seller networks," *Review of Economic Design*, vol. 5, no. 3, pp. 301–331, 2000.

[21] R. E. Kranton and D. F. Minehart, "A theory of buyer-seller networks," *American Economic Review*, vol. 91, no. 3, pp. 485–508, 2001.

[22] M. O. Jackson and A. Watts, "The evolution of social and economic networks," *Journal of Economic Theory*, vol. 106, no. 2, pp. 265–295, 2002.

[23] M. O. Jackson and A. Watts, "On the formation of interaction networks in social coordination games," *Games and Economic Behavior*, vol. 41, no. 2, pp. 265–291, 2002.

[24] S. Skaperdas, "Contest success functions," *Economic Theory*, vol. 7, no. 2, pp. 283–290, 1996.

[25] H. Moulin, "The price of anarchy of serial, average and incremental cost sharing," *Economic Theory*, vol. 36, no. 3, pp. 379–405, 2008.

[26] H. Moulin and A. Watts, "Two versions of the tragedy of the commons," *Review of Economic Design*, vol. 2, no. 1, pp. 399–421, 1997.

[27] A. Watts, "Uniqueness of equilibrium in cost sharing games," *Journal of Mathematical Economics*, vol. 37, no. 1, pp. 47–70, 2002.

[28] M. I. Freidlin and A. D. Wentzell, *Random Perturbations of Dynamical Systems*, Springer, New York, NY, USA, 1984.

[29] H. P. Young, *Individual Strategy and Social Structure*, Princeton University Press, Princeton, NJ, USA, 1998.

[30] H. P. Young, "The evolution of conventions," *Econometrica*, vol. 61, no. 1, pp. 57–84, 1993.

[31] A. Kadet, "Smart money: is your favorite charity spying on you?" *The Wall Street Journal*, vol. 16, 2010.

Growth and Volatility Reconsidered: Reconciling Opposite Views

L. Bisio and L. Ventura

Department of Economics and Law, Sapienza University of Rome, Via del Castro Laurenziano 9, 00161 Rome, Italy

Correspondence should be addressed to L. Ventura; luigi.ventura@uniroma1.it

Academic Editors: L. Grilli, J.-L. Hu, and M. T. Leung

Many contributions in the recent literature have investigated over the relationship between GDP growth and its volatility without getting a clear and unambiguous answer. Besides reassessing the well-known effect of output volatility on growth as benchmark analysis, this study aims at looking into the "black box" of the business cycle volatility by disentangling the impacts of volatility of GDP major components—that is, private consumption, private investment and government expenditure—on growth, simultaneously considered. Our empirical analysis unveils a remarkably robust and strong negative correlation of consumption volatility with mean growth and a positive one with volatility of investment and of public expenditure. If these findings shed some additional light on the (still controversial) relationship between economic fluctuations and growth, they will also make it possible to compare the relative impact of each component, with possibly relevant policy implications. Importantly, this might reconcile opposite views about the issue that different empirical results might originate from the relative importance across empirical studies of the various components of volatility.

1. Introduction

Among the issues economists largely debated upon over the recent decades, the relationship between the volatility of business cycle and output growth deserves a particular attention. Nonetheless, for a long time, long-run growth and business cycle were conceived of as independent phenomena to be analyzed by means of separated tools. This view was strongly supported by Lucas [1] who claimed that the trade-off between growth and business cycle fluctuations was pretty inexistent. Then, the Real Business Cycle (RBC) paradigm [2] pointed to the exogenous stochastic process driving the technological progress as the common root of both trend growth and cyclical fluctuations. However, once the endogenous technological progress hypothesis was introduced into the RBC framework [3, 4] the idea of a causal relationship between the instability of the business cycle and growth gained theoretical support, thereby prompting the subsequent empirical literature on volatility and growth (see Aghion and Saint-Paul [5] for a very interesting analysis of the theoretical evolution on this issue and Gaggl and Steindl [6] for a literature review on growth and cycle).

This paper is meant to contribute to the stream of literature which aimed at verifying both the existence of a statistically significant causal relationship between output volatility and growth and the sign of that relationship. Although no unambiguous evidence has been obtained on this topic so far—also due to the existing differences across studies with respect to the computation of volatility, the sample selections, and the estimation methodologies—the largest consensus suggests that volatility is detrimental for growth. It is worth mentioning the seminal work by G. Ramey and V. A. Ramey [7] which proved the existence of a negative robust relationship between output volatility and average growth, whereby volatility was built as a measure of forecast uncertainty. However, despite their findings were subsequently confirmed by an extensive literature (see, e.g., [8–11]), other relevant empirical studies pointed at a positive impact of output variability on growth [12–14] and, in general an inconclusive evidence comes out of the theoretical debate (from the theoretical point of view the *neo-Schumpeterian* view and the *arrovian* approach attain opposite conclusions on the issue. The former considers "*recessions as opportunities*" [15] because the opportunity cost of efficiency-enhancing activities is lower than in normal times, thus prompting optimizing firms towards engaging in those activities (see, e.g., [5, 16–18]). Therefore, downturns drive positive effects not only on output growth but also on productivity growth that turns out to be countercyclical. By contrast, according to the arrovian approach, as long as production is dominated by external learning [19] or *learning-by-doing*, economic booms stimulate productivity enhancement, whereas economic downturns negatively affect both the short-term and the long-term growth. As a consequence, productivity growth follows a procyclical path (see, e.g., [8, 20, 21])).

To our knowledge, most contributions to the previous literature have mainly aimed at empirically investigating the impact of the volatility of single macroeconomic variables on growth, as for example, government spending [22, 23], investment share of GDP, real exchange rate [24, 25], or inflation [26, 27]. However, notwithstanding the relevance of the results attained so far, it is still quite difficult to make a comparison among the different kinds of volatilities in order to identify the one relatively most detrimental to growth. The only attempt to fill this gap is Furceri's [28] that comparatively evaluates the impact of the volatility of investment, government, and exchange rate, simultaneously considered, onto long-term growth.

In a similar spirit, our purpose is to go beyond the traditional analysis of the relationship between business cycle volatility and growth; as we are confident that the impact of the former on the latter might change depending on the transmission channel considered. Hence, besides reassessing the well-known effect of output volatility on growth as benchmark analysis, this study aims at looking into the "black box" of the business cycle volatility by simultaneously verifying the statistical relevance of the volatility of some of the main components of GDP—private consumption (C), private investment (I), and government expenditure (G)—for growth (we skip net exports for reasons which will become clearer in the sequel). We believe that, by disentangling the impacts of the volatility of GDP main components on growth, not only additional aspects of the (still controversial) relationship between economic fluctuations and growth can be unveiled, but also the relative impact of each component volatility can be compared, with possibly relevant policy implications.

Indeed, there exist several theoretical arguments suggesting how volatility in consumption, private investment, and government expenditure can interact with growth. Concerning consumption and investment volatility, the literature on risk and optimal decisions predicts that *ceteris paribus* a higher degree of risk and volatility implies a higher economic growth rate, on average, because higher profitable investments are associated with more volatility, via a higher degree of technology specialization and a smaller degree of risks diversification [29]. However, as agents are assumed to be risk averse, the ultimate impact of risk on growth crucially depends on the degree of markets completeness: if they were complete, agents could hedge against risks and pursue higher rate-of-return investment plans; if they were incomplete this would not be possible, and a trade-off would emerge between volatility and growth. Hence, risk averse agents would invest in both high and low expected return sectors in order to ensure a larger diversification of their risk, thereby reducing economic volatility and also economic growth. On the other hand, to the extent that risk aversion and insurance market incompleteness induce agents to increase precautionary savings leading to higher capital accumulation rates [30], risk and volatility can be beneficial to growth. Concerning fiscal policy volatility, theory predicts ambivalent outcomes in terms of its impact on growth: if government expenditure comes in the form of automatic stabilizers (among others, see Sachs and Sala-i-Martin [31], Asdrubali et al. [32], and Afonso and Furceri [22]) that offset the negative effects of business cycle shocks, clearly one can expect a beneficial effect of more volatility to investment and growth; by contrast, if a balance discipline must be respected so that government expenditure tends to follow the business cycle rather than contrast it, the volatility of fiscal policy risks to exacerbate the negative effect of adverse shocks to the economy.

A large number of econometric procedures have been implemented throughout the literature to evaluate the relationship between growth and volatility. Although a pure time-series approach was followed by, for example, Caporale and McKiernan [14] and Grier and Perry (2000), several cross-country regressions [7, 33], (Martin and Rogers, 2000) and panel data estimations [8, 10, 11, 34, 35] have been performed to the same purpose. Here we resort to a panel data investigation but, unlike some more recent panel data exercises, we do not average our variables over intervals of time. Indeed, computing volatility as the standard deviation of nonoverlapping time spans leaves no choice but averaging the whole sample over the same time periods. Thus, in order to build our volatility measure, we will rather follow a "rolling windows" approach that yields time-varying variables and allows to preserve the original time dimension of our data set. In other words, GDP growth at time t will be regressed upon measures of volatility computed on the window $t - s$, t, where s is the width of the window. The underlying idea is that growth at time t is influenced by volatility (of the relevant macrovariables) perceived over a window of s years (we will use an $s = 5$ year interval). This assumption seems more reasonable than supposing that the average rate of growth of GDP, over a period of s years, is influenced by the volatility computed over the same spell of time.

This paper is organized as follows. Section 2 presents our dataset, some preliminary evidence emerging from the data, and the methodology employed for the estimation. Section 3 describes our empirical results, while some concluding remarks are drawn in Section 4.

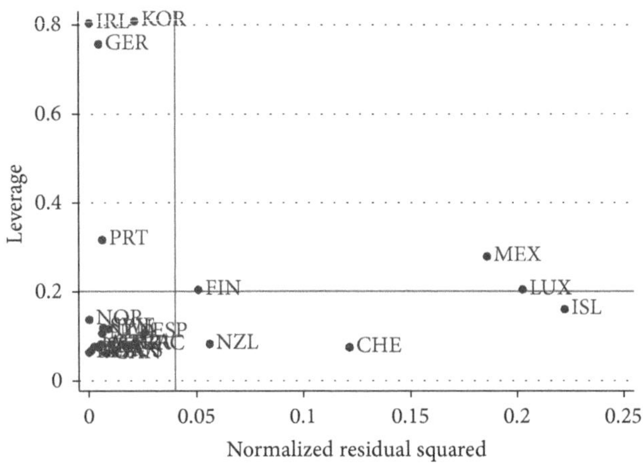

FIGURE 1: Average values of leverage and normalized residuals squared.

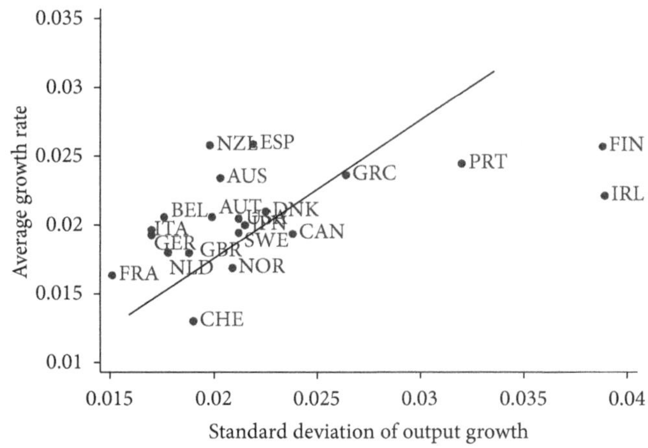

FIGURE 2: Simple correlation of growth and output volatility.

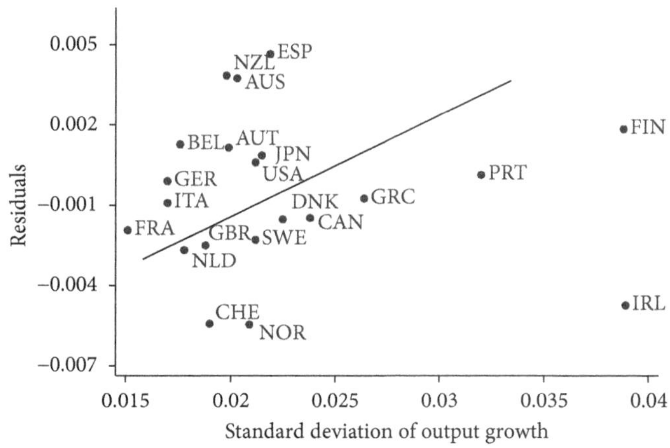

FIGURE 3: Partial correlation of growth and output volatility. (Controlling for the volatility of C, G, and I.)

2. Data, Models, and Methodology

2.1. Data. We use data from Heston et al. [36] and from the Barro-Lee data set [37], both consisting of annual observations (an exception is the schooling variable, which is only available on five-years intervals in the World's Bank data release. We applied a polynomial interpolation method to those series in order to get annual observations to be employed in our model). Our regression analysis focuses on a sample of 25 OECD countries and is performed over the time horizon 1978–2007 (our main sample consists of 25 countries out of the whole 34 OECD countries. Indeed, we retain those countries that joined the OECD before the 1990's in order to preserve a certain degree of homogeneity in terms of technology, development, and quality of data. Consistently, we do not include Turkey, whose data quality is graded "C" according to the Heston et al. [36] data quality scale ranging from A (best quality) to D (worst quality)). However, before turning to the empirical models specification and discussing the econometric strategy, we present some evidence based on some basic preliminary analysis of our data.

Table 4 shows the results of our outliers testing and inspecting procedure, that reveals some extreme values in the case of Iceland, Korea, Luxembourg, and Mexico. These results, combined with the evidence presented in Figure 1 (where the points above the horizontal line have higher-than-average leverage, and points to the right of the vertical line have higher-than-average studentized residuals, based on our benchmark regression), suggest that it may be worth testing our models on a second sample, that is, a subsample of the main one where the above mentioned countries are omitted. Hence, our cross-country dimension is equal to $N = 25$ in the benchmark sample and $N = 21$ for the restricted sample, while our time dimension is equal to $T = 30$.

In what follows we focus on a subsample of 19 OECD countries (compared to our 21-countries restricted sample, we additionally get rid of Ireland and Switzerland presenting outlier values in the government and consumption volatility series, resp.) over the period 1978–2007 and present the simple cross-country correlation between average output growth rate and, respectively, the standard deviation of output, consumption, investment, and government consumption growth rates. What Figures 2, 4, 6, and 8 clearly show is that growth positively correlates with the standard deviations of either GDP and GDP components. However, as simple correlation is likely to hide spurious linkages between variables, we also provide the (more robust) partial correlation measure in Figures 3, 5, 7, and 9, whose y-axes display the residuals of a cross-country population weighted estimation where average growth is regressed against the volatilities of all variables so far mentioned (i.e., GDP, C, I, and G) except the variable whose standard deviation is displayed on the x-axis. Partial correlation confirms the evidence of the positive linkage assessed by simple correlation only in the case of output and government consumption volatility. On the other hand, the sign of the relationship between consumption and investment volatilities to growth is reverted as a clear negative relationship emerges between their standard deviations and the correspondent regressions residuals. It should be noted, however, that partial correlations do not account for the effect of additional explanatory variables, that will be used in our regression analysis.

TABLE 1: List of countries in the main sample and averaged volatilities over the period 1978–2007.

Country	GDP growth	Output volatility	Consumption volatility	Investment volatility	Gov. consumpt. volatility
Australia	0.0234	0.0203	0.0132	0.0785	0.0153
Austria	0.0206	0.0199	0.0170	0.0592	0.0100
Belgium	0.0206	0.0176	0.0124	0.0745	0.0148
Canada	0.0193	0.0238	0.0177	0.0792	0.0161
Denmark	0.0210	0.0225	0.0232	0.0891	0.0169
Finland	0.0257	0.0388	0.0262	0.1030	0.0194
France	0.0163	0.0151	0.0107	0.0554	0.0139
Germany	0.0192	0.0170	0.0142	0.0547	0.0166
Greece	0.0236	0.0264	0.0209	0.0849	0.0402
Iceland	0.0414	0.0404	0.0499	0.1474	0.0197
Ireland	0.0221	0.0389	0.0287	0.1059	0.0408
Italy	0.0196	0.0170	0.0191	0.0502	0.0180
Japan	0.0200	0.0215	0.0160	0.0016	0.0120
Korea	0.0557	0.0519	0.0454	0.1162	0.0230
Luxembourg	0.0384	0.0306	0.0183	0.1010	0.0213
Mexico	0.0139	0.0428	0.0400	0.1404	0.0318
Netherlands	0.0180	0.0178	0.0186	0.0544	0.0189
New Zealand	0.0258	0.0198	0.0184	0.0902	0.0219
Norway	0.0168	0.0209	0.0232	0.0869	0.0158
Portugal	0.0244	0.0320	0.0241	0.1025	0.0282
Spain	0.0258	0.0219	0.0205	0.0629	0.0178
Sweden	0.0194	0.0212	0.0214	0.0887	0.0137
Switzerland	0.0130	0.0190	0.0090	0.0610	0.0176
United Kingdom	0.0179	0.0188	0.0194	0.0683	0.0116
United States	0.0204	0.0212	0.0142	0.0736	0.0163

TABLE 2: Descriptive statistics.

		Descriptive statistics			
Series	Obs	Mean	Std. dev.	Min	Max
GDP growth	750	0.0233	0.0287	−0.1302	0.11639
GDP volatility	750	0.0232	0.0147	0.0036	0.0957
Consumption volatility	750	0.0186	0.0142	0.0022	0.0987
Investment volatility	750	0.0798	0.0476	0.0079	0.323
Government consumption volatility	750	0.0162	0.0100	0.002	0.0646
Investment share of GDP	750	28.81	5.6367	16.0422	53.5848
Education	750	42.23	13.67	9.76	73.42
Population growth	750	0.006	0.0050	−0.0046	0.0241
Initial level of GDP	750	22541.93	8156.53	3980.23	66065.33

Finally, our preliminary data analysis is devoted to verify the time series properties of our panel data. Indeed, we test the stationarity of the series involved in our regressions by applying the [38] (IPS hereafter) test for unit root which seems particularly suitable for our data (the IPS test is based on heterogeneity of the autoregressive parameters of the tested equation, i.e., it allows for heterogeneity in the error variances and the serial correlation structure of the errors). The results of the IPS test, which is based on the well-known Dickey-Fuller procedure, are reported in Table 5. They are evidence that our main variables of interest—that is, the GDP growth rate and the volatilities of GDP components—are stationary, whereas some of our control variables are not. This holds in particular for the initial level of GDP series (cf. the results in Table 5 referring to the log level of GDP) and for education. The use of explanatory nonstationary variables as controls in equations with a stationary dependent variable has already been discussed in the literature [39–41]. However, when nonstationary variables are among the regressors in an expression where the dependent variable is stationary, one may reasonably argue that they are sharing a common trend, thus forming a stationary error correction term. This seems

Table 3: Data sources and descriptions.

Variable name	Definition and construction	Source
GDP growth rate	Percentage growth rate of real GDP per capita in constant prices. Reference year: 1996, Laspeyres index.	Penn World Tables 6.3
GDP volatility	Standard deviation of real GDP growth rate. Yearly series.	Penn World Tables 6.3
Consumption volatility	Standard deviation of real consumption growth rate (real GDP times consumption share of GDP). Yearly series.	Penn World Tables 6.3
Investment volatility	Standard deviation of real Investment growth rate (real GDP times investment share of GDP). Yearly series.	Penn World Tables 6.3
Gov. consumption volatility	Standard deviation of real public consumption growth rate (real GDP times government cons.share of GDP). Yearly series.	Penn World Tables 6.3
Investment share of GDP	Log level of the investment share of real GDP. Yearly series.	Penn World Tables 6.3
Initial GDP	Log level of GDP of the 1st year of the window of which the corresponding volatility is computed. Yearly series.	Penn World Tables 6.3
Population growth rate	Percentage growth rate of population. Yearly series.	Penn World Tables 6.3
Education	Logarithm of the percentage of secondary schooling attained in population aged 25 years and over.	Barro-Lee dataset (2010)

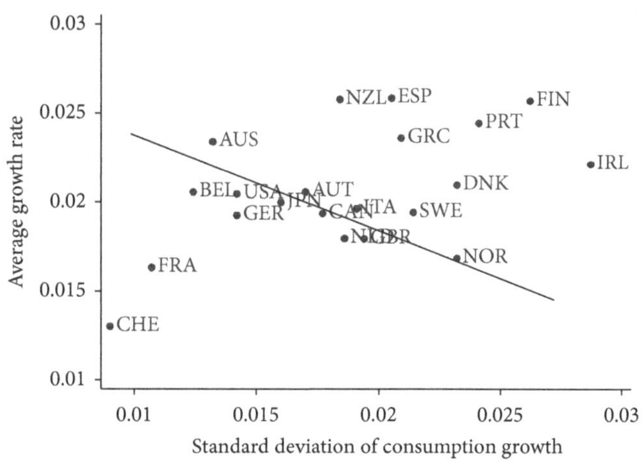

Figure 4: Simple correlation of growth and consumption volatility.

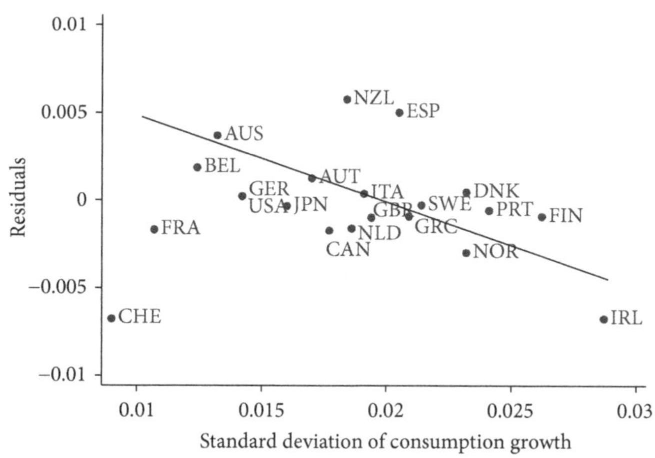

Figure 5: Partial correlation of growth and consumption volatility. (Controlling for the volatility of Y, I, and G.)

Table 4: Outlier testing.

Country	Residuals (|0.2|)	Leverage (0.4)	Cook's D. (0.16)	DFBETA (0.4)
Germany		0.76	0.24	
Iceland	2.61		0.21	0.83
Ireland		0.80		
Korea	1.54	0.81	1.87	2.41
Luxembourg	2.54		0.26	0.87
Mexico	−2.56		0.40	

Note: Studentized residuals, Levarages, Cook's Distance, and DFBETA influence measures are considered. Only countries reporting statistics besides the cutoff values are reported. Cutoff values for each indicator are in parenthesis.

to be the case in our analysis, as it is very likely that the level of education is related to the level of GDP. Moreover, any time-related common factor should be captured by the time dummies included in our models.

2.2. Growth and Volatility: A Static Regression Analysis. We start by estimating a benchmark model, in the spirit of G. Ramey and V. A. Ramey [7], where we regress GDP growth against the volatility of output growth along with a set of conditioning variables that are quite standard within the growth regression literature—documented by Levine and Renelt [42] to be relevant in the context of growth cross-country regressions—and where country and time-specific constants are also considered as follows:

$$g_{it} = \alpha_{i.} + \tau_{.t} + \beta\sigma_{it}^{y} + \theta' X_{it} + \varepsilon_{it},$$
$$\varepsilon_{it} \sim N\left(0, \sigma_{\varepsilon}^{2}\right), \quad i = 1, \ldots, N, \ t = 1, \ldots, T, \tag{1}$$

where g_{it} is the annual growth rate of per capita GDP of country i at time t; $\alpha_{i.}$ and $\tau_{.t}$ represent, respectively, a country and a time-specific fixed effect; σ_{it}^{y} is our measure of output growth volatility, and the vector X_{it} includes a set of control variables, namely, (i) the annual log-level of investment share

TABLE 5: Panel unit root test [38].

Variable	Level		First difference	
	Constant	Constant + trend	Constant	Constant + trend
Log of GDP	12.4454	0.78674	−13.409***	−9.96431***
GDP volatility	−4.9473***	−6.3950***	−19.0850***	−16.803***
Consumption volatility	−4.3329***	−4.0761***	−19.6400***	−16.336***
Investment volatility	−20.811***	−6.1437***	−4.4186***	−18.687***
Gov. consumption volatility	−5.6580***	−2.6002***	−20.813***	−17.653***
Investment share of GDP	−0.7502	−2.8268**	−17.7615***	−14.5888***
Log of population	6.6528	−1.0168	−4.4148***	−3.1863***
Education	−0.2669	1.5139	−3.1892***	$-8.4E+12$***

***, **Rejection of the null hypothesis of the presence of a unit root at 1% and 5% level of significance.
The choice of the optimal lag for the underlying autoregressive equation is based on the Schwarz identification criterion (SIC).

TABLE 6: Dependent variable: growth rate of per capita GDP. Regressors: volatility of GDP growth, consumption growth, investment growth, government consumption growth, and control variables. Sample: OECD countries (25 countries). Horizon: 1978–2007. Annual observations. All regressions include year dummies.

	Static models estimations					
Estimation	FE	FE	FE	FE-IV GMM	FE-IV GMM	FE-IV GMM
GDP volatility	−0.127		0.177	−0.417*		−0.981
	(−0.88)		(0.69)	(−1.93)		(−1.62)
Consumption volatility		−0.549***	−0.613***		−0.907**	−0.525***
		(−3.28)	(−3.46)		(−3.06)	(−2.50)
Investment volatility		0.049	0.012		0.154	0.334*
		(1.18)	(0.21)		(1.56)	(1.77)
Government consumption volatility		0.460***	0.443***		0.323*	0.442***
		(3.83)	(3.72)		(1.86)	(2.71)
Education	0.003	0.003	0.003	0.005	0.002	0.003
	(0.58)	(0.66)	(0.50)	(0.60)	(0.31)	(0.51)
Population growth	−0.736*	−0.823**	−0.863**	0.501	0.340	0.542
	(−1.72)	(−2.04)	(−2.21)	(0.89)	(0.67)	(1.00)
Initial GDP	−0.050***	−0.032**	−0.031**	−0.066***	−0.035**	−0.041**
	(−3.52)	(−2.23)	(−2.20)	(−4.15)	(−2.11)	(−2.58)
Investment share of GDP	0.084***	0.083***	0.084***	−0.106***	−0.084***	−0.082***
	(6.73)	(7.19)	(7.26)	(−3.28)	(−3.22)	(−3.25)
Observations	750	750	750	675	675	675
Instruments	no	no	no	yes	yes	yes
Hansen J statistic (P value)				0.321	0.76	0.87
Kleibergen-Paap Wald F statistic				69.231	41.711	27.638

Note: T-statistics in parenthesis, robust SEs. *Significance at 10%, **significance at 5%, and ***significance at 1%.

of GDP, (ii) the log-level of GDP per capita on the first year of the rolling window over which the corresponding observation of volatility is computed (see below), (iii) a measure for the initial human capital given by the log-percentage of population aged over 25 years who attained a degree of secondary school, and (iv) the annual growth rate of population (a detailed description of the series is provided in Tables 1, 2, and 3). Finally, ε_{it} is a standard error term.

The peculiarity of our model is that our measure of volatility is time varying, whereas previous panel studies on volatility and growth, such as, for example, Kose et al. [10], and Rafferty [34] measure volatility as the standard deviation over 5/10 yearly observations along with averaged observations over the same span for the rest of the variables, which implies a sharp shortening of the time dimension of their panel dataset. By contrast, our measure of volatility is computed as the standard deviation of a five-year rolling window of observations whose last year is contemporaneous to the dependent variable g_{it} (thus, 1974–1978 is the first rolling window and 2003–2007 is the last one). Our dependent variable, on the other hand, is not computed as a mean over a rolling window, but rather as a simple growth rate. This is also relevant from the statistic point of view, as it should prevent our results from being affected by serial correlation

Table 7: Dependent variable: growth rate of per capita GDP. Regressors: lagged growth rate of per capita GDP, volatility of GDP growth, consumption growth, investment growth, government consumption growth, and control variables. Sample: OECD countries (25 countries). Horizon: 1978–2007. All regressions include year dummies.

	Dynamic models estimations					
Estimation	LSDV IV 2sls	LSDV IV 2sls	LSDV IV 2sls	GMM-SYS	GMM-SYS	GMM-SYS
GDP volatility	−0.248		−0.931	−0.053		−0.392
	(−1.59)		(−1.43)	(−0.29)		(−0.56)
Consumption volatility		-0.769^{***}	-0.396^{**}		-0.470^{**}	−0.304
		(−2.83)	(−2.16)		(−2.11)	(−1.26)
Investment volatility		0.169^{*}	0.341^{*}		0.13	0.195
		(1.78)	(1.66)		(1.66)	(0.92)
Government consumption volatility		0.252^{*}	0.372^{***}		0.330^{*}	0.360^{**}
		(1.85)	(2.70)		(2.05)	(2.12)
GDP growth ($t-1$)	0.365^{***}	0.309^{***}	0.299^{***}	0.375^{***}	0.340^{***}	0.345^{***}
	(4.95)	(4.33)	(4.02)	(4.44)	(4.24)	(4.33)
Education	0.004	0.003	0.004	0.007	0.008	0.009
	(0.66)	(0.48)	(0.68)	(0.66)	(0.83)	(0.77)
Population growth	0.100	−0.024	0.16	−0.440	−0.534	−0.522
	(0.22)	(−0.06)	(0.33)	(−0.92)	(−1.08)	(−0.98)
Initial GDP	-0.048^{***}	−0.021	-0.028^{**}	−0.015	−0.013	−0.015
	(−3.90)	(−1.64)	(−2.12)	(−0.77)	(−0.68)	(−0.65)
Investment share of GDP	-0.085^{***}	-0.064^{**}	-0.060^{***}	-0.075^{**}	-0.068^{**}	-0.075^{**}
	(−3.49)	(−3.14)	(−3.00)	(−2.37)	(−2.17)	(−2.24)
Observations	675	675	675	725	725	725
Country dummies	Yes	Yes	Yes	No	No	No
Instruments	Yes	Yes	Yes	Yes	Yes	Yes
Kleibergen-Paap Wald F statistic	140.47	56.569	23.352			
Hansen J/Sargan test (P value)	0.715	0.738	0.654	0.243	0.592	0.558
Arellano-Bond test (AR2)				0.837	0.707	0.752

Note: T-statistics in parenthesis, robust SEs. *Significance at 10%, **significance at 5%, and ***significance at 1%.

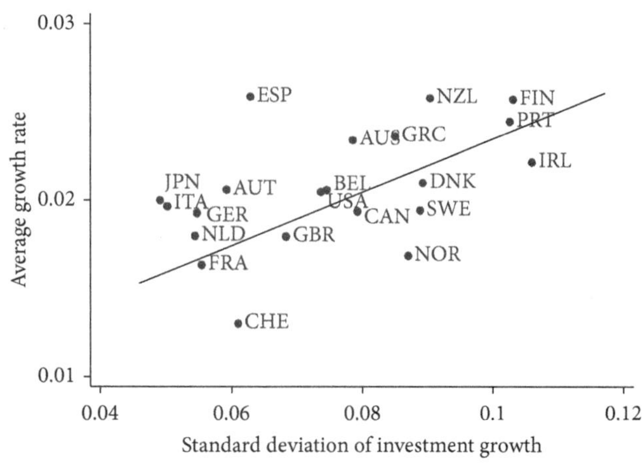

Figure 6: Simple correlation of growth and investment volatility.

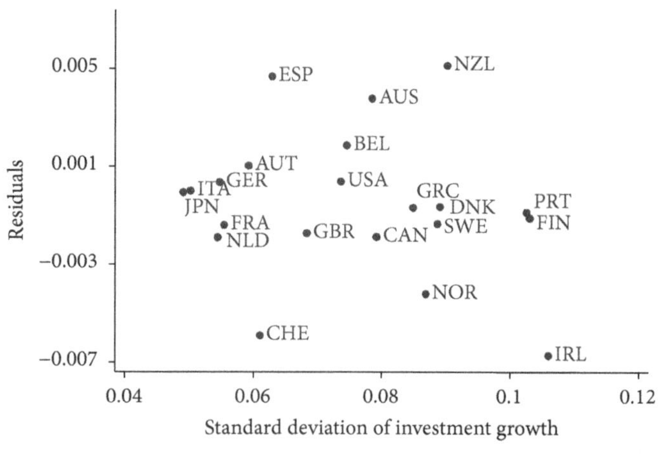

Figure 7: Partial correlation of growth and investment volatility. (Controlling for the volatility of C, G, and I.)

problems. The aim of this regression is to verify the existence of a causal relationship between the growth rate of GDP at time t and the volatility occurring over the previous interval, from $t-5$ to t.

The next step will be checking whether this global relationship is driven by some specific components or whether

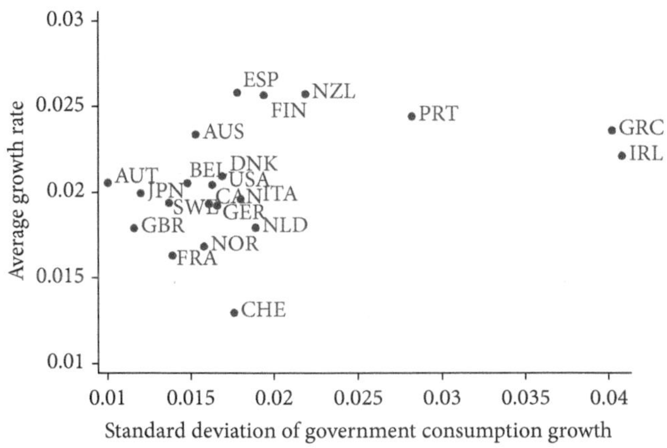

FIGURE 8: Simple correlation of growth and government consumption volatility.

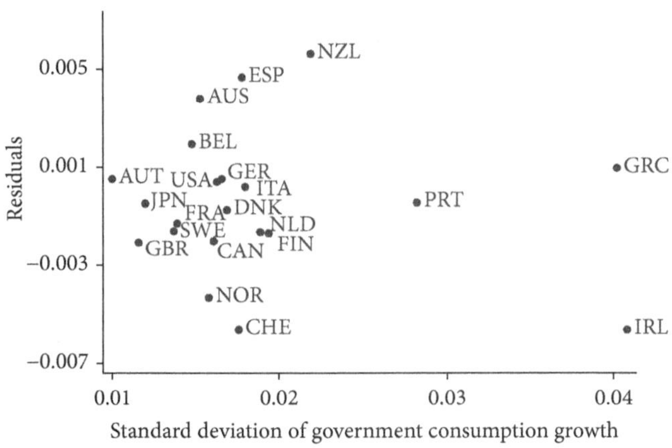

FIGURE 9: Partial correlation of growth and government consumption. (Controlled for volatility of Y, C, and G.)

all of them exert the same influence upon growth. In order to see this, we start from the fundamental accounting identity

$$\mathrm{GDP}_t = C_t + I_t + G_t + NX_t. \quad (2)$$

By dividing both members by GDP_{t-1} we get

$$\frac{\mathrm{GDP}_t}{\mathrm{GDP}_{t-1}} = \frac{C_t}{\mathrm{GDP}_{t-1}} + \frac{I_t}{\mathrm{GDP}_{t-1}} + \frac{G_t}{\mathrm{GDP}_{t-1}} + \frac{NX_t}{\mathrm{GDP}_{t-1}}. \quad (3)$$

Which can also be written as

$$\frac{\mathrm{GDP}_t}{\mathrm{GDP}_{t-1}} = \frac{C_t}{C_{t-1}} s_{t-1}^{C} + \frac{I_t}{I_{t-1}} s_{t-1}^{I} + \frac{G_t}{G_{t-1}} s_{t-1}^{G} + \frac{NX_t}{NX_{t-1}} s_{t-1}^{NX}, \quad (4)$$

where s_{t-1}^{C}, s_{t-1}^{I}, s_{t-1}^{G}, s_{t-1}^{NX} represent the GDP shares of consumption, investments, public expenditure and net exports, respectively. In what follows, we will assume that those shares are approximately constant for the (relatively short) spell of time over which volatilities are computed (the time subscript will thus be omitted). Under this assumption, elementary statistics yield

$$\begin{aligned}
\mathrm{Var}\left(\frac{\mathrm{GDP}_t}{\mathrm{GDP}_{t-1}}\right) = {} & \left(s^C\right)^2 \mathrm{Var}\left(\frac{C_t}{C_{t-1}}\right) + \left(s^I\right)^2 \mathrm{Var}\left(\frac{I_t}{I_{t-1}}\right) \\
& + \left(s^G\right)^2 \mathrm{Var}\left(\frac{G_t}{G_{t-1}}\right) \\
& + \left(s^{NX}\right)^2 \mathrm{Var}\left(\frac{NX_t}{NX_{t-1}}\right) \\
& + 2\left[s^C s^I \mathrm{Cov}\left(\frac{C_t}{C_{t-1}}, \frac{I_t}{I_{t-1}}\right) + s^C s^G \mathrm{Cov}\left(\frac{C_t}{C_{t-1}}, \frac{G_t}{G_{t-1}}\right) + s^C s^{NX} \mathrm{Cov}\left(\frac{C_t}{C_{t-1}}, \frac{NX_t}{NX_{t-1}}\right)\right] \\
& + 2\left[s^I s^G \mathrm{Cov}\left(\frac{I_t}{I_{t-1}}, \frac{G_t}{G_{t-1}}\right) + s^I s^{NX} \mathrm{Cov}\left(\frac{I_t}{I_{t-1}}, \frac{NX_t}{NX_{t-1}}\right) + s^G s^{NX} \mathrm{Cov}\left(\frac{G_t}{G_{t-1}}, \frac{NX_t}{NX_{t-1}}\right)\right].
\end{aligned} \quad (5)$$

Equation (5) shows that the variance of GDP growth can be decomposed into the sum of variances of its various components, multiplied by the square of the corresponding shares, plus the covariances between the components. In the following empirical analysis we are going to consider only the first three components of the overall volatility as expressed by (5)—namely, the volatility of private consumption, investment, and government consumption—as we decided to focus on the internal sources of volatility, and because the variance of net exports is extremely large. In doing so, we are capturing a sizeable portion of the variance of GDP less net exports (around 70%, rising to about 100% if we also take covariances into account, which implies that the impact of the variability of shares is negligible). On the other hand, the share of the first three components of overall GDP volatility over the GDP comprehensive of the trade balance component is slightly larger than one (about 1.11 in some computations), mainly due to the effects of covariances of the three components with net exports.

Hence, estimation of model (6) aims at detecting if the volatility of consumption, investment, and government expenditure influences mean growth in the same direction, or rather if some of them are detrimental and some beneficial to growth. In order to do that, we simply augment Model (1) by consumption (σ_{it}^{c}), investment (σ_{it}^{i}), and government expenditure (σ_{it}^{g}) volatility as separate control regressors, as in the following:

$$g_{it} = \alpha_{i\cdot} + \tau_{\cdot t} + \gamma\sigma_{it}^{c} + \delta\sigma_{it}^{i} + \epsilon\sigma_{it}^{g} + \theta' X_{it} + \varepsilon_{it}. \quad (6)$$

Finally, our last empirical specification (Model (7)) also includes a measure of the overall volatility of GDP growth which will possibly capture the effects of net exports growth volatility and of all the interactions between the various components, and possibly a size effect as follows:

$$g_{it} = \alpha_{i\cdot} + \tau_{\cdot t} + \beta\sigma_{it}^{y} + \gamma\sigma_{it}^{c} + \delta\sigma_{it}^{i} + \epsilon\sigma_{it}^{g} + \theta' X_{it} + \varepsilon_{it}. \quad (7)$$

Turning to the econometric methodology, as our sample of OECD countries represents the universe of countries more likely than a random sample taken from a larger universe of countries, we opt for a fixed-effects model specification. Therefore, we assume that the fixed country-specific ($\alpha_{i\cdot}$) and a fixed period-specific terms ($\tau_{\cdot t}$) are deterministic, respectively, for each country and period and that ε_{it} is a standard random component (an appropriate Hausman test of the fixed effects model versus random effects model was performed over all the model specifications, supporting our intuitive argument in favour of the former). Then, we account for the presence of both country and time effects, respectively, by applying a "within-group" transformation (i.e., we subtract the mean of each variable over time per country from itself) on all variables and by including time-specific dummies. Finally, we perform a robust least square (LS) estimation, which represents our benchmark estimation.

However, since growth equations are likely to be affected by reverse causality issues, we check for the endogeneity of the regressors (the endogeneity test that we perform is defined as the difference of two Sargan-Hansen statistics: one for the equation with the smaller set of instruments (where the suspect regressor(s) are treated as endogenous) and one for the equation (with the larger set of instruments) where the suspect regressors are treated as exogenous. See Baum et al. [43]). Test results show both the investment growth volatility and the investment share of GDP to be endogenous with respect to GDP growth, thus implying the inconsistency of the LS estimates. The lack of independence between the regressors distribution and the error term call for an instrumental variables (IV) approach. Concerning the choice of the instruments, we take advantage of the panel dimension of our data by using the lagged values of the endogenous variables as predeterminates, with respect to contemporaneous growth. A second concern is that a plain two-step least square (2SLS) IV estimator, though providing consistent coefficient estimates, implies a loss of efficiency and the inconsistency of standard errors estimates in the presence of heteroskedasticity, which might possibly affect the testing procedures and results in our models (both the Pagan-Hall and the Breusch-Pagan statistics indicate that the null hypothesis of homoscedasticity is rejected at the 1% level). However, the issue of inefficiency can be tackled by means of the generalized method of moments (GMM) that allows for an efficient estimation in the presence of heteroscedasticity, by resorting to linear orthogonality conditions (Baum et al. [43] provides a useful guide to IV and GMM estimation and their implementation in STATA). Our estimates of models (1), (6) and (7) are thus derived by a two-step efficient GMM estimator, where each variable found to be endogenous—namely, investment volatility and investment GDP share—is instrumented, respectively, by its second lag and its second and third lag (these regressions are performed using the *xtivreg2* program in STATA [44]). The validity of the instruments employed is tested by means of the Wald F-statistics based on the Kleibergen-Paap rk statistics which is robust in presence of heteroscedasticity. It excludes the hypothesis of weak instruments in both cases as it exceeds the rule of thumb, suggested by Staiger and Stock that the F statistic must be larger than 10. As for the exogeneity of the instruments, in both cases we rely on the Hansen-J statistics which strongly accept the exogeneity hypothesis of the instruments in both cases. (See Baum et al. [43] for a detailed explanation of test implementation in STATA and for references). Finally, it is worthwhile noticing that, besides being efficient, our estimation results are also consistent with respect to either heteroscedasticity or autocorrelation because of the Newey-West specification employed for the estimation of the long-run GMM covariance matrix (the Newey-West approach is based on the Bartlett kernel function (which enters the formula of the feasible long-run covariance matrix of moment condition) whose *bandwidth* is chosen according to the common criterion which sets it equal to $T^{1/3}$, where T is the panel time dimension. See Baum et al. [43] and the references therein).

2.3. Growth and Volatility: A Dynamic Panel Approach. Even though current growth rates are not likely to affect our measures of volatility (which is computed over the preceding 5-annual observations window), our results might be biased to the extent that persistent innovations to growth affect future growth rates, as it is argued, for example, in Fatàs and Mihov [23]. For this reason, we re-estimate our models (1), (6), and (7) including the lagged output growth rates as additional regressor as in a dynamic panel estimation framework as follows:

$$g_{it} = \alpha_{i\cdot} + \tau_{\cdot t} + \rho g_{it-1} + \beta\sigma_{it}^{y} + \theta' X_{it} + \varepsilon_{it},$$

$$g_{it} = \alpha_{i\cdot} + \tau_{\cdot t} + \rho g_{it-1} + \beta\sigma_{it}^{y} + \gamma\sigma_{it}^{c} + \delta\sigma_{it}^{i} + \epsilon\sigma_{it}^{g} + \theta' X_{it} + \varepsilon_{it},$$

$$g_{it} = \alpha_{i\cdot} + \tau_{\cdot t} + \rho g_{it-1} + \gamma\sigma_{it}^{c} + \delta\sigma_{it}^{i} + \epsilon\sigma_{it}^{g} + \theta' X_{it} + \varepsilon_{it}, \quad (8)$$

where the previous notation holds.

However, estimating dynamic panel models with unobservable country fixed effects is not a straightforward task. Besides the well-known "dynamic panel bias" that would arise if a naive ordinary least square (OLS) approach was applied to a dynamic fixed-effects model—whereby the lagged dependent variable would turn out to be endogenous to the fixed effects in the error term—usual strategies employed to treat and estimate fixed-effects models, like the least square dummy variable (LSDV) or the "within-group transformation" estimators, are also well known to yield biased estimated coefficients. Anyway, the magnitude of such a bias was found to be inversely correlated with the time dimension of panel; that is, it approaches zero as T approaches infinity [45], implying that those estimators

TABLE 8: Dependent variable: growth rate of per capita GDP. Regressors: volatility of GDP growth, consumption growth, investment growth, government consumption growth, and control variables. Sample: OECD countries (21 countries). Horizon: 1978–2007. Annual observations. All regressions include year dummies.

	Static models estimations—restricted sample					
Estimation	FE	FE	FE	FE-IV GMM	FE-IV GMM	FE-IV GMM
GDP volatility	−0.806		0.038	−0.583**		−0.214
	(−0.41)		(0.15)	(−2.24)		(−0.66)
Consumption volatility		−0.941***	−0.953***		−0.881***	−0.816***
		(−4.63)	(−4.56)		(−4.07)	(−3.48)
Investment volatility		0.105**	0.096*		−0.025	0.016
		(2.37)	(1.74)		(−0.41)	(0.22)
Government consumption volatility		0.293***	0.291***		0.268*	0.285*
		(2.68)	(2.65)		(1.65)	(1.75)
Education	0.005	0.005	0.005	0.006	0.004	0.005
	(1.27)	(1.23)	(1.24)	(0.69)	(0.58)	(0.62)
Population growth	−0.497	−0.331	−0.335	0.761	0.922	0.920
	(−1.14)	(−0.86)	(−0.87)	(1.14)	(1.49)	(1.50)
Initial GDP	−0.066***	−0.054***	−0.054***	−0.077***	−0.065***	−0.065***
	(−3.32)	(−2.85)	(−2.84)	(−3.51)	(−3.18)	(−3.22)
Investment share of GDP	0.056***	0.062***	0.062***	−0.089***	−0.080***	−0.079***
	(4.79)	(5.82)	(5.82)	(−3.95)	(−3.00)	(−2.99)
Observations	630	630	630	567	567	567
Instruments	no	no	no	yes	yes	yes
Hansen J statistic (P value)				0.118	0.234	0.258
Kleibergen-Paap Wald F statistic				90.809	89.438	90.061

Note: T-statistics in parenthesis, robust SEs. *Significance at 10%, **significance at 5%, and ***significance at 1%.

perform well only when the time dimension of the panel is large enough—which is the case for most macropanel data (over the last two decades an extensive literature has delt with this issue especially in the context of microeconometrics—that usually deals with wide (large N) and short (small T) panel datasets—providing a number of alternative suitable econometric strategies). Judson and Owen [46] compare the performance of alternative estimators in the context of a dynamic fixed-effects model for narrow (small N) and long (large T) panels typical of macrodata (they run a Monte-Carlo approach experiment in the spirit of Kiviet [47] in order to compare the efficiency of the LSDV estimator, the LSDV corrected (LSDVC) estimator by Kiviet [47], the Anderson and Hsiao [48] IV difference estimator, and the Arellano and Bond [49] GMM difference estimator, according to different dataset dimensions and degrees of persistence of the lagged dependent variable). Among their findings, they also stress that (i) the difference in the efficiency of those estimators becomes quite small for "large enough" N and T and that (ii) when the outperforming corrected LSDV estimator by Kiviet [47] cannot be implemented (Bruno [50] provides a STATA routine able to implement a LSDVC estimator which, however, is not viable in presence of endogenous regressors other than the lagged dependent variable, which unfortunately is our case) and when $T = 30$, the LSDV represents a more than satisfactory alternative to the Anderson and Hsiao [48] and Arellano and Bond [49] GMM difference strategies, because the magnitude of the bias is relatively small (Harris and Mátyás [51] show that when N is small enough, the LSDV estimator performs just as well as the Arellano and Bond [49] GMM difference estimator). By relying on this evidence, in order to estimate our dynamic models (8) we resort to the LSDV approach. Moreover, in order to confer robustness to our LSDV estimates results, we repeat the estimation employing a restricted one-step "GMM system" estimator [52, 53] as other studies do, like for example, Edwards's [35]. The GMM system estimator belongs to the group of consistent estimators for dynamic panel fixed-effects models that have been proposed in the literature in order to tackle the inconsistency of LSDV in that context (these techniques share the common features of expunging fixed effects by first-differencing the data and of relying upon internal instrumentation of the lagged dependent variable that, once first-differenced, turns out to be correlated with the first-differenced error term. Anderson and Hsiao [48] exploit a simple 2SLS - IV approach using the second lags of the dependent variable (either in difference or in levels) as instruments; Arellano and Bond [49] resort to a GMM approach to derive a larger number ($T - 1$) of internal instruments (in levels) to instrument the endogenous lagged differenced term, which gains efficiency with respect to Anderson and Hsiao approach). Besides, the GMM system is particularly suitable to the extent that data used in the model suffer from some degree of persistence—whereby lagged level of persistent variables would be only weak instruments for the stationary first-differenced term, as it would be the case

Table 9: Dependent variable: growth rate of per capita GDP. Regressors: lagged growth rate of per capita GDP, volatility of GDP growth, consumption growth, investment growth, government consumption growth, and control variables. Sample: OECD countries (21 countries). Horizon: 1978–2007. Annual observations. All regressions include year dummies.

	Dynamic models estimations—restricted sample					
Estimation	LSDV IV 2sls	LSDV IV 2sls	LSDV IV 2sls	SYS-GMM	SYS-GMM	SYS-GMM
GDP volatility	−0.339**		−0.089	−0.135		0.700
	(−1.99)		(−0.40)	(−0.63)		(1.54)
Consumption volatility		−0.586***	−0.560***		−0.386**	−0.562**
		(−3.65)	(−3.14)		(−2.17)	(−2.15)
Investment volatility		−0.020	−0.001		−0.059	−0.222*
		(−0.43)	(−0.02)		(−1.01)	(−1.79)
Government consumption volatility		0.235**	0.242**		0.291*	0.289*
		(2.04)	(2.06)		(1.79)	(1.72)
GDP growth ($t-1$)	0.478***	0.430***	0.428***	0.473***	0.432***	0.451***
	(7.30)	(6.92)	(6.89)	(4.14)	(3.58)	(3.53)
Education	0.004	0.004	0.004	−0.004	−0.001	−0.001
	(0.70)	(0.72)	(0.73)	(−0.32)	(−0.02)	(−0.13)
Population growth	0.220	0.267	0.268	0.111	−0.112	−0.007
	(0.50)	(0.63)	(0.63)	(0.16)	(−0.22)	(−0.01)
Initial GDP	−0.036**	−0.032**	−0.034**	−0.012	−0.012	−0.012
	(−2.23)	(−2.23)	(−2.24)	(−0.56)	(−0.74)	(−0.62)
Investment share of GDP	−0.072***	−0.063***	−0.062***	−0.135**	−0.094*	−0.117***
	(−3.72)	(−3.40)	(−3.40)	(−2.47)	(−1.69)	(−2.66)
Observations	567	567	567	609	609	609
Country dummies	Yes	Yes	Yes	No	No	No
Instruments	Yes	Yes	Yes	Yes	Yes	Yes
Kleibergen-Paap Wald F statistic	212.340	202.231	201.867			
Hansen J/Sargan test (P value)	0.713	0.571	0.562	0.182	0.215	0.214
Arellano-Bond test (AR2) (P value)				0.862	0.745	0.768

Note: T-statistics in parenthesis, robust SEs. *Significance at 10%, **significance at 5%, and ***significance at 1%.

with the GMM difference estimator. However, when the time dimension of the panel is large, an evident drawback of the GMM approach is that it implies the proliferation of the number of instruments, which tends to explode in T. Using too many instruments can overfit the endogenous variables and bias the coefficient estimates, which is among the reasons both difference and system GMM are recommended for short (small T) and large (large N) panels, as argued in Roodman [54, 55]. Therefore, in order both to preserve the reliability of the estimates and to improve the performance of Sargan tests for the joint validity of the instruments, our strategy aims at the limitation of instruments proliferation by both limiting the number of lags used as instruments in the GMM system regressions and resorting to a "collapsed" form of the instrumenting matrix [54].

3. Results

3.1. Main Regressions. Tables 6–9 contain the results of our main regressions' estimates. In particular, Tables 6 and 7 contain results relative to the whole panel, whereas Tables 8 and 9 contain results relative to the restricted sample of countries. In fact, from the descriptive statistics and from the diagnostic analysis of our main sample, the presence of some extreme outlier countries can be easily detected (see Tables 1 and 4). Thus, in order to verify the robustness of our benchmark results, we exclude these countries from our OECD sample, thus resorting to a restricted sample over which we test again our empirical models. Results of the static and dynamic models estimations are displayed, respectively, in Tables 6, 7, 8, and 9. Hansen-J and Sargan tests output for the exogeneity of the instruments employed in either 2SLS and GMM estimations is always provided when IV regressions results are presented, whereas the Arellano and Bond [49] tests for autocorrelation in the error structure are provided only when GMM system estimations output is presented. It is worth noticing that the null hypothesis for all these tests should be accepted for valid estimations, which is always the case in our regressions.

First of all, we can see from our tables that the Ramey and Ramey type of result is confirmed both in our static and in our dynamic models, either on the complete or on the restricted sample, although the (negative) coefficient of volatility is sometimes not statistically significant. In particular, it is worth stressing that, regardless of the sample chosen, GDP

Table 10: Dependent variable: growth rate of per capita GDP. Regressors: volatility of GDP growth, consumption growth, investment growth, government consumption growth, and control variables. Sample: OECD countries (25 countries). Horizon: 1978–2007. Annual observations. All regressions include year dummies. All regressions are population weighted.

	Static models weighted estimations					
Estimation	FE	FE	FE	FE-IV 2sls	FE-IV 2sls	FE-IV 2sls
GDP volatility	−0.073		0.311	−0.476***		−1.790**
	(−0.89)		(1.55)	(−3.94)		(−2.84)
Consumption volatility		−0.687***	−0.766***		−1.337***	−0.882***
		(−5.75)	(−5.90)		(−6.79)	(−4.68)
Investment volatility		0.086***	0.116		0.202***	0.625***
		(2.83)	(0.21)		(3.08)	(3.11)
Government consumption volatility		0.066	0.036		−0.058	0.136
		(0.57)	(0.753)		(−0.34)	(0.73)
Education	0.006	0.007*	0.008**	0.003	0.006	0.006
	(1.45)	(1.94)	(2.03)	(0.55)	(0.95)	(0.99)
Population growth	−0.048	−0.203	−0.223	1.332***	1.05**	1.297***
	(−0.15)	(−0.65)	(−0.72)	(2.88)	(2.38)	(2.70)
Initial GDP	−0.042***	−0.016**	−0.017**	−0.057***	−0.100	−0.022*
	(−5.63)	(−2.21)	(−2.05)	(−5.18)	(−0.81)	(−1.69)
Investment share of GDP	0.115***	0.110***	0.110***	−0.132***	−0.108***	−0.119***
	(11.44)	(11.07)	(11.05)	(−5.19)	(−4.44)	(−4.28)
Observations	750	750	750	675	675	675
Instruments	no	no	no	yes	yes	yes
Sargan statistic (*P* value)				0.807	0.514	0.852
Kleibergen-Paap Wald *F* statistic				133.016	87.75	40.079

Note: T-statistics in parenthesis, robust SEs. *Significance at 10%, **significance at 5%, and ***significance at 1%.

volatility coefficient always turns out to be significantly negative in the context of the static IV regressions; that is, once we properly account for endogeneity which is found to affect investment volatility and the investment share of GDP. According to these estimates, an increase by 10% in the volatility of GDP brings about a reduction in mean growth by 0.09% in the main sample and by 0.13% in the restricted sample. What we infer from this evidence is that disregarding endogeneity would imply a substantially downward biased significance of coefficient estimates. On the other hand, volatility of GDP always fails to be statistically significant within the dynamic regression context, regardless of the estimation strategy employed. Then, we also observe that when volatility of GDP is included in addition to volatility of consumption, investments, and public expenditure, it is never statistically significant at standard significance level, although the sign of its coefficient is always negative.

Concerning the sign of the impact of the different components of volatility on mean growth, the most striking and seemingly very robust result is the negative and almost always statistically significant coefficient attached to the volatility of consumption. It is also worth stressing that the magnitude of its negative impact onto growth is slightly above that implied by (mean) output volatility, as a 10% increase in consumption volatility determines a 0.12% and a 0.16% drop in average GDP growth, respectively, in the two sample considered in the static context (as for this parameter we observe statistically significant estimated coefficients across the models (cf. Tables 6–9); we discuss the average of these estimates). As for the dynamic regression framework, we note that the negative influence of consumption volatility growth is somehow mitigated in both the samples as, on average, the estimated impacts of a 10% increase of consumption volatility onto average GDP growth drop to 0.08% and 0.09%, respectively. As we argued in the introduction, this might be taken to mean that what is really harmful to economic growth is market incompleteness, revealed by the fact that volatility of production and income cannot be dampened by real or financial markets and spill over to consumption. Moreover, volatility in consumption directly affects agents and makes them more vulnerable and less prone to accept additional risks, which might endanger their willingness to engage in more risky and on average more profitable investment opportunities.

On the same ground, the result concerning the impact of public expenditure volatility on mean growth is also quite remarkable. The sign of the coefficient is positive and almost always statistically significant across model specifications, estimations strategies, and samples, suggesting in a fairly robust way that volatility in public expenditure is not harmful, but rather beneficial for growth. The magnitude of the estimated impact of a 10% change in public expenditure volatility ranges between 0.07% and 0.05% for the main sample and between 0.045% and 0.042% for the restricted sample, respectively, in the static and dynamic models. This result lends some support to the view that public expenditures

Table 11: Dependent variable: growth rate of per capita GDP. Regressors: lagged growth rate of per capita GDP, volatility of GDP growth, consumption growth, investment growth, government consumption growth, and control variables. Sample: OECD countries (25 countries). Horizon: 1978–2007. Annual observations. All regressions include year dummies. All regressions are population weighted.

	Dynamic models weighted estimations					
Estimation	LSDV	LSDV	LSDV	LSDV IV 2sls	LSDV IV 2sls	LSDV IV 2sls
GDP volatility	−0.042		0.396*	−0.271***		0.436*
	(−0.46)		(1.92)	(−2.71)		(1.76)
Consumption volatility		−0.583***	−0.683***		−0.515***	−0.630***
		(−4.67)	(−5.06)		(−3.51)	(−3.85)
Investment volatility		0.074***	−0.200		−0.120	−0.114
		(2.38)	(−0.34)		(−0.31)	(−1.64)
Government consumption volatility		0.013	−0.030		−0.075	−0.122
		(0.11)	(−0.20)		(−0.49)	(−0.79)
GDP growth $(t-1)$	0.183***	0.142***	0.142***	0.430***	0.399***	0.399***
	(4.70)	(3.59)	(3.61)	(8.65)	(7.92)	(7.92)
Education	0.004	0.005	0.005	0.005	0.005	0.005
	(0.86)	(1.19)	(1.28)	(0.88)	(1.00)	(0.98)
Population growth	−0.282	−0.378	−0.414	0.518	0.360	0.346
	(−0.87)	(−1.17)	(−1.28)	(1.32)	(0.92)	(0.77)
Initial GDP	−0.032***	−0.139	−0.120	−0.036***	−0.019*	−0.017
	(−4.07)	(−1.59)	(−1.34)	(−3.68)	(−1.80)	(−1.56)
Investment share of GDP	0.092***	0.093***	0.093***	−0.096***	−0.099***	−0.096***
	(8.20)	(8.30)	(8.30)	(−4.96)	(−4.98)	(−4.99)
Observations	725	725	725	675	675	675
Country dummies	Yes	Yes	Yes	Yes	Yes	Yes
Instruments	No	No	No	Yes	Yes	Yes
Kleibergen-Paap Wald F statistic				275.699	269.17	268.73
Sargan test (P value)				0.136	0.166	0.208

Note: T-statistics in parenthesis, robust SEs. *Significance at 10%, **significance at 5%, and ***significance at 1%.

become more volatile when it is used to dampen economic fluctuations, originating from both idiosyncratic and aggregate shocks.

On the other hand, the results concerning volatility in the investment component of GDP growth are less clear cut, at least in terms of statistical significance of the estimated coefficients. If in the case of the benchmark sample the investment volatility coefficients become statistically significant only once we control for endogeneity in the context of the IV regressions and are not statistically significant in the non-IV case, the opposite occurs in the case of the restricted sample (cf. Tables 6 and 8). Hence, we argue that unobserved characteristics imply a downward bias of the coefficient's significance in the former case, whereas a spurious relationship—that we eliminate by resorting to the IV strategy—occurs in the latter. However, across most model specifications, except for the dynamic model estimated on the restricted sample, volatility of investments exerts a positive impact on mean growth. If we recall that volatility of investment *demand* is what we are really talking about, then more volatility can be interpreted as a larger sensitivity of investments to aggregate economic fluctuations, which is a necessary condition for the efficient working of such mechanisms as the ones advocated by neo-Schumpeterian's opportunity cost argument (see e.g., [5, 16, 18, 56]).

Finally, the sign of the other regressors, which we added as control variables following Levine and Renelt [42], meets our prior expectations though with some exceptions that will be duly stressed in the following paragraph. First of all, as expected, dynamic models estimations show that lagged GDP growth is always strongly and significantly correlated to current growth. Then, the negative and statistical significant estimated coefficient of the initial level of GDP can be interpreted as a proof of the betaconvergence hypothesis. Moreover, as all models specifications adopted are endowed with structural variables and country-specific fixed effects, we can interpret that result as verifying the conditional betaconvergence hypothesis. We interpret the fact that the coefficient attached to the initial level of GDP estimated within the static models is slightly higher than its counterpart estimated within the dynamic models, as evidence that the presence of the lagged growth rate term might partially capture the "catching-up" effect.

According to our results, a higher level of education fosters more growth, though the estimated coefficient never achieves standard statistical significance. However, it is likely

TABLE 12: Dependent variable: growth rate of per capita GDP. Regressors: volatility of GDP growth, consumption growth, investment growth, government consumption growth, and control variables. Sample: OECD countries (21 countries). Horizon: 1978–2007. Annual observations. All regressions include year dummies. All regressions are population weighted.

	Static models weighted estimations—restricted sample					
Estimation	FE	FE	FE	FE-IV 2sls	FE -IV 2sls	FE-IV 2sls
GDP volatility	0.319***		0.513**	0.224		0.859***
	(2.99)		(2.48)	(1.55)		(3.15)
Consumption volatility		−1.038***	−1.09***		−1.165***	−1.25***
		(−7.43)	(−7.78)		(−6.53)	(−7.02)
Investment volatility		0.139***	0.017		0.089**	−0.107
		(4.68)	(0.29)		(2.27)	(−1.44)
Government consumption volatility		0.003	−0.020		−0.052	−0.106
		(0.03)	(−0.19)		(−0.36)	(−0.73)
Education	0.004	0.007**	0.007**	−0.002	0.002	0.002
	(1.33)	(2.11)	(2.22)	(−0.41)	(0.48)	(0.31)
Population growth	0.623*	0.626*	0.620*	2.36***	2.079***	2.059***
	(1.85)	(1.92)	(1.91)	(5.00)	(4.60)	(4.62)
Initial GDP	−0.039***		−0.023**	−0.0452***	−0.029**	−0.024**
	(−4.00)		(−2.45)	(−3.56)	(−2.38)	(−1.99)
Investment share of GDP	0.085***		0.080***	−0.097***	−0.091***	−0.089***
	(8.44)		(8.56)	(−4.91)	(−4.83)	(−4.80)
Observations	630	630	630	567	567	567
Instruments	no	no	no	yes	yes	yes
Hansen J statistic (P value)				0.339	0.541	0.560
Kleibergen-Paap Wald F statistic				170.679	171.291	175.060

Note: T-statistics in parenthesis, robust SEs. *Significance at 10%, **significance at 5%, and ***significance at 1%.

that the slow-moving behavior of this variable is absorbed by the country fixed effects which are always included in the regressions presented, as they capture any unobservable slow-moving country characteristic by construction. Indeed, we proved that carrying out OLS regressions that do not account for country specific effects provides positive and significant coefficients estimates for education in almost all models specifications and for both samples (the results of these estimations are available upon request).

As for the estimates of the impact of population growth rates on GDP growth, results are quite nonrobust across estimation strategies, models, and samples employed. In fact, the expected negative sign of the estimated coefficient is verified only by static non-IV regressions, showing statistical significance only when the complete sample is considered. Turning to dynamic models estimations, population growth coefficient reverts to positive sign but never appears statistically significant at standard levels.

Eventually, another unexpected result comes from the estimated coefficient of investment share of GDP in the context of the IV static and dynamic regressions, as it appears to be significatively negative. By contrast, the expected positive and statistically significant sign is only provided by the non-IV estimates. However, as this variable is verified to be endogenous across all models specifications and samples, we tend to rely on the (counterintuitive) results provided by the instrumented estimates, possibly generated by a convergence-like mechanism.

3.2. Population-Weighted Regressions. The results so far are obtained from models that assign all countries equal weights, regardless of their relative size. In other words, results are equally influenced by, for example, the USA and Sweden notwithstanding the substantial differences in their population size. Therefore, as additional robustness check, we run a set of population-weighted regressions for both static and dynamic models and for both complete and restricted samples. The estimations strategies do not differ from those employed in our benchmark not-weighted regressions. However, since the GMM approach is not allowed when weights are employed, we resort to the 2SLS-IV method when we need to run instrumented variables regressions in order to account for endogeneity. This experiment is intended to verify whether the evidence provided by our main regressions is driven by small countries, and the corresponding results are presented in Tables 10, 11, 12, and 13. Broadly speaking, we see that the impact of overall GDP volatility on growth is more ambiguous and seems to crucially depend on the sample: significantly negative for the overall sample, while being significantly positive for the restricted sample. Moreover, unlike in the unweighted regressions, the impact of overall GDP volatility often plays a statistically significant role—with a positive sign—when the three distinct sources of volatility are included. At this point, it is maybe useful to remember the interpretation of this coefficient, which should capture the impact of volatility in net trades and, though probably to a lesser extent, the impact of covariances among the various

TABLE 13: Dependent variable: growth rate of per capita GDP. Regressors: lagged growth rate of per capita GDP, volatility of GDP growth, consumption growth, investment growth, government consumption growth, and control variables. Sample: OECD countries (21 countries). Horizon: 1978–2007. Annual observations. All regressions include year dummies. All regressions are population weighted.

	Dynamic models weighted estimations—restricted sample					
Estimation	LSDV	LSDV	LSDV	LSDV IV 2sls	LSDV IV 2sls	LSDV-IV IV 2sls
GDP volatility	0.197*		0.511**	0.006		0.584**
	(1.78)		(2.40)	(0.04)		(2.40)
Consumption volatility		−0.825***	−0.889***		−0.731***	−0.800***
		(−5.61)	(−5.97)		(−4.46)	(−4.84)
Investment volatility		0.094***	−0.026		0.019	−0.113*
		(2.95)	(−0.44)		(0.53)	(−1.69)
Government consumption volatility		−0.052	−0.070		−0.124	−0.159
		(−0.47)	(−0.63)		(−0.96)	(−1.23)
GDP growth ($t-1$)	0.331***	0.272***	0.267***	0.497***	0.457***	0.445***
	(7.95)	(6.43)	(6.34)	(10.16)	(9.14)	(8.96)
Education	0.001	0.003	0.003	0.002	0.005	0.004
	(0.21)	(0.86)	(0.87)	(0.55)	(1.04)	(0.90)
Population growth	0.104	0.161	0.187	0.58	0.525	0.549
	(0.29)	(0.46)	(0.54)	(1.42)	(1.30)	(1.36)
Initial GDP	−0.025**	−0.017*	−0.146	−0.021*	−0.013	−0.011
	(−2.51)	(−1.73)	(−1.50)	(−1.89)	(−1.22)	(−0.95)
Investment share of GDP	0.049***	0.053***	0.052***	−0.063***	−0.064***	−0.063***
	(4.66)	(5.12)	(5.05)	(−4.17)	(−4.23)	(−4.20)
Observations	609	609	609	567	567	567
Country dummies	yes	yes	yes	yes	yes	yes
Instruments	no	no	no	yes	yes	yes
Hansen J/Sargan test (P value)				0.178	0.196	0.200
Kleibergen-Paap Wald F statistic				348.850	344.011	346.559

Note: T-statistics in parenthesis, robust SEs. *Significance at 10%, **significance at 5%, and ***significance at 1%.

components of volatility. Investment volatility is still linked to more growth, except in the case of the dynamic estimation on the restricted sample. On the other hand, the volatility in public expenditure ceases to be significant for all model specifications and all samples. Once again, the most robust and clear cut relationship remains the negative one between consumption volatility and mean growth.

4. Concluding Remarks

This paper tries to complement the existing empirical literature on volatility and growth by decomposing volatility of GDP and using some of the components (consumption, investment, and public expenditure) in standard growth equations *à la* G. Ramey and V. A. Ramey [7] that are estimated by a variety of econometric methods, on an OECD cross country panel dataset, in order to assess the robustness of the results. The underlying idea is that key to understanding the reasons why GDP volatility should influence mean growth in either way is an assessment of the drivers of such a volatility (in other words whether it is consumption, investment, or public expenditure that makes GDP unstable should really make a difference).

We suggest that attaching a positive or negative sign to the impact of the various components of GDP volatility could also help solving the apparent lack of unanimity affecting the results presented in the recent empirical literature, whose contributions make clear that different estimation techniques and, above all, different samples, may yield different results.

Among the various components of overall GDP growth volatility we focus on consumption, investments, and public expenditure volatility, leaving out volatility in net trades and the covariances between all of these variables. The most striking result we obtain is a remarkably robust and strong negative relationship between consumption volatility and mean growth. This we interpret as evidence that lack of markets completeness discourage riskier and more profitable investments and depress consumption, by fostering more precautionary savings. On the other hand, once we control for this particular factor, investment volatility is often positively associated to mean growth, as well as volatility in government expenditures.

It is worth recalling that our measures of volatility relate to the demand side of the economy. It would also be interesting, as a future extension of this work, to relate mean growth to other measures of volatility, computed from variables related to the supply side of an economy, such as the volatility in the returns of labour and capital, and productivity.

References

[1] R. E. Lucas Jr., *Models of Business Cycles*, Basil Blackwell, New York, NY, USA, 1987.

[2] E. Kydland and E. C. Prescott, "Time to build and aggregate fluctuations," *Econometrica*, vol. 50, no. 6, pp. 1345–1370, 1982.

[3] G. W. Stadler, "Business cycle models with endogenous technology," *American Economic Review*, vol. 80, no. 4, pp. 763–778, 1990.

[4] R. G. King and S. Rebelo, "Public policy and economic growth: developing neoclassical implications," *Journal of Political Economy*, vol. 98, no. 5, pp. S126–S150, 1990.

[5] P. Aghion and G. Saint-Paul, "Virtues of bad times: interaction between productivity growth and economic fluctuations," *Macroeconomic Dynamics*, vol. 2, no. 3, pp. 322–344, 1998.

[6] P. Gaggl and S. Steindl, "Business cycles and growth: a survey," WIFO Working Papers 308, 2007.

[7] G. Ramey and V. A. Ramey, "Cross-country evidence on the link between volatility and growth," *The American Economic Review*, vol. 85, pp. 1138–1151, 1995.

[8] P. Martin and C. A. Rogers, "Stabilization policy, learning-by-doing, and economic growth," *Oxford Economic Papers*, vol. 49, no. 2, pp. 152–166, 1997.

[9] V. Hnatkovska and N. Loayza, "Volatility and growth," in *Managing Economic Volatility and Crises: A Practitioner's Guide*, J. Aizenman and B. Pinto, Eds., Cambridge University Press, Cambridge, UK, 2005.

[10] M. A. Kose, E. S. Prasad, and M. E. Terrones, "How do trade and financial integration affect the relationship between growth and volatility?" *Journal of International Economics*, vol. 69, no. 1, pp. 176–202, 2006.

[11] J. Imbs, "Growth and volatility," *Journal of Monetary Economics*, vol. 54, no. 7, pp. 1848–1862, 2007.

[12] R. C. Kormendi and P. G. Meguire, "Macroeconomic determinants of growth: cross-country evidence," *Journal of Monetary Economics*, vol. 16, no. 2, pp. 141–163, 1985.

[13] K. B. Grier and G. Tullock, "An empirical analysis of cross-national economic growth, 1951–1980," *Journal of Monetary Economics*, vol. 24, no. 2, pp. 259–276, 1989.

[14] T. Caporale and B. McKiernan, "The relationship between output variability and growth: evidence from post war UK data," *Scottish Journal of Political Economy*, vol. 43, no. 2, pp. 229–236, 1996.

[15] J. A. Schumpeter, *Capitalism, Socialism, and Democracy*, Harper and Brothers, New York, NY, USA, 1976, Harper Colophon edition.

[16] S. Davis and J. C. Haltiwanger, "Gross job creation, gross job destruction, and employment reallocation," *The Quarterly Journal of Economics*, vol. 107, no. 3, pp. 819–863, 1992.

[17] C. R. Bean, "Endogenous growth and the procyclical behaviour of productivity," *European Economic Review*, vol. 34, no. 2-3, pp. 355–363, 1990.

[18] R. Caballero and M. Hammour, "The cleansing effect of recessions," *American Economic Review*, vol. 84, no. 5, pp. 383–398, 1991.

[19] K. J. Arrow, "The economic implications of learning by doing," *Review of Economic Studies*, vol. 29, pp. 155–173, 1962.

[20] A. Shleifer, "Implementation Cycles," *Journal of Political Economy*, vol. 94, no. 6, pp. 1163–1190, 1986.

[21] K. Blackburn and A. Pelloni, "On the relationship between growth and volatility," *Economics Letters*, vol. 83, no. 1, pp. 123–127, 2004.

[22] A. Afonso and D. Furceri, "Government size, composition, volatility and economic growth," *European Journal of Political Economy*, vol. 26, no. 4, pp. 517–532, 2010.

[23] A. Fatàs and I. Mihov, "Policy volatility, institutions and economic growth," *Review of Economics and Statistics*, vol. 95, no. 2, pp. 362–376, 2013.

[24] G. Schnabl, "Exchange rate volatility and growth in small open economies at the EMU periphery," *Economic Systems*, vol. 32, no. 1, pp. 70–91, 2008.

[25] P. Aghion, P. Bacchetta, R. Rancière, and K. Rogoff, "Exchange rate volatility and productivity growth: the role of financial development," *Journal of Monetary Economics*, vol. 56, no. 4, pp. 494–513, 2009.

[26] R. Judson and A. Orphanides, "Inflation, volatility and growth," *International Finance*, vol. 2, no. 1, pp. 117–138, 1999.

[27] F. Al-Marhubi, "Cross-country evidence on the link between inflation volatility and growth," *Applied Economics*, vol. 30, no. 10, pp. 1317–1326, 1998.

[28] D. Furceri, "Long-run growth and volatility: which source really matters?" *Applied Economics*, vol. 42, no. 15, pp. 1865–1874, 2010.

[29] F. Black, *Business Cycles and Equilibrium*, Blackwell, Cambridge, Mass, USA, 1987.

[30] L. Mirman, "Uncertainty and optimal consumption decisions," *Econometrica*, vol. 39, pp. 179–185, 1971.

[31] J. Sachs and X. Sala-i-Martin, "Fiscal federalism and optimum currency areas: evidence for Europe from the US," NBER Working Paper 3885, 1991.

[32] P. Asdrubali, B. E. Sørensen, and O. Yosha, "Channels of interstate risk sharing: United States 1963–1990," *Quarterly Journal of Economics*, vol. 111, no. 4, pp. 1080–1110, 1996.

[33] R. Lensink, H. Bo, and E. Sterken, "Does uncertainty affect economic growth? An empirical analysis," *Review of World Economics*, vol. 135, no. 3, pp. 393–396, 1999.

[34] M. Rafferty, "The effects of expected and unexpected volatility on long-run growth: evidence from 18 developed economies," *Southern Economic Journal*, vol. 71, no. 3, pp. 582–591, 2005.

[35] J. A. Edwards, "Dynamics of the cross-country growth/volatility relationship," *Global Economy Journal*, vol. 7, no. 2, article 4, 2007.

[36] A. Heston, R. Summers, and B. Aten, "Penn World Table Version 6.3," 2010.

[37] R. Barro and J. W. Lee, "A new data set of educational attainment in the world, 1950–2010," NBER Working Paper 15902, 2010.

[38] K. S. Im, M. H. Pesaran, and Y. Shin, "Testing for unit roots in heterogeneous panels," *Journal of Econometrics*, vol. 115, no. 1, pp. 53–74, 2003.

[39] H. S. Esfahani, "Understanding economic growth in specific contexts: an overview of the first phase of global research project 'explaining growth,'" in *Diversity in Economic Growth: Global Insights and Explanations*, Edward Elgar Publishing, Glos, UK, 2009.

[40] W. Easterly and A. Kraay, "Small states, small problems? Income, growth, and volatility in small states," *World Development*, vol. 28, no. 11, pp. 2013–2027, 2000.

[41] L. Pritchett, "A conclusion to cross national growth research: a foreword 'to the countries themselves'," in *Explaining Growth. A Global Research Project*, G. McMahon and L. Squire, Eds., chapter 6, 2003.

[42] R. Levine and D. Renelt, "A sensitivity analysis of cross-country growth regressions," *American Economic Review*, vol. 82, no. 4, pp. 942–963, 1992.

[43] C. F. Baum, M. E. Schaffer, and S. Stillman, "Enhanced routines for instrumental variables/generalized method of moments estimation and testing," *The Stata Journal*, vol. 7, no. 4, pp. 465–506, 2007.

[44] Schaffer, "XTIVREG2: Stata module to perform extended IV/2SLS, GMM and AC/HAC, LIML and k-class regression for panel data models," Statistical Software Components S456501, Boston College Department of Economics, 2005.

[45] S. J. Nickell, "Biases in dynamic models with fixed effects," *Econometrica*, vol. 49, no. 6, pp. 1417–1426, 1981.

[46] R. A. Judson and A. L. Owen, "Estimating dynamic panel data models: a guide for macroeconomists," *Economics Letters*, vol. 65, no. 1, pp. 9–15, 1999.

[47] J. F. Kiviet, "On bias, inconsistency, and efficiency of various estimators in dynamic panel data models," *Journal of Econometrics*, vol. 68, no. 1, pp. 53–78, 1995.

[48] T. W. Anderson and C. Hsiao, "Formulation and estimation of dynamic models using panel data," *Journal of Econometrics*, vol. 18, no. 1, pp. 47–82, 1982.

[49] M. Arellano and S. Bond, "Some tests of specification for panel data: Monte Carlo evidence and an application to employment equations," *The Review of Economic Studies*, vol. 58, pp. 277–297, 1991.

[50] G. S. F. Bruno, "XTLSDVC: stata module to estimate bias corrected LSDV dynamic panel data models," Statistical Software Components S450101, Boston College Department of Economics, 2005.

[51] M. N. Harris and L. Mátyás, "A comparative analysis of different IV and GMM estimators of dynamic panel data models," *International Statistical Review*, vol. 72, no. 3, pp. 397–408, 2004.

[52] M. Arellano and O. Bover, "Another look at the instrumental variable estimation of error-components models," *Journal of Econometrics*, vol. 68, no. 1, pp. 29–51, 1995.

[53] R. Blundell and S. Bond, "Initial conditions and moment restrictions in dynamic panel data models," *Journal of Econometrics*, vol. 87, no. 1, pp. 115–143, 1998.

[54] D. Roodman, "How to do xtabond2: an introduction to "Difference" and "System" GMM in Stata," Center For Global Development Working Paper 103, 2006.

[55] D. Roodman, "A short note on the theme of too many instruments," Center For Global Development Working Paper 125, 2007.

[56] G. Saint-Paul, "Productivity growth and the structure of the business cycle," *European Economic Review*, vol. 37, pp. 861–890, 1993.

14

John Nyman and the Economics of Health Care Moral Hazard

Sander Kelman[1] and Albert Woodward[2]

[1] *1500 Sawyer Avenue, Manasquan, NJ 08736, USA*
[2] *CBHSQ, SAMHSA, US Department of Health and Human Services, 1 Choke Cherry Road, Rockville, MD 20050, USA*

Correspondence should be addressed to Sander Kelman; sanderkelman@gmail.com

Academic Editors: M. J. Larson, I. Shoji, and J. Zarnikau

In 2003, John Nyman published *The Theory of Demand for Health Insurance*. His principal contributions are (1) to replace the previously unexamined axiom of risk avoidance with the axiom of welfare maximization; (2) to uncover a misinterpretation in the literature on moral hazard, namely, the insurance payoff as a price reduction, rather than as an income transfer. The immediate consequence of these reformulations is to recognize insurance-induced health care utilization as resulting in an increase in social welfare. Despite its evident validity and enormous implications, Nyman's work has received very little attention or recognition in the health economics literature.

1. Introduction

Although it remains to be seen whether the US can bring its per capita health care costs into line with other industrial nations [1], the US, after nearly 100 years of effort, passed national health care legislation in 2010. The Affordable Care Act, as it is widely known, passed with expectations of eventually bringing the nation close to a state of universal health care coverage. The legislative and other debates leading up to passage covered a wide range of topics, but one important concept—health care moral hazard—was never explicitly encountered in the debate.

The absence of moral hazard in the debate appears to be an aberration. For more than 40 years one of the central tenets of health care economics has been the presumption that universal coverage would induce a rather substantial degree of moral hazard and therefore would reduce national economic welfare correspondingly.

Among economists, these tenets are rooted analytically in a framework known as *welfare economics*, the objective of which seeks the circumstances leading to improved or maximized *human welfare*. The nature of the framework and, more pointedly, the manner in which that framework has been mobilized to characterize the health insurance policy payoff results in a habitual conclusion that more insurance-induced health care utilization results in a decline in human welfare. Consistent with that result had been the omnipresent policy caution that extensions of health insurance coverage to the general population were to be avoided.

In 2003, John Nyman published *The Theory of Demand for Health Insurance* [2] that uncovered a number of what he argued to be critical errors in the way in which the insurance payoff has been understood through the lens of *welfare economics*, and that the cumulative effect of these errors has been to introduce a decided bias in the formulation of health coverage policy. The book is slim by page count, but momentous in its findings and implications. His analysis is stunning, with potentially revolutionary implications for the scientific-economic basis of health care finance; yet, ten years on, there appears to be little notice, pro or con, in the usual professional locations. This paper attempts to elaborate and inform that state of affairs.

Nyman's book concerns itself with the formulation of a coherent "theory of the *demand*[1] for health insurance." To the casual observer, this may appear to belabor the obvious; in fact, what Nyman presents overturns decades of questionable orthodoxy and brings economic theory into coincidence with widespread lay American and professional international thinking about health care finance and many of the practices in all other developed countries. Moreover, he does it without stepping outside the analytical norms of traditional economics.

Nyman's book is not for everyone. Much of his argument proceeds in the language, geometry, and mathematics of *welfare economics*, a particularly rarified, but respected subdiscipline within the canon of contemporary economics[2]. Nyman's conclusions, however, and particularly the implications of those conclusions are for everyone.

2. Background

Many in the US health care field, including health economists, have supported the idea of universal coverage. The tenets of the professional discipline of health economics, however, have not supported the notion of such coverage [3, 4].

The modern professional economic argument on the subject began with Arrow in 1963 [5]. Arrow's argument is based on the widespread and *strong*[3] assumption that consumers are averse to the risk of uncertain events[4] such as unpredictable medical expenses. While this assumption may appear to be self-evident, it means more in economic parlance than the vernacular words connote. To economists, *risk aversion* refers to the presumed tendency of people to prefer the certainty of a *fair insurance premium*[5] to the uncertainty of actuarially equivalent *self-insurance* ("going naked"). Believing health insurance premiums at the time to be largely *fair*, but observing a widespread lack of insurance coverage, Arrow concluded that this was a notable instance of *market failure*, a technical expression denoting the failure of the marketplace, through private incentives, to make available goods and services which are demonstrably part of the *optimal*, or *welfare maximizing*, output of the economy or otherwise revealed or understood to be highly meritorious [6].

An important analytical challenge to Arrow's argument was introduced shortly thereafter by Pauly [7]. In it Pauly argues that the lack of widely available insurance against most health care costs may be for good and rational economic reasons, not *market failure*. In particular, he points to *moral hazard*, the curious coinage of insurance underwriters to characterize the greater *demand* for services when covered by insurance than when not covered. Pauly's argument is straightforward: (1) people covered by health insurance—once the premium is paid—face much less expensive health care services than do those in similar clinical circumstances, but without insurance; (2) since it is less expensive, they purchase more of it ("sliding down their *demand curve*" for medical care services); (3) increased utilization leads, in successive periods, to higher premiums, taxes, and foregone wage increases to pay for it; and (4) the resulting increased (premium) costs of coverage make insurance less attractive, and, so goes Pauly's argument, many people refrain from its purchase[6,7].

While the foregoing argument is advanced to take exception to Arrow's finding of a *market failure* for health insurance coverage, Pauly further argues that, given the presence of *moral hazard*, any effort to extend health insurance coverage, private or public, is likely to have the effect of reducing the level of *economic welfare* across the population [7, page 534]. More than anything, this questionable implication of Pauly's argument has resulted in the aversion of economists, and especially health economists, to any significant expansion of health care coverage, referenced above.

Pauly views the insurance payoff as an artificial reduction in price, resulting in an increase in purchase of medical care services (and a reduction in the purchase of all other things), and, from fairly settled *welfare economic theory*, this results in an unambiguous decline in *welfare*[8].

While somewhat obliquely stated in the original, it should have been clear from Pauly's original comment that this argument was intended to apply only or primarily to the relatively inexpensive and predictable elements of medical care, "visits to a physician's office... dental care, eyeglasses or drugs" [7, page 535]. In 1983, he restated this qualification and persisted that, "the relevant theory, empirical evidence, and policy analysis for *moral hazard* in the case of serious illness have not been developed. This is one of the most serious omissions in the current literature" [8]. Given the extent to which *moral hazard* has dominated economist thinking on health care finance—expensive as well as inexpensive—for several decades, the neglect of this qualification is remarkable.

3. Implications and Consequences of the Original Moral Hazard Argument

Feldstein [9] set the tone for much of the empirical research to follow Pauly's comment. In this 1973 study, Feldstein inferred that, on the subject of American health insurance of the time, the *welfare* losses resulting from *moral hazard* exceeded the gains from *risk avoidance* (insurance coverage). To attenuate this disturbing perception, he recommended raising the coinsurance rate on health insurance to 66 percent. Over the next several decades, many others replicated these inferences [10]. One other study worthy of note in this regard is the RAND Health Insurance Experiment, conducted mostly during the 1980s [11].

Instead of merely a footnote qualifying Arrow's paean to universal coverage in favor of some form of catastrophic coverage, Pauly's comment launched a generation of professional work purporting to document the loss in *welfare* suffered by American health care consumers as a result of the tax exemption of employer-based insurance, first- or near-first-dollar coverage (where it existed), and copayments beneath the substantial level determined by some economists to be "optimal" [10]. By the late 1970s, this reasoning led, among other things, to a policy posture of avoiding the extension of public financing of health insurance in favor of a panoply of punitive, behavior modifying and micromanaging measures to restrict this tendency to *moral hazard*: higher deductibles and coinsurance, care management, prepayment, gatekeepers, utilization review, voluntary and mandatory second opinions, chronic disease management, and so forth, all of which underlies much of the contemporary physician displeasure with the health insurance system. Initially (in the 1970s and 80s) this emphasis was said to be erected in order to insert discipline into the markets for health care services, so that when some version of universal coverage came along, it would not be wasted in welfare-reducing *moral hazard* [12]. Eventually, with the exception of one year during the Carter and one or two during the Clinton administrations, there was no serious progress until the Obama administration. This is largely where the main contours of the theoretical and empirical discourse remained until the past few years with the publication of Nyman's book and articles [13].

4. The Argument from Nyman

Nyman's argument can be recapitulated as follows.

The present theory and analysis of the economics of the demand for health insurance is encumbered by serious anomalies and other difficulties. What is needed is a new formulation starting from first principles, but without the necessity of deviating from any of the fundamentals of modern *welfare economics*.

In particular, *risk avoidance*, the long-standing behavioral assumption underlying the study of the demand for health insurance, is both theoretically untenable and empirically rejected.

Risk avoidance, as specified above, has formed the basis of all discussions of the economics of the demand for any type of insurance for nearly the past 60 years [14].

This axiom presumes that people purchase insurance because they prefer the certain loss of paying the premium to taking their chances with actuarially equivalent risky outcomes (self-insurance). The degree to which people are presumed *risk averse* is measured by the extent to which they are willing to pay a premium that exceeds the sum of actuarially equivalent, self-insurance outlays[9]. But this makes no sense in the case of health insurance, argues Nyman, since much of the high-end health care services normally covered by health insurance policies are out of the reach of most people's self-insurance capabilities. If you cannot afford to pay out of pocket for it, you are not buying health insurance against it for *risk-avoidance* purposes. In other words, if you cannot afford to pay the costs associated with the unforeseen and expensive covered health care interventions, then the premium for the policy covering those interventions is not the actuarial equivalent of the financial circumstances you face. Your purchase behavior, in this situation, therefore, is not driven by what economists refer to as *risk avoidance*[10].

Additionally, argues Nyman, "the demand for insurance has nothing to do with the demand for certainty, because uncertainty exists with or without insurance. Even if the consumer has insurance, the uncertainty is whether the consumer will remain healthy and incur the loss of the premium or become ill and receive an (insurance payment)" [2, page 54], and even with the payment, it remains uncertain whether the consumer's health status will improve, with obvious and serious economic and other implications.

Moreover, continues Nyman, empirically, all of the scientific research to date on Prospect Theory[11] [15, 16], which extends to all aspects of economic chance taking, suggests that people generally prefer uncertain losses to certain losses of the same expected magnitude. These consistent empirical findings cannot be consistent with an axiom that posits a predictable preference for a certain loss over actuarially equivalent uncertain losses, and where empirical findings regularly contradict prevailing theory, the theory ought to be in question.

In place of the traditional *risk avoidance* formulation of consumer motivation, Nyman substitutes the historically prior and more general and familiar, "*weaker,*" premise, namely, that consumers base their purchase decisions regarding health insurance on their effort to maximize *expected utility*[12]. This formulation has the added benefit of rendering the theory of the *demand* for health insurance consistent with the theory of demand for everything else.

The second anomaly in the contemporary economics of health insurance is the treatment of the insurance payoff as a reduction in price, leading to an increase in utilization.

Beginning with Pauly [7] all discussions of health care *moral hazard* have adopted the surprisingly arbitrary convention, as described above, that treats the insurance payoff as making the purchase of covered health care services by insured persons as if those services are available to those insured persons at substantially reduced prices (deductibles and coinsurance). The problem with this is neither logical inconsistency nor empirical contradiction as was the case with *risk avoidance*. In this case the problem is an error in adducing the *welfare* implications of the insurance-induced increase in utilization. The argument is as follows.

Fundamentally, argues Nyman, consumers *demand* health insurance in order to obtain income transfers from the insurance pool in the event of sickness.

Having discarded *risk avoidance* and using the *weaker*[13] Bernoulli [17] *welfare maximization* premise, Nyman postulates that consumers attempt to maximize their utility by purchasing health insurance, in order to have access to income transfers, which are the payoffs from the insurance pool in the event that they are sick. This enables them to purchase needed, often expensive, health care services that they would never have been able to afford without insurance. Normally in economic discourse, "affordability" refers to discussions of purchases of which people with low incomes cannot avail themselves; in this case the subject is health care services which form the standard of care in treating many serious conditions, services which are not affordable out of pocket even by a significant majority of the population.

These services are the often life-saving diagnostic and therapeutic interventions: non-X-ray diagnostic radiology, heart surgery, organ and bone-marrow transplants, therapeutic radiology, chemotherapy, and many, many others. These interventions cost tens and even hundreds of thousands of dollars for a single application and in most instances would not be purchased were it not for widespread insurance coverage[14]. These are presumably the services about which Pauly argued that the relevant theory, empirical evidence, and policy analysis for *moral hazard* in the case of serious illness had not been developed [8]. Arguably, Nyman's new formulation of the *demand* for health insurance offers a plausible answer to Pauly's honorably modest qualification of his own work.

Given this new formulation of the *demand* for health insurance, economic theory suggests that much of the resulting increase in health care utilization represents an improvement in *economic welfare*, not the worsening that has been argued for the past 40 years.

The immediate consequence of this shift in motivational specification of the *demand for health insurance* brings with it a major change in the economic implications of the insurance payoff. Nyman's characterization of the insurance payoff is as the payment of a *transitory income* transfer to the insured from the insurance pool. This results in the insured consumer *demanding* more health care at every price than he/she had previously (to the income transfer, not to the holding of insurance). By the same long-standing *welfare economics* invoked above, this increased demand from increased income results in an unambiguous increase in *utility* or *welfare*.

By retaining the stronger *risk-avoidance* assumption and thereby overlooking the likely unaffordability of the sickness outcome in the Friedman and Savage scenario [18], economists from Pauly forward have been blinded to the income transfers inherent in the insurance payoff and have, instead, viewed the insurance payoff as merely reducing the price at which health care services are available to members of the insurance pool.

They do not account in the theory for how the price declines. But the insurance payoff is as much a component of *transitory income* [19] as are winnings at the gaming table. It would be difficult to overstate either the centrality or the wrong headedness of both the *risk aversion* assumption and the insurance payoff/price reduction convention for determining the *welfare* implications of holding health insurance.

Nyman is not denying the presence of *moral hazard*—the tendency to purchase more as prices decline. He is differing with the prior formulation of the consumer demand for health insurance, the characterization of the insurance payoff to sick insured individuals, and, therefore, the *welfare* implications of greater insurance coverage.

Following on this reformulation, Nyman distinguishes between *efficient* and *inefficient moral hazard*. Each is a component of the total *welfare* effect of the measurable increase in utilization resulting from increased insurance coverage. *Efficient moral hazard* is that component of the utilization increases attributable solely to the increase in income the transfer affords. From well-developed *welfare theory*, this results in an unambiguous increase in *welfare*. *Inefficient moral hazard* is that component of the increase attributable to the fact that the utilization is purchased at deductible and coinsurance rates, not full price. As reviewed in Section 2, this latter component results in an unambiguous reduction in welfare.

While the theory in question is considerably more complicated even than this discussion, it is not a distortion to say that the *moral hazard* argument of the past 40 years, as it has been applied to health insurance policy, contains an error (or at least an unrecognized assumption) that is often the barb of introductory microeconomic course pedagogy—the error of confusing a *movement along a demand curve* with a *shift in the demand schedule*. More specifically until Nyman, economists have erred in interpreting the insurance-induced increase in health care expenditure as a movement downward along a given individual's *demand curve* in response to the appearance of a reduction in price. Instead, what Nyman sees is an outward shift in the individual's *demand curve*, resulting from the income transfer originating in policy-holder premium payments. The "pivot point" of the two interpretations is in the analytical choice between *risk avoidance* and *welfare maximization* (see Friedman and Savage [18] versus Bernoulli [17]), and the *welfare* implications of the two perspectives are starkly different. According to the orthodox theory, based on *risk avoidance*, all *moral hazard* is *inefficient*.

Indeed there is another respect in which the old *moral hazard* argument is in theoretical default. Within the presently-accepted *welfare economic* or *general equilibrium* framework, one can imagine people purchasing health insurance on the basis of either *risk avoidance* or *welfare maximization*. In either case, premium payments are made into an insurance pool. Of the people making the payments, some remain healthy throughout the term of the contract. Others do not and, if covered, submit claims for needed services; if approved, payments are made to insureds, effectively increasing their income and purchasing power. As a result, according to Nyman, the correct formulation of the insurance payoff is using the pool to transfer income from all premium payers to those who are or become sick and are covered and authorized for needed services; this transfer is a form of *transitory income* [19] enabling the purchase of otherwise unaffordable services[15]. Welfare is unquestionably increased[16].

From the point of view of the traditional theory, however, insureds are viewed, not as receiving an income transfer from the pool, but rather facing prices significantly beneath market prices for covered health care services. Within this (traditional) theory, the insurance pool ceases to be a part of the theory. It disappears once the insurance premium is paid. Under Nyman's theory premium payments are made to the pool, and income transfers are made from the pool to qualifying insureds, which use it (only) to purchase covered and authorized services. Providers, in turn, use the money to pay suppliers, purchase equipment, hire labor, and so forth. As theory, the reduced price formulation is seriously truncated.

This is the crux of Nyman's contribution—to extend the Pauly formulation in favor of the more tenable and theoretically consistent view that health insurance results in a system of income transfers from the healthy to the sick, and that these transfers often result in *net welfare increases*. Boldly put, in the face of nearly 40 years of economists trumpeting the *welfare*-reducing effects of health insurance coverage, Nyman insists, with arguably ample justification, that the truth, on balance, is just the reverse.

Substantively, in place of the decried *always inefficient moral hazard* is the additional services purchased by insureds, which most would never have been able to afford, the purchase of which, when sick, is the new, posited reason for the purchase of the insurance. In light of Nyman's contribution, prior estimates of the welfare loss due to *moral hazard* [9] have been severely overstated. Nyman concludes in a careful theoretical-empirical analysis [2, page 98] that only 31 percent of insurance-induced utilization is welfare decreasing *inefficient moral hazard*; whereas 69 percent is *efficient moral hazard*, income increases affording people throughout most of the Nation's income distribution the ability to purchase otherwise unaffordable—and arguably effective—care.

Nyman's preliminary empirical exploration suggests the possibility, and even likelihood that valuing the total of *efficient* and *inefficient moral hazard* leads to significantly positive net social benefits.

In an effort to provide an empirical illustration of these ideas, Nyman cites [2, page 110–114] credible recent studies which reveal a 25% increased risk of mortality among the uninsured, ages 25–65, a valid estimate of the value of an additional year of life within that age interval of $100,000, and excess per capita health care expenditures among the insured of this age group (relative to those uninsured) of $976 (1996). Based on these estimates, if coverage were to be extended to the 40 million uninsured in 1996, the year to which the estimates apply (now in 2013, several million greater) Americans' one-year welfare increases from improved mortality alone would be valued at $123 billion, and welfare reductions due to the traditional *(inefficient) moral hazard* (of purchasing health care at prices beneath its cost of production) would be valued at $39 billion, with a one-year net social benefit of $84 billion "or a welfare gain from *moral hazard* that is more than three times its cost" and over $2,000 per uninsured person.

Nyman discusses a variety of qualifications in using these numbers, but concludes that the $84 billion estimate is a very conservative one for the narrow question he addresses. For those who believe that a proper estimate of net social benefits should be an important contributor to policy selection, this is an extremely important finding.

If the prior work of Pauly, Feldstein, Newhouse, Manning, and others was actually an impediment to improved coverage, then Nyman's work, if it stands up, should remove that impediment. The difficulty of measuring the effects of moral hazard, however, is a barrier to overcoming this impediment. Moreover, should these formulations and findings hold up upon further investigation, Nyman, 40 years later, reinstates Arrow's original conclusion that serious gaps in coverage strongly suggest an important instance of *market failure*. Following on that, economists should then trumpet the consequent economic desirability of increased social financing for the achievement of universal—but not necessarily first dollar—coverage against health care expenses. Should these formulations and findings hold up, we may expect these new preferences to be revealed in future polling of health economists.

5. Consequences and Implications

The first corollary of Nyman's work is that the *welfare* implications of *moral hazard* are now reversed. In the traditional formulation, insurance is seen to reduce the price of medical treatments leading to distortions in patterns of consumer purchase that unambiguously reduce *welfare*. According to Nyman's formulation, insurance provides income transfers from the insurance pool to sick insureds, enabling them to avail themselves of expensive, standards of care not otherwise affordable for serious illnesses. Because this increase in income enables the insureds to increase their purchases of medical treatments at each price level, this leads to general increases in welfare[17]. Practical implications of this include a need to rethink and recalculate optimal copayment levels, income tax exemption on employment-based health insurance, and optimal insurance policy design. Following on that is the implication that greater coverage or elimination of the uninsured is not only good politics in some circles, but it is also good economics in any circles[18].

A final implication is the appearance that something other than mere analytic discourse is involved in this discussion of the past 40 years. In the US a unique coincidence exists of rather parlous health care coverage and a rather aggressive economic doctrine which, in effect, tends to justify that stinginess. Neither exists to any significant degree in other advanced countries[19]. There is no suggestion here of a vulgarly conceived conspiracy to suppress doctrines that would have the effect of universalizing health care coverage. What we have shown is that there is a serious scientific question about the validity of the contemporary doctrine of *moral hazard*, and that its popularity is greatest, nay, almost uniquely held—in a country with the least generous health care coverage, suggesting that the study of the doctrine of *moral hazard* belongs not only in the field of Economic Science but also in that of the Sociology of Knowledge.

6. Response to the Argument

Despite what appears to be a major challenge, the response to Nyman's work by health economists appears to be one of benign neglect followed by begrudging, albeit limited, acceptance among some. Standard reviews of the book—generally positive and summarizing Nyman's work—have appeared in four journals that can be considered peer-reviewed, professional journals of economics, health care policy, or insurance [20–23]. The book has not been reviewed in some of the leading economic or health services journals in which one would expect great interest, even if negative[20]. Nyman's theory has been the inspiration of a favorable article in *The New Yorker* in August 2005 [24][21]. It is explained in at least two health economics textbooks that have achieved several editions[22], is taught in college and university health economics or policy courses, and has spawned related theoretical and empirical work [25, 26].

The first critical review concerning Nyman's theory appeared several years before his book's publication. Blomqvist [27], while directing an entire article in response to an article by Nyman appearing earlier in the same journal [13] embodying much of the argument in the book under review, largely skirts the issues Nyman raises, damns with faint praise, and otherwise dismisses the argument. A recent article provides indirect empirical support of Nyman's measurement of efficient moral hazard by estimating that inefficient moral hazard does not contribute as much dead weight loss to the economy as might be expected [28]. Another recent article cites Nyman's concept of income transfer effect in unemployment insurance [29].

On April 1, 2010, at a Book Forum at the American Enterprise Institute, in Washington, DC, Mark Pauly presented an overview of a book he had recently published [30] (http://www.aei.org/events/2010/04/01/emhealth-reform-without-side-effects-making-markets-work-for-individual-health-insuranceem/), offering his views on health care reform. There were two discussants of Pauly's book; the first was John Nyman. The moderator, in introducing Mr. Nyman, said that "... he's written quite extensively in the field of health policy, including challenging some of Mark's earlier theories of moral hazard..." to which Mr. Pauly was heard to interject, "Well, we agree". To this day, there has been no published explanation of this comment of agreement.

Contrast the reception of Nyman's work to the recent resurrection of Arrow's article [5] that was published more than four decades ago. Arrow's article provided the basis of a special-issue tribute of the *Journal of Health Politics, Policy, and Law* in 2001, with articles from many of the nation's leading health economists and a response by Arrow [31]. The present paper attempts to call attention to how Nyman's work has been so overlooked, whereas an article 40 years old—and largely rejected within 5 years of publication—is the subject of a captive journal issue. Arguably, John Nyman is no Kenneth Arrow... at least not yet, and, certainly, Arrow is due his tribute.

All of this is underscored by two recent presidential addresses to leading economic groups. In his address to the 2006 meeting of the American Society of Health Economists, Joseph Newhouse offers a retrospective on the tradeoff between *moral hazard* and *risk avoidance* since Zeckhauser [14], though he also credits the earlier Arrow [5] and Pauly [7]. The content is brief and celebratory. No untoward ideas are considered; neither Nyman nor his ideas are mentioned or cited.

Martin Feldstein, in his address to the 2006 meeting of the American Economic Association, offers a thoughtful, undogmatic synthesis of his thinking after 40 years study of social insurance. Health insurance is treated only in a 2-page section on Medicare, but not so short that the analytical principles of *risk avoidance* and trading off risk reduction against *moral hazard* could not be avowed. Again, no contradictory ideas are acknowledged; neither Nyman nor his ideas are cited.

There has been no review and discussion in journals or conferences as panel sessions, for example, of the American Economics Association, Academy Health, or Health Services Research. This lack of a full debate subsequent to the book's publication raises several questions. Why has not there been more notice of the work and its implications for health policy? Why have not the health policy and health economics annual meetings, journals, and other publications presented or debated the work? If it is wrong, it should be challenged in the usual arenas of scholarly debate. If the burden of opinion after open debate is that the work is found wanting, then it should be dismissed. Surely, standard scholarly practice is to engage the argument and see where the dust settles.

The response of the leadership of the field perhaps can be best understood within the sociology of knowledge that explains changes in science [32]. Half a century ago Kuhn introduced a new way of thinking about these changes, which is called the theory of scientific revolutions [33]. Nyman's theory does not appear to fit within the widely understood notion of Kuhn's scientific revolution. Kuhn's notion views the various scientific disciplines as based on fundamental ideas and assumptions. At critical points in the development of the disciplines some of those ideas or assumptions are thought, generally by newer practitioners of the field, to be in some types of theoretical or empirical errors. Even in those cases where the new ideas are revealed to be superior to what they are challenging, the process of its adoption is often protracted.

Clearly Nyman is not in any way challenging the fundamentals of *welfare economics*, though that compartment of the larger economic enterprise has taken its licks over the years. On the other hand, the Friedman-Savage (risk aversion) formulation of the demand for insurance has been settled economic doctrine for more than 50 years, and Nyman points out that it is inapplicable to the circumstances of health insurance coverage anywhere. Premiums paid for health insurance policies for the majority of the population are not the actuarial equivalent of what they would be paying where they are uninsured. As such the theory is seriously flawed. As a result the insurance payoff has been misinterpreted as a reduction in the price of the covered services rather than as an income transfer from the insurance fund to the sick insured. The welfare implications, as discussed previously, are reversed with major policy implications.

Nyman's reinterpretation of the insurance payoff clearly presents a challenge to the health care *moral hazard* analysis that has been a fundamental element of health economics doctrine for almost 50 years. And as in other fields and sciences, the withdrawal of previously dominant, now flawed ideas from scientific discourse is indeed a protracted process.

7. Conclusions and Reflections

John Nyman has, in a sense, "revolutionized" the economic theory of the *demand* for health insurance [25]. His principal contributions are (1) to replace the previously unexamined—and flawed—axiom of *risk avoidance* with that of *welfare maximization*; (2) to uncover a serious error or misinterpretation in the literature on *moral hazard*, namely, the practice of his predecessors to characterize the insurance payoff as a price reduction, rather than as an income transfer (and a lesser price reduction). The immediate consequence of these reformulations is to recognize insurance-induced health care utilization as, on balance, resulting in an increase in *social welfare*, not, as argued by others for the past 40 years, an unambiguous reduction in *welfare*.

Acknowledgment

The views expressed in the article are solely the authors' view and not the US Department of Health and Human Services.

Endnotes

1. Perhaps the most deceptive is the term, "*demand*," which, in ordinary parlance suggests an "unyielding insistence," but in economic parlance indicates merely the consumer's placid willingness to purchase certain quantities of a given commodity at various prices. Throughout this text, the expression "*demand for health insurance*" has no connection to legislative passage of extended or universal health insurance coverage. The analytical issues discussed have enormous implications for such policy issues.
2. For a more accessible version, see [11].
3. We use the terms *strong* and *weak* in this discussion in the philosophic logical sense of narrow or restrictive and broad or enabling, respectively.
4. Traditionally, *risk* and *uncertainty* have been used in technical economic discussions to connote distinct ideas about the unknown future. *Risk* was used to connote circumstances in which the range of outcomes, and their probabilities were "known"; *uncertainty*, when neither was "known." In this discussion, as with the preponderance of the literature on this subject, the two terms are used interchangeably.
5. That is, a premium equal to the value of expected health care outlays faced and insured against.
6. There is a considerable level of disingenuousness in this argument and all of the related subsequent work. The clear implication of Pauly's discussion is that there but for *moral hazard* virtually all Americans would be covered by lower cost health insurance coverage. Aside from the problem of determining the portion of the growth in per capita health care costs of the past 40 years attributable to *moral hazard* and that portion to demographic and technological changes and the general level of inflation, it seems rather clear that most of today's 60 million uninsured and seriously underinsured cannot afford health insurance because of the cost relative to their income, independent of the premium elevation resulting from *moral hazard*.
7. In fairness, Arrow did note the troubling presence of *moral hazard* and the need for copayments to control them, but, until Pauly's comment, did not suggest the possibility that insurance-induced overconsumption, rather than *market failure* might be responsible for large gaps in coverage.
8. Briefly, the reason argued for the theoretical decline in *welfare* is due to a distortion in the prices faced by insured persons. Because insured persons face prices for insured medical care that is well below the market prices for those services, they purchase much more of it than they would if they faced market prices and much less of other commodities, the prices of which are largely unchanged. According to this theory, consumers are presumed to purchase goods and services in amounts that are driven by the equalization of price ratios to the corresponding ratios of gratification intensity from the commodities in question. But because the prices faced by insured persons are not market prices, they are actually obtaining lesser levels of welfare than if everyone faced market prices.
9. This excess normally would be due to such things as inaccurately high actuarial claims estimates and insurance company administrative expenses, such as advertising, claims processing, and profit taking.
10. Indeed, though this is not part of Nyman's argument, most holders of autoinsurance would never be able to cover out of pocket, or even borrow to finance, many of the costs of autoaccident liability events (and it is therefore, interestingly, obligatory); the same holds for small-owner business property coverage.
11. For which Daniel Kahneman, a psychologist, was awarded the Nobel Prize in Economic Science in 2002.
12. In a poignant but awkward hesitation, Arrow, coawarded the Nobel Prize in Economic Science in 1972 (the fourth year of the award), begins his discussion of "The Theory of Ideal Insurance" by stating that "The expected-utility hypothesis, due originally to Daniel Bernoulli [17], is plausible and is the most analytically manageable of all hypotheses that have been proposed to explain behavior under uncertainty. In any case, the results to follow probably would not be significantly affected by moving to another mode of analysis. It is further assumed that individuals are normally risk averters."
13. That is, "broader," "more inclusive," and "less restrictive".
14. This is not to suggest that all health care utilization, *après* Nyman, is efficient and appropriate. It is only to caution that what excesses do exist—and they are enormous in the US—is not a simple matter of price-reducing insurance.
15. Strictly speaking, this is not the usual textbook increase in income, since it can only be used to purchase covered health care services, not from the usual, broad panoply of consumer commodities. Yet, it is certainly a form of income, and it does enable the consumer to purchase more than without this transfer, and the consumer's *welfare* is arguably greater—where the *efficient* outweighs the *inefficient* component—than in the absence of the coverage and the services this transfer affords.
16. Even within this new framework for understanding the insurance payoff, the old *inefficient moral hazard* is still present, but a lesser portion of the welfare effect of the utilization increase (see [2]).
17. Assuming that the absolute value of *efficient moral hazard* exceeds that of *inefficient moral hazard*.
18. Of course, everything is relative. Extending health care coverage to all Americans still depends on the increased benefits, calculated according to the new metric, to be greater than those benefits that result from spending a similar amount on other non-health areas of potential benefit.
19. Michel Grignon, Personal Communication.

20. *Journal of Health Economics, Health Economics, European Journal of Health Economics, and Journal of Risk and Uncertainty*, and the *American Economic Review*.
21. Ironically, even in *The New Yorker*, and by as notable a writer as Malcolm Gladwell, none of Nyman's actual contribution to the policy discussion is included in the article.
22. One text is *Health Economics: theory, insights, and industry studies*, by Rexford Santerre and Stephen Neun, published by South-Western/Cengage Learning, now in its fifth edition. The other text is *The Economics of Health and Health Care*, by Sherman Folland, Allen Goodman, and Miron Stano, published by Prentice Hall, now in its sixth edition.

References

[1] G. F. Anderson and B. K. Frogner, "Health spending in OECD countries: obtaining value per dollar," *Health Affairs*, vol. 27, no. 6, pp. 1718–1727, 2008.

[2] J. A. Nyman, *The Theory of Demand for Health Insurance*, Stanford University Press, Stanford, Calif, USA, 2003.

[3] R. Feldman and M. A. Morrisey, "Health economics: a report on the field," *Journal of Health Politics, Policy and Law*, vol. 15, no. 3, pp. 627–646, 1990.

[4] V. R. Fuchs, "Economics, values, and health care reform," *American Economic Review*, vol. 86, no. 1, pp. 1–24, 1996.

[5] K. J. Arrow, "Uncertainty and the welfare economics of medical care," *American Economic Review*, vol. 53, no. 5, pp. 941–973, 1963.

[6] R. A. Musgrave and P. B. Musgrave, *Public Finance in Theory and Practice*, McGraw-Hill Book Company, New York, NY, USA, 5th edition, 1989.

[7] M. V. Pauly, "The economics of moral hazard: comment," *American Economic Review*, vol. 58, no. 3, pp. 531–537, 1968.

[8] M. Pauly, "More on moral hazard," *Journal of Health Economics*, vol. 2, no. 1, pp. 81–85, 1983.

[9] M. S. Feldstein, "The welfare loss of excess health insurance," *Journal of Political Economy*, vol. 81, no. 2, pp. 251–280, 1973.

[10] S. Folland, A. C. Goodman, and M. Stano, *The Economics of Health and Health Care*, Macmillan Publishing Company, New York, NY, USA, 1993.

[11] J. A. Nyman, "American health policy: cracks in the foundation," *Journal of Health Politics, Policy and Law*, vol. 32, no. 5, pp. 759–783, 2007.

[12] P. J. Feldstein, *Health Care Economics*, John Wiley & Sons, New York, NY, USA, 3rd edition, 1988.

[13] J. A. Nyman, "The economics of moral hazard revisited," *Journal of Health Economics*, vol. 18, no. 6, pp. 811–824, 1999.

[14] R. Zeckhauser, "Medical insurance: a case study of the tradeoff between risk spreading and appropriate incentives," *Journal of Economic Theory*, vol. 2, no. 1, pp. 10–26, 1970.

[15] D. Kahneman and A. Tversky, Eds., *Choices, Values, and Frames*, Cambridge University Press, Cambridge, UK, 2000.

[16] D. Kahneman and A. Tversky, "Prospect theory: an analysis of decision under risk," *Econometrica*, vol. 47, pp. 263–291, 1979.

[17] D. Bernoulli, "Exposition of a new theory on the measurement of risk," *Econometrica*, vol. 22, pp. 23–36, 1954, Translated by Louise Sommer.

[18] M. Friedman and L. J. Savage, "The utility analysis of choices involving risk," *Journal of Political Economy*, vol. 66, no. 4, pp. 279–304, 1948.

[19] M. Friedman, *The Theory of the Consumption Function*, Princeton University Press, Princeton, NJ, USA, 1957.

[20] W. J. Boyes, "The theory of demand for health insurance," *Inquiry*, vol. 41, no. 1, pp. 106–107, 2004, Review of J. Nyman.

[21] R. Hirth, "The theory of demand for health insurance," *Journal of Economic Literature*, vol. 42, pp. 188–189, 2004, Review of J. Nyman.

[22] J. G. Eisenhauer, "The theory of demand for health insurance: a review essay," *Journal of Insurance Issues*, vol. 29, no. 1, pp. 71–87, 2006.

[23] M. Grignon, "The theory of demand for health insurance," *The Journal of Risk and Insurance*, vol. 72, no. 1, pp. 184–190, 2005, Review of Nyman.

[24] M. Gladwell, "The moral hazard myth," *The New Yorker*, vol. 81, no. 25, p. 44, 2005.

[25] D. Stone, "Behind the Jargon moral hazard," *Journal of Health Politics, Policy and Law*, vol. 36, no. 5, pp. 887–896, 2011.

[26] J. P. Geyman, "Moral hazard and consumer-driven health care: a fundamentally flawed concept," *International Journal of Health Services*, vol. 37, no. 2, pp. 333–351, 2007.

[27] A. Blomqvist, "Does the economics of moral hazard need to be revisited? A comment on the paper by John Nyman," *Journal of Health Economics*, vol. 20, no. 2, pp. 283–288, 2001.

[28] L. J. Bates, K. Mukherjee, and R. E. Santerre, "Medical insurance coverage and health production efficiency," *Journal of Risk and Insurance*, vol. 77, no. 1, pp. 211–229, 2010.

[29] R. Chetty, "Moral hazard versus liquidity and optimal unemployment insurance," *Journal of Political Economy*, vol. 116, no. 2, pp. 173–234, 2008.

[30] M. V. Pauly, "Health reform without side effects: making markets work for individual health insurance," American Enterprise Institute Book Forum, Washington, DC, USA, 2010, http://www.aei.org.

[31] M. A. Peterson, "Special issue: Kenneth arrow and the changing economics of health," *Journal of Health Politics, Policy and Law*, vol. 26, no. 5, pp. 823–828, 2001.

[32] S. Keen, *Method, Debunking Economics*, chapter 7, Pluto Press, 2001.

[33] T. S. Kuhn, *The Structure of Scientific Revolution*, University of Chicago Press, Chicago, Ill, USA, 1963.

15

Lead, Follow or Cooperate? Sequential versus Collusive Payoffs in Symmetric Duopoly Games

Marco A. Marini and Giorgio Rodano

Department of Computer, Control and Management Engineering, Sapienza University of Rome, Via Ariosto 25, 00185 Rome, Italy

Correspondence should be addressed to Marco A. Marini; marini@dis.uniroma1.it

Academic Editors: M. E. Kandil and M. Tsionas

In many strategic settings comparing the payoffs obtained by players under full cooperation to those obtainable at a sequential (Stackelberg) equilibrium can be crucial to determine the outcome of the game. This happens, for instance, in repeated games in which players can break cooperation by acting sequentially, as well as in merger games in which firms are allowed to sequence their actions. Despite the relevance of these and other applications, no full-fledged comparisons between collusive and sequential payoffs have been performed so far. In this paper we show that even in symmetric duopoly games the ranking of cooperative and sequential payoffs can be extremely variable, particularly when the usual linear demand assumption is relaxed. Not surprisingly, the degree of strategic complementarity and substitutability of players' actions (and, hence, the slope of their best replies) appears decisive to determine the ranking of collusive and sequential payoffs. Some applications to endogenous timing are discussed.

1. Introduction

Standard game-theoretic settings dealing with the emergence of cooperation usually weight the stream of players' payoffs colluding a finite or infinite number of periods to those obtained by defecting one period and then playing simultaneously *à la* Nash (noncooperatively) afterward. The possibility that players defect from the collusive outcome as leaders or followers in every stage game is usually not considered. An exception to this approach is contained, for instance, in Mouraviev and Rey [1], who study the role of price (or quantity) leadership in facilitating firm collusion in an infinitely repeated setting. They show that, under price competition and, to a much lesser extent, under quantity competition, the possibility that players sequence their actions in every stage may help to sustain collusion. This happens because the presence of a deviating leader makes it easy for the follower to punish such defection.

In general, the focus on the link between timing and collusion is not entirely new within the economic literature. For instance, in some classical contributions on cartels and mergers under oligopoly, colluding firms are assumed to act as Stackelberg leaders [2–6]. Moreover, a few recent papers on mergers and R&D agreements consider different timing structures, where groups of firms can either act as leaders or followers (e.g., [7–10]). In these and other potentially interesting economic applications, it is crucial to compare the payoff under collusion to those under noncooperative sequential play to determine the outcome of the game.

While the literature comparing leader and follower's (as well as simultaneous Nash) payoffs has a long-standing tradition (see [11, 12] or [13] for references), the number of papers that compares collusive and sequential outcomes even in a simple duopoly framework appears, at the best, scant. If, on the one hand, it has been proved that in regular symmetric duopoly games with single-valued best-replies and monotone payoffs on rivals' actions (denoted *monotone spillovers*), when actions are *strategic complements,* the follower's payoff dominates which of the leader and the opposite holds under *strategic substitutes* (e.g., [13–15]. In particular, by relaxing the assumption of complements or substitutes actions, [13] proves that either the leader's payoff dominates that of the follower (which is also dominated by the simultaneous Nash) or, in turn, is dominated by the follower's. Dowrick [16], Amir [17], Amir and Grilo [18], Amir et al. [15], Currarini and Marini [19, 20], and Von Stengel and Zamir [21] all present various leader-follower payoff comparisons between single players or coalitions. On the other hand, the relationship between fully cooperative and sequential payoffs has been scarcely explored. To the best of our knowledge, in an oligopoly setup with quantities acting as strategic substitutes, Levin [6, 22] has provided a comparison between prices, quantities, and social welfare in Cournot, Stackelberg, and monopoly equilibria. In a symmetric setting, Figuières et al. [23] have considered, in turn, symmetric conjectural, simultaneous Nash and Pareto-optimal interior equilibria. However, their model assumes symmetric conjectures for players, and, therefore, their main results do not apply to the analysis of a Stackelberg equilibrium, which is naturally asymmetric.

Our paper considers a class of symmetric duopoly games and shows that the ranking of cooperative and sequential payoffs can be extremely variable. In particular, when actions are *strategic substitutes* and *spillovers negative*, it is shown that, rather surprisingly, the leader can earn in some cases a higher profit than the equal-split cooperative (efficient) payoff, and this occurs, in particular, when players' best replies are very (and negatively) sloped. This is because the leader can exploit in full her first-mover advantage when the follower strongly reduces his strategy in response. Exactly the reverse occurs in a game with *strategic substitutes* and *positive spillovers*. Here the leader can do better than under symmetric collusion when the follower is not very reactive. A similar but opposite reasoning applies to the case of *strategic complements*: with *negative spillovers*, equal-split cooperative payoffs are lower than follower's payoff when best replies are very flat, and the opposite under *positive spillovers*. In this paper we also provide a taxonomy of all feasible ranking of payoffs and actions of players arising in simultaneous, sequential, and collusive equilibria when actions are either strategic complements or substitutes.

At the end of the paper we discuss some possible implications of our results. To this aim, we introduce an elementary endogenous timing game in which players can decide the timing of their cooperative or noncooperative strategies. Thus, we show that when binding agreements among players are allowed, intertemporal cooperation is in general more vulnerable to defection than cooperation occurring at just one stage.

The paper is organized as follows. The next section introduces the basic setup of the paper. Section 3 presents some results concerning players' equilibrium strategies and payoffs. To understand the forces at work, some simple examples of price and quantity competition are briefly presented. Section 4 applies some of the paper results to the issue of endogenous intertemporal cooperation Section 5 concludes.

2. The Setup

We assume two players $i = 1, 2$ with identical strategy sets $X_i = X \subset \mathbb{R}_+$ and symmetric payoffs $u_i(x_i, x_j) : X^2 \to \mathbb{R}$, that is, such that, for every profile $(x_i, x_j) \in X^2$, $u_i(x_i, x_j) = u_j(x_j, x_i)$. We restrict payoffs to be either strictly positive or strictly negatively monotone on rival's strategy. We talk, in turn, of *positive* (PS) and *negative spillovers* (NS). Moreover, players' actions are defined *strategic complements* (*substitutes*) if and only if, for every $i = 1, 2$ and $j \neq i$, the payoff $u_i(x_i, x_j)$ exhibits increasing (decreasing) differences in $(x_i, x_j) \in X^2$, that is, $u_i(x_i, x_j') - u_i(x_i, x_j'') \geq 0$ (≤ 0) for every $x_j'', x_j' \in X$ with $x_j'' > x_j'$. It is well known that, with smooth players' payoffs, increasing (decreasing) differences hold if and only if $\partial^2 u_i/(\partial x_i \partial x_j) \geq (\leq) 0$ [24]. We will assume, in what follows, strictly increasing or strictly decreasing differences of players' payoffs, which, in turn, imply strictly increasing or strictly decreasing players' best-replies.

We can now define the behaviour of players in the different scenarios. Under perfect collusion, players are assumed to set cooperatively their strategy profile

$$\mathbf{x}^c = \left(x_i^c, x_j^c\right), \tag{1}$$

where, for every ith player,

$$x_i^c = \arg\max_{x_i} \sum_{i=1,2} u_i\left(x_i, x_j\right). \tag{2}$$

The above formulation implies that the two players possess transferable utilities. No side payments are explicitly allowed and, therefore, payoff allocation only depends on the strategies played by the two players at the (efficient) profile (1). In the following analysis we will assume a *symmetric* cooperative solution, namely, $x_i^c = x_j^c = x^c$ and, therefore, $u_i(x^c, x^c) = u_j(x^c, x^c)$. We show in Appendix that, for a large class of games (such as games with strict quasiconcave payoff functions and convex strategy sets), the cooperative solution is symmetric. (See also [25, 26].) Depending on the model applications such solution can be interpreted, in turn, as the formation of a merger (or a cartel), or as tacit collusion. When players are assumed to move simultaneously and noncooperatively, they play *à la* Nash, and the equilibrium strategy profile is

$$\mathbf{x}^n = \left(x_i^n, x_j^n\right), \tag{3}$$

where, for every $i, j = 1, 2$ and $j \neq i$

$$x_i^n = \arg\max_{x_i} u_i\left(x_i, x_j^n\right). \tag{4}$$

By symmetry, if the Nash equilibrium $\mathbf{x}^n$ of the duopoly game is unique, it must be symmetric: $x_i^n = x_j^n = x^n$. Finally, when players act sequentially, we assume that the relevant equilibrium concept is the Stackelberg (subgame perfect Nash) equilibrium, that is, the profile

$$\mathbf{x}^s = \left(x_i^s, r_j\left(x_i^s\right)\right), \tag{5}$$

where, for the leader (henceforth player i)

$$x_i^s = \arg\max_{x_i} u_i\left(x_i, r_j\left(x_i\right)\right) \tag{6}$$

and, for the follower (henceforth player j), $r_j : X \to X$ such that

$$r_j\left(x_i\right) = \arg\max_{x_j} u_j\left(x_i, x_j\right). \tag{7}$$

Note that if players' payoffs are continuous and strictly quasiconcave, best replies are continuous and single valued. In addition, if players' strategy sets are compact and convex, Brower's fixed-point theorem ensures the existence of a Nash equilibrium $\mathbf{x}^n$ of the simultaneous move game. The existence of a Stackelberg equilibrium $\mathbf{x}^s$ requires both the continuity of the leader's payoff on her action as well as a follower's continuous best reply, implying that the leader faces a continuous maximization problem over a compact set. In turn, the existence of the cooperative equilibrium $\mathbf{x}^c$ does not pose particular problems when players' payoffs are continuous and strategy sets compact. The uniqueness of equilibria (1)–(5) is, in general, a more demanding property. When not specifically stated differently, we will assume it.

3. Main Results

It is well known that, in symmetric duopoly games with monotone spillovers and single-valued best replies, if actions are strategic substitutes (and best-replies decreasing), players' payoffs under equilibria ((3)–(5)) respect the following inequality:

$$u^L \geq u^N \geq u^F, \tag{8}$$

where u^N indicates a player's payoff at the simultaneous Nash equilibrium (3), and u^L and u^F denote, respectively, the leader and the follower's payoffs at the subgame perfect Nash (Stackelberg) equilibrium (5). Since we have assumed strictly increasing or strictly decreasing players' best-replies and monotone spillovers, we can exclude the trivial interior equilibria in which $\mathbf{x}^n = \mathbf{x}^s$ and, therefore, $u^L = u^N = u^F$. As a result, (8) becomes

$$u^L > u^N > u^F. \tag{9}$$

When, conversely, players' actions are strategic complements (and best-replies increasing), it is obtained that

$$u^F > u^L > u^N. \tag{10}$$

This means that, when (9) holds, since all players prefer to lead and none to follow, in the endogenous timing game *à la* Hamilton and Slutsky [27]—known as *extensive form game with observable delay*—where two players declare simultaneously their intention to play *early* or *late* a given strategic game, there exists a unique pure subgame perfect Nash equilibrium in which players end up playing simultaneously. If, conversely, (10) holds, both sequential (Stackelberg) equilibria, with either order of play among players, are supported as subgame perfect Nash equilibrium of the extended game.

In what follows, some of the results presented do not strictly require the monotonicity of players' best-replies (implied, in turn, by the property of increasing or decreasing differences of players' payoffs). However, for simplicity, our main results are characterized for two well-known classes of duopoly games in which actions are, in turn, strategic complements and substitutes. The first result is rather trivial, and it is simply based on (8)–(10) and on the Pareto-efficiency of the symmetric collusive outcome.

Proposition 1. *In all symmetric duopoly games in which players' actions are strategic complements (substitutes), the symmetric collusive payoff of every player must be higher than leader's (follower's) equilibrium payoff at the sequential game, namely,* $u^C > u^L$ ($u^C > u^F$).

Proof. Suppose by contradiction that, if duopoly game actions are strategic complements, $u^C \leq u^L$. By (10), $u^C \leq u^L < u^F$ and using symmetry, $2u^C < u^L + u^F$, contradicting the efficiency of the cooperative strategy profile $\mathbf{x}^c$. The same occurs when actions are strategic substitutes and $u^C \leq u^F$. □

Corollary 2. *In all symmetric duopoly games in which players' actions are strategic complements (substitutes), the following payoff ranking arises:* $u^C > u^L > u^N$ ($u^C \geq u^N > u^F$).

Proof. This is obtained by combining symmetry, the results of Proposition 1, and the efficiency of the cooperative allocation. □

However, to obtain a complete ranking of players' payoffs, it remains to be ascertained if, in turn, $u^C \geq u^F$ or $u^F > u^C$ for actions that are strategic complements and $u^C \geq u^L$ or $u^L > u^C$ for actions that are strategic substitutes. As a first step we focus our attention on games with strategic complements.

3.1. Games with Strategic Complements. We present here some results on the relationship between players' equilibrium strategies and their payoffs when actions are strategic complements. The next result provides a sufficient condition for the follower's payoff to overcome the symmetric collusive payoff.

Proposition 3. *In all symmetric duopoly games with strategic complements and negative (NS) (positive (PS)) spillovers, if at the Stackelberg equilibrium the leader plays a strategy that is lower (higher) than that played under collusion, namely,* $x_i^s < x^c$ ($x_i^s > x^c$), *the following payoff ranking arises:* $u^F > u^C > u^L > u^N$.

Proof. If, at the Stackelberg equilibrium, player i ($i = 1, 2$) as leader plays a strategy such as $x_i^s < x^c$ (under NS) and $x_i^s > x^c$ (under PS), thus, for the follower

$$u_j\left(x_i^s, r_j\left(x_i^s\right)\right) \geq u_j\left(x_i^s, x^c\right) > u_j\left(x^c, x^c\right), \tag{11}$$

where the first inequality stems from the Nash property of best-reply $r_j(\cdot)$ and the second from the property of monotone spillovers and the fact that $x^c > x_i^s$ under NS and $x^c < x_i^s$ under PS. Thus, by symmetry, $u_j(x_i^s, r_j(x_i^s)) = u^F$ and $u_j(x^c, x^c) = u^C$ and, by Proposition 1, it follows that $u^F > u^C > u^L > u^N$. Example 4 below shows that the condition is only sufficient and, by no means, necessary for the result. Figures 1 and 2 illustrate the two cases of proposition under NS and PS. □

Example 4 (Cournot with strategic complements). Let two firms face an inverse demand function $P(Q) = (1 + Q)^{-b}$,

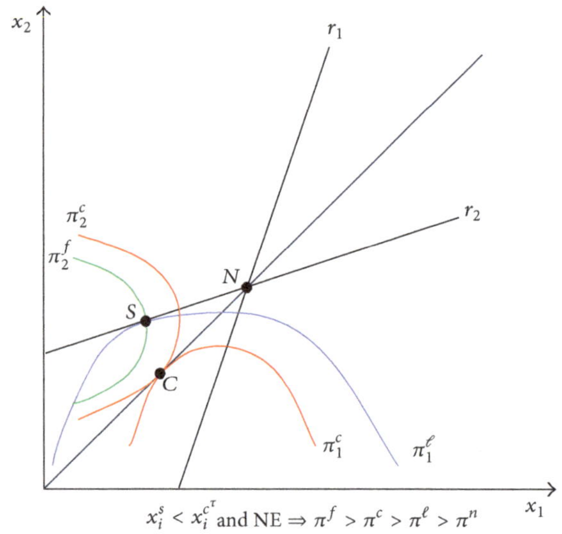

FIGURE 1: Duopoly game with strategic complements and negative externalities—red: coop. isoprofits; blue: leader's isoprofit; green: follower's isoprofit.

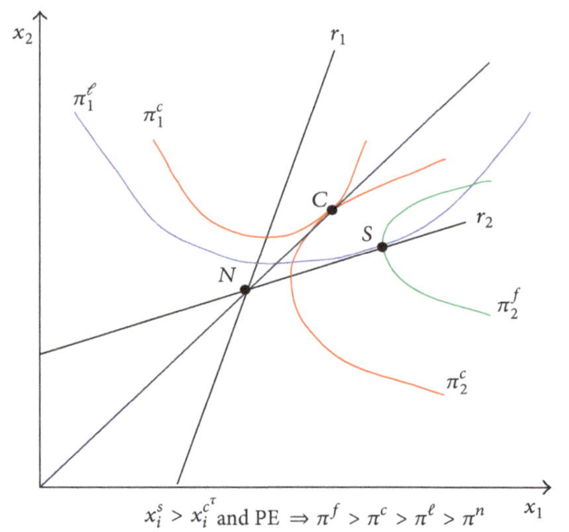

FIGURE 2: Duopoly Game with strategic complements and positive externalities—red: coop. isoprofits; blue: leader's isoprofit; green: follower's isoprofit.

where $Q = (q_1 + q_2)$ and $b > 1$, and, for simplicity, production costs set to zero. Every firm payoff is $u_i(q_i, Q) = (1 + Q)^{-b} q_i$, $i = 1, 2$, and it is easy to see that spillovers are negative and quantities act as strategic complements, yielding increasing best replies. Simple computations show that the equilibrium quantities are, respectively, $q^n = 1/(b - 2)$, $q_i^s = 1/(b - 1)$, $q_j^s = b/(b-1)^2$, and $q^c = 1/(2(b - 1))$. Equilibrium payoffs are $u^N = (b - 2)^{-1}(b/(b-2))^{-b}$, $u^L = (b - 1)^{-1}(b^2/(b-1)^2)^{-b}$, $u^F = (b-1)^{-2} b (b^2/(b-1)^2)^{-b}$, and $u^C = (2b-2)^{-1}(b/(b-1))^{-b}$. It is straightforward to see that, for $b > 2$, $q^n > q_j^s > q_i^s > q^c$ and $u^C \geq u^F > u^L > u^N$. Figure 4 illustrates this case. For $1 < b < 2$, there is a switch in the

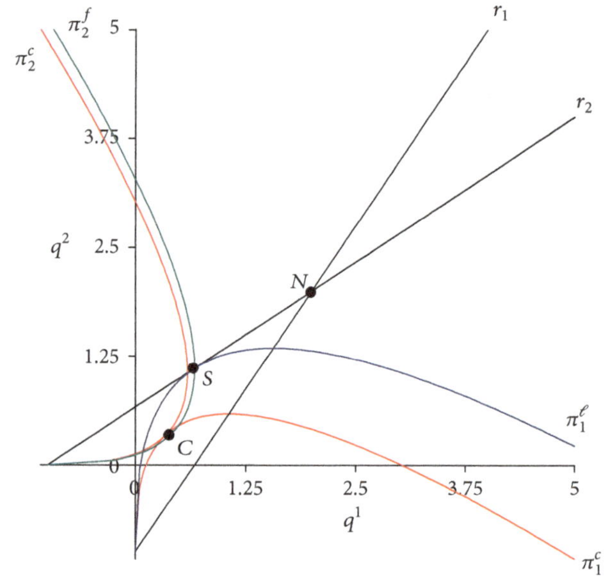

FIGURE 3: Numerical example (Cournot with strategic complements)—case $b = 2.5$. Red: coop. isoprofits; blue: leader's isoprofit; green: follower's isoprofit.

ranking of payoffs and $u^F > u^C > u^L > u^N$. Note that, for $1 < b \leq 2$, firm's best replies are not contraction and, for this range of parameters, a simultaneous (Cournot) pure strategy Nash equilibrium does not exist. However, since $q_i^s = 1/(b-1)$ and $q^c = 1/(2(b - 1))$, $q^c < q_i^s$ holds for any level of b. This proves that the condition of Proposition 3 is only sufficient and not necessary for inequality $u^F > u^C$ to arise. This is illustrated in Figure 4. As in the standard Cournot duopoly, lower isoprofit curves for firm 1 (or isoprofit curves more on the left for firm 2) correspond to higher profit levels.

The next proposition illustrates the relation between leader's and follower's strategy at any Stackelberg equilibrium in which the follower obtains a higher payoff than under collusion. Together with Proposition 3, it helps to see that, when strategies are complements (and best-replies increasing), a Stackelberg equilibrium always lies below the 45-degree line under negative externalities and above the 45-degree line under positive spillovers (see Figures 2, 3, and 4).

Proposition 5. *In all symmetric duopoly games with strategic complements, if the follower's payoff at the Stackelberg equilibrium is higher than the payoff obtained at the symmetric cooperative equilibrium, namely,* $u^F > u^C$, *the strategy level of the follower is higher (lower) than the leader's under negative (positive) externalities, namely,* $x_j^s > x_i^s$ *under NS and* $x_j^s < x_i^s$ *under PS, where* $x_j^s = r_j(x_i^s)$.

Proof. Assume that $x_j^s < x_i^s$ under NS and $x_j^s > x_i^s$ under PS. Thus,

$$u_j(r_j(x_i^s), r_j(x_i^s)) > u_j(x_i^s, r_j(x_i^s)) > u_j(x^c, x^c), \quad (12)$$

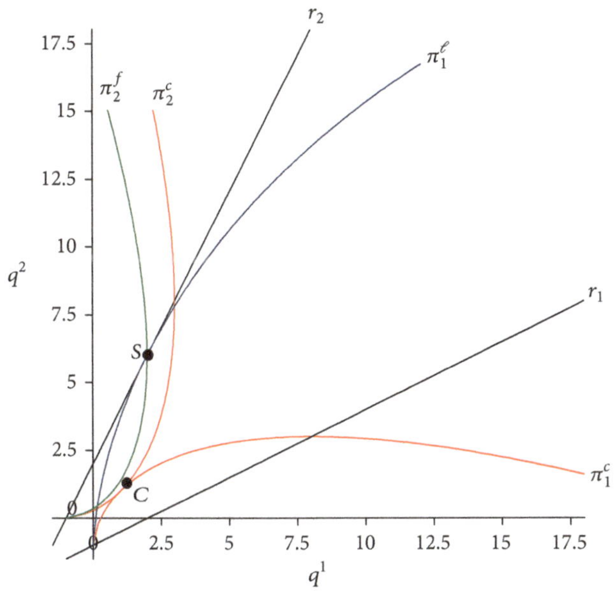

FIGURE 4: Numerical example (Cournot with strategic complements)—case $b = 1.5$. Red: coop. isoprofits; blue: leader's isoprofit; green: follower's isoprofit.

where the first inequality is due to monotone spillovers and the second to the fact that $u^F > u^C$. Since by symmetry $u_j(x) = u_i(x)$ for any strategy profile x in which $x_i^n = x_j^n$,

$$u_i\left(r_j\left(x_i^s\right), r_j\left(x_i^s\right)\right) + u_j\left(r_j\left(x_i^s\right), r_j\left(x_i^s\right)\right) > u_i\left(x^c, x^c\right) + u_j\left(x^c, x^c\right), \tag{13}$$

which contradicts the efficiency of x^c. □

The next proposition characterizes instead the order of strategies in the standard case in which the collusive agreement yields a higher payoff for a player than playing as a follower the sequential game. Again, to make things simple, we assume that Stackelberg and simultaneous Nash equilibrium differ, that is, $\mathbf{x}^s \neq \mathbf{x}^n$.

Proposition 6. *In all symmetric duopoly games with strategic complements, if the symmetric collusive payoff is at least as high as the follower's payoff at the Stackelberg equilibrium; namely, $u^C \geq u^F$, the following ranking between equilibrium strategies arises: $x^n > x_j^s > x_i^s \geq x^c$ under NS and $x^c \geq x_i^s > x_j^s > x^n$ under PS, where $x_j^s = r_j(x_i^s)$, for $i, j = 1, 2$ and $j \neq i$.*

Proof. The fact that $x_i^s \geq x^c$ under negative spillovers (NS) and $x_i^s \leq x^c$ under positive spillovers (PS) whenever $u^C \geq u^F$ is directly implied by Proposition 3. The remaining inequalities are standard (see, for instance, Amir et al., [28]): taking player i in the role of leader,

$$u_i\left(x_i^s, r_j\left(x_i^s\right)\right) > u_i\left(x^n, x^n\right) \geq u_i\left(x_i^s, x^n\right), \tag{14}$$

where the first inequality is due to the fact that $\mathbf{x}^s \neq \mathbf{x}^n$ and the second by the Nash property of $\mathbf{x}^n$. Thus, (14) directly implies that $r_j(x_i^s) = x_j^s < x^n$ under NS and $r_j(x_i^s) = x_j^s > x^n$ under PS. Given that players' actions are strategic complements (and best-replies increasing), it also follows that $x_i^s < x^n$ under NS and $x_i^s > x_i^n$ under PS, since both Stackelberg and simultaneous Nash profiles lie along the increasing follower's best reply. Finally, since the simultaneous Nash equilibrium is symmetric and lies on the 45-degree line, the latter inequalities ($x_i^s < x^n$ under NS and $x_i^s > x_i^n$ under PS) forcefully imply that x^s lies above the 45-degree line under NS and below this line under PS. Hence, $x_j^s > x_i^s$ under NS and $x_j^s < x_i^s$ under PS, and this concludes the proof. □

So far, we have shown that, in duopoly games with strategic complements, two main strategy-payoff equilibrium combinations are possible in the nontrivial case in which $\mathbf{x}^s \neq \mathbf{x}^n$.

Proposition 7. *In all symmetric duopoly games with strategic complements (i) under negative spillovers (NS), if $x^n > x_j^s > x_i^s \geq x^c$, both payoff rankings may arise as follows: $u^C \geq u^F > u^L > u^N$ or $u^F > u^C > u^L > u^N$, while, for $x^n > x_j^s \geq x^c > x_i^s$, it follows that $u^F > u^C > u^L > u^N$. (ii) Under positive spillovers (PS), if $x^c \geq x_i^s > x_j^s > x^n$ both payoff-rankings $u^C \geq u^F > u^L > u^N$ or $u^F > u^C > u^L > u^N$ may arise, while if $x_i^s > x^c \geq x_j^s > x^n$, the only possible payoff ranking is $u^F > u^C > u^L > u^N$.*

Proof. It follows straightforwardly by Corollary 2 and Propositions 1, 3, and 5. □

However, as the next example illustrates, in duopoly games with strategic complements (as, for instance, the classical price duopoly game), the case in which the follower's payoff overcomes the collusive payoff remains a rather unusual event. When the follower's best reply is a contraction, it is unlikely that the leader's equilibrium strategy is so low (high) under NS (PS) for the follower to overcome the symmetric collusive payoff. To obtain this, the (increasing) best replies have to be very flat under NS (see Example 4) and very steep under PS.

Example 8 (Bertrand with differentiated products and strategic complements). Let firm i's ($i = 1, 2$) market demand be $q_i(p_i, p_j) = (1 - p_i + \beta p_j)^b$, where p_i and p_j denote the prices charged by the two firms. Let also $b > 0$, $0 < \beta < 1$, and let production costs be normalized to zero for both firms. Payoffs are, therefore, simply given by $u_i(p_i, p_j) = (1 - p_i + \beta p_j)^b p_i$. Note that, for $\beta > 0$, these payoffs exhibit increasing differences and best replies are increasing (prices act as strategic complements). Externalities are positive. When the game is played simultaneously and noncooperatively, the equilibrium payoffs are $u^N = (b - \beta + 1)^{-1-b}(\beta - 1 + b - \beta + 1)^b$, while, when the game is played sequentially, the leader obtains

$$u^L = \left(b - \beta^2 + 1\right)^{-1} (b + 1)^{-1} \left(b + \beta + 1\right) \Delta, \tag{15}$$

for

$$\Delta = \left(\frac{\beta\left(b\beta^2 - \beta - b\beta - b^2 - 2b - 1\right)}{(b+1)^2\left(\beta^2 - b - 1\right)} - \frac{b+\beta+1}{2b+b^2-\beta^2-b\beta^2+1} + 1 \right)^b, \tag{16}$$

and the follower

$$u^F = (b+1)^{-2}\left(\beta^2 - b - 1\right)^{-1}\left(b\beta^2 - \beta - b\beta - b^2 - 2b - 1\right)\Gamma \tag{17}$$

for

$$\Gamma = \left(\frac{\beta(b+\beta+1)}{2b+b^2-\beta^2-b\beta^2+1} - \frac{\left(b\beta^2 - \beta - b\beta - b^2 - 2b - 1\right)}{(b+1)^2\left(\beta^2 - b - 1\right)} + 1 \right)^b. \tag{18}$$

Finally, when the two firms decide to merge and act as a monopolist, every firm obtains

$$u^C = ((\beta - 1) + (b+1)(1-\beta))^b((b+1)(1-\beta))^{b-1}. \tag{19}$$

Simple calculations show that, for all reasonable values of the parameters, the typical payoff ranking is $u^C > u^F > u^L > u^N$. Moreover, the following ranking of players' actions (prices) obtains $p^c > p_i^s > p_j^s > p^n$. Figure 5 depicts this case for $\beta = 0.5$ and $b = 1$. No substantial modifications of the above rankings are obtained by manipulating parameters of the model.

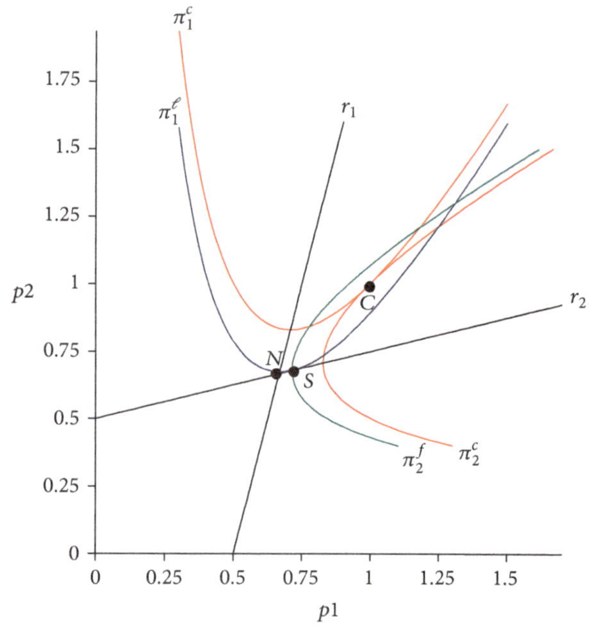

FIGURE 5: Numerical example (price competition with strategic complements)—case $b = 1$ and $\beta = 0.5$. Red: coop. isoprofits; blue: leader's isoprofit; green: follower's isoprofit.

3.2. Games with Strategic Substitutes. When players' actions are strategic substitutes, it can be shown that there are only two possible rankings of equilibrium strategies and payoffs under either negative or positive externalities. These are characterized in the next proposition.

Proposition 9. *(i) In all symmetric duopoly games with strategic substitutes, the following rankings between equilibrium strategies can arise: either $x_i^s > x_j^n > x_j^s \geq x^c$ or $x_i^s > x^n \geq x^c \geq x_j^s$ under NS and $x_j^s \geq x^c \geq x_i^n > x_i^s$ or $x^c > x_j^s > x^n > x_i^s$ under PS, where $x_j^s = r_j(x_i^s)$, $i, j = 1, 2$. (ii) Moreover, only two alternative payoff rankings are possible: either $u^C \geq u^L > u^N > u^F$ or $u^L > u^C \geq u^N > u^F$.*

Proof. (i) Similarly to Proposition 6 we can write, for player i acting as a leader,

$$u_i\left(x_i^s, r_j\left(x_i^s\right)\right) > u_i\left(x_i^n, x^n\right) \geq u_i\left(x_i^s, x^n\right), \tag{20}$$

where the first inequality stems from the fact that $\mathbf{x}^s \neq \mathbf{x}^n$ and the second from the property of the Nash equilibrium. Therefore, it follows that $r_j(x_i^s) = x_j^s < x^n$ under NS and $r_j(x_i^s) = x_j^s > x^n$ under PS. Moreover, since actions are strategic substitutes, $x_i^s > x^n$ under NS and $x_i^s < x^n$ under PS, given that both profiles $\mathbf{x}^s$ and $\mathbf{x}^n$ lie along the follower's (decreasing) best reply. Thus, $x_i^s > x^n > x_j^s$ under NS and $x_j^s > x^n > x_i^s$ under PS. By the symmetry and monotonicity of players' payoffs and by the efficiency of the cooperative strategy profile, we obtain also that $x^c \leq x_i^n$ under NS and $x^c \geq x_i^n$ under PS. We remain, therefore, with the following two inequalities: either $x_i^s > x^n > x_j^s \geq x^c$ or $x_i^s > x^n > x^c \geq x_j^s$ under NS, and $x_j^s \geq x^c \geq x^n > x_i^s$ or $x^c \geq x_j^s > x^n > x_i^s$ under PS. Both cases may arise. (ii) From Proposition 1 we know that $u^C \geq u^N > u^F$ when actions are strategic substitutes. Given that $u^L > u^N$, it follows that only two rankings are possible: either $u^C \geq u^L > u^N > u^F$ or $u^L > u^C \geq u^N > u^F$, as also the numerical example below illustrates. □

Example 10 (Cournot duopoly with strategic substitutes). Let assume an inverse demand function given by $P(Q) = (1 - Q)^b$, with $Q = (q_1 + q_2) < 1$, $b > 0$ and zero production costs for both firms. The payoffs can be obtained as $u_i(q_i, Q) = (1 - Q)^b q_i$, for $i = 1, 2$. For $b > 0$ payoffs exhibit decreasing differences and, therefore, players best replies are decreasing. Spillovers are negative. When the game is played simultaneously *à la* Nash firms' equilibrium payoffs are given by $u^N = b^b(b+2)^{-(b+1)}$. When the game is played *à la* Stackelberg, the leader obtains $u^L = b^{2b}(b+1)^{-(2b+1)}$ and the follower $u^F = b^{(2b+1)}(b+1)^{-(2b+2)}$, respectively. Finally, when the two firms collude, they obtain each $u^C = b^b 2(b+1)^{-(b+1)}$. Simple computations show that for $b \geq 1$ (linear or convex

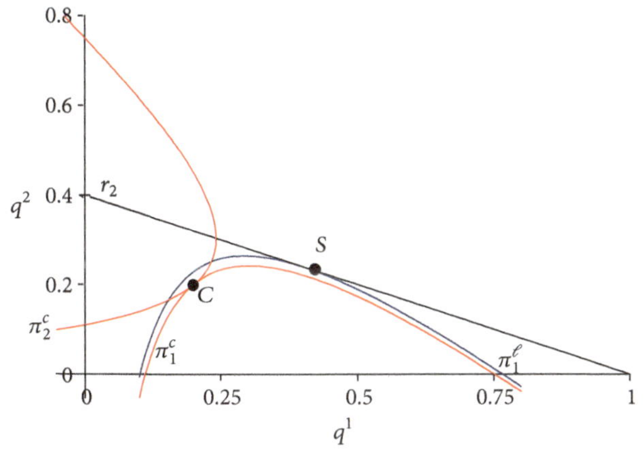

FIGURE 6: Numerical example (Cournot with strategic substitutes)—case $b \geq 1$. Red: coop. isoprofits; blue: leader's isoprofit.

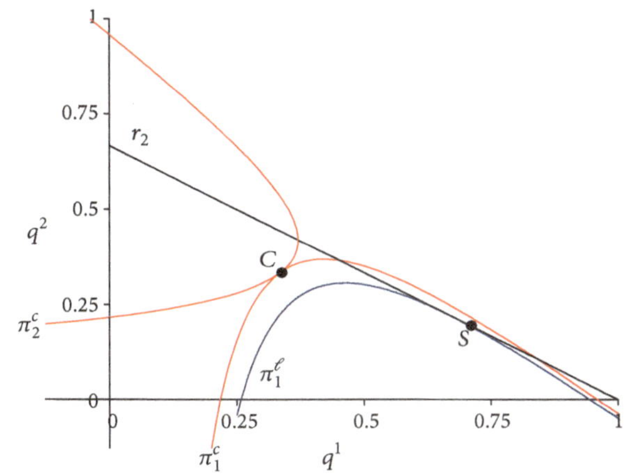

FIGURE 7: Numerical example (Cournot with strategic substitutes)—case $0 < b < 1$. Red: coop. isoprofits; blue: leader's isoprofit.

demand), $u^C \geq u^L > u^N > u^F$, with the equal sign holding only for $b = 1$. Figure 6 depicts this relation among players' payoffs. When, instead, $0 < b < 1$ (concave demand), the payoff ranking is the following: $u^L > u^C > u^N > u^F$. Figure 7 illustrates this case. Figure 8 shows instead that the ranking $u^L > u^C$ arises when the inverse demand is strongly concave (which occurs for a very low b) and that the dominance of leader's payoff over the collusive payoff may occur in both cases in which the follower's strategy is either higher or lower than the collusive strategy.

4. Endogenous Timing and Collusion

In order to check some of the potential consequences of our results, we introduce here a simple setting that extends Hamilton and Slutsky's [27] endogenous timing game (known as *extended game with observable delay*) by including in this game the possibility for players to commit to full cooperation. The game runs as follows. At an initial stage players announce simultaneously their purpose to play *early*

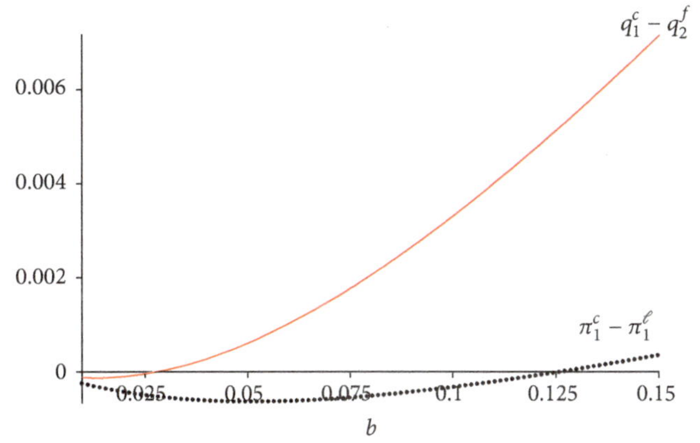

FIGURE 8: Numerical example—red line: $(x^{c^t} - x_j^s)$ = Coop. output – follower's output; black dotted line: $(\pi^c - \pi^\ell)$ = coop. payoff – leader's payoff. $b = 0.1, \ldots, 0.15$.

or *late* a duopoly game and their intention to cooperate or not with the rival. The rules of the game are rather simple: when *both* players announce their intention to cooperate, the agreement is binding and players collude at the selected time. Otherwise, they play independently with the timing as prescribed by their own announcement. This game basically requires the *unanimity* of players to cooperate. Note that there exist many real life examples in which the willingness of people to take a joint action and the timing of their action are highly complementary, as for example, friends deciding whether to spend or not a holiday together, firms deciding if signing or not a R&D agreement, and so on. Our aim here is to check for the existence of subgame perfect Nash equilibria (in pure strategies) (SNE) of such *cooperation-timing* duopoly game.

Formally, the game can be described as follows. We let, at a pre-play stage denoted t_0, the two players announce simultaneously their intention to cooperate or not with the rival, as well as the timing $\tau = (t_1, t_2)$ they intend to play a given duopoly game. Every player's announcement set A_i, for $i = 1, 2$ and $j \neq i$, can be defined as

$$A_i = [(\{i, j\}, t_1), (\{i, j\}, t_2), (\{i\}, t_1), (\{i\}, t_2)], \quad (21)$$

where the first two announcements express collusive intentions, while the remaining two correspond to the usual (noncooperative) timing choices (*early*, *late*) of Hamilton and Slutsky's [27] game. Players' announcement space $A = A_1 \times A_2$ contains 16 different announcement profiles $a \in A$ which, in turn, induce the following set $\mathscr{C}$ of time-cooperation *configurations* $C(a)$:

$$\begin{aligned}\mathscr{C}(A) = \big[&(\{1,2\}^{t_1}), (\{1,2\}^{t_2}), (\{1^{t_1}, 2^{t_2}\}),\\ &(\{1^{t_2}, 2^{t_1}\}), (\{1\}^{t_1}, \{2\}^{t_1}), (\{1\}^{t_2}, \{2\}^{t_2}),\\ &(\{1\}^{t_1}, \{2\}^{t_2}), (\{1\}^{t_2}, \{2\}^{t_1})\big].\end{aligned} \quad (22)$$

Differently from Hamilton and Slutsky [27], here the two players are allowed to cooperate and form an alliance either at period t_1 or t_2 or across periods. Players are allowed to cooperate either during one period or across time, that is, sequencing their cooperative strategy over time. They are not allowed instead to cooperate twice, once in period 1 and once in period 2. We assume that in order to be signed, a binding agreement endowed with a specific timing requires the *unanimity* of all players. Formally, for $i = 1, 2$, $j \neq i$, $k = 1, 2$ and $\tau = (t_1, t_2)$,

$$C(a) = (\{i^{\tau_i}, j^{\tau_j}\}) \quad \text{iff } a_i = (\{i, j\}, \tau_k) \quad \text{for } i = 1,2 \text{ and } k = 1,2, \quad C(a) = (\{i\}^{\tau_h}, \{j\}^{\tau_l}) \text{ otherwise.} \tag{23}$$

The above rule prescribes that, if both players agree to cooperate, they can behave collusively in just one period or alternate their collusive strategy over time. However, if just one player disagrees on cooperation, both players end up playing independently in their own preferred time.

The notion used to define the stability of a given time configuration $C(a)$ is simply the Nash equilibrium of the corresponding announcement profile.

Definition 11 (Nash-stability). A configuration $C(a) \in \mathscr{C}(A)$ is Nash-stable if and only if $C = C(a^*)$, with a^* possessing the following property:

$$u_i(x(C(a^*))) \geq u_i(x(C(a_i', a_j^*))), \tag{24}$$

for any $a_i' \in A_i$, for all $i = 1, 2$ and $j \neq i$.

When a timing-configuration $C = C(a^*)$ is Nash-stable, this implies, in turn, that the profile $\sigma^* = (a^*, x^*)$ is a subgame perfect Nash equilibrium (SNE) of the extended game. The only warning is that, in the equilibrium path in which players decide cooperatively, they are assumed to behave as a single maximizing entity. Formally, when the announcement profile induces a collusive behavior, players are assumed to sign a binding agreement. A similar approach is taken in the so called endogenous coalition formation literature (see Ray and Vohra [29, 30], Yi [31], Ray [32], and Marini [33] for surveys.) The next proposition illustrates the main implications of our simple model.

Proposition 12. *The endogenous timing-cooperation game played by two symmetric players can give rise to the following cases: (i) under strategic complements, for $u^C \geq u^F$, the set of stable configurations is given by*

$$\mathscr{C}^* = [(\{1,2\}^{t_1}), (\{1,2\}^{t_2}), (\{1^{t_1}, 2^{t_2}\}), (\{1^{t_2}, 2^{t_1}\}), (\{1\}^{t_1}, \{2\}^{t_2}), (\{1\}^{t_2}, \{2\}^{t_1})]. \tag{25}$$

(ii) Under strategic complements, for $u^F > u^C$,

$$\mathscr{C}^* = [(\{1,2\}^{t_2}), (\{1\}^{t_1}, \{2\}^{t_2}), (\{1\}^{t_2}, \{2\}^{t_1})]. \tag{26}$$

(iii) Under strategic substitutes, for $u^C \geq u^L$,

$$\mathscr{C}^* = [(\{1,2\}^{t_1}), (\{1,2\}^{t_2}), (\{1^{t_1}, 2^{t_2}\}), (\{1^{t_2}, 2^{t_1}\}), (\{1\}^{t_1}, \{2\}^{t_1})], \tag{27}$$

and (iv) under strategic substitutes, for $u^L > u^C$,

$$\mathscr{C}^* = [(\{1,2\}^{t_1}), (\{1\}^{t_1}, \{2\}^{t_1})]. \tag{28}$$

Proof. (i) When players' actions are strategic complements and $u^C \geq u^F$, Proposition 1 proved that the following ranking between players' payoffs:

$$u^C \geq u^F > u^L > u^N. \tag{29}$$

Therefore, any cooperative announcement $a = (\{i, j\}, \tau)$ expressed by both players is a Nash equilibrium of the extended time-cooperation game for any $\tau = (t_1, t_2)$, since no player can deviate profitably by announcing either $a_i' = (\{i\}, t_1)$ or $a_i'' = (\{i\}, t_2)$ inducing, in turn, a duopoly played either simultaneously or sequentially. Therefore, all cooperative configurations $(\{i, j\}^{\tau})$ or $(\{i^{t_h}, j^{t_l}\})$ are supported as SNE of the extended game. The noncooperative sequential configuration $(\{i\}^{t_1}, \{j\}^{t_2})$ is also a Nash equilibrium announcement, since, by deviating unilaterally, a player can only induce a noncooperative simultaneous play, obtaining, according to (29), a lower payoff. (ii) When $u^F > u^C$, the cooperative configurations $(\{i, j\}^{t_1})$ and $(\{i^{t_h}, j^{t_l}\})$ are no longer Nash-stable since each player can profitably deviate as a follower by announcing $a_i'' = (\{i\}, t_2)$. Both sequential noncooperative configurations can instead be supported as SNE, since full collusion (at time two) is in this case profitable only for the leader and not for the follower. (iii) When players' actions are strategic substitutes and $u^C \geq u^L$, by Proposition 1,

$$u^C \geq u^L > u^N > u^F. \tag{30}$$

Here all cooperative agreements are Nash equilibrium announcements for any $\tau = (t_1, t_2)$. Also all noncooperative simultaneous configurations $(\{i\}^{t_1}, \{j\}^{t_1})$ are stable, since by deviating unilaterally with an announcement $a_i'' = (\{i\}, t_2)$, a player ends up playing sequentially as a follower, receiving a lower payoff. (iv) Finally, when $u^L > u^C$, the cooperative configurations $(\{i, j\}^{t_2})$ and $(\{i^{t_2}, j^{t_2}\})$ are not stable since players can deviate by announcing $a_i' = (\{i\}, t_1)$ and obtaining a higher payoff as a leader. The simultaneous (noncooperative) configuration played at time 1 is also stable since no player can deviate as a leader, but only as a follower, and the latter deviation is no profitable. □

Our simple extension of Hamilton and Slutsky [27] has helped to reach at least one clear-cut conclusion. It is as follows: intertemporal cooperation (or cooperation across time) is, overall, the most vulnerable form of cooperation among players. This is because such type of cooperation may be subject to the objections of players in the role of leaders and followers more frequently than if cooperation takes place just in a single period.

5. Concluding Remarks

This paper has presented a first attempt to connect two usually distinct issues concerning players' strategic interaction: one dealing with their timing of play and the other with their capacity to collude. We have shown that the nature of interaction between players in the strategic setting (duopoly game) plays a crucial role for the decision of players to sign or not a binding agreement and to sequence or not their strategies.

Appendix

Lemma A.1 (existence of a symmetric cooperative equilibrium). *Let players' payoffs be continuous and strictly quasiconcave and their strategy set be compact and convex. Then, the strategy profile* $x^c \in \arg\max_{\mathbf{x}\in X^2} \sum_{i=1,2} u_i(\mathbf{x})$ *is such that* $x_i^c = x_j^c$.

Proof. Compactness of each X implies compactness of X^2. Continuity of each player's payoff $u_i(\mathbf{x})$ on $\mathbf{x}$ implies the continuity of the social payoff function $\sum_{i=1,2} u_i(\mathbf{x})$. Existence of an efficient profile $x^c \in X^2$ directly follows. We prove that, under our assumptions, such a strategy profile is symmetric. Suppose $x_i^c \neq x_j^c$. By symmetry we can derive from $\mathbf{x}^c$ a new vector $\tilde{\mathbf{x}}$ permuting the strategies of players i and j such that

$$\sum_{i=1,2} u_i(\tilde{\mathbf{x}}) = \sum_{i=1,2} u_i(\mathbf{x}^c), \qquad \text{(A.1)}$$

and hence, by the strict quasiconcavity of all $u_i(\mathbf{x})$, for all $\delta \in (0,1)$ we have that

$$\sum_{i=1,2} u_i(\delta\tilde{\mathbf{x}} + (1-\delta)\mathbf{x}^c) > \sum_{i=1,2} u_i(\mathbf{x}^c). \qquad \text{(A.2)}$$

Since, by the convexity of X, the strategy vector $(\delta\tilde{\mathbf{x}} + (1-\delta)\mathbf{x}^c) \in X^2$, we obtain a contradiction. □

Conflict of Interests

The authors declare that there is no conflict of interests regarding the publication of this paper.

Acknowledgments

The authors wish to thank Christian Ewerhart, Attila Tasnadi, Jacquelin Morgan, Maria Luisa Petit, George Zaccour, and the participants at the Oligo workshop in Budapest, the MDEF workshop in Urbino, the SING7 conference in Paris, and seminar audience at CREI Roma III and Sapienza University for their useful comments and discussions.

References

[1] I. Mouraviev and P. Rey, "Collusion and leadership," *International Journal of Industrial Organization*, vol. 29, no. 6, pp. 705–717, 2011.

[2] C. d'Aspremont, A. Jaquemin, J. Gabszewicz, and J. Weymark, "On the stability of dominant cartels," *Canadian Journal of Economics*, vol. 14, pp. 17–25, 1982.

[3] C. d'Aspremont and J. J. Gabszewicz, "On the stability of collusion," in *New Developments in the Analysis of Market Structure*, J. Stiglitz and G. F. Mathewson, Eds., MIT Press, Boston, Mass, USA, 1986.

[4] M. Donsimoni, N. Economides, and H. Polemarchakis, "Stable cartels," *International Economic Review*, vol. 27, pp. 317–327, 1986.

[5] A. Daughety, "Beneficial concentration," *American Economic Review*, vol. 80, no. 5, pp. 1231–1237, 1990.

[6] D. Levine, "Horizontal mergers: the 50-percent benchmark," *American Economic Review*, vol. 80, no. 5, pp. 1238–1245, 1990.

[7] S. Huck, K. A. Konrad, and W. Müller, "Big fish eat small fish: on merger in Stackelberg markets," *Economics Letters*, vol. 73, no. 2, pp. 213–217, 2001.

[8] J. S. Heywood and M. McGinty, "Leading and merging: convex costs, Stackelberg, and the merger paradox," *Southern Economic Journal*, vol. 74, no. 3, pp. 879–893, 2008.

[9] M. Escrihuela-Villar and R. Faulí-Oller, "Mergers in asymmetric Stackelberg markets," *Spanish Economic Review*, vol. 10, no. 4, pp. 279–288, 2008.

[10] M. Marini, M. L. Petit, and R. Sestini, "Strategic timing in R&D agreements," *Economics of Innovation and New Technology*, 2013.

[11] E. van Damme and S. Hurkens, "Endogenous Stackelberg leadership," *Games and Economic Behavior*, vol. 28, no. 1, pp. 105–129, 1999.

[12] E. van Damme and S. Hurkens, "Endogenous price leadership," *Games and Economic Behavior*, vol. 47, no. 2, pp. 404–420, 2004.

[13] B. von Stengel, "Follower payoffs in symmetric duopoly games," *Games and Economic Behavior*, vol. 69, no. 2, pp. 512–516, 2010.

[14] E. Gal-Or, "First mover and second mover advantages," *International Economic Review*, vol. 26, pp. 649–653, 1985.

[15] R. Amir, I. Grilo, and J. Jin, "Demand-induced endogenous price leadership," *International Game Theory Review*, vol. 1, pp. 219–240, 1999.

[16] S. Dowrick, "von Stackelberg and Cournot duopoly: choosing roles," *The RAND Journal of Economics*, vol. 17, no. 2, pp. 251–260, 1986.

[17] R. Amir, "Endogenous timing in two-player games: a counterexample," *Games and Economic Behavior*, vol. 9, no. 2, pp. 234–237, 1995.

[18] R. Amir and I. Grilo, "Stackelberg versus Cournot equilibrium," *Games and Economic Behavior*, vol. 26, no. 1, pp. 1–21, 1999.

[19] S. Currarini and M. Marini, "A sequential approach to the characteristic function and the core in games with externalities," in *Advances in Economic Design*, M. Sertel and A. Kara, Eds., Springer, Berlin, Germany, 2003.

[20] S. Currarini and M. Marini, "A conjectural cooperative equilibrium in strategic form games," in *Game Practise and the Environment*, C. Carraro and V. Fragnelli, Eds., Kluwer Academic Press, Norwell, Mass, USA, 2004.

[21] B. von Stengel and S. Zamir, "Leadership games with convex strategy sets," *Games and Economic Behavior*, vol. 69, no. 2, pp. 446–457, 2010.

[22] D. Levine, "Stackelberg, Cournot and collusive monopoly: performance and welfare comparison," *Economic Inquiry*, vol. 26, pp. 317–330, 1988.

[23] C. Figuières, M. Tidball, and A. Jean-Marie, "On the effects of conjectures in a symmetric strategic setting," *Research in Economics*, vol. 58, no. 1, pp. 75–102, 2004.

[24] D. M. Topkis, *Supermodularity and Complementarity*, Princeton University Press, Princeton, NJ, USA, 1998.

[25] S. W. Salant and G. Shaffer, "Optimal asymmetric strategies in research joint ventures," *International Journal of Industrial Organization*, vol. 16, no. 2, pp. 195–208, 1998.

[26] D. Leahy and P. J. Neary, "Symmetric research joint ventures: cooperative substitutes and complements," *International Journal of Industrial Organization*, vol. 23, pp. 5381–6397, 2005.

[27] J. H. Hamilton and S. M. Slutsky, "Endogenous timing in duopoly games: Stackelberg or Cournot equilibria," *Games and Economic Behavior*, vol. 2, no. 1, pp. 29–46, 1990.

[28] M. Amir, R. Amir, and J. Jin, "Sequencing R&D decisions in a two-period duopoly with spillovers," *Economic Theory*, vol. 15, no. 2, pp. 297–317, 2000.

[29] D. Ray and R. Vohra, "Equilibrium binding agreements," *Journal of Economic Theory*, vol. 73, no. 1, pp. 30–78, 1997.

[30] F. Bloch, "Coalition formation in games with spillovers," in *The Endogenous Formation of Economic Coalitions*, C. Carraro, Ed., Fondazione Eni Enrico Mattei Series on Economics and the Environment, Elgar, Cheltenham, UK, 2003.

[31] S. S. Yi, "The endogenous formation of economic coalitions: the partition function approach," in *The Endogenous Formation of Economic Coalitions*, C. Carraro, Ed., Fondazione Eni Enrico Mattei Series on Economics and the Environment, pp. 80–127, Elgar, Cheltenham, UK, 2003.

[32] D. Ray, *A Game-Theoretic Perspective on Coalition Formation*, Oxford University Press, Oxford, UK, 2007.

[33] M. A. Marini, "Games of coalition and network formation: a survey," in *Networks, Dynamics and Topology*, A. Naizmada, S. Stefani, and A. Torriero, Eds., Springer, London, UK, 2009.

16

Long-Term Effects of Expiration of Derivatives on Indian Spot Volatility

Sunita Narang[1] and Madhu Vij[2]

[1] *Acharya Narendra Dev College, University of Delhi, Delhi 110019, India*
[2] *Faculty of Management, University of Delhi, Delhi 110007, India*

Correspondence should be addressed to Sunita Narang; narang.sunita20@gmail.com

Academic Editors: M. T. Leung, S. Managi, and K. P. Upadhyaya

This paper examines the impact of expiration of derivatives on spot volatility of Indian capital market. The review of the literature shows that the previous Indian studies have covered a period of only 4–6 years after the introduction of derivative trading in India in 2000. They are unanimous about volume effect but not about return and volatility effect. This paper uses regression techniques and one symmetric and three asymmetric GARCH models, namely, TGARCH, EGARCH, and PGARCH, to evaluate the impact. It uses daily data on popular index S&P CNX Nifty of National Stock Exchange of India, during a period of more than a decade from June 12, 2000 to January 10, 2012. Findings of the study show that spot returns, volume, and volatility are high on expiration day and they build up further on the day after expiry which shows that the Indian market is weakly efficient. The expiration effect is mainly due to concentration of volumes in near-month contracts and absence of physical settlement.

1. Introduction

Derivatives were introduced on two major exchanges of India, namely, National Stock exchange (NSE) and Bombay Stock Exchange (BSE) in 2000. During this time Indian government took many decisions to bring major structural changes in the market. NSE acted as a catalytic agent in reforming the micro structure, market practices, and trading volumes of the Indian securities market. It is dominating the derivative segment with more than 99% of the market share in 2011-12. The exchanges manage their respective cash and derivative segments which have been well integrated with uniform trade practices and trade timings. Screen-based trading allows the arbitrageurs to use computer programs for identifying arbitrage conditions and ensures quick execution of orders. Index and stock-based derivatives are traded in monthly series, the expiration date for each series being the last Thursday of the expiry month, that is, Indian market experiences the quadruple witching day. At any point of time, three monthly series are traded side by side and are cash settled on the expiration or an early exercise.

As derivative contracts call for cash settlement on the expiration day, the trading and manipulation activities of speculators and unwinding of cash positions by arbitrageurs in the cash markets sometimes cause distortion to price, volume, and volatility near the expiration day. If many arbitrageurs liquidate at the same time and in the same direction, price and volatility effects are possible. Speculators can also make deliberate attempts to manipulate prices. The severity of these effects partially depends on the stock market procedures for accommodating order imbalances. Considering the fact that a large number of derivative transactions take place on this day, the magnitude of these potential side effects can be large. Also, since index arbitrage is typically executed with expensive computer technology, the potential benefits are reaped by only a small number of institutional investors, but the side effects are suffered by all market participants.

During 2001–08, highly liquid index futures and options provided a simple and efficient arbitrage opportunity to traders. Futures and options contracts were cash settled so there was no direct pressure due to delivery demands on the cash market on expiration days. As opposed to these facilitators of a smooth arbitrage, short sales in the cash market were banned during this period by the Indian market regulator SEBI which may have constrained the arbitrage transactions requiring a short position in the cash market.

After 2008, the ban on shortsales was lifted. Since then there is significant increase in use of computer programs for doing arbitrage, known as algorithmic trading. It is yet to be seen if these changes have altered the impact of expiration day on the volatility of Indian spot market.

2. The Literature Review

Many previous studies have pointed towards significant expiration effects in terms of high volume and volatility. The studies [1–8] found significant volume effects on account of expiration days. Apart from higher volume, the studies [9–12] also found evidence of a reversal of the index. The studies [6, 13–15] found increased volatility in individual stock returns. [16] for TSE 300 Index and [17] for Spanish Exchange found that price reversals, higher trading volume, and higher volatility are associated with expiration days. On the other hand, [18, 19] found no significant expiration-day effect on cash-market volatility. This indicates that world over researchers are unanimous about the volume effect of expiration day. The impact on returns and volatility, however, is not clear. Some studies show return reversal whereas others do not. Similarly, some researchers report high volatility and others find it insignificant.

In case of India, most of the studies are reporting significant expiration effect during a period of 4–6 years after introduction of derivatives in 2000 [1, 7, 8]. Indian researchers also agree on volume effects while, the results regarding price effects and volatility effects are mixed [1, 2, 7, 8]. Since researchers in India and abroad are not unanimous about volatility effect, it needs to be further examined whether and to what extent the expiration effects add to higher than normal volatility and whether this volatility has a detrimental effect. Our study proposes to use a longer period to get comprehensive results on all the three variables, namely, return, volume, and volatility, for this emerging market by using econometric models.

3. Data

NSE established itself as the market leader in the futures and options segment since the inception of derivative trading in 2000. Its benchmark index, S&P CNX Nifty, is a well diversified index consisting of 50 liquid stocks; hence, the study considers Nifty as a proxy for the Indian stock market and uses its time series data to see the impact of derivative expiration on stock market volatility. The impact of expiration-day is evaluated during post derivative period; hence, daily closing prices of approximately 13 years, from June 12, 2000 to January 10, 2012, have been collected from the website of NSE. The total period has approximately 2393 days out of which 127 days are the expiration days and 126 days are non expiration days.

To separate the impact of US market (proxy for world) from that of domestic market on volatility, the data of S&P 500 index is used as an additional independent variable. S&P 500 is widely regarded as the best single gauge of the US equities market; this world-renowned index includes a representative sample of 500 leading companies in leading industries of the US economy. The correlation coefficient of Nifty and S&P 500 shows that they are highly correlated and the US market significantly affects the Indian market. We have also collected the volume data of Nifty spot index to evaluate the impact of derivative expiration on it.

4. Econometric Technique

For analysis of impact of derivative expiration we calculate the return series by taking log of first difference of the daily closing prices of S&P Nifty and S&P 500 US index. Trading volume is also calculated using logarithms. Current financial time series exhibit the phenomena of volatility clusters and if it is not captured then the empirical findings are not reliable. Hence, we have used GARCH(1,1) model, proposed by [20], to capture this effect.

GARCH models display some limitations in capturing stylized characteristics of the data like heavy tails, asymmetric (leverage) effect, volatility clustering. The most important feature is asymmetric effect which was discovered by [21], and confirmed by the findings of [22–24], among others. This effect results when predictable volatility increases more due to unexpected drop in price (bad news) than unexpected increase in price (good news) of same magnitude. According to [21, 25], this is due to leverage effect. A drop in price increases financial leverage, which makes the stock riskier and increases its volatility. Many researchers treat leverage effect same as asymmetric volatility. We are capturing the asymmetric effect using three models, namely, EGARCH model by [23], TGARCH model by [26], and PGARCH model by [27, 28].

Finally, there is a variety of statistics to evaluate and compare forecast errors in the volatility forecasting literature. The most popular measures used in the literature include mean error (ME), root mean square error (RMSE), mean absolute percentage error (MAPE), and mean absolute error (MAE). We have chosen measures of RMSE, MAE, and MAPE for comparing the performance of various GARCH models we have used.

5. Method

5.1. Impact of Derivative Expiration on Spot Volume. We analyse the impact of derivative expiration on spot volume using regression technique with a dummy variable for expiration day. This variable takes the value of 1 on the last Thursday of the month when derivative contracts expire in India and 0 otherwise. Apart from this we also employ dummy variable for next day and see its impact on the spot volume. Next, we take the Thursday prior to expiry day as the non expiration day and employ dummy variable for assessing its impact on spot volume.

5.2. Impact of Derivative Expiration on Spot Return and Volatility. Second, we employ GARCH and its asymmetric counterparts to examine the impact of expiration day, next day, and non expiration day on spot return and spot volatility using dummy variables. We also use multiplicative volume dummies to find the impact of expiration day, next day, and non expiration day volumes on spot return and volatility.

6. Empirical Results

6.1. Descriptive Statistics. To observe the preliminary difference in returns of expiry day, its next day and non expiry day, we start with descriptive statistics of these days (see Table 1).

The results in Table 1 show that the mean and unconditional variance of returns is highest during next days and lowest during non expiration days. The skewness statistics indicates higher probability of getting higher returns on next day compared to expiry day. Its positive value during non expiration days suggests high probability of getting lower returns. The kurtosis and JB statistics indicate that next day returns are more normal than expiry day returns while returns are highly non normal during non expiry days.

Table 1: Descriptive statistics of expiration and nonexpiration periods.

	Expiry day	Next day	Nonexpiry day
Mean	0.0033	0.0034	0.0010
Std. Dev.	0.0132	0.0166	0.0094
Skewness	−0.2523	−0.4475	0.4988
Kurtosis	4.5947	3.9711	7.9259
Jarque Bera	14.11***	8.72**	255.75***
No. of Obs.	127	126	126

**indicates significance at 5%.

***indicates that values are significant at 1%.

6.2. Impact of Derivative Expiration on Spot Volume. To reveal any effects of expiration day and its next day on the trading volume of the Nifty spot index, regression model was evaluated with the following results:

$$\begin{aligned} \text{Ln}(\text{vol}_t) &= 2.1374 * c + 0.8829 * \text{Ln}(\text{vol}_{t-1}) \\ &\quad + 0.1319 * \text{Expday}, \\ \text{Ln}(\text{vol}_t) &= 2.0648 * c + 0.8877 * \text{Ln}(\text{vol}_{t-1}) \\ &\quad + 0.1479 * \text{Nextday}, \end{aligned} \quad (1)$$

where $\text{Ln}(\text{vol}_t)$ is the logarithm of trading volume on day t and $\text{Ln}(\text{vol}_{t-1})$ is the volume on previous day. Expday and Nextday are the dummies for expiration day and its next day, respectively.

The results show that the coefficients of the dummies for both expiration day and its next day are positive and significant (1%) and the magnitude is higher on the next day. This shows that expiration period increases the spot volume and that there is no reversal in volume during this period. We could not find the presence of autocorrelation and heteroscedasticity in the volume data hence OLS is an appropriate method.

Next, we see the impact of non expiration day on spot volume as follows:

$$\begin{aligned} \text{Ln}(\text{vol}_t) &= 2.1216 * c + 0.8842 * \text{Ln}(\text{vol}_{t-1}) \\ &\quad - 0.0225 * \text{NExpday}. \end{aligned} \quad (2)$$

The results in the previous equation show that the coefficient of non expiry day is negative and insignificant. Consequently, it can be concluded that derivative expiration has a significant positive effect on the volume of Nifty.

6.3. Impact of Derivative Expiration on Spot Return and Volatility. To evaluate the impact of expiry day and its volume on spot return and volatility we augment the GARCH return and volatility equations with the dummies of expiry day, its multiplicative dummy with volume; next day, its multiplicative dummy with volume; and non expiry day and its multiplicative dummy with volume. The results are shown in Tables 2, 3, and 4.

The results in Table 2 show that the impact of expiry day its volume is highly significant (1%) and positive on both spot return and volatility under Ged distribution.

The results in Table 3 show highly significant (1%) and positive impact of next day and its volume on spot returns and volatility under Ged distribution.

By comparing Tables 2 and 3 we can see that the impact of next day on return and volatility is higher than the impact of expiry day, suggesting continuation of an upward pressure. This indicates that no price or volatility reversal is taking place. This implies that expiration period is profitable for Indian market participants. Apart from this, we also note that the volumes are also higher on next day compared to expiry day. These volumes are partially responsible for high returns and volatility during expiration period. The results in Table 4 suggests that impact of non expiration day is positive and insignificant on returns and negative and insignificant on volatility. This implies that Indian market experiences significant expiration effects in terms of high returns, volumes, and volatility.

7. Conclusions

The analysis of post derivative period for expiration effect indicates that return, volume, and volatility are high on expiry day, and all these variables further increase on next day, indicating continuation of upward pressure. This indicates negative price, volume, and volatility reversal. The volume on expiry and next days is partially responsible for high returns and volatility on these days.

High volumes on these days may be attributed to various reasons: unwinding of large position; discretionary liquidity trading; and more active trading by informed traders during this period [29].

Although, Indian government has tried to implement physical settlement but it is yet to take off; hence, the cash settlement feature of derivatives may be contributing to high returns during these days. Increase in returns on both expiry and next day could also be due to flow of new information into the market which implies that Indian market is weakly efficient [30]. According to [6], if the underlying market is deep and if suppliers of liquidity are quick to respond to

Table 2: Impact of expiry day and its volume on spot return and volatility.

	Garch(1,1)	TGarch(1,1)	EGarch(1,1)	PGarch(1,1)
Nifty(−1)	0.0404***	0.0527***	0.0318**	0.0426***
S&P 500(−1)	0.2103***	0.2111***	0.2163***	0.2186***
Expday	0.0032***	0.0030***	0.0033***	0.0038***
Expday * Lnvol	0.0002***	0.0002***	0.0002***	0.0002***
Alpha	0.1499***	0.0600***	0.1398***	0.1264***
Gamma	—	0.1859***	−0.0429***	0.5389***
Beta	0.8125***	0.7918***	0.9375***	0.8317***
Expday	4.34*E* − 005	5.41*E* − 05*	0.3971***	0.0023**
Expday * Lnvol	2.36*E* − 006	2.82*E* − 06*	0.0226***	0.0001**
LogL	6947.2	6954.69	6938.1	6957.73
RMSE	0.021030	0.021006	0.020998	0.020976
MAE	0.010981	0.010959	0.010945	0.010934
MAPE	177.39	170.14	166.13	156.25

*indicates significance at 10%.
**indicates significance at 5%.
***indicates that values are significant at 1%.

Table 3: Impact of next day and its volume on spot return and volatility.

	Garch(1,1)	TGarch(1,1)	EGarch(1,1)	PGarch(1,1)
Nifty(−1)	0.0358**	0.0437***	0.0208	0.0264*
S&P 500(−1)	0.2119***	0.2136***	0.2144***	0.2147***
Nextday	0.0039***	0.0043***	0.0046***	0.0047***
Nextday * Lnvol	0.0002***	0.0002***	0.0002***	0.0003***
Alpha	0.1526***	0.0671**	0.1378***	0.1269***
Gamma	—	0.1813***	−0.0331**	0.5367***
Beta	0.8119***	0.7974***	0.9479***	0.8411***
Nextday	5.3*E* − 05*	6.13*E* − 05**	0.4269***	0.0029***
Nextday * Lnvol	2.96*E* − 06*	3.37*E* − 06**	0.0235***	0.0002***
LogL	6952.92	6958.54	6940.28	6962.28
RMSE	0.021008	0.020954	0.020959	0.020954
MAE	0.010950	0.010914	0.010916	0.010914
MAPE	171.34	146.57	148.39	146.25

*indicates significance at 10%.
**indicates significance at 5%.
***indicates that values are significant at 1%.

Table 4: Impact of nonexpiry day and its volume on spot return and volatility.

	Garch(1,1)	TGarch(1,1)	EGarch(1,1)	PGarch(1,1)
Nifty(−1)	0.0358**	0.0408**	0.0226	0.0216
S&P 500(−1)	0.2164***	0.2194***	0.2285***	0.2297***
NExpday	0.0005	0.0002	0.0002	0.0002
NExpday * Lnvol	4.85*E* − 005	1.47*E* − 005	9.77*E* − 006	1.21*E* − 05
Alpha	0.1507***	0.0689**	0.1229***	0.1192***
Gamma	—	0.1766***	−0.0188	0.4774***
Beta	0.8152***	0.7987***	0.9557***	0.8554***
NExpday	−1.65*E* − 005	−2.37*E* − 005	0.0505	−0.0006
NExpday * Lnvol	−8.61*E* − 007	−1.21*E* − 006	0.0035	−3.39*E* − 05
LogL	6966.97	6973.63	6592.78	6973.36
RMSE	0.021012	0.020949	0.020964	0.020932
MAE	0.010938	0.010918	0.010921	0.010917
MAPE	173.16	149.18	150.27	148.35

**indicates significance at 5%.
***indicates that values are significant at 1%.

selling or buying pressure, the price effects of large arbitrage unwinding will be small. The results of our study indicate significant effect on price which means that the market mechanisms in India are not well designed to offset surprise imbalances and there is a need to further increase the depth of markets.

High volatility on both expiry and next day indicates that investors are undecided and prefer to roll over their position. It could also be due to manipulation activities. This temporary increase in volatility cannot destabilize the markets in long run. Further, our study shows that non expiry days contribute to insignificant return and volatility. Thus, we conclude that Indian market experiences significant expiration effect.

The study proves that Indian spot market experiences high volume and volatility during expiration of near-month derivative contracts. Large gaps exist in the range of derivative products that are traded actively. Most of the trading happens in near month contracts. On a typical trading day in the middle of the month, about 98 percent of the turnover comes from near-month contracts, while less than 0.5 percent comes from the far-month series. Of the individual stocks traded in the futures and options market, far-month contracts of only about 10 percent are traded. The concentration of volumes in the near-month series means that this is speculators' market. The manipulation by speculators is the main reason behind high volatility during and after expiry of these contracts. The impact of expiry day volume on return and volatility shows that positive and significant causality is running from volume to return and volatility which means that prices are speculative and traders take large spot positions to cover their risk resulting in high volatility during expiration period. This implies that volumes in near-month contracts should be regulated. Further, regulators should take necessary steps to curb volatility whenever volumes increase to a higher than normal level during expiration. This can also be achieved by popularising far-month contracts.

References

[1] B. S. Bodla and K. Jindal, "Equity derivatives in India: growth pattern and trading volume effects," *ICFAI Journal of Derivatives Markets*, vol. 5, pp. 62–82, 2008.

[2] S. S. Debasish, "Investigating expiration day effects in stock index futures in India," *Journal of Economics and Behavioral Studies*, vol. 1, pp. 9–19, 2010.

[3] A. G. Karolyi, "Stock market volatility around expiration days in Japan," *Journal of Derivatives*, vol. 4, no. 2, pp. 23–43, 1996.

[4] P. F. Pope and P. K. Yadav, "The impact of option expiration on underlying stocks: the UK evidence," *Journal of Business Finance & Accounting*, vol. 19, pp. 329–344, 1992.

[5] C. Schlag, "Expiration-day effects of stock index derivatives in Germany," *European Financial Management*, vol. 2, pp. 69–95, 1996.

[6] H. R. Stoll and R. E. Whaley, "Expiration-day effects of the all ordinaries share price index futures: empirical evidence and alternative settlement procedures," *Australian Journal of Management*, vol. 22, no. 2, pp. 139–174, 1997.

[7] N. Tripathy, "Expiration and week effect: empirical evidence from the Indian derivative market," *International Review of Business Research Papers*, vol. 6, pp. 209–219, 2010.

[8] V. Vipul, "Futures and options expiration-day effects: the Indian evidence," *The Journal of Futures Markets*, vol. 25, no. 11, pp. 1045–1065, 2005.

[9] H. R. Stoll and R. E. Whaley, *Expiration Day Effects of Index Options and Futures*, Monograph Series in Finance and Economics, Monograph 1986-3, New York University, 1986.

[10] H. R. Stoll and R. E. Whaley, "Program trading and expiration-day effects," *Financial Analysts Journal*, vol. 43, no. 2, pp. 16–18, 20–28, 1987.

[11] H. R. Stoll and R. E. Whaley, "Program trading and individual stock returns: ingredients of the triple-witching brew," *The Journal of Business*, vol. 63, no. 1, pp. S165–S192, 1990.

[12] H. R. Stoll and R. E. Whaley, "Expiration-day effects: what has changed?" *Financial Analysts Journal*, vol. 47, no. 1, pp. 58–72, 1991.

[13] Y.-F. Chow, H. H. M. Yung, and H. Zhang, "Expiration day effects: the case of Hong Kong," *The Journal of Futures Markets*, vol. 23, no. 1, pp. 67–86, 2003.

[14] D. Lien and L. Yang, "Availability and settlement of individual stock futures and options expiration-day effects: evidence from high-frequency data," *The Quarterly Review of Economics and Finance*, vol. 45, no. 4-5, pp. 730–747, 2005.

[15] H. M. Maniar, R. Bhatt, and D. M. Maniyar, ""Expiration hour effect of futures and options markets on stock market"a case study on NSE (National Stock Exchange of India)," *International Review of Economics and Finance*, vol. 18, no. 3, pp. 381–391, 2009.

[16] T. W. Chamberlain, C. S. Cheung, and C. C. Y. Kwan, "Expiration-day effects of index futures and options: some Canadian evidence," *Financial Analysts Journal*, vol. 45, no. 5, pp. 67–71, 1989.

[17] M. Illueca and J. A. LaFuente, "New evidence on expiration-day effects using realized volatility: an intraday analysis for the Spanish stock exchange," *The Journal of Futures Markets*, vol. 26, no. 9, pp. 923–938, 2006.

[18] P. Corredor, P. Lechón, and R. Santamaría, "Option-expiration effects in small markets: the Spanish stock exchange," *The Journal of Futures Markets*, vol. 21, no. 10, pp. 905–928, 2001.

[19] D. Lien and L. I. Yang, "Options expiration effects and the role of individual share futures contracts," *The Journal of Futures Markets*, vol. 23, no. 11, pp. 1107–1118, 2003.

[20] T. Bollerslev, "Generalized autoregressive conditional heteroskedasticity," *Journal of Econometrics*, vol. 31, no. 3, pp. 307–327, 1986.

[21] F. Black, "Studies in stock price volatility changes," in *Proceedings of the Business Meeting of the Business and Economics Statistics Section*, pp. 177–181, American Statistical Association, 1976.

[22] K. R. French, G. W. Schwert, and R. F. Stambaugh, "Expected stock returns and volatility," *Journal of Financial Economics*, vol. 19, no. 1, pp. 3–29, 1987.

[23] D. B. Nelson, "Conditional Heteroskedasticity in asset returns: a new approach," *Econometrica*, vol. 59, pp. 347–370, 1991.

[24] G. Schwert, "Stock volatility and the crash of "87"," *Review of Financial Studies*, vol. 3, pp. 77–102, 1990.

[25] A. A. Christie, "The stochastic behavior of common stock variances. Value, leverage and interest rate effects," *Journal of Financial Economics*, vol. 10, no. 4, pp. 407–432, 1982.

[26] L. R. Glosten, R. Jagannathan, and D. E. Runkle, "On the relation between the expected value and the volatility of the nominal excess return on stocks," *Journal of Finance*, vol. 48, no. 5, pp. 1779-1801, 1983.

[27] S. Taylor, *Modeling Financial Time Series*, John Wiley & Sons, New York, NY, USA, 1986.

[28] G. Schwert, "Why stock market volatility change over time?" *Journal of Finance*, vol. 44, pp. 1115–1153, 1989.

[29] A. R. Admati and P. Pfleiderer, "A theory of intraday patterns: volume and price variability," *Review of Financial Studies*, vol. 1, pp. 3–40, 1988.

[30] E. F. Fama, "Multi-period consumption-investment decisions," *American Economic Review*, vol. 60, pp. 163–174, 1970.

Exchange Rate Determination and Forecasting: Can the Microstructure Approach Rescue Us from the Exchange Rate Disparity?

Guangfeng Zhang,[1] Qiong Zhang,[2] and Muhammad Tariq Majeed[3]

[1] *GREQAM, School of Economics, Aix-Marseille University, Marseille 13236, France*
[2] *School of Public Administration, Sichuan University, Chengdu 610000, China*
[3] *School of Economics, Quaid-i-Azam University, Islamabad 45320, Pakistan*

Correspondence should be addressed to Guangfeng Zhang; guangfeng.f.zhang@gmail.com

Academic Editors: M. E. Kandil and A. Rodriguez-Alvarez

Using two measures of private information and high-frequency transaction data from the leading interdealer electronic broking system Reuters D2000-2, we examine the association between exchange rate return and contemporaneous order flow and the predictability power of lagged order flow on the future exchange rate return. Our empirical analysis demonstrates that at high frequency (5, 10, 15, 20, 25, and 30 min) there exists strong positive association between exchange rate returns and contemporaneous order flow. However, the results indicate weak predictability of order flow on the future exchange rate return.

1. Introduction

In exchange rate economics one conventional common sense about exchange rates is that exchange rates follow a random walk process for frequencies less than annual, such as daily, weekly, or even monthly. However, exchange rates show some trend, cyclicality, or general history dependence at lower frequencies. In contrast to macroeconomic fundamental analysis at lower frequencies, studies on microstructure approaches to exchange rates focus on the movements in exchange rates at high frequency. In particular, microstructure approaches emphasize how exchange rates respond to order flow, which measures the net transaction pressure between buy and sell forces in the actual FX market.

The theoretical frameworks for microstructure approaches to exchange rates have been sequentially built by Lyons [1] and Evans and Lyons [2]. In particular, the portfolio-shift model proposed by Evans and Lyons [2] is initially set up in a customer-dealer trading environment to show how order flow impacts exchange rates. Evans and Lyons apply the trading model to daily data obtained from the customer-dealer transaction platform Reuters D2000-1 to examine the exchange rate Deutsche mark/US dollar and Japanese yen/US dollar over May 1 to August 31, 1996. As a result, Evans and Lyons find that order flow can be a good series to determine the exchange rate movement at daily frequency. Similarly, empirical studies have applied this theoretical framework to various high-frequency data from diverse interdealer trading platforms. Killeen et al. [3] study the daily exchange rate German mark/French franc traded on the electronic broking system (EBS) in 1998. Hau et al. [4] study EBS data over 1998 to 1999 on the exchange rate German mark against US dollar. Berger et al. [5] study the intraday EBS data on the exchange rate US dollar/Japanese yen and Euro/US dollar spanning over January 1999 to February 2004. Ito and Hashimoto [6] study the intraday EBS data on the exchange rate US dollar/Japanese yen over January 4, 1998 to October 31, 2003 and Euro/US dollar over January 3, 1999 to October 31, 2003. Relevant studies also have examined the data from central banks. Rime [7] applies weekly data from Norges Bank for the exchange rate Deutsche mark/US dollar, British pound/US dollar, and Swiss franc/US dollar over July 1995 to September 1999. Payne [8] employs the tick-by-tick real-time foreign exchange trading data of Deutsche mark/US dollar from the interdealer FX trading system Reuters D2000-2. Overall, these studies consistently confirm a significant positive association between exchange rates and the corresponding contemporaneous order flow.

We aim to revisit the association between exchange rates and contemporaneous order flow and the predictability of the lagged order flow on the future exchange rate. Our study uses the intraday high-frequency transaction data from one of the leading interdealer electronic broking systems, Reuters D2000-2. We implement the empirical analysis via two different measures of order flow. Our analysis demonstrates that at high frequency (5, 10, 15, 20, 25, and 30 min) there exists a strong positive association between exchange rate return and contemporaneous order flow. However, our empirical study shows weak predictability of order flow on the future exchange rate return. We also investigate the feedback trading in the FX market, but in our case this common theoretical hypothesis is rejected in our empirical analysis.

Comparing with relevant researches, our study is distinct from others in terms of the approach to measure order flow, the approach to implement the contemporaneous association and future prediction, and our particular data set. First, we use two different measurements of order flow to identify the impact of order flow on the contemporaneous exchange rate and the prediction of order flow on the future exchange rate. Related researches usually adopt the number of the net transactions (number of buyer-initiated trade minus number of seller-initiated trade) to proxy the absolute value of order flow, which is originally defined as the net value between the buyer-initiated trade and seller-initiated trade. We use the net transaction values in our empirical study though the number of transactions is adopted in relevant studies. In particular, in our empirical analysis, we also use the ratio of the absolute order flow to the trade flow to proxy order flow. Second, we examine the possible endogeneity of the contemporaneous order flow from the feedback trading and possible nonlinearity involved in the association. Third, we separately examine the contemporaneous determination of the exchange rate and the prediction power of the lagged order flow on the future exchange rate return. In the analysis of prediction, we identify the relative weak predictability of the history order flow on the future return, the weak historical dependence of order flow, and the high market efficiency in the actual FX market. Finally, it is worth mentioning that we use the transaction data for the exchange rate Deutsche mark/US dollar from one of the leading brokered interdealer trading system, Reuters D2000-2. Relevant researches have extensively examined the transaction data from customer-dealer platform, central banks, direct interdealer transaction platform Reuters D2000-1, and broker interdealer transaction platform EBS. As we discussed in the survey section that the data from different source usually represent different characteristics of the trading agents in the FX market, which makes the association using the data from this different source worth revisiting.

The structure of this paper is as follows. Section 2 briefly introduces the theoretical issue about the association between exchange rates and order flow. Section 3 describes the data and constructs the series used in our empirical analysis. Section 4 introduces the methodology arrangements adopted in our empirical study. Section 5 reports the results of our empirical studies. Section 6 concludes this paper.

2. Theoretical Issue

The theoretical models proposed by Lyons [1] and Evans and Lyons [2] are designed to fit the structure of the actual foreign exchange trading process. The two models are termed as, respectively, hot-potato trading and portfolio-shift model. Particularly, Evans and Lyons [2] frame the real market-markers' behaviours in the FX market. Their model captures the important aspects of exchange rate determinations caused by the actual foreign exchange transactions between the market participants. For more details about the model details, see Lyons [1] and Evans and Lyons [2]. We summarize the relationship between the exchange rate return Δp_t and the order flow x_t in the specification as follows:

$$\Delta p_t = \alpha + \beta x_t + \varepsilon_t. \quad (1)$$

As the theoretical model suggested, the positive net transaction pressure between buying and selling increases the value of the exchange rate which is defined as the domestic price of the foreign currency. The coefficient β on order flow x_t should take positive value. On the contrary, the negative net transaction pressure decreases the value of the exchange rate. As to the association between exchange rate return Δp_t and order flow x_t, practical studies are concerned with the causation relationship between these two series. Representative studies, such as those of Killeen et al. [3] and Payne [8], use the VAR structure and Johansen cointegration procedure to examine the long-run association involved. They demonstrate a long-run cointegration relationship between exchange rates and order flow, but a single direction of causality from order flow to the exchange rate return. According to the theoretical framework of Evans and Lyons [2], our empirical study examines the impact of order flow on the contemporaneous exchange rate return and the predictability of order flow on the future exchange rate return.

3. Data Description and Construction

Our empirical analysis uses the real transaction data for the exchange rate Deutsche mark/US dollar over October 6 to October 10, 1997. The data comes from one of the leading electronic FX transaction platforms, Reuters D2000-2, which is updated to D3000-2 now. The original dataset contains two data files. One dataset records the real-time quotes for the exchange rate Deutsche mark against US dollar, which includes the time stamp, the best bid price, and the best ask price at a particular time. The other dataset records the real-time trade, which includes the time stamp, the trade quantity, the trade direction, and the trade price. The vast majority of transactions on Deutsche mark/US dollar take place between 6 am and 6 pm, Monday to Friday although foreign exchange transaction takes place on the Reuters system D2000-2 24 hours a day and 7 days a week. The empirical analyses in

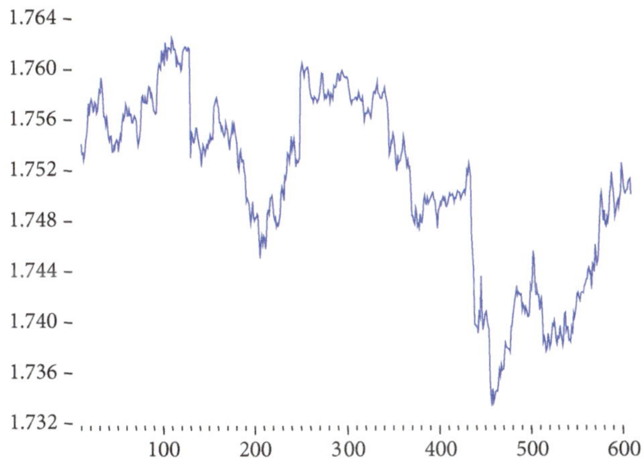

FIGURE 1: Exchange rate Deutsche mark/US dollar (5-minute frequency).

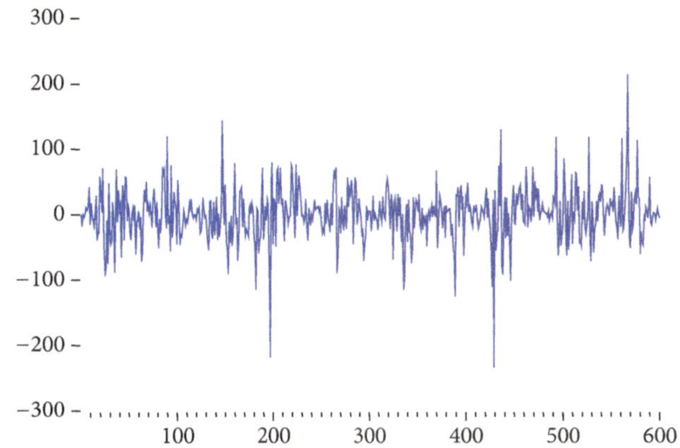

FIGURE 2: Order flow (5-minute frequency).

the following sections are based on the subsample, which includes a vast number of trades and provides us with a considerable power to test the impact of order flow on the exchange rate.

The dataset has distinguishing features which are worth mentioning. The first noticeable feature is that the dataset contains the real transaction prices instead of the indicative quotes which are often used in the relevant applied studies. The midquote is a typical proxy for the trade price. However, one fact is that the midquote may not represent a true state of the market especially when the market is thin or the market is one-sided (i.e., strong buying pressure or selling pressure). Thus, the midquote may not be representative. Although our sample span is relatively short, which is five days from October 6 to October 10, 1997, our attention is focused on the association between the exchange rate return and order flow at extra high frequency that makes the time span of the sample long enough to our analysis. Figure 1 shows the exchange rate dynamics at 5-minute frequency. Another feature of the dataset is that it contains the exact transaction values for each trade instead of the number of the transactions which is often adopted in the relevant literatures; see, for example, Evans and Lyons [9]. Finally, with the trade direction indicator (i.e., buying or selling) and the corresponding contemporaneous transaction value, we can calculate the total transaction value and order flow for each individual period.

In our empirical analysis, we adopt two versions of measurements for order flow. According to FX microstructure theories, when the trade direction is positive it indicates that the actual trade is initiated by buyer, the trade is termed as the buyer-initiated trade. On the contrary, when the trade direction is negative it indicates that the real trade is initiated by seller, the trade is termed as the seller-initiated trade. Order flow x_t at time t is defined as the net value between buyer-initiated trades B_t and the seller-initiated trades S_t, which is calculated by the following formula:

$$x_t = S_t - B_t. \tag{2}$$

We demonstrate order flow x_t in Figure 2, which graphically shows that order flow is a stationary I(0) process. Alternatively, we adopt another measurement for order flow, advocated by Ito and Hashimoto [6]. The measurement defines order flow as the ratio of the net trade pressure $(S_t - B_t)$ to the corresponding contemporaneous total trade quantity Q_t which is equal to the sum of the two-sided trades, $(S_t + B_t)$. We term this order flow as order flow ratio, $x\text{Ratio}_t$. $x\text{Ratio}_t$ is calculated by the following formula:

$$x\text{Ratio}_t = \frac{(S_t - B_t)}{(S_t + B_t)}. \tag{3}$$

Why we introduce this measurement for order flow? The intuition behind this measure is the fact that the whole market activities vary from time to time. The ratio $x\text{Ratio}_t$ can measure the degree of market activeness. We demonstrate the principle in the following typical artificial example (Ito and Hashimoto [6]): when the market is active during a particular time period, we can have a buyer-initiated trade $B_t = 1000$ and a seller-initiated trade $S_t = 990$. But we can only have a buyer-initiated trade $B_t = 100$ and a seller-initiated trade $S_t = 90$ when the market is calm. In the two scenarios, we have the same quantity of order flow x_t, which is 10. However, order flow ratio $x\text{Ratio}_t$ is, respectively, 0.001 and 0.01 in the two cases. This example indicates the different characteristics between these two different measurements. Figure 3 demonstrates order flow ratio $x\text{Ratio}_t$ at 5-minute frequency, which is apparently different from the plot in Figure 2.

To examine the association between exchange rates and order flow at high-frequency and check the persistence of the relationship, we use 5-minute frequency as the interval basis and aggregate order flow to order flow 10-minute, 15-minute, 20-minute, 25-minute, and 30-minute frequencies. We construct the change in the log of the spot exchange rate (DM/\$ times 100000) as the exchange rate return Δp_t. The interdealer order flow x_t is measured contemporaneously with the exchange rate return Δp_t. Tables 1 and 2 show, respectively, the descriptive statistics for the two measurements of order flow at various frequencies.

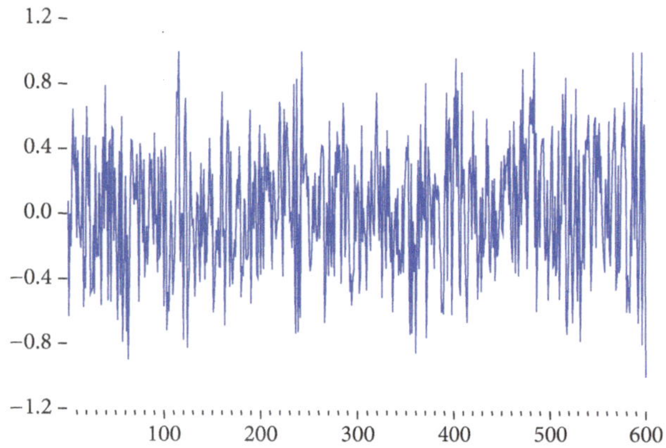

FIGURE 3: Order flow ratio (5-minute frequency).

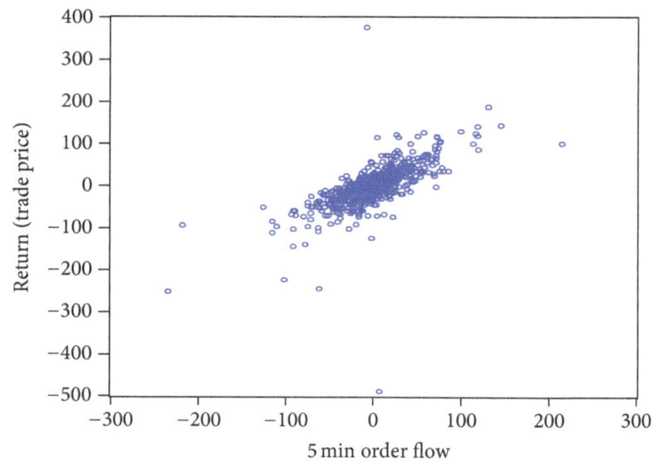

FIGURE 4: DM/USD exchange rate return and order flow (5-minute frequency).

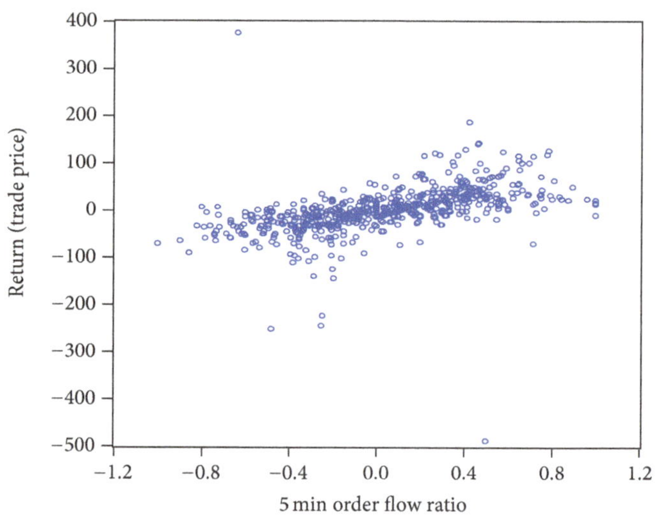

FIGURE 5: DM/USD exchange rate return and order flow ratio (5-minute frequency).

4. Analysis Concerns and Arrangements

Our primary goal is to examine the association between exchange rates and contemporaneous order flow and investigate the predictability of order flow on the future exchange rate. Before the formal implementation, we discuss several issues involved in the actual analysis. The first concern is the possible endogeneity of order flow in the actual association between exchange rates and order flow, which is usually due to the simultaneity between foreign exchange trading and quoting. Another concern is the possible nonlinearity involved in the association between exchange rates and order flow.

4.1. Endogeneity. Relevant studies demonstrate that order flow carries information and has permanent effect on exchange rates. Meanwhile, it is necessary to focus on the joint determination between exchange rates and order flow, which is mostly of concern in the feedback trading. Feedback trading means that the foreign exchange trading determines the movements of exchange rates meanwhile exchange rate levels impact the foreign exchange trading. Relevant empirical studies usually accept the assumption that trade (order flow) precedes the quotes (trading prices). Under this implication, the VAR structure of Hasbrouck [10] has been frequently used in exchange rate modelling, such as Payne [8] and Killeen et al. [3], to assess how informative order flow is. These studies include the contemporaneous order flow in the exchange rate return equation while they exclude the contemporaneous exchange rate return from the trade (order flow) equation. The nonstandard VAR approach logically removes the endogeneity issue from the simultaneity between the two series. However, there are arguments, such as Lyons [1] and Daníelsson and Love [11], that there is contemporaneous feedback trading between trades and quotes.

To check the simultaneity between the exchange rate and order flow, we adopt the 5-minute interval data as the analysis basis. The intuition behind this choice is that when the tick-by-tick data is aggregated into low-frequency data the feedback trade effect can be identified easily. Love and Payne [12] address that the notation of feedback trading which allows order flow to respond to price movements at frequency of less than one minute is somewhat dubious. Daníelsson and Love [11], using nonstandard VAR specification and instrumental variable (IV) method, find that if the data are sampled at anything other than at the highest frequency then any feedback trading may well appear contemporaneous and the trading in period t depends on the asset return in that interval.

Mapping the feedback trading to our single-direction equation estimation, we are concerned with the endogeneity of order flow in the single-direction association that we have to identify whether order flow is endogenous in our specification. On the presence of the endogeneity coming from the jointly simultaneous determination between the exchange rate and the contemporaneous order flow, we should use instrument techniques to handle the endogeneity issue in the regression. Compared with OLS estimation, instrument variable estimation (IV) and the generalized methods of moments (GMM) estimation are for the consistency at presence of endogeneity. However, results from IV and GMM hold cost of the loss of efficiency if there is no endogeneity involved in the specified equation. We firstly regress the exchange rate return on order flow at 5-minute and 30-minute frequencies and check the correlation between order flow and the regression residuals. The results reject the hypothesis that there is correlation between order flow and the residual term of the equation.

4.2. Nonlinearity. The majority of the empirical studies we discussed above confirm the positive association between exchange rates and order flow in a linear specification. Meanwhile, there is possible nonlinearity involved in the relationship, which matters significantly in our short-span sample. Payne [8] identifies nonlinearity in the association and then he creates a nonlinear VAR in his empirical analysis. Evans and Lyons [13] directly use nonparametric method in their empirical analysis, which avoids the drawbacks of the direct parametric linear specification. We demonstrate the scatter-plots between the exchange rate return and order flow at two frequencies (5-minute and 30-minute) in Figures 4, 5, 6, and 7. These figures indicate clearly a systematic, approximately linear positive relation between exchange rates and order flow at both 5-minute and 30-minute frequencies. We conclude that the relationship is clearly not the result of a small number of outliers and no nonlinearity is evident in the association.

Given that we have justified the linear association between exchange rates and order flow at both frequencies, we can proceed to estimate the specific association. In the following subsections, we introduce the arrangement for estimating the contemporaneous relationship between exchange rate return and the contemporaneous order flow and the arrangement for investigating the prediction ability of order flow on the future exchange rate return at high frequency.

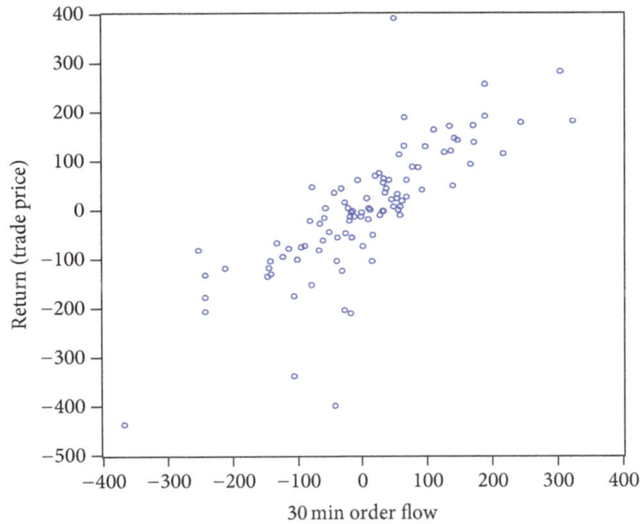

FIGURE 6: DM/USD exchange rate return and order flow (30-minute frequency).

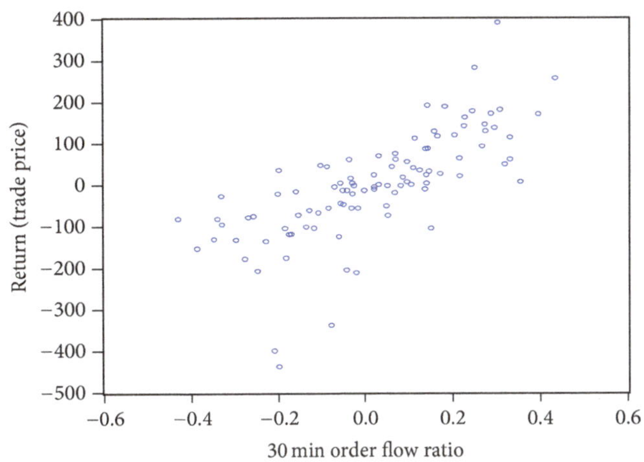

FIGURE 7: DM/USD exchange rate return and order flow ratio (30-minute frequency).

4.3. Contemporaneous Price Impact. The positive order flow represents net buying pressure and the negative order flow represents net selling pressure. Thus, we expect that buying pressure raises the transaction prices and selling pressure lowers the transaction prices. In the studies we discussed in previous sections the return equation includes both the contemporaneous and lagged order flows as the explanatory determinants, such as those of Evans and Lyons [2] and Payne [8]. Slightly different, at this stage we only include the contemporaneous order flow in the determination regression and examine the contemporaneous association between the exchange rate movement and order flow at various frequencies (5, 10, 15, 20, 25, and 30 minutes). According to the two different measurements of order flow we discussed in the data description section, our practical contemporaneous regression equations are specified as follows. For order flow, we have

$$\Delta p_{t,h} = c + \alpha x_{t,h} + \varepsilon_{t,h} \tag{4}$$

and for order flow ratio, we have

$$\Delta p_{t,h} = c + \alpha * x\text{Ratio}_{t,h} + \varepsilon_{t,h}, \tag{5}$$

where $\Delta p_{t,h}$ denotes the exchange rate return over a horizon h. $x_{t,h}$ and $x\text{Ratio}_{t,h}$ represent, respectively, the two different measurements of order flow over the same horizon. $\varepsilon_{t,h}$ is the error term. The horizon h is initially set up at 5-minute frequency to calculate order flow. We aggregate the 5-minute order flow to order flow at 10-minute, 15-minute, 20-minute, 25-minute, and 30-minute frequencies.

4.4. Future Price Prediction. To directly investigate the prediction power of order flow on the future exchange rate return, we only include the lagged exchange rate returns and lagged order flow in the return equation. Corresponding to

TABLE 1: Order flow descriptive statistics at different horizons.

	5 minutes	10 minutes	15 minutes	20 minutes	25 minutes	30 minutes
Mean	0.881667	1.763333	2.645000	3.526667	4.408333	5.290000
Median	1.500000	5.000000	8.000000	4.000000	1.000000	6.000000
Maximum	215.0000	269.0000	356.0000	410.0000	283.0000	324.0000
Minimum	−234.0000	−197.0000	−321.0000	−279.0000	−345.0000	−366.0000
Std. dev.	39.64055	58.94865	76.67211	90.37102	102.3269	115.9329

This table reports some summary statistics for order flow, measured in millions of dollars, at 5-minute frequency, and aggregated to 10-minute, 15-minute, 20-minute, 25-minute, and 30-minute frequencies.

TABLE 2: Order flow ratio descriptive statistics at different horizons.

	5 minutes	10 minutes	15 minutes	20 minutes	25 minutes	30 minutes
Mean	0.031845	0.027866	0.026526	0.029278	0.025767	0.020082
Median	0.032796	0.043438	0.043140	0.015080	0.001379	0.023331
Maximum	1.000000	0.736842	0.709924	0.684211	0.531429	0.435780
Minimum	−1.000000	−0.729167	−0.725191	−0.531469	−0.517647	−0.428571
Std. dev.	0.392208	0.304738	0.270706	0.236041	0.219407	0.195233

This table reports some summary statistics for order flow ratio measured at 5-minute frequency and aggregated to 10-minute, 15-minute, 20-minute, 25-minute, and 30-minute frequencies.

the two contemporaneous determination equations above, we specify the two prediction associations as follows:

$$\Delta p_t = \beta_0 + \sum_{i=1}^{m} \gamma_i \Delta p_{t-i} + \sum_{i}^{m} \delta_i x_{t-i} + \varepsilon_t, \quad (6)$$

$$\Delta p_t = \beta_0 + \sum_{i=1}^{m} \gamma_i \Delta p_{t-i} + \sum_{i}^{m} \delta_i x\text{Ratio}_{t-i} + \varepsilon_t, \quad (7)$$

where Δp_t denotes the exchange rate return from period $t-1$ to t. x_{t-i} is the lagged order flow. We regress the exchange rate return on the lagged order flow and lagged exchange rate return at 5 minutes and 10 minutes, respectively. We choose 5 as the maximum lag m for both the exchange rate return and order flow. With the maximum lag 5, we aim to test whether the predictability of order flow can be ahead of half-hour when the data is measured at 5-minute frequency and one-hour when the data is measured at 10-minute frequency. Considering the discontinuity of the data (we only focus on period from 06:00 am to 06:00 pm in our contemporaneous analysis), we separately examine the prediction power of order flow in the Granger-causality regressions, based on the data from the five different days.

5. Empirical Data Analysis

During the test whether order flow is endogenous in the contemporaneous regression, we fail to accept the hypothesis that the order flow is correlated with the regression residual term. Moreover, this conclusion is valid for the two measurements of order flow at all the chosen frequencies. Thus, we accept the validity of the assumption that trading precedes the quoting. For relevant studies, see those of Evans and Lyons [2], Berger et al. [5], and Ito and Hashimoto [6].

5.1. Contemporaneous Price Impact. Before the actual estimation, we firstly investigate whether the two measurements of order flow in our study, order flow and order flow ratio, are stationary processes. Killeen et al. [3] find a long-run cointegration relation between exchange rate levels and cumulated order flow. In our relative short sample, we expect that the two measures of order flow are stationary processes, which are shown in Figures 2 and 3. Table 3 reports the unit root test results for the two measurements of order flow at 5-minute and 30-minute frequencies. The tests confirm that order flow and order flow ratio are consistently I(0) series at 10-minute, 15-minute, 20-minute, and 25-minute frequencies.

According to (4) and (5), we use OLS to implement the estimation of the contemporaneous association. Tables 4 and 5 report the estimation results for the impact of order flow on the contemporaneous exchange rate return. For the two measurements of order flow, the results suggest that all the coefficient estimates are statistically significant and correctly signed at all frequencies. The magnitudes of the coefficients on order flow imply that the contemporaneous impact of order flow is significant. The determination coefficient R-squares ranges from 47 percent to 61 percent for the case of order flow and varies from 26 percent to 52 percent for the case of order flow ratio. These results are consistent with the study of Evans and Lyons [9]. We also separately regress the exchange rate return on order flow for the five days of our sample and the estimates are significantly close to those we report here.

Our coefficient estimates reported in Tables 4 and 5 are consistent with our theoretical hypothesis. Meanwhile, they are different in magnitude from the estimates of Evans and Lyons [9]. We think one possible reason could be because our estimate is concerned the association between the exchange rate return with order flow at a higher frequency, that is, 5-minute and 10-minute frequencies, and so forth. However,

TABLE 3: Tests for a unit root in the data (order flow and order flow ratio).

Horizon, h	Level τ_μ	1st difference τ_μ	Level τ_τ	1st difference τ_τ
5-minute				
x_t	−20.60183	−13.58463 (9)	−20.65302	−13.57312 (9)
$x\text{Ratio}_t$	−21.05210	−15.15247 (7)	−21.15086	−15.13972 (7)
30-minute				
x_t	−10.55059	−12.63489 (1)	−10.68869	−12.56727 (1)
$x\text{Ratio}_t$	−10.69478	−10.59656 (2)	−11.26808	−10.53929 (2)

The symbols x_t and $x\text{Ratio}_t$ denote, respectively, order flow and order flow ratio (see the text for data source and exact definitions). The reported numbers in the columns are the Dickey-Fuller statistics for the null hypothesis that the sum of the coefficients in the autoregressive representation of the variables sum to unity. τ_μ is the test statistic allowing for only constant in mean and τ_τ is the test statistic allowing for both constant and trend in mean. The numbers in parenthesis after these statistics indicate the lag length used in the autoregression, determined by the Schwarz information criterion. For the test statistics, the null hypothesis is that the series in question is I(1).

TABLE 4: Estimates of (4) at different horizons.

Horizon, h	Beta-hat (OF)	R-squared
5-minute	0.9083667 (0.0389624)	0.4757
10-minute	0.9149569 (0.0491146)	0.5388
15-minute	0.9182686 (0.0572092)	0.5667
20-minute	0.9525129 (0.0640856)	0.6004
25-minute	0.8624387 (0.0727042)	0.5421
30-minute	0.8703092 (0.0695521)	0.6135

The net order flow (OF) represents the net value of buyer-initiated trade minus the seller-initiated trade, measured in millions of dollars; numbers in the parenthesis are the standard errors for the corresponding coefficient estimates.

Evans and Lyons's analysis is based on the aggregated daily data. We can observe in Tables 4 and 5 that when the data frequency gets lower the impact of order flow gets larger. We also observe the sensitivities of the approaches to measure order flow. The exchange rate return is more sensitive to order flow ratio than order flow.

5.2. Prediction Analysis. To investigate the prediction of lagged order flow on future exchange rate return, we estimate (6) and (7) with OLS. Tables 6 and 7 separately report, for the five days, the estimation results for the regression of the exchange rate return on the lagged exchange rate return and lagged order flow. Table 6 is for the case that net order flow is taken as the explanatory variable and Table 7 is for the case that order flow ratio is taken as the explanatory variable. Generally, all the results indicate weak prediction power of order flow on the future exchange rate return. In the case of order flow at five-minute frequency, reported in Table 6, except in day 3 and day 5, the coefficients on the first lagged order flow are not significant and wrongly signed. Other coefficients on lagged order flow during the five days are also not statistically significant and wrongly signed. In the case of order flow ratio, reported in Table 7, the coefficients are not statistically significant even positively signed. Similarly, at 10-minute frequency, reported in Tables 8 and 9, only in day 3 the coefficients on the first lagged order flow and order flow ratio appear to be correctly sighed and significant. The F-statistics for the regressions show lagged order flow are not jointly different from zero though in some cases the adjusted R-squares are not essentially zero.

Overall, the estimation results reported in Tables 6, 7, 8, and 9 suggest that lagged order flow has weak predictability of the future exchange rate return. For the majority the impact is not beyond 10 minutes. This result is consistent with those of Berger et al. [5] and Ito and Hashimoto [6]. The results also appear to confirm the conventional wisdom in the academic literatures that the exchange rate follows a random walk process at frequency less than annual such as daily, weekly, or even monthly.

5.3. Market Efficiency. Due to the significant impact of order flow on the contemporaneous exchange rate return and weak prediction of lagged order flow on the future exchange rate return, we investigate the serial dependence involved in order flow. We investigate the autocorrelation of order flow at 5 minutes and 10 minutes, which are shown in Figures 8, 9, 10, and 11. The figures indicate that within 95 percent confidence intervals the autocorrelation is centered at zero, shown as shaded areas. Within the entire sample span, the highest level (positive) of autocorrelations is only found at lag 1 at 5-minute frequency. The weak autocorrelation is consistent with the prediction analysis results that order flow has weak prediction on exchange rates at 5-minute frequency.

For the data at 10-minute frequency, the autocorrelation of order flow is demonstrated in Figures 10 and 11. According to the figures, apparently, we cannot find strong autocorrelations involved, even at the first lag. Thus, there is no significant impact on the exchange rate return beyond 10 minutes.

The weak autocorrelation in order flow, demonstrated in Figures 8 to 11, indicates how poorly informative a dealer's

TABLE 5: Estimates of (5) at different horizons.

Horizon, h	Beta-hat (OFR)	R-squared
5-minute	0.6821226 (0.04672573)	0.2618
10-minute	1.363381(0.1159284)	0.3177
15-minute	2.049136 (0.1991693)	0.3495
20-minute	3.133242 (0.2923226)	0.4349
25-minute	3.403084 (0.3952186)	0.3827
30-minute	4.765898 (0.4607529)	0.5196

The net order flow ratio (OFR) represents the ratio of net order flow to the corresponding contemporaneous trade quantity over the same period, measured in millions of dollars; numbers in the parenthesis are the standard errors for the corresponding coefficient estimates.

TABLE 6: Granger's causality estimation of (6) (5-minute frequency).

	Day 1	Day 2	Day 3	Day 4	Day 5
Order flow					
L1	−0.118071 (0.19506)	−0.137330 (0.16762)	0.218996 (0.16716)	−0.220818 (0.23302)	0.293388 (0.20688)
L2	−0.120591 (0.19228)	−0.088450 (0.16622)	−0.060422 (0.16300)	−0.013327 (0.23357)	−0.299061 (0.20852)
L3	0.108081 (0.19130)	−0.172152 (0.16703)	0.268007 (0.15693)	−0.447154 (0.23714)	−0.410111 (0.20512)
L4	−0.190258 (0.18857)	−0.311102 (0.16644)	−0.051263 (0.15932)	−0.014220 (0.23410)	0.235299 (0.21190)
L5	−0.022752 (0.18485)	0.270998 (0.15131)	−0.096563 (0.15590)	0.167554 (0.23372)	−0.269974 (0.20186)
Exchange rate return					
L1	0.150455 (0.17953)	0.256772 (0.16881)	0.023109 (0.17056)	0.257228 (0.17044)	−0.135055 (0.17139)
L2	0.064654 (0.17867)	−0.043441 (0.16814)	−0.086769 (0.16403)	0.148246 (0.17029)	0.031216 (0.17199)
L3	−0.015274 (0.17925)	0.217579 (0.16979)	−0.239797 (0.16118)	0.330404 (0.17486)	0.255290 (0.16949)
L4	0.172611 (0.17717)	0.385293 (0.16870)	−0.093093 (0.16256)	0.106227 (0.17636)	−0.215438 (0.17468)
L5	−0.169169 (0.17404)	−0.245181 (0.15871)	−0.055984 (0.16353)	−0.232155 (0.17743)	0.121239 (0.17028)
Constant	2.816570 (4.10656)	−0.516888 (4.00396)	−5.881906 (3.26599)	−1.067474 (5.48496)	7.343517 (5.01448)
Adjusted R-sq	−0.013954	0.047594	0.020127	0.030615	0.038009
F-statistic	0.844486	1.564692	1.232112	1.356878	1.446467
P value	0.5872	0.1277	0.2796	0.2110	0.1707

This table reports the results of the regressions of the exchange rate return at 5-minute frequency on five lags of order flow and five lags of exchange rate returns over the five days in the sample. Standard errors are reported in the parentheses below the coefficient estimates. The F-statistics and P value are from the F-tests, which indicate lagged order flow coefficients are not jointly different from zero.

trading information is to other dealers in the FX market. Consistent with this fact, the portfolio-shift model of Evans and Lyons [2] truly indicates that the initial order flow in the first two-round trades does not suggest much actual market information to all the involved dealers who always attempt to avoid revealing their own inventory positions and trading motivations. Specifically, the price (exchange rate) in the portfolio-shift model is assumed purely to be determined by the market makers existing in the FX market. Meanwhile, in the interdealer market these market makers are various financial institutions that always attempt to protect themselves and make speculation with informed information. Thus, the information based on the posttrade order flow cannot reflect all information of the prices.

5.4. Daily Forecasting of Order Flow on Exchange Rates. Additionally, we examine the predictability of order flow on the future exchange return with the daily frequency data used by Evans and Lyons [2]. Table 10 reports the Granger-causality regression results of Deutsche mark/US dollar and Japanese yen/US dollar on the lagged exchange rate returns

TABLE 7: Granger's causality estimation of (7) (5-minute frequency).

	Day 1	Day 2	Day 3	Day 4	Day 5
Order flow ratio					
L1	0.0127747 (1.35864)	−0.1026879 (1.64811)	1.431332 (1.32566)	0.9731951 (1.74083)	1.370567 (1.59191)
L2	0.1546971 (1.35789)	−0.0067625 (1.64395)	1.739592 (1.28954)	−0.8501948 (1.76384)	0.2341238 (1.57967)
L3	1.132090 (1.36198)	−1.984280 (1.62947)	0.9612191 (1.26949)	−1.539022 (1.77396)	−1.961865 (1.60199)
L4	−1.763775 (1.35909)	−2.677360 (1.68247)	0.4618692 (1.26981)	0.8257213 (1.76976)	−0.2814629 (1.53728)
L5	−0.0692894 (1.35542)	3.401814 (1.69208)	−2.043698 (1.22580)	1.084196 (1.78272)	−1.630415 (1.56783)
Exchange rate return					
L1	0.066245 (0.13549)	0.151886 (0.13252)	0.058555 (0.14190)	0.088925 (0.11628)	−0.031734 (0.13489)
L2	−0.055129 (0.13503)	−0.133859 (0.13305)	−0.219643 (0.13753)	0.188863 (0.11694)	−0.157064 (0.13524)
L3	−0.023257 (0.13392)	0.182826 (0.13239)	−0.101251 (0.13789)	0.111203 (0.11765)	0.071740 (0.13608)
L4	0.144834 (0.13323)	0.243417 (0.13497)	−0.123974 (0.14026)	0.019763 (0.11721)	−0.066863 (0.13152)
L5	−0.190439 (0.13387)	−0.274561 (0.13508)	−0.006818 (0.13651)	−0.166060 (0.11667)	0.037412 (0.13267)
Constant	3.880461 (3.89964)	−0.495662 (4.02191)	−5.822364 (3.36141)	−2.927650 (6.20530)	6.910383 (5.13380)
Adjusted *R*-sq	−0.013033	0.045517	0.031465	−0.008714	−0.023858
F-statistic	0.854623	1.538870	1.367102	0.902379	0.736689
P value	0.5778	0.1362	0.2060	0.5339	0.6884

This table reports the results of the regressions of the exchange rate return at the 5-minute frequency on five lags of order flow and five lags of exchange rate returns over the five days in the sample. Standard errors are reported in the parentheses below the coefficient estimates. The *F*-statistics and *P* value are from the *F*-tests, which indicate lagged order flow coefficients are not jointly different from zero.

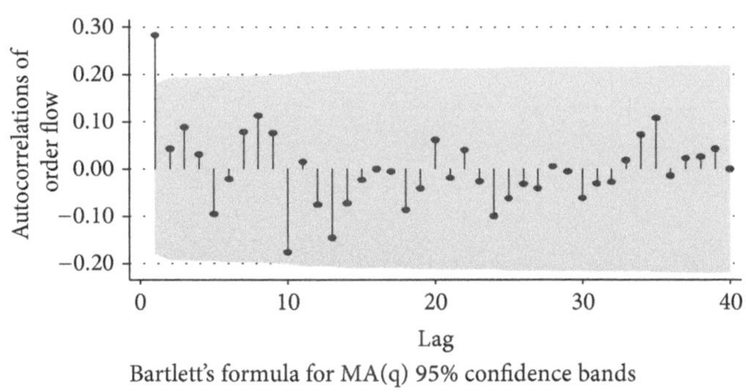

FIGURE 8: DM/USD order-flow autocorrelations (5-minute frequency). Shaded region denotes 95% confidence interval.

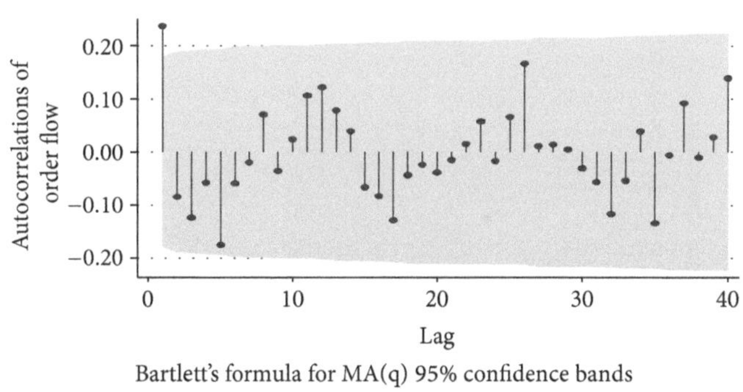

FIGURE 9: DM/USD order-flow-ratio autocorrelations (5-minute frequency). Shaded region denotes 95% confidence interval.

and lagged order flow at the daily frequency. The coefficients on the first lag of order flow are clearly positive but not statistically significant. The *F*-statistic and *P* values indicate that the lagged order flow have no any predictive power on the future exchange rate return.

6. Conclusions

The microstructure theories suggest that order flow carries information and has permanent effects on exchange rates. Using the transaction data on the exchange rate Deutsche mark/US dollar from one of the popular trading platforms, Reuters D2000-2, we examine the association between the exchange rate and order flow. Our analysis demonstrates that at intraday high-frequency order flow is a valuable determinant for the contemporaneous exchange rate returns. However, our experiments of the prediction of order flow on the future exchange rate indicate that the impact of order flow on the future exchange rate is quite vulnerable. Actually, the prediction on the future exchange rate return cannot go

TABLE 8: Granger's causality estimation of (6) (10-minute frequency).

	Day 1	Day 2	Day 3	Day 4	Day 5
Order flow					
L1	0.136435 (0.34967)	−0.089633 (0.26324)	0.526039 (0.30753)	−0.447771 (0.36917)	−0.446635 (0.30271)
L2	−0.308135 (0.35084)	−0.263654 (0.26533)	0.091605 (0.28730)	−0.401649 (0.37418)	−0.404804 (0.28665)
L3	0.688376 (0.33985)	0.209682 (0.26306)	−0.326159 (0.29723)	0.702109 (0.37023)	0.184541 (0.28903)
L4	−0.039688 (0.33378)	−0.481917 (0.26637)	0.235170 (0.29056)	0.272496 (0.37699)	−0.180359 (0.30057)
L5	0.035736 (0.32321)	0.214257 (0.25365)	−0.150053 (0.26986)	−0.086382 (0.37463)	0.153250 (0.28587)
Exchange rate return					
L1	−0.191310 (0.32897)	0.231504 (0.28081)	−0.429302 (0.30579)	0.570028 (0.26693)	0.223603 (0.29134)
L2	0.196840 (0.33985)	0.287834 (0.28982)	−0.283998 (0.30125)	0.312146 (0.27584)	0.268175 (0.26696)
L3	−0.642743 (0.32175)	−0.265260 (0.31380)	0.201120 (0.31266)	−0.582852 (0.26878)	−0.262002 (0.27343)
L4	−0.036487 (0.31441)	0.392224 (0.30960)	−0.266103 (0.29923)	0.047003 (0.27626)	0.169784 (0.28404)
L5	−0.132261 (0.30469)	−0.000436 (0.30732)	0.043512 (0.29192)	−0.256454 (0.27060)	−0.308772 (0.27394)
Constant	10.20020 (10.1838)	−0.338317 (8.30204)	−11.89428 (8.39075)	−6.790016 (11.6759)	16.56448 (11.4245)
Adjusted R-sq	−0.040912	−0.023319	−0.066581	0.157572	0.028411
F-statistic	0.791690	0.879226	0.669151	1.991340	1.154979
P value	0.6368	0.5592	0.7462	0.0583	0.3465

This table reports the results of the regressions of the exchange rate return at the 10-minute frequency on five lags of order flow and five lags of exchange rate returns over the five days in the sample. Standard errors are reported in the parentheses below the coefficient estimates. The F-statistics and P value are from the F-tests, which indicate lagged order flow coefficients are not jointly different from zero.

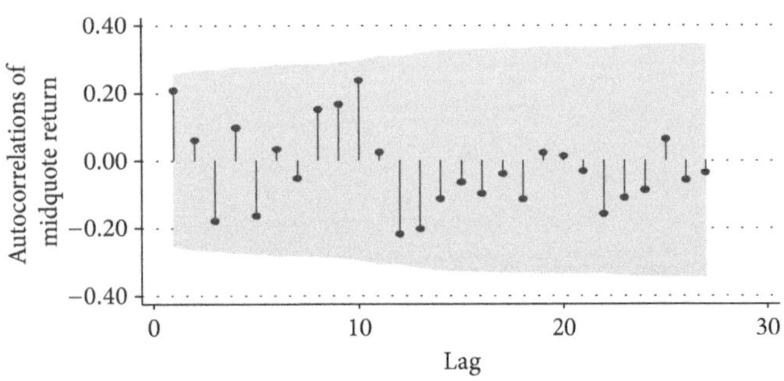

FIGURE 10: DM/USD order-flow autocorrelations (10-minute frequency). Shaded region denotes 95% confidence interval.

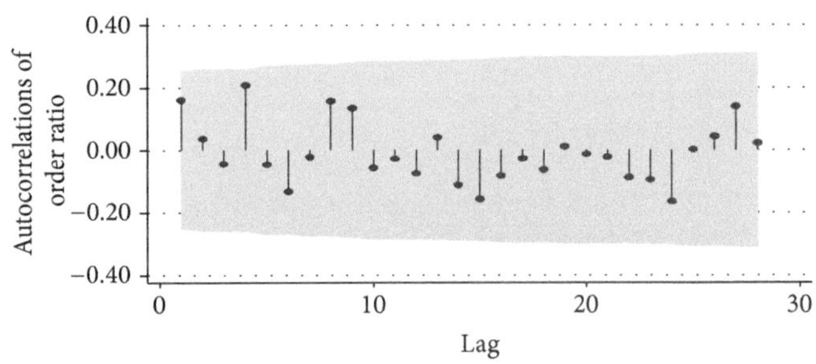

FIGURE 11: DM/USD order-flow-ratio autocorrelations (5-minute frequency). Shaded region denotes 95% confidence interval.

beyond ten minutes. In the single equation analysis, we also investigate the possible reverse causality from the exchange rate return to order flow, which is termed as the feedback trading. However, our empirical analysis shows that order flow cannot be an endogenous variable in the contemporaneous determination relationship. We also investigate the historical dependence between sequential order flows, but we find the weak link between two close foreign exchange trades.

Market participants in the interdealer FX market always attempt to make profits with informed information. This feature determines that these individual market participants always attempt to be invisible to others. Thus, in the sequential foreign exchange trades, these dealers' positions are not easy to be used by others as the basis to judge the future foreign exchange rate movement direction. It is difficult to use order flow to predict the future exchange rate return, which

Table 9: Granger's causality estimation of (7) (10-minute frequency).

	Day 1	Day 2	Day 3	Day 4	Day 5
Order flow ratio					
L1	1.452997 (4.18435)	−7.161375 (5.87120)	7.000977 (4.40539)	−5.381639 (5.81161)	−1.991782 (5.01936)
L2	−4.756718 (4.17151)	−1.148140 (5.90187)	1.539089 (4.53134)	0.8427163 (5.69368)	−7.019992 (4.94556)
L3	4.300887 (4.61385)	1.098973 (5.76261)	−5.782016 (4.45942)	3.622646 (5.65865)	4.424921 (5.41766)
L4	−4.682226 (4.72272)	−3.561131 (5.42382)	1.078133 (4.47422)	−3.700085 (5.70355)	−7.256623 (5.66760)
L5	−3.082177 (4.76887)	9.458012 (5.45826)	−3.866186 (4.19091)	0.0341534 (6.02435)	−2.922525 (5.54956)
Exchange rate return					
L1	−0.175783 (0.21753)	0.437584 (0.25799)	−0.291414 (0.24866)	0.439126 (0.19050)	−0.037015 (0.24979)
L2	0.150516 (0.21630)	0.443720 (0.24984)	−0.212081 (0.25728)	−0.032820 (0.19146)	0.095924 (0.23262)
L3	−0.267521 (0.22922)	−0.475691 (0.26724)	0.232605 (0.24993)	−0.299533 (0.18394)	−0.344220 (0.24029)
L4	0.153912 (0.23201)	0.019291 (0.24813)	−0.104209 (0.23884)	0.322982 (0.19069)	0.254912 (0.24888)
L5	0.096837 (0.23303)	−0.138886 (0.24878)	0.171748 (0.23178)	−0.248077 (0.19084)	−0.059125 (0.23752)
Constant	4.471015 (9.39785)	0.431035 (8.03827)	−8.303744 (8.55325)	−2.577605 (15.1951)	15.47169 (11.0835)
Adjusted R-sq	−0.099520	0.073591	−0.047717	0.0277	0.0123
F-statistic	0.520285	1.421015	0.758618	1.15	1.07
P value	0.8663	0.2038	0.6665	0.3491	0.4083

This table reports the results of the regressions of the exchange rate return at the 10-minute frequency on five lags of order flow and five lags of exchange rate returns over the five days in the sample. Standard errors are reported in the parentheses below the coefficient estimates. The F-statistics and P value are from the F-tests, which indicate lagged order flow coefficients are not jointly different from zero.

Table 10: Granger's causality estimation of return (Evans and Lyons [2] data).

Daily frequency	Deutsche mark/US dollar	Japanese yen/US dollar
Order flow		
L1	3.58 (5.8)	3.44 (7.3)
L2	9.72 (7.7)	−1.33 (9.9)
L3	−1.75 (7.7)	−5.29 (9.8)
L4	3.29 (8.1)	2.87 (9.7)
L5	1.40 (5.8)	−1.07 (7.1)
Exchange rate return		
L1	−0.074 (0.21)	−0.07 (0.16)
L2	−0.46 (0.21)	−0.04 (0.17)
L3	0.10 (0.21)	−0.15 (0.16)
L4	−0.06 (0.22)	0.003 (0.17)
L5	−0.10 (0.12)	0.014 (0.13)
Constant	−0.000515 (0.00057)	0.002442 (0.00131)
Adjusted R-sq	−0.012987	−0.059870
F-statistic	0.905130	0.581988
P value	0.5339	0.8227

This table reports the results of the regressions of the exchange rate returns on five lags of order flow and five lags of exchange rate returns. Standard errors are reported in the parentheses after the coefficients. The F-statistics and P value are from the F-tests, which indicate lagged order flow coefficients are not jointly different from zero.

indicates that private information, based on public macro fundamentals, might only temporarily impact on exchange rate variations.

References

[1] R. K. Lyons, "A simultaneous trade model of the foreign exchange hot potato," *Journal of International Economics*, vol. 42, no. 3-4, pp. 275–298, 1997.

[2] M. D. D. Evans and R. K. Lyons, "Order flow and exchange rate dynamics," *Journal of Political Economy*, vol. 110, no. 1, pp. 170–180, 2002.

[3] W. P. Killeen, R. K. Lyons, and M. J. Moore, "Fixed versus flexible: lessons from EMS order flow," NBER Working Papers 8491, 2001.

[4] H. Hau, W. Killeen, and M. Moore, "How has the euro changed the foreign exchange market?" DNB Staff Reports 79, 2003.

[5] D. W. Berger, A. P. Chaboud, S. V. Chernenko, E. Howorka, and J. H. Wright, "Order flow and exchange rate dynamics in electronic brokerage system data," International Finance Discussion Papers 830, 2006.

[6] T. Ito and Y. Hashimoto, "Price impacts of deals and predictability of the exchange rate movements," NBER Working Paper 12682, 2006.

[7] D. Rime, *U.S. Exchange Rates and Currency Flows*, SIFR Research Report Series no. 4, Stockholm Institute for Financial Research, Stockholm, Sweden, 2001.

[8] R. Payne, "Informed trade in spot foreign exchange markets: an empirical investigation," *Journal of International Economics*, vol. 61, no. 2, pp. 307–329, 2003.

[9] M. Evans and R. Lyons, "Order flow and exchange rate dynamics," BIS Paper 2, 1999.

[10] J. Hasbrouck, "Measuring the information content of stock trades," *The Journal of Finance*, vol. 46, no. 1, pp. 179–207, 1991.

[11] J. Daníelsson and R. Love, "Feedback trading," *International Journal of Finance and Economics*, vol. 11, no. 1, pp. 35–53, 2006.

[12] R. Love and R. Payne, "Macroeconomic news, order flows and exchange rates," FMG Discussion Papers dp475, 2003.

[13] M. Evans and R. Lyons, "Understanding order flow," NBER Working Paper 11748, National Bureau of Economic Research, Inc., Cambridge, Mass, USA, 2005.

18

The Respective Effects of Being Observed and Sanctioned in Modified Dictator and Ultimatum Games

Agnès Festré[1] and Pierre Garrouste[2]

[1] *University of Picardie (France) and GREDEG, University of Nice-Sophia Antipolis, UMR n° 6227, 250 rue Albert Einstein, 06560 Valbonne Cedex, France*
[2] *University of Nice-Sophia Antipolis and GREDEG, UMR n° 6227, 250 rue Albert Einstein, 06560 Valbonne Cedex, France*

Correspondence should be addressed to Agnès Festré; festre@gredeg.cnrs.fr

Academic Editors: I. Shoji and E. Silva

We experiment within a laboratory the respective effects of being observed and sanctioned in both a dictator and an ultimatum game. We obtain the classical results that individuals do not play the subgame perfect equilibria. We also show that being observed increases the offers made by the proposer in the dictator game but this effect is difficult to identify in the ultimatum game. We also find that in the dictator game, the more the individuals are sensitive to observation the less they are to sanction.

1. Introduction

A common result from the recent literature showing that individuals do follow social norms is that sanctions are effective tools to help enforce social norms (This is the case in dictator games [1], ultimatum games [2, 3], prisoner dilemma games [1], or public goods games [4, 5]. Similar results are found in third-party sanction experiments ([6–8] for an evolutionary game theoretical interpretation.) Some experiments show however that such an assumption can be falsified. According to Fehr and Schmidt [9], agents' efforts are lower when principals condition a fine on the deviation from a desired effort level. Fehr and Gächter [10] or Fehr and List [11] not only show that positive incentives can crowd out motivations but also that sanctions may undermine agents' motivations.) What is however less appreciated in the economic literature is that individuals not only anticipate the sanction and its level, but also modify their behavior when others are watching them. Lewitt and Levin [12] show for instance that depending on the level of scrutiny that results from the fact that "people are aware that their behavior is being monitored, recorded, and subsequently scrutinized" [12, page 59]), individuals may behave differently in laboratory and field experiments. They suggest that scrutiny in lab experiment leads to overestimate the importance of prosocial behaviors relative to environments without such scrutiny due to an "artificially" induced moral/social cost in labs. However, they mainly refer to scrutiny as emanating from the experimenter. By contrast, we test whether being observed by a third party affects individuals' decisions and compare this effect with the sanction effect. This attempt is of both theoretical and empirical interest. From the theoretical viewpoint, it permits to disentangle the sanction effect from the scrutiny effect, in contrast to experiments such as public good games with sanctions in which the two effects are usually blended. Moreover, it addresses the controversial issue of whether fairness is inspired by *regard for others* (fairness is an intrinsic feature of human beings) or whether it results from external forces, for example, *regard by others*. A growing literature is now investigating this question in dictator game settings (see for a survey [13]).

From the empirical viewpoint, our attempt suggests that a comparative cost-benefit analysis of the scrutiny versus sanction effect could provide useful information for deciding whether it is more efficient to rely on both rather than on the more important of the two effects only.

In order to test this intuition, we provide experiments that not only show, as in Fehr and Fischbacher [1], that

(1) a third party (the observer of the game) or a second party (the recipient or the responder) does sanction a first party (the proposer) when his/her offer is deemed to be unfair, but also that (2) the proposer is likely to modify his/her offer when a third party is simply informed about the amount of the offer. We use a within design (and a control experiment), that is, a sequence of dictator (DG) and ultimatum (UG) games between randomly selected pairs of proposer/recipient and introduce at a certain step the fact that a third party is first informed about the transfer from the proposer to the recipient of the pair he is assigned to, and thereafter has the option to sanction (at no cost but under some restricted conditions, see below) unfair offers by deducting a certain amount from the proposer's remaining share. We also ran a control treatment in order to control for learning effects (see below).

Our results show that the relative effects of observation and sanction strongly depend on the institutional setting. In the DG, regard by others has a dramatic effect on the level of the offers, whereas in the UG this effect is difficult to corroborate. In the DG, we observe a negative relationship between the observation effect and the sanction effect. In the UG, the relative effect of observation versus sanction is more ambiguous, since it is hard to disentangle the effects of observation and sanction from competing effects derived from risk aversion attributes of proposers and receivers on one hand, and from expectations by proposers of the level of acceptation (or refusal) of receivers on the other hand. In a nutshell, the fact that the proposer can be sanctioned by both the receiver and the observer makes it difficult to discriminate between the relative effects of those two types of sanction. Consequently, more specific research needs to be done in order to disentangle the observation/sanction effect from the risk aversion/expectation effect.

Related literature concerns the effect of observation by the experimenter or the recipient in dictator and ultimatum games and its various interpretations following the seminal paper by Hoffman et al. [14]. In this paper, Hoffman et al. provide a DG experiment that ensures experimenter-subject anonymity (double-blind treatment) and shows that dictators tend to give more when observed by the experimenter, hence suggesting that "fairness" might not be "'own' preference, but a derivative of judgment by others." [14, page 349].

Dana et al. [15] confirm this intuition by introducing a costly exit option to a DG. They show that one-third of participants are willing to exit in a public game but not in another study where the game is private, concluding that giving often reflects a desire not to violate other's expectations rather than a concern for others' welfare per se. Similarly, Andreoni and Bernheim [16] develop a theory that accounts for dictator giving on the basis of the assumption that "people like to be perceived as fair" [16, page 1608].

At the opposite, Bolton and Zwick [17] and Bolton et al. [18] find no significant experimenter anonymity effect. Bolton and Zwick [17] run experiments where they compare three games: a UG, an "impunity game" with full observation by the experimenter for both and a "zero knowledge game" (UG without experimenter observation). They find that although the "impunity game" and DGs are very similar in their design, dictators in the "impunity game" demonstrate an unwillingness to leave anymore than the minimum, regardless of the minimum which is 5% or 45% of the pie. They conclude that the anonymity hypothesis cannot explain the difference between their results and the findings of Forsyth et al. (1994) in DGs with full experimenter observation. Rather they suggest that the difference could be explained by apparently minor differences in respective designs regarding the possible choices available for subjects; in the "impunity game," there are a limited number of division choices; in the DG of Forsyth et al. (1994), the division is unrestricted. Bolton et al. [18] further explore this intuition by designing experiments that vary in the number of repetitions and the cardinal number of possible splitting. They conclude that dictators determine how much money they should keep, and consequently how much they should give in gifts, on the basis of the total amount available for the entire experimental session, and not on the basis of what is available per game. In other terms, dictators in the "impunity game" appear to be less generous than those in DG studies when considered on a per game basis. But when viewed on the basis of the entire experiment they appear equally, and therefore consistently, generous.

Other contributions by Bohnet and Frey [19, 20], Frohlich et al. [21], Burnham [22], and Haley and Fessler [23] test the recipient anonymity hypothesis in prisoner's dilemma, DGs, or UGs and show, again, that results are very sensible to experimental design. Although Frohlich et al. [21] support Hoffman et al. [14] findings that increasing anonymity across recipients reduces dictator's offers, they point out that DG experiments designed to create conditions of privacy and anonymity have a flaw, since they may engender doubts on subjects regarding the existence of pairings (such statements in the instructions as "you will not be paired with any of these people," meaning that subjects will be paired exclusively with people sitting in a different room may raise doubts about the very pairing. Note that this suggests that double-blind DG experiments lead to overestimating systematically the role of self-interest in individual's motivations, a claim which stands in complete contradiction with Lewitt and Levin [12]) and the disposition of any money they share. Bohnet and Frey [20] explore further the intuition of Hoffman et al. [24] that the language used to explain the experimental task affects "subjects" degree of social distance from the experimenter and expectations of reciprocity" [24, page 653]. They show that silent one-way identification suffices to raise solidarity in prisoner's dilemma and dictator games, suggesting that social distance (and not only expectations of reciprocity) matters. By contrast, Burnham [22] shows that reducing recipient anonymity may increase offers. Photographs, conceived as a "precise step from total anonymity towards the rich and uncontrolled communication of nonlaboratory experiments" [22, page 134], are introduced in a UG and induce results consistent with Schelling's "identifiable victim" that when people know more about the recipient, they give more. Moreover, they suggest that perceived privacy may be more important than the actual level of privacy (note that this is in line with recent findings in neurobiology [25] showing that behavior influenced by peers indicates a true change in attitude such that social influence induces a true change in perception and

TABLE 1: Payoffs of the sequence of DGs in *Treatment 1*.

Players	Payoffs		
	Step 1	Step 2	Step 3
A	A $\rightarrow 10 - p_1$	A $\rightarrow 10 - p_2$	A $\rightarrow 10 - p_3 - S$
B	B $\rightarrow p_1$	B $\rightarrow p_2$	B $\rightarrow p_3$
C	C $\rightarrow 0$	C $\rightarrow E[G_2]$ with $1 < G_2 < 5$	C $\rightarrow S$, if $S \leq \sum_{i=1}^{6} (10 - p_3^i)/6$ Or C $\rightarrow E[G_3]$ with, $1 < G_3 < 5$ $S > \sum_{i=1}^{6} (10 - p_3^i)/6$

not merely a desire of conformity (see [26]). Haley and Fessler [23] introduce tacit visual cues in the form of stylized eyes or auditing cues (via the use of sound-deadening earmuffs) suggesting subjects that are being observed by others. They show that when using a computer displaying eyespots almost twice as many participants gave money to their partners in a DG as compared with the control treatment.

Other related papers explore the effect of different modes of communication between subjects. Ellingsen and Johannesson [27], Xiao and Houser [28, 29], Mohlin and Johannesson [30], and Andreoni and Rao [31] introduce the possibility of feedback (verbal written communication) from recipient to dictators. Results suggest that anticipated verbal feedback is equivalent to the effect of the recipient punishment power in UGs [27] or is an expression of disapproval that plays as a substitute for monetary punishments [28], but unfortunately does not permit to discriminate between interpretations of fairness in terms of social norms and "relationship" interpretations, which claim that communication increases empathy or decreases the social distance [30].

The remainder of the paper is organized as follows. In Section 2, we describe the two treatments that we ran. In Section 3, we compare the effects of the existence of a third party on the level of the propositions in the modified DGs and UGs. In Section 4, we focus on the level of sanctions as well as their effects on the propositions. In Section 5, we look at the receiver's behavior in the UG, and finally we discuss our results in Section 6.

2. Description of the Two Treatments (*Treatment 1* and *Control Treatment*)

The two treatments that we ran are designed as follows.

The within design of *Treatment 1* is made of two periods of three steps.

(i) The first period is a sequence of three DGs and consists of a first step where a proposer and a responder are alone, a second step where a proposer and a responder who both know that a third party (the observer) is informed about the sharing of the pie, and a third step identical to the second except that the observer is now allowed to sanction (at no cost) the proposer.

(ii) The second period is a sequence of three UGs with the same three steps as described for DGs.

In order to prevent responders from retaliating against proposers, we randomly matched responders at the beginning of the second period with one of the existing pair of proposer/observer. Although retaliation behavior is interesting in itself (in particular, it occurred during the pilot), we prefer to neutralize it in order to avoid pollution of the results.

Moreover, in order to avoid the reluctance to punish associated with costly sanctions, we assume that sanction is costless for the punisher. We are also justified in holding that social disapproval is not necessarily costly for those who sanction a given behavior. For instance, answering an opinion poll that asks a given question such as "would you say that the President's decision is: excellent, good, bad, very bad, no opinion" is not costly (if we except an opportunity cost that we may approximate to the show-up fee) and can be assimilated to a sort of sanction. Furthermore, the fact that citizens in democratic societies can sanction a politician by voting against him can be considered as costless for them. When a teacher gives low grades to bad pupils, it is not costly for him. *Deciding* to put a fine is not costly for the policeman even if it is so for the society (Bruno Frey suggests another experiment with both a constant cost of the sanctions and positive as well as negative sanctions. We also work on a between design as kindly suggested by Werner Güth and Jean-Louis Rullière.) We can give many examples that are in line with this idea of costless social sanctions.

Accordingly, the design of the *Treatment 1* may be summarized as follows.

Each participant played the whole sequence of three DGs and three UGs five times one after the other.

All subjects were informed about the extensive form of the game and the exchange rate between Euros and ECU (experimental currency unit). The exchange rate was 1 ECU = 0.1 euro. Thus, Player A knew, for instance, that C will be informed about the sharing of the pie at the second step and that he could punish him at the third step of both the DG and UG. The experimental instructions can be found in Appendix A.1, and the payoffs are summarized in Table 1 (for the sequence of DGs) and Table 2 (for the sequence of UGs) below, where p_1 defines the offer of proposer (A) at the first step, p_2 at the second step, and p_3 at the third step of the DG. p_4 defines the offer of proposer (A) at the first step, p_5 at the second step, and p_6 at the third step of the UG. Finally, S defines the sanction (the amount C deducts from A's remaining share).

TABLE 2: Payoffs of the sequence of UGs in *Treatment 1*.

Players	Payoffs		
	Step 1	Step 2	Step 3
A	$A \rightarrow 10 - p_4$ or $A \rightarrow 0$	$A \rightarrow 10 - p_5$ or $A \rightarrow 0$	$A \rightarrow 10 - p_6 - S$ or $A \rightarrow 0$ or $A \rightarrow -S$
B	$B \rightarrow p_4$ or $B \rightarrow 0$	$B \rightarrow p_5$ or $B \rightarrow 0$	$B \rightarrow p_6$ or $B \rightarrow 0$
C	$C \rightarrow 0$	$C \rightarrow E[G_5]$ with $1 < G_5 < 5$	$C \rightarrow S$, If $S \leq \max(10 - p_6^1)$ and $p_6 = 0$ or $C \rightarrow E[G_6]$ with $1 < G_6 < 5$ if $S > \max(10 - p_6^1)$

Subjects received a show-up fee of 5 euro in all experiments; as it is the practice, this show-up fee is not considered part of type A players' endowment, but is included when we report subjects' average earnings in some of the results below. Moreover, in the second step of both the DG and the UG, the third party gets a random amount G_2 with $1 < G_2 < 5$.

In order to avoid too obvious strategic behaviors, we implemented sanctioning rules. Because the sanctions are costless for the punishers, they have indeed the possibility to take all what the proposers keep. In the DG, the sanction cannot be greater than the mean of the remaining shares of all proposers, otherwise it is a random amount G_3 with $1 < G_3 < 5$. In the UG, the sanction cannot be greater than the maximum of the remaining shares of proposers but can be equal to zero, otherwise it is a random amount G_6 with $1 < G_6 < 5$ (see Figure 1(a)).

Subjects interacted anonymously and were never informed of other players' identities. The subjects were students or people who have voluntarily registered to the LEEP (Laboratoire d'Economie Expérimentale de Paris) platform dedicated to experimental economics at the University of Paris. Each subject participated in only one treatment.

The experiments were computerized using the REGATE software designed by Ferriol [32], and the program was set up by Maxim Frolov from the Centre d'Economie de la Sorbonne of the University of Paris 1.

The instructions (see Appendix A) were distributed and read aloud. The subjects then filled out a questionnaire that allowed their understanding of the rules of the game. They answered privately the questions. The answers were mainly correct and we read the right answers aloud.

The specific roles of proposer (A), recipient (B), and observer (C) were randomly assigned to the subjects inside 6 distinct groups drawn at random at the beginning of the experiment. Moreover, as already mentioned, subjects of type B were randomly reallocated in one of the existing group at the end of the first period.

Each session lasted roughly 1:30 h and subjects earned on average 95.71 ECU. We ran 6 sessions of *Treatment 1* during the period December 2008 through January 2009 (the data of the experiments are available on the following site: http://hp.gredeg.cnrs.fr/Pierre_Garrouste/donneesCumulees Au23022009.xls. We have decided to eliminate seven (out of a total of 180) observations considered as too irrational. More precisely, they were corresponding to offers of 9 and 10 in the two first steps of the two games).

We also ran a *Control Treatment* (*Treatment 2*) that permits us to control for learning and partly for order effects. The design of this treatment is the following:

(i) a first step with three standard dictator games played successively followed by

(ii) a second step with three standard ultimatum games played successively.

Those two steps were run for five times, and 3 sessions were played on May 2010 (see Tables 3 and 4 and Appendix A.2).

3. The Effects of the Existence of a Third Party on Offers in the Modified DGs and UGs

Theoretically (see Tables 5 and 6 for the theoretical equilibrium payoffs), introducing a third party who is only informed about the sharing of the pie should have no effect on the proposer's offer in the DG as well as in the UG. The theoretical solution of the DG corresponds to a proposal of zero, that is,

$$p_j^i = 0, \quad \text{for } i = 1, \ldots, 6, \ j = 1, 2 \tag{1}$$

(where i defines the six As and j the steps), while in the UG it corresponds to the minimum possible proposition (in our experiments, one ECU), that is.

$$p_j^i = 1, \quad \text{for } i = 1, \ldots, 6, \ j = 4, 5, 6. \tag{2}$$

The empirical results give a completely different picture; the existence of the third party increases the level of the propositions in the two games (see Appendices B, C, and D for the statistics of the results). In the DG, the mean of the differences in terms of offers by the proposers between the case where the third party is not informed (the opaque

TABLE 3: Payoffs of the sequence of DGs in *Control Treatment*.

Players	Payoffs Step 1	 Step 2	 Step 3
A	A → $10 - p_1$	A → $10 - p_2$	A → $10 - p_3$
B	B → p_1	B → p_2	B → p_3

TABLE 4: Payoffs of the sequence of UGs in *Control Treatment*.

Players	Payoffs Step 1	 Step 2	 Step 3
A	A → $10 - p_4$ or A → 0	A → $10 - p_5$ or A → 0	A → $10 - p_6$ or A → 0
B	B → p_4 or B → 0	B → p_5 or B → 0	B → p_6 or B → 0

TABLE 5: Theoretical payoffs in each step (1, 2, 3) of the sequence of DGs for players A, B, and C.

	A	B	C
1	10	0	0
2	10	0	G_2
3	0	0	10

TABLE 6: Theoretical payoffs in each step (1, 2, 3) of the sequence of UGs for players A, B, and C.

	A	B	C
1	9	1	0
2	9	1	G_5
3	9	1	G_6

case) and the case where he is only informed (the open case) noted that $p_2 p_1$ reaches 0.32 and is significantly different from zero ($\Pr(|T| > |t|) = 0.03$), and in the UG (noted $p_5 p_4$), this mean is equal to 0.28 and is significantly different from zero ($\Pr(|T| > |t| = 0.02$) (see Appendix E). The mean of the differences between the case with sanctions and the open case is, respectively, 1.12 (with $\Pr(|T| > |t|) = 0.00$) for the DG ($p_3 p_1$) and 0.34 for the UG ($p_6 p_4$) (with $\Pr(|T| > |t|) = 0.02$) (see Appendix E).

In the *Control Treatment* (where the theoretical equilibria are, respectively, a nil offer in the DG and an offer of 1 ECU in the UG), the respective values are the following: for the standard DG the mean of the differences between the second and the first steps is −0.20 but is not significant ($\Pr(|T| > |t|) = 0.16$), and the mean of the differences between the third and the second steps is 0.01 and is also not significant ($\Pr(|T| > |t|) = 0.91$) (see Appendix E). This is very different from the results obtained in *Treatment 1*, and this suggests that the presence of an observer impacts on the proposer's behavior. For the standard UG the means are significant (resp. 0.28 ($\Pr(|T| > |t|) = 0.02$) and 0.23 ($\Pr(|T| > |t|) = 0.01$), but when the propositions are accepted this mean becomes −0.04 and is not significant ($\Pr(|T| > |t|) = 0.46$). When a proposition is refused, the next proposition is higher and the mean of the differences between the two propositions (the next proposition minus the refused one) is 1.04 and is highly significant ($\Pr(|T| > |t|) = 0.00$). This is in line with the standard results. We will discuss the results below.

What we also found interesting is that for *Treatment 1*, the regressions of the differences between offers in the case of sanctions and the open case on the differences between the proposals in the open case and the opaque case suggest that the existence of a third party increases (at the margin) offers by proposers more than the sanction does. When we regress the differences (in both the DG and the UG) between the sanction case and the open one on the opaque case and the open one, we obtain a coefficient of −0.41 in the DG and of −0.37 in the UG (see Appendix G). This means that the marginal effect of the presence of a third party being informed about the sharing of the pie is higher than the marginal effect of being sanctioned by the same third party. In other words, as far as the level of offers is concerned, the higher is the marginal effect of being observed by someone, the lower is the marginal effect of the sanction. This result suggests the existence of self-reputational motives guiding individual behavior (see, e.g., [33]).

4. Third Party's Sanctions in Modified DGs and UGs

As we already discussed, there is only one possible equilibrium resulting from the sequence of DGs played in *Treatment 1* (see Table 5). It corresponds to the situation where the proposer keeps the whole pie. In this case, the sanction S is equal to the size of the pie and the proposer gets nothing. This equilibrium corresponds to a gain of 0 for every proposer and the responder and 10 for the third party. The reasoning is as follows. if one of the proposers keeps less than 10, say 9, the mean of the amounts the proposers want to keep is 9.83. In this case, the proposer who keeps 9 may encounter a loss of −.83 (because the third party can take up to 9.83) while the others can win (10–9.83). Therefore, he had better not to deviate from keeping the whole pie. The other solution could be when the proposers keep a value less or equal to $E[G_3]$ (G_3 is what the third party obtains when his sanction is strictly higher than the average value which the six proposers want to keep in the DG. In the UG, G_3 is what the third party obtains when the responder accepts the offer or when his sanction is strictly higher than the highest value of what the proposers want to keep if the responder refuses the proposer's offer. In the two games, it is defined as a random value drawn between 1 and 5). In this case, the third party has no interest to punish the proposer, since he obtains less (the sanction) than what the random draw gives him. This solution is however unstable because the proposers are better off if they keep a higher amount. Just because the sanction needs to be less than the mean of the amount kept by all proposers, if five proposers decide to keep, say 3, the sixth proposer has interest to keep 4 since the mean is 3.16 and since, according to the rules of the game, the third party cannot take him higher than 3.16. But the other proposers have also interest to keep 4. This reasoning can be reproduced until 10 is reached.

Two-sample Wilcoxon rank-sum (Mann-Whitney) test

var2	Obs	Rank sum	Expected
1	124	16524	15438
2	124	14352	15438
Combined	248	30876	30876

Unadjusted variance	319052.00
Adjustment for ties	−21031.43
Adjusted variance	298020.57

Ho: prop1 (var2 == 1) = prop1 (var2 == 2)

z = 1.989

Prob > $|z|$ = 0.0467

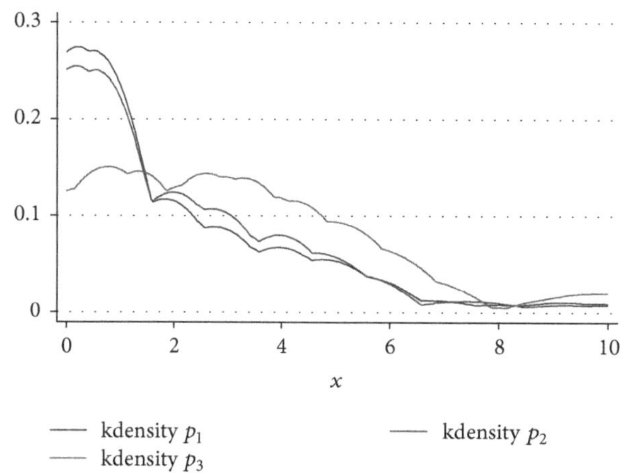

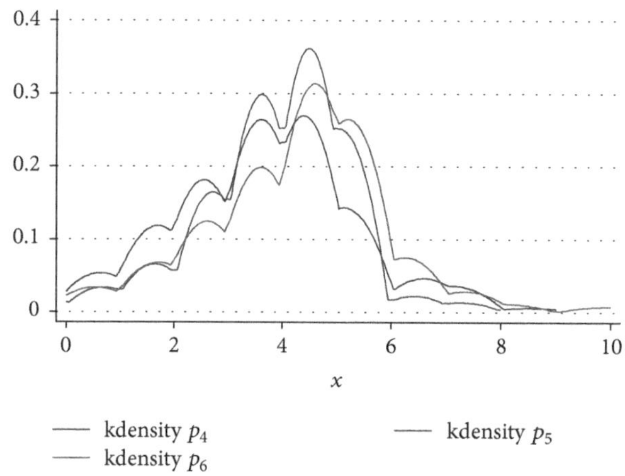

FIGURE 1

More generally a proposer i if rational has to keep

$$10 - p_3^i < \frac{\sum_{i=1}^{6}\left(10 - p_3^i\right)}{6}. \tag{3}$$

That is

$$\frac{\sum_{i=1}^{6} p_3^i}{6} > p_3^i. \tag{4}$$

This condition holds, and we obtain a unique equilibrium if and only if

$$p_3^i = 0 \quad \forall i = 1, \ldots, 6. \tag{5}$$

The unique equilibrium has the following characteristics. the proposers keep 10 and the third parties' sanctions (SDG, for sanction in the DG) are 10. For the UG, the result is slightly different. The proposer offers 9, which the responder accepts (the perfect subgame equilibrium), and the third party cannot sanction (SUG, for sanction in the UG) the proposer just because the recipient accepts the offer.

Table 7

	Step 1	Step 2	Step 3	Total for period 1
A	$10 - p_1$	$10 - p_2$	$10 - p_3 - S$	$30 - p_1 - p_2 - p_3 - S$
B	p_1	p_2	p_3	$p_1 + p_2 + p_3$
C	0	G_2	S if $S \leq \text{avg}(10 - p_3)$ otherwise G_3	$G_2 + S$ or $G_2 + G_3$

Table 8

	Step 1	Step 2	Step 3	Total for the period 2
A	$10 - p_1$ or 0	$10 - p_1$ or 0	$10 - p_3 - S$ or 0	$30 - p_1 - p_2 - p_3 - S$ or 0 or $20 - p_1 - p_2$ or $20 - p_2 - p_3$ or $20 - p_1 - p_3$ or $20 - p_1 - p_2 - S$ or $20 - p_2 - p_3 - S$ or $10 - p_1 - S$ or $10 - p_2 - S$ or $10 - p_3 - S$ or $0 - S$
B	p_1 or 0	p_2 or 0	p_3 or 0	$p_1 + p_2 + p_3$ or 0 or p_1 or p_2 or p_3 or $p_1 + p_2$ or $p_2 + p_3$ or $p_1 + p_3$
C	0	G_5	S if $p_3 = 0$ and $S \leq \max(10 - p_3)$ otherwise G_6	$G_5 + G_6$ or $G_5 + S$

The empirical results tell a different story. If the mean of the sanctions (S) is 4.37 for the DG and 4.78 for the UG (the difference between the two equals 0.41 and is significant ($\Pr(|T| > |t|) = 0.094$), the mean of the corresponding offers are, respectively, 2.49 and 4.25 for the DG and the UG. The first result (the means of the sanctions) is due to the difference between the rules governing sanctions in the two games, respectively. In the DG, the sanction needs not to be higher than the mean of the amounts kept by the proposers, whereas in the UG it needs not to be higher than the highest amount kept by the proposers. It seems rational for the third parties to punish more in the modified UG than in the modified DG. What is however interesting is that whereas sanctions rules are different, the effect of the existence of a third party is not affected by this difference. The difference between the offers in the two games is due to the fact that in the UG, responders are allowed to refuse offers from proposers even in the two first steps of the game when no sanction is allowed. The differences between offers made at the same steps in the two games give a strange result. If the differences are the same in the two first steps (2.33 and 2.31, resp.), the difference between the third steps is less important (1.4). Accordingly, the effect of the difference in the rules of sanctioning is less important than the effect of the difference in the rules of the game (to be allowed or not to refuse the offers).

Another result lies in the relations between sanctions and offers. When we regress (we have tested positively the normality of the distribution. We then have used an OLS regression) the last propositions on the second ones and on the sanctions, we find a negative and significant relationship between the last proposition and the sanction in the ultimatum game (−0.18) (no significant relationship between the last proposition and the previous one), but a positive and significant one between the last proposition and the second one in the dictator game (0.038) and no significant relationship between the last proposition and the sanction (see Appendix F). We find similar result when we test the two following models:

$$\text{(i) } p_3 = \alpha_d \cdot p_1 + \beta_d \cdot p_2 + \mu_d \cdot \text{SDG} + b_d$$
$$\text{(ii) } p_6 = \alpha_u \cdot p_4 + \beta_u \cdot p_5 + \mu_u \cdot \text{SUG} + b_u,$$

where β_d and μ_u are both significant (0.31 and −0.18, resp.) but the other parameters are not.

That means that the first offers do not influence the third ones in both games and that although the second assignments to B do not influence the third ones in the UG, they do in the DG. Finally the level of the sanction influences the last assignments but only in the UG.

5. The Second Party's "Sanctions" in the UG in the Two Treatments

Theoretically, the recipient rejects the proposition only if it is nil. If rational, he/she has to accept all nonnil propositions. In *Treatment 1*, the percentage of rejected propositions is 27.4%. The average level of propositions that are rejected is 2.49 with standard deviation of 0.13, while the mean of the level of the propositions that are accepted is 4.29 with standard deviation of 1.29. We see that the accepted propositions are not far from a fifty-fifty solution. This is a classical experimental result. We controlled for the gender and the age and found no significant impacts.

The number of the propositions that are rejected is significantly different in the *Control Treatment* as compared to *Treatment 1* (22.2% and 27.4%, resp.). The average level of the propositions that are rejected is 2.41 (with standard deviation of 1.45), whereas the average level of propositions that are accepted is 3.92 (standard deviation of 1.29).

6. Discussion

Our experimental design allows us to validate some now well-accepted experimental findings on one hand, and to obtain interesting new results on the other hand. The results, however, depend on the type of game involved. Some of them are valid in the DG as well as in the UG, but others are only observed in the DG. What is common to the two games lies in the fact that they diverge significantly from theoretical results. The offers are never nil in the DG and never equal to one ECU in the UG.

We also show that sanctions are efficient; proposers are induced to increase their offers in the fear of monetary losses. In the UG, offers are always higher than predicted by the perfect subgame equilibrium. Those two findings are well documented in the literature. What is however more surprising and original is the idea that in the DG, individuals increase their offers when they know that somebody else knows the level of their offer. Consequently, the percentage of individuals whose propositions increase from one step to the next is always higher than the percentage of those whose propositions decrease (see Appendix D). Moreover, the difference between the propositions in the second and first steps in the two games played *Treatment 1* (i.e., $p_2 p_1$ in the DG and $p_5 p_4$ in the UG) is significantly positive. This "somebody is watching you" effect must be supplemented by the fact that the more the effect of "being regarded by others" the less the effect of the sanction and vice versa. The fact that subjects' choices are modified when they are scrutinized can corroborate the two theoretical interpretations we have already in our introductory survey of related literature. First, individuals' behavior may be considered as guided by self-reputational motives [15, 16, 33]. Second, individuals can be conceived as strong reciprocators [34] in the sense that they internalize the possible reactions of others; the fact that somebody is aware of my decisions makes me behaving in conformity with what the others consider as fair. It is the reason why the more they react to people scrutiny the less they react to expected sanction, just because they internalize a norm of fairness.

What seems however confusing lies in the fact that in the UG, we do not find similar findings. Appendix D shows that while the percentages of proposers who increase their offers are higher in the two games (DG and UG) in *Treatment 1* than those who decrease them, it is the opposite in the *Control Treatment*, but only for the DG. Moreover, if the difference between the first and the second offers, as well as between the third and the second in the DG, is significantly positive in *Treatment 1* but not the *Control Treatment*, those differences are always significant in the UG and in the two kinds of experiments (1 and 2). This result shows that the UG is more complex, because the proposer first takes into account the risk that the receiver may reject his/her offer and second increases his/her offer in case of rejection. Everything is as if those two effects were at least as important as the "somebody is watching you" effect.

Finally, we need to explain why the sanctions are negatively related with the offers in the UG and not in the DG. In the UG, the relation is intuitive since the higher the offer the less the sanction. This result is in line with the interpretation that individuals (here, the third parties) are reciprocators and accordingly, when proposers expect a sanction they increase their offers. This effect is however impossible to identify precisely, because it is blended with the expectation of the proposer regarding the receiver's decision (he accepts or refuses). What is less intuitive is that in the DG, the proposers do not seem to be reactive to sanction. The explanation lies in the fact that the dictator seems more sensible to observation than to sanction. Another explanation might be that third parties internalize dictators' behaviors as being truly "unfair," and that dictators know that they are perceived this way. This explanation is corroborated by the fact that in 21.1% of the cases the sanctions are nil as compared to 3.8% in the UG.

Those results need however to be strengthened by further investigation. A first improvement could be made by designing DG experiments that permit to discriminate more accurately between interpretations in terms of conformity and in terms of social distance ("somebody is watching you" effect) and to better control for order effects. Then we plan to run UG experiments that permit to disentangle the relative effects of subjects' attitude towards risk and observation by a third party.

Appendices

A. Instructions

A.1. Instructions for Treatment 1. This is an experience on decision making within a group. If you follow the instructions carefully, you could win money which would be paid in cash at the end of the experience.

ECU (experimental currency unit) is the currency used during the experience, and all conversions will be made in ECU. At the end of the session, your profit will be paid in euros at the rate of 1 ECU = 0.1 euro.

You will participate in the experience for 5 times of two periods each. Prior to the first period, the participants are divided randomly into groups of 3. Therefore, there are 6 groups of three participants each. Within each group, each participant will be identified by a letter A, B, or C. The decisions to be made by each participant during the two periods are detailed in the remaining instructions. At the end of the first period, the Bs are redistributed randomly within the groups, while the As and Cs are not. At the end of the second period, the roles will be reassigned randomly and both periods are played 5 times.

The first period contains three steps carried out as follows.

Step 1. C does not participate in this step. A receives 10 ECUs. A has the possibility of sending part of this amount to B, namely x_1, the amount sent to B from A. At the end of this first step, A has $10 - p_1$ ECU and B has p_1 ECU.

• t test $p_2p_1 == 0$

One-sample t test

Variable	Obs	Mean	Std. err.	Std. dev.	[95% conf. interval]	
p_2p_1	135	−0.2074074	0.1468656	1.706425	−0.4978821	0.0830673

Mean = mean (p_2p_1) $t = -1.4122$
Ho: mean = 0 Degrees of freedom = 134

Ha: mean < 0 Ha: mean ! = 0 Ha: mean > 0
$\Pr(T < t) = 0.0801$ $\Pr(|T| > |t|) = 0.1602$ $\Pr(T > t) = 0.9199$

• t test $p_3p_2 == 0$

One-sample t test

Variable	Obs	Mean	Std. err.	Std. dev.	[95% conf. interval]	
p_3p_2	135	0.0148148	0.1346474	1.564462	−0.2514943	0.2811239

Mean = mean (p_3p_2) $t = 0.1100$
Ho: mean = 0 Degrees of freedom = 134

Ha: mean < 0 Ha: mean ! = 0 Ha: mean > 0
$\Pr(T < t) = 0.5437$ $\Pr(|T| > |t|) = 0.9126$ $\Pr(T > t) = 0.4563$

• t test $p_5p_4 == 0$

One-sample t test

Variable	Obs	Mean	Std. err.	Std. dev.	[95% conf. interval]	
p_5p_4	135	0.2814815	0.122464	1.422904	0.039269	0.523694

Mean = mean (p_5p_4) $t = 2.2985$
Ho: mean = 0 Degrees of freedom = 134

Ha: mean < 0 Ha: mean ! = 0 Ha: mean > 0
$\Pr(T < t) = 0.9885$ $\Pr(|T| > |t|) = 0.0231$ $\Pr(T > t) = 0.0115$

• t test $p_6p_5 == 0$

One-sample t test

Variable	Obs	Mean	Std. err.	Std. dev.	[95% conf. interval]	
p_6p_5	135	0.237037	0.0970587	1.12772	0.0450719	0.4290022

Mean = mean (p_6p_5) $t = 2.4422$
Ho: mean = 0 Degrees of freedom = 134

Ha: mean < 0 Ha: mean ! = 0 Ha: mean > 0
$\Pr(T < t) = 0.9920$ $\Pr(|T| > |t|) = 0.0159$ $\Pr(T > t) = 0.0080$

Figure 2

Step 2. A receives 10 ECUs once again. A can choose to send part of this amount to B, namely x_2, the amount sent to B from A. C is informed of the value of the amount p_2 that A chose to send to B. C receives a random amount between 1 and 5 ECUs. At the end of this step, A has $(10 - p_2)$ ECU and B has p_2 ECU and C has the random amount between 1 and 5 ECUs, the amount of which is represented by G_2.

Step 3. A receives 10 ECUs. A can choose to send part of this amount to B, namely x_3, the amount sent to B from A. C is informed of the value of the amount p_3 that A chose to send to B. C has the possibility of withdrawing from As profit, a share of the amount $(10 - p_3)$ that A keeps, the amount of which is represented by S. During the third step, the profits are as follows. A keeps a profit equal to $10 - p_3 - S$. B has a profit equal to p_3. C makes a profit equal to S if S is less than or equal to the average of the 6 $(10 - p_3)$ proposed by the six As who are participating in the experience, otherwise it is a random amount G_3 of between 1 and 5.

At the end of the third step, the profits are calculated for all participants of the first period and then the second period is started. See Table 7.

Example 1

Step 1. A receives 10. A gives 0 to B. A obtains 10 − 0 and B 0 ($p_1 = 0$).

Table 9

Variable	Obs	Mean	Std. Dev.	Min	Max
p_1	173	1.34104	1.750214	0	6
p_2	173	1.66474	2.149303	0	10
p_3	173	2.791908	2.527188	0	10
p_4	173	3.647399	1.594852	0	8
p_5	173	3.936416	1.299151	0	8
p_6	173	4.283237	1.672488	0	10
p_2p_1	173	.3236994	1.961657	−5	10
p_3p_2	173	1.127168	2.733515	−10	10
p_3p_1	173	1.450867	2.845674	−5	10
p_5p_4	173	.2890173	1.652252	−5	5
p_6p_5	173	.3468208	2.030567	−6	9
p_6p_4	173	.6358382	2.196797	−6	10

Table 10

Variable	Obs	Mean	Std. Dev.	Min	Max
p_1	135	1.459259	1.972811	0	10
p_2	135	1.251852	1.567956	0	6
p_3	135	1.266667	1.920821	0	10
p_4	135	3.22963	1.786937	0	7
p_5	135	3.511111	1.434473	0	7
p_6	135	3.748148	1.391437	0	8
p_2p_1	135	−.2074074	1.706425	−10	5
p_3p_2	135	.0148148	1.564462	−5	9
p_3p_1	135	−.1925926	1.528321	−10	5
p_5p_4	135	.2814815	1.422904	−4	4
p_6p_5	135	.237037	1.12772	−3	5
p_6p_4	135	.5185185	1.647485	−5	5

Table 11

	p_2p_1	p_3p_2	p_3p_1	p_5p_4	p_6p_5	p_6p_4
p_2p_1	1.0000					
p_3p_2	−0.3005	1.0000				
p_3p_1	0.4007	0.7535	1.0000			
p_5p_4	−0.0111	0.0060	−0.0019	1.0000		
p_6p_5	−0.0517	0.0737	0.0352	−0.3021	1.0000	
p_6p_4	−0.0561	0.0726	0.0311	0.4729	0.6971	1.0000

Table 12

	p_2p_1	p_3p_2	p_3p_1	p_5p_4	p_6p_5	p_6p_4
p_2p_1	1.0000					
p_3p_2	−0.5663	1.0000				
p_3p_1	0.5368	0.3913	1.0000			
p_5p_4	−0.0127	−0.0220	−0.0367	1.0000		
p_6p_5	−0.0635	0.2729	0.2085	−0.1814	1.0000	
p_6p_4	−0.0544	0.1678	0.1111	0.7395	0.5278	1.0000

Step 2. A receives 10. A gives 3 to B. A obtains 7, B 3 and C a profit between 1 and 5.

Table 13

	p_2p_1	p_3p_2	p_3p_1	p_5p_4	p_6p_5	p_6p_4
Equal 0	55.6	36.5	39.3	40.4	43.8	27.0
Negative	19.7	17.4	13.3	22.5	23.0	25.3
Positive	24.7	46.1	47.2	37.1	33.1	47.8

Table 14

	p_2p_1	p_3p_2	p_3p_1	p_5p_4	p_6p_5	p_6p_4
Equal 0	61.5	65.2	57.8	43.7	47.4	36.3
Negative	24.4	18.5	25.2	20.0	20.7	20.7
Positive	14.1	16.3	17.0	36.3	31.9	43.0

Table 15

Treatment	Mean of the Differences between the propositions	values
1	2-1	**.323** **(0.031)**
	3-2	**1.127** **(0.000)**
Control	2-1	−.207 (0.16)
	3-2	.0148 (0.912)

Inside parenthesis the values of $\Pr(|T| > |t|)$.
In bold values significant (at 1% or 5%).

Table 16

Treatment	Mean of the Differences between the propositions	Decisions A	Decisions R
1	5-4	**−.435** **(0.001)**	**1.367** **(0.000)**
	6-5	−.142 (0.084)	**1.425** **(0.002)**
Control	5-4	**−.345** **(0.007)**	**1.653** **(0.000)**
	6-5	.0142 (0.918)	**1.179** **(0.000)**

Inside parenthesis the values of $\Pr(|T| > |t|)$.
In bold values significant (at 1% or 5%).

Step 3. A receives 10. A gives 3 to B. If the average donations to B is 5, C can take S such as $3 \leq S \leq 7$ to A. In this case, A obtains $7 - S$, B obtains 3 and C obtains S, if $S \leq 5$ (average of donations to B), otherwise A receives an amount between 1 and 5.

The second period has two steps carried out as follows.

Step 1. C does not participate in this step. A receives 10 ECUs. C has the possibility of sending part of this amount to B, namely p_1, the amount sent to B from A. B can accept or

Table 17

	p_3	p_6
p_2	0.372***	
	(0.08)	
SDG	0.081	
	(0.06)	
p_5		0.164
		(0.09)
SUG		−0.179**
		(−0.07)
_cons	1.906***	4.463***
	(0.35)	(0.50)

Table 18

	p_3p_2	p_3p_1	p_3p_1
p_2p_1	−0.419***		0.581***
	(0.102)		(0.102)
p_3p_2		0.784***	
		(0.052)	
_cons	1.263***	0.567***	1.263***
	(0.202)	(0.154)	(0.202)
r2	0.090	0.568	0.161

Table 19

	p_6p_5	p_6p_4	p_6p_4
p_5p_4	−0.371***		0.629***
	(0.090)		(0.090)
p_6p_5		0.754***	
		(0.059)	
_cons	0.454***	0.374**	0.454***
	(0.150)	(0.122)	(0.150)
r2	0.091	0.486	0.224

refuse this share. If B refuses, A and B gain nothing. If B accepts, A has $10 - p_1$ ECU and B has p_1 ECU.

Step 2. A receives 10 ECUs again. A can choose to send part of this amount to B, namely p_2, the amount sent to B from A. B can accept or refuse this share. If B refuses, A and B gain nothing. If B accepts, A has $10 - p_2$ ECU and B has p_2 ECU. C is informed of the value of the amount p_2 that A chose to send to B. C receives an amount equal to 5 ECU if B refuses the share or a random amount between 1 and 5 ECUs if B accepts the share.

Step 3. A receives 10 ECUs again. A can choose to send part of this amount to B, namely p_3, the amount sent to B from A. B can accept or refuse this share. If B refuses, A and B gain nothing. If B accepts, A has $10 - p_3$ and B has p_3. C is informed of the value of the amount p_3 that A chose to send to B. C has the possibility of receiving an amount on A's profit, represented by S. During the third step, the profits are as follows. A keeps a profit equal to $10 - p_3 - S$ if B accepts the share or $0 - S$ if B refuses it. B has a gain equal to p_3 if he accepts the share and 0 otherwise. C makes a profit equal to S if the share is not made, that is to say if B refuses it and if S is less than the highest value $(10 - p_3)$ that the A participants who are making the experiment keep, otherwise C receive a random amount G_6 which is between 1 and 5.

At the end of the third step, the profits are calculated for all the participants of the second period. See Table 8.

Example 2

Step 1. A receives 10. A gives 4 to B. If B accepts, B obtains 4 and A obtains 6. If B refuses, A and B have 0.

Step 2. A receives 10. A give 5 to B. If B accepts, B obtains 5 and A obtains 5. If B refuses, A and B have 0. In both cases, C obtains a profit between 1 and 5.

Step 3. A receives 10. A gives 3 to B. If B accepts, B obtains 3, A obtains 7, and C obtains a profit between 1 and 5. If B refuses, A obtains $0-S$ and C obtains S. If, for example, the maximum number of proposals made to B is 5 and $S = 4$ then A loses 4, B obtains nothing, and C obtains 4.

A.2. Instructions for the Control Treatment. This is an experience on decision making within a group. If you follow the instructions carefully, you could win money which would be paid in cash at the end of the experience.

ECU (experimental currency unit) is the currency used during the experience, and all conversions will be made in ECU. At the end of the session, your profit will be paid in euros at the rate of 1 ECU = 0.1 euro.

You will participate in the experience for 5 times of two periods each. Prior to the first period, the participants are divided randomly into groups of 2. Therefore, there are 10 groups of two participants each. Within each group, each participant will be identified by a letter A or B. The decisions to be made by each participant during the two periods are detailed in the remaining instructions. At the end of the first period, the Bs are redistributed randomly within the groups while the As are not. At the end of the second period, the roles will be reassigned randomly and both periods are played 5 times.

The first period contains three steps carried out as follows.

Step 1. A receives 10 ECUs. A has the possibility of sending part of this amount to B, namely p_1, the amount sent to B from A. At the end of this first step, A has $10 - p_1$ ECU and B has p_1 ECU.

Example 3. If A sends 3 to B, A gets 7 (10 − 3) and B gets 3.

Step 2. This step is the same as the previous step.

Step 3. This step is the same as the previous step.

The second period has two steps carried out as follows.

Step 1. C does not participate in this step. A receives 10 ECUs. C has the possibility of sending part of this amount to B, namely p_1, the amount sent to B from A. B can accept or refuse this share. If B refuses, A and B gain nothing. If B accepts, A has $10 - p_1$ ECU and B has p_1 ECU.

Example 4. If A sends 2 ECUs to B and if B refuses, A and B get nothing. If B accepts, A gets 8 (10 − 2) and B gets 2.

Step 2. This step is the same as the previous step.

Step 3. This step is the same as the previous step.

In the following:

(i) p_i is the proposition made by A at step i

(ii) $p_2p_1 = p_2 - p_1$ (more generally $p_np_{(n-i)} = p_n - p_{(n-i)}$)

(iii) SDG and SUG are, respectively, the sanctions in the DG and UG.

B. Descriptive Statistics

Treatment 1. See Table 9.

Control Treatment. See Table 10.

C. Correlations Matrices

First Experiments. See Table 11.

Control Treatment. Table 12.

D. Percentages of Changes of the Propositions

Treatment 1. See Table 13.

Control Treatment. See Table 14.

E. Significance of the Differences between the Propositions

Treatment 1. See Figure 1.

Control Treatment. See Figure 2.

Summary

(i) *The DGs.* See Table 15.

(ii) *The UGs.* See Table 16.

F. Regressions of the Last Propositions (p_3 (in the DG) and p_6 (in the UG)) on the Previous Propositions (resp. p_2 and p_5) and the Sanctions, in the UG (SUG) and the DG (SDG)

See Table 17.

G. Regressions of the Differences on the Differences

(i) *In the DGs.* See Table 18.

(ii) *In the UGs.* See Table 19.

References

[1] E. Fehr and U. Fischbacher, "Third-party punishment and social norms," *Evolution and Human Behavior*, vol. 25, no. 2, pp. 63–87, 2004.

[2] W. Güth and R. Tietz, "Ultimatum bargaining behavior. A survey and comparison of experimental results," *Journal of Economic Psychology*, vol. 11, no. 3, pp. 417–449, 1990.

[3] C. Camerer, G. F. Loewenstein, and M. Rabin, Eds., *Advances in Behavioral Economics*, Princeton University Press, Princeton, NJ, USA, 2003.

[4] E. Fehr and S. Gächter, "Cooperation and punishment in public goods experiments," *American Economic Review*, vol. 90, no. 4, pp. 980–994, 2000.

[5] D. Masclet and M. C. Villeval, "Punishment, inequality, and welfare: a public good experiment," *Social Choice and Welfare*, vol. 31, no. 3, pp. 475–502, 2008.

[6] C. J. Turillo, R. Folger, J. J. Lavelle, E. E. Umphress, and J. O. Gee, "Is virtue its own reward? Self-sacrificial decisions for thesake of fairness," *Organizational Behavior and Human Decision Processes*, vol. 89, no. 1, pp. 839–865, 2002.

[7] E. Fehr and S. Gächter, "Altruistic punishment in humans," *Nature*, vol. 415, no. 10, pp. 137–140, 2002.

[8] J. P. Carpenter and P. H. Matthews, "Norm enforcement: the role of third parties," *Journal of Institutional and Theoretical Economics*, vol. 166, no. 2, pp. 239–258, 2010.

[9] E. Fehr and K. M. Schmidt, "Fairness, incentives, and contractual choices," *European Economic Review*, vol. 44, no. 4–6, pp. 1057–1068, 2000.

[10] E. Fehr and S. Gächter, "Do incentive contracts undermine voluntary cooperation?" Working Paper, University of Zurich, 2002.

[11] E. Fehr and J. A. List, "The hidden costs and returns of incentives-trust and trustworthiness among CEOs," *Journal of the European Economic Association*, vol. 2, no. 5, pp. 743–771, 2004.

[12] S. D. Levitt and J. A. List, "What do laboratory experiments measuring social preferences reveal about the real world?" *Journal of Economic Perspectives*, vol. 21, no. 2, pp. 153–174, 2007.

[13] A. K. Koch and H. T. Normann, "Giving in dictator games: regard for others or regard by others?" *Southern Economic Journal*, vol. 75, no. 1, pp. 223–231, 2005.

[14] E. Hoffman, K. McCabe, K. Shachat, and V. Smith, "Preferences, property rights, and anonymity in bargaining games," *Games and Economic Behavior*, vol. 7, no. 3, pp. 346–380, 1994.

[15] J. Dana, D. M. Cain, and R. M. Dawes, "What you don't know won't hurt me: costly (but quiet) exit in dictator games," *Organizational Behavior and Human Decision Processes*, vol. 100, no. 2, pp. 193–201, 2006.

[16] J. Andreoni and B. D. Bernheim, "Social image and the 50-50 norm: a theoretical and experimental analysis of audience effects," *Econometrica*, vol. 77, no. 5, pp. 1607–1636, 2009.

[17] G. E. Bolton and R. Zwick, "Anonymity versus punishment in ultimatum bargaining," *Games and Economic Behavior*, vol. 10, no. 1, pp. 95–121, 1995.

[18] G. E. Bolton, K. Zwick, and E. Katok, "Dictator game giving: rules of fairness versus acts of kindness," *International Journal of Game Theory*, vol. 27, no. 2, pp. 269–299, 1998.

[19] I. Bohnet and B. S. Frey, "Social distance and other-regarding behavior in dictator games: comment," *American Economic Review*, vol. 89, no. 1, pp. 335–339, 1999.

[20] I. Bohnet and B. S. Frey, "The sound of silence in prisoner's dilemma and dictator games," *Journal of Economic Behavior and Organization*, vol. 38, no. 1, pp. 43–57, 1999.

[21] N. Frohlich, J. Oppenheimer, and J. Moore, "Some doubts about measuring self-interest using dictator experiments: the costs

of anonymity," *Journal of Economic Behavior and Organization*, vol. 46, no. 3, pp. 271–290, 2001.

[22] T. C. Burnham, "Engineering altruism: a theoretical and experimental investigation of anonymity and gift giving," *Journal of Economic Behavior and Organization*, vol. 50, no. 1, pp. 133–144, 2003.

[23] K. J. Haley and D. M. T. Fessler, "Nobody's watching? Subtle cues affect generosity an anonymous economic game," *Evolution and Human Behavior*, vol. 26, no. 3, pp. 245–256, 2005.

[24] E. Hoffman, K. McCabe, and V. L. Smith, "Social distance and other-regarding behavior in dictator games," *American Economic Review*, vol. 86, no. 3, pp. 653–660, 1996.

[25] G. S. Berns, J. Chappelow, C. F. Zink, G. Pagnoni, M. E. Martin-Skurski, and J. Richards, "Neurobiological correlates of social conformity and independence during mental rotation," *Biological Psychiatry*, vol. 58, no. 3, pp. 245–253, 2005.

[26] M. F. Mason, R. Dyer, and M. I. Norton, "Neural mechanisms of social influence," *Organizational Behavior and Human Decision Processes*, vol. 110, no. 2, pp. 152–159, 2009.

[27] T. Ellingsen and M. Johannesson, "Anticipated verbal feedback induces altruistic behavior," *Evolution and Human Behavior*, vol. 29, no. 2, pp. 100–105, 2008.

[28] E. Xiao and D. Houser, "Emotion expression in human punishment behavior," *Proceedings of the National Academy of Sciences of the United States of America*, vol. 102, no. 20, pp. 7398–7401, 2005.

[29] E. Xiao and D. Houser, "Emotion expression and fairness in economic exchange," Working Paper, Interdisciplinary Center for Economic Science (ICES), George Mason University, 2007.

[30] E. Mohlin and M. Johannesson, "Communication: content or relationship?" *Journal of Economic Behavior and Organization*, vol. 65, no. 3-4, pp. 409–419, 2008.

[31] J. Andreoni and J. M. Rao, "The power of asking: how communication affects selfishness, empathy, and altruism," *Journal of Public Economics*, vol. 95, no. 7-8, pp. 513–520, 2011.

[32] S. Ferriol, "Regate-ng software," 2011, http://regate-ng.gate.cnrs.fr/~sferriol/debian/.

[33] R. Bénabou and J. Tirole, "Incentives and prosocial behavior," *American Economic Review*, vol. 96, no. 5, pp. 1652–1678, 2006.

[34] E. Fehr and U. Fischbacher, "The economics of strong reciprocity," in *Moral Sentiments and Material Interests, The Foundations of Cooperation in Economic Life*, H. Gintis, S. Bowles, and E. Fehr, Eds., MIT Press, Cambridge, UK, 2005.

19

A Model of Endogenous Growth: The Case of an Innovative Economy

Constantin Chilarescu[1] and Ioana Viasu[2]

[1] *Laboratory CLERSE, University of Lille 1, Cité Scientifique, 59655 Villeneuve d'Ascq Cedex, France*
[2] *Faculty of Economics and Business Administration, West University of Timisoara, Strada J. H. Pestalozzi, Nr. 16, 300115 Timisoara, Romania*

Correspondence should be addressed to Constantin Chilarescu; constantin.chilarescu@univ-lille1.fr

Academic Editors: D. M. Hanink, B. Junquera, Y. Shiftan, and J. Zarnikau

The main aim of this paper is to bring some improvements to the model developed by Funke and Strulik, having as starting point the basic model proposed by Grossman and Helpman. We will prove that the competitive equilibrium solution is locally unique. Nevertheless, at least as regards the stability of equilibrium point, we confirm the results obtained by Funke and Strulik.

1. Introduction

A large number of papers have been published in the last years on this subject, following the line developed by Grossman and Helpman [1]. Among them, to our knowledge, the first are the papers of Romer [2] and Eriksson [3]. Eriksson works out a model that is only a slight modification to those developed by Grossman and Helpman. The formal model of the economy of Romer has three sectors. The research sector uses human capital and the existing stock of knowledge to produce new knowledge. The intermediate-goods sector uses the designs from the research sector together with forgone output to produce the large number of intermediates that are in fact durable goods that are available for use in final goods production at any time. The final goods sector uses labor, human capital, and the set of intermediates that are available to produce final output. Output can be either consumed or saved as new capital.

Few years later, the balanced growth path of the endogenous growth model with physical capital, human capital, and R&D has been explored by Funke and Strulik [4] and then by Arnold [5] (henceforth FSA). FSA suggest that the typical advanced economy follows three development phases, characterized by physical capital accumulation, human capital formation, and innovation. In their paper, FSA claim that consumption goods, investment goods, and intermediate goods are all produced with the same technology and they can be transformed one to one without further cost from output of the industrial sector which is produced with Cobb-Douglas technology. In other words, one unit of each intermediate can be obtained from one unit of final output.

Gómez [6] analyzes the equilibrium dynamics of this model and corrects the analysis of FSA. Sequeira [7] incorporates an erosion effect into the endogenous growth model and claims that this effect significantly improves the fit between the model and the data.

Iacopetta [8, 9] extends the earlier analysis of FSA and argues that other sequences of the phases of development are possible and shows that the model can generate a trajectory in which innovation precedes human capital formation. This trajectory accords with the observation that the rise in formal education is followed with a considerable lag in the process of industrialization.

In order to obtain our results, we follow the line developed by Grossman and Helpman, more exactly, the model proposed in Chapter 5. They consider the case of an economy where capital goods and intermediate inputs each have only a single use and the final output is either consumed or invested. In their model, labor is used in R&D, in the production of intermediates and final goods.

We concentrate our analysis only on the case of an innovative economy and the paper is organized as follows. In the next section we argue and develop the differential equations that describe the dynamics of all variables of the model. The third section gives a complete characterization of the balanced growth path. Section four studies the stability conditions and the final section presents some conclusions and numerical simulations.

2. A Model of Growth with Innovation

In this section we develop a model of endogenous growth with innovation and derive the differential equations that describe the dynamics of the economy. Without loss of generality, we suppose that the economy is populated by a large and constant number of identical individuals, normalized to one, so that all the variables can be interpreted as per capita quantities. Each individual is endowed with one unit of time. There are three types of sectors in this model: the final output sector, the R&D sector, and the educational sector. Without loss of generality we introduce the following assumptions.

(a) The first sector produces the final output and the technology requires inputs, besides intermediates, labor, and physical capital. Capital is measured in units of consumption goods. Output can be either consumed or saved as new capital. The market for the final good y is assumed to be perfectly competitive and therefore the price of this good equals its marginal production cost. Final output y is produced according to a Cobb-Douglas production function

$$y = \gamma k^{\beta} d^{\eta} h_y^{1-\beta-\eta}, \tag{1}$$

where $\gamma > 0$, β, and η are positive elasticity parameters with $\beta + \eta \leq 1$, k is physical capital, h_y denotes the share of human capital employed to produce the final output, and d is an index of intermediate goods,

$$d = \left(\int_0^n x(i)^{\alpha} di \right)^{1/\alpha}, \tag{2}$$

where $n = n(t)$ is a measure of products invented before time t and can be considered as the number of available varieties. $x(i)$ represents the input of component i in the production of final good, and $0 < \alpha < 1$ controls the elasticity of substitution between intermediates, $\varepsilon = 1/(1-\alpha)$.

(b) In the second sector, specialized R&D firms devote resources to invent new products. Invention of new products is determined solely by the share of human capital devoted to research activity, denoted here by h_d. The measure of products invented evolves according to the following differential equation:

$$\dot{n} = \delta h_d, \tag{3}$$

where $\delta > 0$ is an efficiency parameter.

(c) Once a product was invented, a R&D firm obtains a perpetual patent, which allows the firm to sell these new products to the final good sector at a price chosen to maximize its profit. Whether the owner of the patent manufactures itself the good or licenses others to do so, it can extract the same monopoly profit. Intermediate goods are produced by labor alone, under monopolistic competition, and therefore, in order to fulfill the conditions for market clearing, we need to consider this kind of labor in the model. In fact intermediate goods are durable goods used by the final output sector. Since the intermediates are assumed not to depreciate, the value of one unit of it is the present discounted value of the infinite stream of rental income that it generates.

(d) The third sector is the educational sector. Each individual can spend a part of his time in the education sector, in order to raise its level of human capital. This process is proportional to the share of human capital devoted to education, denoted here by h_e and is described by the following differential equation:

$$\dot{h} = \xi h_e, \tag{4}$$

where $\xi > 0$ is an efficiency parameter.

Under these assumptions we are now able to determine the monopolist price of each intermediates. The derivative of function d, defined by (2), with respect to $x(j)$, is given by

$$\frac{d}{dx(j)} [d] = d^{1-\alpha} x(j)^{\alpha-1}, \tag{5}$$

and therefore

$$p(j)^d = d^{1-\alpha} x(j)^{\alpha-1} p_d \tag{6}$$

is the price of intermediate $x(j)$ in terms of d, where p_d is the unit price of d. By assuming in a formal way that the marginal and average cost of production is constant, normalized to one, the lemma of Shephard provides the following prices, in terms of y

$$p_d = \eta \frac{y}{d}, \qquad r = \beta \frac{y}{k}, \qquad w = (1-\beta-\eta) \frac{y}{h_y}, \tag{7}$$

where w is the price of labor employed for the production of capital good. In the same terms, substituting p_d from (7) into (6), the price of any intermediate $x(j)$, denoted here by $p(j)$, will then be given by

$$p(j) = \frac{\eta y}{d^{\alpha}} x(j)^{\alpha-1}. \tag{8}$$

This price is paid by the final output sector, for a unit of $x(j)$, to monopolist producer. As we can observe, this price is dependent on $x(j)$. Therefore, the demand function for an intermediate $x(j)$ at price $p(j)$ will be

$$x(j) = \left[\frac{d^{\alpha}}{\eta y} \right]^{1/(\alpha-1)} p(j)^{1/(\alpha-1)}. \tag{9}$$

Facing the demand function (9), the monopolist supplier of intermediate x_j maximizes operating profits

$$\pi(j) = (p(j) - w)\, x(j). \tag{10}$$

The optimal price will therefore be given by

$$p_j = \frac{w}{\alpha}. \tag{11}$$

To simplify, we denote by p_x this unique price. In a symmetric equilibrium, the quantity supplied for all intermediates is the same; that is, $x(j) = x$, and therefore

$$d^{\alpha} = nx^{\alpha}. \tag{12}$$

Substituting this result into (8) yields

$$p_x = \frac{\eta y}{nx}. \tag{13}$$

Equating the two prices yields the total quantity of intermediates required by the sector of production:

$$nx = \frac{\alpha\eta}{1-\beta-\eta} h_y. \tag{14}$$

Regardless of its composition, $X = nx$ measures the quantity of labor used in manufacturing intermediates. We denote by h_m this quantity of labor; that is,

$$h_m = \frac{\alpha\eta}{1-\beta-\eta} h_y. \tag{15}$$

Let (u_d, u_m, u_e, u_y) be the amount of unit time necessary to innovation, to manufacture intermediates, to education and, respectively, to produce the final output. Then, we have, $h_y = hu_y$, $h_d = hu_d$, $h_m = hu_m$, and $h_e = hu_e$ and the full employment requires:

$$u_y + u_d + u_m + u_e = 1. \tag{16}$$

Under this hypothesis, (15) can therefore be written as

$$u_m = \frac{\alpha\eta}{1-\beta-\eta} u_y, \tag{17}$$

and the above identity becomes

$$\frac{1-\beta-\eta(1-\alpha)}{1-\beta-\eta} u_y + u_d + u_e = 1. \tag{18}$$

Substitution of d from (12) and nx from (14) into (1) provides the final form of production function:

$$y = Ak^{\beta} h_y^{1-\beta} n^{\eta(1-\alpha)/\alpha}, \quad A = \gamma \left(\frac{\alpha\eta}{1-\beta-\eta}\right)^{\eta}. \tag{19}$$

Successively substitution of w from (7), p_j from (11), and x from (14) into (10) provides a profit equal to

$$\pi = \frac{\eta(1-\alpha)}{n} y. \tag{20}$$

If v is the market price of an intermediate, then, in a general equilibrium, free entry into R&D requires

$$w = \delta v \Longleftrightarrow g_v = \frac{\dot{v}}{v} = \frac{\dot{w}}{w} = g_w, \tag{21}$$

where g_z denotes the growth rate of variable z. The equilibrium in the capital market requires that the interest rate equals the dividend rate π/v plus the rate of capital gain $\dot{v}/v$ and thus we can write

$$g_v = \frac{\dot{v}}{v} = r - \frac{\pi}{v} = g_w. \tag{22}$$

Substituting π from (20), v from (21) and w from (7) we obtain

$$g_w = r - \frac{\delta\eta(1-\alpha)}{1-\beta-\eta} \frac{h_y}{n}. \tag{23}$$

The next two equations describe the dynamics of the budget constraint and the dynamics of physical capital

$$\dot{a} = ra + w(1-u_e)h - c, \tag{24}$$

$$\dot{k} = y - c. \tag{25}$$

Subject to the budget constraint equation (24) and to the development of skill equation (4) and using as state variables (h, a) and as control variables (c, u_e), we can write the following optimization problem:

$$\max_{\{c,u_e\}} \int_0^{\infty} \frac{c^{1-\theta} - 1}{1-\theta} e^{-\rho t} dt, \tag{26}$$

where $\rho > 0$ denotes the time preference rate and $\theta > 0$ denotes the intertemporal elasticity of substitution. The Hamiltonian is given by

$$J = \frac{c^{1-\theta} - 1}{1-\theta} + \lambda\left[ra + w(1-u_e)h - c\right] + \mu\xi h u_e. \tag{27}$$

The first derivatives of Hamiltonian with respect to c, u_e, h, and a provide the following system of differential equations:

$$g_c = \frac{\dot{c}}{c} = \frac{r-\rho}{\theta}, \qquad g_w = \frac{\dot{w}}{w} = r - \xi, \tag{28}$$

where g_z denotes the growth rate of variable z. Combining (23) with the second equation of the above system we can determine the following relation

$$u_y = \frac{\xi(1-\beta-\eta)}{\delta\eta(1-\alpha)} \frac{n}{h}, \tag{29}$$

from where it immediately follows

$$g_{u_y} = g_n - g_h. \tag{30}$$

After log-differentiating equation (19) with respect to time, the output growth rate is then determined by

$$g_y = \beta g_k + (1-\beta)\left(g_h + g_{u_y}\right) + \frac{\eta(1-\alpha)}{\alpha} g_n, \quad (31)$$

and substitution of the above result provides

$$g_y = \beta g_k + \frac{\alpha(1-\beta) + \eta(1-\alpha)}{\alpha} g_n. \quad (32)$$

Equations (3) and (25) can also be written as

$$g_n = \delta \frac{h}{n} u_d, \qquad g_k = \frac{1}{\beta} r - \frac{c}{k}. \quad (33)$$

Log-differentiation of r and w from (7) provides

$$g_r = -\frac{1-\beta}{\beta} r + (1-\beta)\frac{c}{k} + \frac{\alpha(1-\beta) + \eta(1-\alpha)}{\alpha} g_n, \quad (34)$$

$$g_w = g_y - \left(g_h + g_{u_y}\right) = g_y - g_n \Longrightarrow g_n = g_y - g_w \quad (35)$$

and after some algebraic manipulations yields

$$g_n = \frac{\alpha}{\eta(1-\alpha) - \alpha\beta}\left(\beta\frac{c}{k} - \xi\right). \quad (36)$$

Substituting (36) into (34) and denoting by $\chi = c/k$ and $\psi = n/h$ enable us to write down the following system of differential equations in terms of (r, χ, ψ):

$$\begin{aligned} g_r &= -\frac{(1-\beta)}{\beta} r + \frac{\eta(1-\alpha)}{\eta(1-\alpha) - \alpha\beta}\chi - A, \\ A &= \frac{\xi[\alpha(1-\beta) + \eta(1-\alpha)]}{\eta(1-\alpha) - \alpha\beta}, \\ g_\chi &= -\frac{\theta - \beta}{\beta\theta} r + \chi - \frac{\rho}{\theta}, \\ g_\psi &= g_n + \frac{\xi}{\delta}(B + g_n)\psi - \xi, \\ B &= \frac{\xi[1 - \beta - \eta(1-\alpha)]}{\eta(1-\alpha)}. \end{aligned} \quad (37)$$

To understand the dynamics of our system, two supplementary differential equations will be necessary, that is, the first equation of system (28) and

$$g_n = \frac{\alpha\beta}{\eta(1-\alpha) - \alpha\beta}\chi - \frac{\alpha\xi}{\eta(1-\alpha) - \alpha\beta}. \quad (38)$$

3. Balanced Growth Equilibrium

In this section, we focus our analysis on the balanced growth equilibrium, characterized by the fact that all variables grow at constant but possible different rates, and the shares of human capital in its different uses are constant. The system described above reaches the balanced growth path (BGP) if there exists t_* (possibly infinite), such that for all $t \geq t_*$, $g_{u_y} = g_{u_d} = g_{u_e} = 0$, and $g_k = g_c = g_y = g \neq g_h = g_n$, where g_z denotes the growth rate of variable z. The following proposition gives our first main result that characterizes the balanced growth path.

Proposition 1. *Let $\xi > \rho$ and $\theta > \theta_M$. Then the above system reaches the BGP and the following statements are valid:*

$$\begin{aligned} r_* &= \frac{\theta\xi[\alpha(1-\beta) + \eta(1-\alpha)] - \eta\rho(1-\alpha)}{\theta[\alpha(1-\beta) + \eta(1-\alpha)] - \eta(1-\alpha)}, \\ \chi_* &= \frac{(\theta - \beta) r_* + \beta\rho}{\beta\theta}, \qquad \psi_* = \frac{\delta\left(\xi - g_{n_*}\right)}{\xi\left(B + g_{n_*}\right)}, \\ g_{n_*} &= \frac{\alpha(\beta\chi_* - \xi)}{\eta(1-\alpha) - \alpha\beta}, \qquad g_* = \frac{r_* - \rho}{\theta}, \\ u_{y_*} &= \frac{(1 - \beta - \eta)\left(\xi - g_{n_*}\right)}{\eta(1-\alpha)\left(B + g_{n_*}\right)}, \qquad u_{e_*} = \frac{\alpha(\beta\chi_* - \xi)}{\xi[\eta(1-\alpha) - \alpha\beta]}, \\ u_{d_*} &= \frac{\alpha\left(\xi - g_{n_*}\right)}{\xi\left(B + g_{n_*}\right)} \frac{\beta\chi_* - \xi}{\eta(1-\alpha) - \alpha\beta}, \qquad u_{m_*} = \frac{\alpha\eta}{1 - \beta - \eta} u_{y_*}, \end{aligned} \quad (39)$$

where

$$\begin{aligned} \theta_m &= \frac{\eta(1-\alpha)}{\alpha(1-\beta) + \eta(1-\alpha)}, \\ \theta_M &= 1 - \frac{\rho}{\xi} \frac{\alpha(1-\beta)}{\alpha(1-\beta) + \eta(1-\alpha)}. \end{aligned} \quad (40)$$

Proof of Proposition 1. According to (30), constancy of u_y implies that, at equilibrium, the growth rate of n equals the growth rate of h; that is, $g_{n*} = g_{h*}$, and therefore $g_{\psi*} = 0$. Constancy of g_{c_*} implies the constancy of r_*; that is, $g_{r_*} = 0$. Therefore $g_{y_*} = g_{k_*}$, and thus χ is also constant in the steady state; that is, $g_{\chi_*} = 0$ and therefore we have $g_* = g_{y_*} = g_{k_*}$, where we denote by g_{z*} the equilibrium's growth rate of variable z. From the second equation of (28) we observe that r_* should be at least greater than ξ. Analyzing r_* we conclude that the only acceptable alternative that ensures $r_* > \xi$ is $\theta > \theta_m$. This condition also ensures the positivity of χ_* if $\theta > \beta$. A simple computation procedure shows that $\eta(1-\alpha) - \alpha\beta > 0$, that is, $\alpha < \alpha_m$, implies that $\beta\chi_* - \xi > 0$ and $\eta(1-\alpha) - \alpha\beta < 0$, that is, $\alpha > \alpha_m$, implies that $\beta\chi_* - \xi < 0$ and therefore g_{n_*} and u_{e_*} are both positive. What we need now is to find conditions that ensure positivity of $\xi - g_{n_*}$. Obviously we have $\theta_m < \theta_M$. By direct computation we find that $\xi - g_{n_*} > 0$ for all $\alpha > 0$ and for all $\theta > \theta_M$. Because $u_{y_*} > 0, u_{d_*} > 0, u_{e_*} > 0, u_{m_*} > 0$ and $u_{y_*} + u_{d_*} + u_{e_*} + u_{m_*} = 1$ we obviously have $\{u_{y_*}, u_{d_*}, u_{e_*}, u_{m_*}\} \in (0, 1)$. The other relations follow immediately by direct computation and thus the proof is completed. □

4. Stability Property of the BGP

In this section we investigate the stability properties of the BGP found in the previous section. For our analysis we need to consider the system (37):

$$\dot{r} = \left[-\frac{(1-\beta)}{\beta}r + \frac{\eta(1-\alpha)}{\eta(1-\alpha)-\alpha\beta}\chi - A\right]r = f_1,$$
$$\dot{\chi} = \left[-\frac{\theta-\beta}{\beta\theta}r + \chi - \frac{\rho}{\theta}\right]\chi = f_2, \quad (41)$$
$$\dot{\psi} = \left[g_n + \frac{\xi}{\delta}(B+g_n)\psi - \xi\right]\psi = f_3.$$

The study of stability equilibrium that we can examine here, that is, around the BGP, is called asymptotic stability or attracting and it describes how solutions that starts near the equilibrium point BGP converge to BGP. This is a local notion of stability. We will prove that the competitive equilibrium solution is locally unique; that is, the BGP is determinate, if the Jacobian of the reduced system has at least one eigenvalue with negative real part. There are two elements that are irrelevant for our analysis. We denote these two elements by a and, respectively, by b. The Jacobian evaluated at BGP is given by

$$J_* = \begin{pmatrix} J_{11} & J_{12} & 0 \\ J_{21} & J_{22} & 0 \\ a & b & J_{33} \end{pmatrix}, \quad (42)$$

where

$$J_{11} = -\frac{(1-\beta)}{\beta}r_*, \qquad J_{12} = \frac{\eta(1-\alpha)}{\eta(1-\alpha)-\alpha\beta}r_*,$$
$$J_{21} = -\frac{\theta-\beta}{\beta\theta}\chi_*, \quad (43)$$
$$J_{22} = \chi_*, \qquad J_{33} = \xi - g_{n_*} > 0.$$

Let ω_1, ω_2, ω_3 be the three eigenvalues of Jacobian J. First observe that $\xi - g_{n_*} > 0$ and therefore $\omega_3 > 0$; the third eigenvalue of J_* is positive. The following proposition gives the necessary and sufficient conditions which ensure the local saddle-point stability of the BGP.

Proposition 2. *Let $\xi > \rho$ and $\theta > \theta_M$. Then the following statements are valid.*

(i) *If $\alpha > \alpha_m$, then the BGP is a saddle-point equilibrium.*

(ii) *If $\alpha < \alpha_m$, then the BGP is an unstable equilibrium,*

where $\alpha_m = \eta/(\eta+\beta)$.

Proof of Proposition 2. The matrix J_* has as an immediate property, the fact that two of its eigenvalues are the eigenvalues of the matrix $J1_*$:

$$J1_* = \begin{pmatrix} J_{11} & J_{12} \\ J_{21} & J_{22} \end{pmatrix}. \quad (44)$$

By direct computation we obtain

$$\mathrm{Det}(J1_*) = \frac{\theta[\alpha(1-\beta)+\eta(1-\alpha)]-\eta(1-\alpha)}{\theta[\eta(1-\alpha)-\alpha\beta]}r_*\chi_*,$$
$$\mathrm{Tr}(J1_*) = \theta\xi[\alpha(1-\beta)+\eta(1-\alpha)] - \xi[\alpha(1-\beta)+\eta(1-\alpha)] + \alpha\rho(1-\beta), \quad (45)$$

where $\mathrm{Det}(J1_*)$ is the determinant of $J1_*$ and $\mathrm{Tr}(J1_*)$ is the trace of $J1_*$. First observe that $\mathrm{Tr}(J1_*) > 0$ for all $\theta > \theta_M$. Examining the signs of $\mathrm{Det}(J1_*)$ we can claim the following.

(i) If $\alpha > \alpha_m$, then $\mathrm{Det}(J1_*) < 0$ and therefore the real part of ω_1 is negative and the real part of ω_2 is positive and $|\omega_1| < \omega_2$.

(ii) If $\alpha < \alpha_m$, then $\mathrm{Det}(J1_*) > 0$ and therefore the real part of ω_1 is positive and the real part of ω_2 is positive

and thus the proof is completed. □

We conclude this section by noting that in our model there is not an upper limit for θ as it is the case of the cited paper of Manuel Gomez. Also we clarified some questionable aspects of the model developed by FSA and later analyzed by Manuel Gomez, Iacopetta, and Tiago Sequeira.

5. Conclusions

In this paper we explored the equilibrium dynamics of an innovative economy, via an endogenous growth model with physical capital, human capital, and R&D. In the second section we developed a model of endogenous growth with innovation and derive the differential equations that describe the dynamics of the economy. We proved in the third section that, under general fairly conditions, the model reaches the balanced growth path and determined the values of all variables at BGP. Finally, the previous section was dedicated to investigate the stability properties of the BGP.

The main results proposed by our paper are given in Propositions 1 and 2. As we can observe, these results make some light on the general properties of the model.

We close this final section with some numerical simulations in order to confirm the theoretical aspects presented in our paper. As it was observed by Jorgenson and Fraumeni [10, page 17], analysing the US economy for the period 1973–1986, physical capital input is the most important source of growth and therefore $\eta < \beta$ seems to be evident. For our simulation procedure we consider the following benchmark values.

(a) $\beta = 0.25$, $\eta = 0.20$, $\xi = 0.05$, $\delta = 0.1$, $\rho = 0.03$, $A = 1$, $\theta = 2$, and $\alpha = 0.4$. This parametrization yields the following equilibrium:

$\theta_m = 0.2857$, $\theta_M = 0.5714$, $\alpha_m = 0.444$, $r_* = 0.0533$, $\chi_* = 0.2017$, $\psi_* = 0.3077$, $g_* = 0.0117$, $g_{n_*} = 0.0083$, $u_{y_*} = 0.7051$, $u_{d_*} = 0.0256$, $u_{e_*} = 0.1667$, $u_{m_*} = 0.1026$, $\mathrm{Det}(J_1) = 0.1936$, and $\mathrm{Tr}(J_1) = 0.0417$ and the eigenvalues are $\omega_1 = 0.0208 + 0.4395i$, $\omega_2 = 0.0208 - 0.4395i$, and $\omega_3 = 0.0417$. As we can observe, in this case, the equilibrium is unstable.

(b) $\beta = 0.25$, $\eta = 0.20$, $\xi = 0.05$, $\delta = 0.1$, $\rho = 0.03$, $A = 1$, $\theta = 2$, and $\alpha = 0.5$. This parametrization yields the following equilibrium:

$\theta_m = 0.2105$, $\theta_M = 0.5263$, $\alpha_m = 0.444$, $r_* = 0.0524$, $\chi_* = 0.1982$, $\psi_* = 0.2467$, $g_* = 0.0112$, $g_{n_*} = 0.0088$, $u_{y_*} = 0.6784$, $u_{d_*} = 0.0218$, $u_{e_*} = 0.1765$, $u_{m_*} = 0.1233$, $\mathrm{Det}(J_1) = -0.1764$, and $\mathrm{Tr}(J_1) = 0.0412$ and the eigenvalues are $\omega_1 = -0.3999$, $\omega_2 = 0.4411$, and $\omega_3 = 0.0412$. As we can observe, in this case, the equilibrium is saddle path stable.

References

[1] G. M. Grossman and E. Helpman, *Innovation and Growth in the Global Economy*, The MIT Press, Cambridge, Mass, USA, 1991.

[2] P. Romer, "Endogenous technological change," *Journal of Economic History*, vol. 98, no. 5, pp. 71–102, 1990.

[3] C. Eriksson, "Market failures in the R&D growth model with endogenous labor supply," *Journal of Public Economics*, vol. 61, no. 3, pp. 445–454, 1996.

[4] M. Funke and H. Strulik, "On endogenous growth with physical capital, human capital and product variety," *European Economic Review*, vol. 44, no. 3, pp. 491–515, 2000.

[5] L. G. Arnold, "Endogenous growth with physical capital, human capital and product variety: a comment," *European Economic Review*, vol. 44, no. 8, pp. 1599–1605, 2000.

[6] M. A. Gómez, "Transitional dynamics in an endogenous growth model with physical capital, human capital and R and D," *Studies in Nonlinear Dynamics and Econometrics*, vol. 9, no. 1, article 5, 2005.

[7] T. N. Sequeira, "Transitional dynamics of an endogenous growth model with an erosion effect," *Manchester School*, vol. 76, no. 4, pp. 436–452, 2008.

[8] M. Iacopetta, "Phases of economic development and the transitional dynamics of an innovation-education growth model," *European Economic Review*, vol. 54, no. 2, pp. 317–330, 2010.

[9] M. Iacopetta, "Formal education and public knowledge," *Journal of Economic Dynamics and Control*, vol. 35, no. 5, pp. 676–693, 2011.

[10] D. W. Jorgenson and B. M. Fraumeni, "Education and productivity growth in a market economy," *Atlantic Economic Journal*, vol. 21, no. 2, pp. 1–25, 1993.

Permissions

The contributors of this book come from diverse backgrounds, making this book a truly international effort. This book will bring forth new frontiers with its revolutionizing research information and detailed analysis of the nascent developments around the world.

We would like to thank all the contributing authors for lending their expertise to make the book truly unique. They have played a crucial role in the development of this book. Without their invaluable contributions this book wouldn't have been possible. They have made vital efforts to compile up to date information on the varied aspects of this subject to make this book a valuable addition to the collection of many professionals and students.

This book was conceptualized with the vision of imparting up-to-date information and advanced data in this field. To ensure the same, a matchless editorial board was set up. Every individual on the board went through rigorous rounds of assessment to prove their worth. After which they invested a large part of their time researching and compiling the most relevant data for our readers. Conferences and sessions were held from time to time between the editorial board and the contributing authors to present the data in the most comprehensible form. The editorial team has worked tirelessly to provide valuable and valid information to help people across the globe.

Every chapter published in this book has been scrutinized by our experts. Their significance has been extensively debated. The topics covered herein carry significant findings which will fuel the growth of the discipline. They may even be implemented as practical applications or may be referred to as a beginning point for another development. Chapters in this book were first published by Hindawi Publishing Corporation; hereby published with permission under the Creative Commons Attribution License or equivalent.

The editorial board has been involved in producing this book since its inception. They have spent rigorous hours researching and exploring the diverse topics which have resulted in the successful publishing of this book. They have passed on their knowledge of decades through this book. To expedite this challenging task, the publisher supported the team at every step. A small team of assistant editors was also appointed to further simplify the editing procedure and attain best results for the readers.

Our editorial team has been hand-picked from every corner of the world. Their multi-ethnicity adds dynamic inputs to the discussions which result in innovative outcomes. These outcomes are then further discussed with the researchers and contributors who give their valuable feedback and opinion regarding the same. The feedback is then collaborated with the researches and they are edited in a comprehensive manner to aid the understanding of the subject.

Apart from the editorial board, the designing team has also invested a significant amount of their time in understanding the subject and creating the most relevant covers. They scrutinized every image to scout for the most suitable representation of the subject and create an appropriate cover for the book.

The publishing team has been involved in this book since its early stages. They were actively engaged in every process, be it collecting the data, connecting with the contributors or procuring relevant information. The team has been an ardent support to the editorial, designing and production team. Their endless efforts to recruit the best for this project, has resulted in the accomplishment of this book. They are a veteran in the field of academics and their pool of knowledge is as vast as their experience in printing. Their expertise and guidance has proved useful at every step. Their uncompromising quality standards have made this book an exceptional effort. Their encouragement from time to time has been an inspiration for everyone.

The publisher and the editorial board hope that this book will prove to be a valuable piece of knowledge for researchers, students, practitioners and scholars across the globe.

List of Contributors

Brian Petersen
Environmental Studies, Western Michigan University, 1903West Michigan Avenue, Kalamazoo, MI 49008, USA

Adam M. Wellstead
Department of Social Sciences, Michigan Technological University, 1600 Townsend Street, Houghton, MI 49931, USA

Dadson Awunyo-Vitor
Department of Agricultural Economics, Agribusiness and Extension, Kwame Nkrumah University of Science and Technology, Kumasi, Ghana

Ramatu M. Al-Hassan and Daniel B. Sarpong
Department of Agricultural Economics and Agribusiness, University of Ghana, Legon, Ghana

Juan Acosta-Ballesteros, M. del Pilar Osorno-del Rosal and Olga M. Rodríguez-Rodríguez
Departamento de Analisis Economico, Facultad de Ciencias Economicas y Empresariales, Universidad de La Laguna, Campus de Guajara, S/C de Tenerife, 38071 La Laguna, Spain

Xuyang Chen and Maxime Fougère
Employment and Social Development Canada, 140 Promenade du Portage, Phase 4, Gatineau, QC, Canada

Joachim Kaldasch
EBC Hochschule, Alexanderplatz 1, 10178 Berlin, Germany

Ryan Petter and Wallace E. Tyner
Department of Agricultural Economics, Purdue University, 403West State Street, West Lafayette, IN 47907-2056, USA

Rui Alpalhão
Department of Finance, ISCTE Business School, Avenida das Forcas Armadas, 1649-026 Lisbon, Portugal

Joachim Kaldasch
EBC Hochschule Berlin, Alexanderplatz 1, 10178 Berlin, Germany

Nicholas Tsounis
Department of International Trade, Technological Institute of Western Macedonia Kastoria Campus, 52100 Kastoria, Greece
Adjunct Faculty, Hellenic Open University, Greece

Dimitrios Serenis
Department of International Trade, Technological Institute of Western Macedonia Kastoria Campus, 52100 Kastoria, Greece

Vladimir N. Pokrovskii
Moscow State University of Economics, Statistics and Informatics, Moscow 119501, Russia

John F. McDonald and Houston H. Stokes
Department of Economics, University of Illinois at Chicago, Chicago, IL 60680, USA

Alison Watts
Department of Economics, Southern Illinois University, Carbondale, IL 62901, USA

L. Bisio and L. Ventura
Department of Economics and Law, Sapienza University of Rome, Via del Castro Laurenziano 9, 00161 Rome, Italy

Sander Kelman
1500 Sawyer Avenue, Manasquan, NJ 08736, USA

Albert Woodward
CBHSQ, SAMHSA, US Department of Health and Human Services, 1 Choke Cherry Road, Rockville, MD 20050, USA

Marco A. Marini and Giorgio Rodano
Department of Computer, Control and Management Engineering, Sapienza University of Rome, Via Ariosto 25, 00185 Rome, Italy

Sunita Narang
Acharya Narendra Dev College, University of Delhi, Delhi 110019, India

Madhu Vij
Faculty of Management, University of Delhi, Delhi 110007, India

Guangfeng Zhang
GREQAM, School of Economics, Aix-Marseille University, Marseille 13236, France

Qiong Zhang
School of Public Administration, Sichuan University, Chengdu 610000, China

Muhammad Tariq Majeed
School of Economics, Quaid-i-Azam University, Islamabad 45320, Pakistan

Agnès Festré
University of Picardie (France) and GREDEG, University of Nice-Sophia Antipolis, UMR nº 6227, 250 rue Albert Einstein, 06560 Valbonne Cedex, France

Pierre Garrouste
University of Nice-Sophia Antipolis and GREDEG, UMR nº 6227, 250 rue Albert Einstein, 06560 Valbonne Cedex, France

Constantin Chilarescu
Laboratory CLERSE, University of Lille 1, Cite Scientifique, 59655 Villeneuve d'Ascq Cedex, France

Ioana Viasu
Faculty of Economics and Business Administration, West University of Timisoara, Strada J. H. Pestalozzi, Nr. 16, 300115 Timisoara, Romania